Betrayed

SECRECY, LIES, AND CONSEQUENCES

Frederic H Martini

Rugged Land
New York, NY

Published in the United States by Rugged Land
9 Barrow Street, Sixth Floor, New York, NY 10014
www.ruggedland.com

ISBN-13: 9780996636353
Printed in the United States of America

Cover design by Brandi Doane McCann,
http://www.ebook-coverdesigns.com

Table of Contents

PART 2: PEACE, POLITICS, AND INJUSTICE

Dedication

To my father - better late than never

Frederic C. Martini (1918-1995)

Photographs and chapter notes for each chapter can be found in the related section of the author's website: https://www.fredericmartini.com

Introduction

On 22 July 1944, Hitler issued a decree that all Allied airmen captured in France should be turned over to the SS for execution. On 11 April 1945, the Dora Concentration Camp at Nordhausen was liberated, and American forces entered the associated underground V-2 rocket factory known as the Mittelwerk. These two seemingly unconnected events would irrevocably disrupt the lives of 168 Allied airmen who had the misfortune to fall into the hands of the Gestapo in 1944.

This is a story of betrayal, lies, secrecy, and consequences. It begins in June 1944, six days after the Normandy invasion, and extends to the current day. Although many people are involved, there are really three major players: my father, Frederic C. Martini, who was one of the affected airmen; the German rocket engineer Wernher von Braun, who was involved with the conception and operation of the Mittelwerk; and the intelligence services of the US government.

The issues raised by this tale are as relevant today as they were in 1945. At that time, Army Intelligence (G-2), Naval Intelligence, and the Office of Strategic Services (OSS) had been operating with few constraints for several years. Their leadership ranks had come to believe that because they knew secrets withheld from other agencies of government, they were in the best position to make key decisions on national security. Some of those decisions were misguided, others unethical, and a few illegal. All were hidden by a comprehensive and wide-ranging security program that used a combination of dissembling, disinformation, lies, and "alternative facts" to further their goals.

Secret programs brought hundreds of former Nazis, including SS officers and suspected war criminals, to the US to prepare for an anticipated war against the Soviet Union. The groups imported included Wernher von Braun and other members of the V-2 rocket program. Their wartime histories were secret, the existence of the Mittelwerk was secret, and the fact that the skilled slave laborers at Dora came from Buchenwald Concentration Camp where 168 Allied airmen had been held, was secret. The security lid covering von Braun, Dora, Buchenwald, and the Buchenwald airmen did not lift for decades, while the public at large remained completely oblivious.

For almost 40 years, my father and the other American airmen held at Buchenwald were told by the government they had suffered to defend that they were either delusional or liars. The Army, the Veterans Administration, and the US Congress denied their experiences and refused to provide substantive support for the mental and physical damage they had endured.

When I started working on this story, I knew only the barest details. I was always aware that my father was haunted by the war. His mood swings, especially his sudden rages, were simply part of our daily lives.

He seldom spoke about the war, but as a child, I overheard his conversations with other veterans, and once I reached adulthood, he would sometimes tell a story to illustrate a point about wars and history. By the time his health started failing and his battles with the Veteran's Administration heated up, I was away at college, then graduate school, and then building a career. I occasionally heard about my parents' frustrations, but didn't learn just how extensive the problems were. My father felt that it should be his battle, not mine.

After my father died, my mother moved to Hawaii, where I had settled with my wife and son. In 2010, as she was getting prepared to shift to an assisted living facility nearby, I started going through her "stuff" to see what she might want to take with her. I was stunned to find several sealed boxes labeled "Fred Military" and "Fred VA," each packed with documents. I also found vacuum-packed bags of correspondence from WWII. That cache of evidence was the catalyst for this seven-year project.

It has been a wild ride, taking me to Normandy and Paris, to the US National Archives (NARA/College Park) in Maryland, to the National Air and Space Museum (NASM) in Virginia, to the US Holocaust Memorial Museum in DC, to various WW II museums, and into the navigator's chair on a B-17 flight. What started as a story about the trials and tribulations of one Buchenwald airman dealing with the Veterans Administration soon led me into the labyrinth of Project Paperclip, the postwar importation of Nazi engineers, and the oppressive and sometimes heavy-handed application of government secrecy. It became a story about my father as a "friendly fire" casualty of decisions made in the interest of national security by intelligence agencies operating in the absence of public, congressional, or executive oversight.

This is a true story, not a novel. The narrative has been based on declassified records, survivors' accounts (either published, recorded, or filmed), and war crimes trials and depositions. However, there are multiple uncertainties to be expected when attempting to reconstruct events that occurred more than 70 years ago, based on multiple accounts that may or may not overlap. These men were under extreme stress, and each airman's perspective was so limited that none were aware of everything that happened. Over time, memories fade or change, and in most cases, the airmen did not talk about these events until decades later. Where conflicting accounts exist, the narrative follows the consensus view. And although the events are documented, with few exceptions, the thoughts of those involved had to be inferred from what their actions and patterns of behavior reveal about their personalities.

Prologue

1 A.M. The house is cold and silent. His wife and son are asleep, but he hates going to sleep, for his dreams are too terrible. He's been at home for the last week, after losing his job because he can't stand on his aching feet all day. He dresses quietly, donning his leather jacket against the chill. He goes to the bedside bureau and quietly begins tossing clothing into a pile on the floor. His wife, awakened, asks him what's wrong. He doesn't have an answer for her — his actions have a momentum of their own.

Soon the pile contains all of his uniform gear, from his socks to his dress uniform with various medals attached. He gathers the pile in his arms and goes out of the room and down the stairs and passes through the dark kitchen through the back door and onto the porch. Each painful step is a reminder of the horrors of Germany and his humiliation at home.

It is a relatively quiet neighborhood, but a passing car backfires. With no grasp of the intervening moments, he finds himself crouching, pressed against the wall of the house, his clothes scattered before him and down the steps to the small, enclosed back yard. He is gasping and shaking. As he regains a semblance of control, he gathers up his things and moves from the stairs to the far back corner of the yard, where a burn barrel stands empty.

The November sky is clear and moonless, and the stars above glitter like shards of broken glass. It is a chilly night, but not bitterly cold, yet he is shivering as he stuffs his gear into the barrel. A moment's search locates the Mason jar that holds the gasoline for fire starting, and he pours a generous amount over the piled clothing. When he pulls a matchbook from his pants pocket, lights a match, and drops it into the barrel, the saturated contents ignite with a whoosh.

He watches the fire for a time as if hypnotized, and then with a start realizes that his task is still incomplete. He shrugs off his leather flight jacket and tosses it onto the flames. By chance, the jacket lands with the chest up, with his name in view, and the sight of that familiar jacket, and the flames, and the pitiless sky trigger an avalanche of memories that he fights to suppress. As he stands in the radiated warmth of his burning history, with his emotions a mixture of frustration, rage, and grief, his wife watches from the porch in silence. But his actions, although cathartic, change nothing. His troubles are far from over.

Part 1: Wartime

There is only one thing certain about war, that it is full of disappointments and also full of mistakes.

WINSTON CHURCHILL, 27 APRIL 1941

CHAPTER 1

12 June 1944, Great Ashfield, England

-◁⊟▷-

At 0230, Staff Sergeant Fred Martini was awakened by a sharp tap on the forehead and a bright flashlight in the eyes. The flashlight was held by Major Vincent Masters, who told Fred to be on the truck in 30 minutes, before moving on to the next airman on his wake-up list. Fred rummaged in the darkness for his kit bag in the knapsack stuffed under his berth, while in the bunk above him, he could hear his friend Sam getting his gear together. Still a bit muzzy headed, he got to his feet and headed to the softly lit washroom. After hastily using the facilities, washing his face, and shaving, he returned to his bunk, again in darkness, and quietly donned his uniform, taking it off the hangers hooked on the rails at the foot of his bunk.

The small Quonset hut barracks held the noncommissioned officers from two flight crews of the 385th Bomb Group (BG), but only Fred's had been awakened for duty. As Fred and the five other sergeants left the barracks, they crossed the dirt road toward a line of GMC 6x6 trucks, their headlights damped and deflected downward by horizontal strips of electrical tape. They picked one and climbed up into the uncovered cargo area, moving to the front as bomber crews from other barracks climbed in behind them. From the hour and the crowd, Fred knew that this would be a combat mission rather than a training exercise, and he assumed that comparable pickups were being made at the barracks areas of the 548th, 549th, and 550th Squadrons.

Although there were narrow, wooden bench seats available, most of the men chose to stand, knowing that the ride over the unpaved, rain-rutted roads would be brief but bouncy. Once everyone was aboard, someone banged on the roof of the cab, and the truck revved up and headed to the mess hall just over a half-mile away.

Fred braced himself and scanned the skies to see what kind of a day it would be. The predawn hours were cool and clear. The temperature hovered around 50°F, with a dampness in the air that was a lingering reminder of the heavy rains that had cancelled missions two days earlier. A quarter moon struggled to cast its light from just above the eastern horizon. Although partially obscured by a layer of low cloud, the moon still provided enough light to silhouette the tips of three trees that stood alongside Runway 24. The buildings, planes, and the airfield itself were all in darkness, blacked out or unlit to make it harder for a German pilot to locate. The night air carried a mixture of smells dominated by oily smoke, diesel exhaust, and aviation fuel, and Fred knew that some of those smells lingered from the bombing of the field three weeks earlier that destroyed a maintenance hangar and blew the B-17 bomber "Powerful Katrina" to smithereens. He had been hiding under a Jeep feeling extremely vulnerable while that air raid was underway — that was not a favorite memory. But then the industrially tainted air mass parted, and there was a gust from the surrounding countryside that triggered memories of spring growth and flowers. Fred found it a bit unsettling. It was a transition from wartime to peacetime in the space of a moment.

The truck soon reached the end of the access road and made a hard right as it turned toward the communal mess hall. Fred looked around the truck at his crew, some still half asleep. They had been through so much together already — months of intense training, nine combat missions, and two crash landings — that they had been welded into a cohesive unit.

Like most aircrews in the Army Air Corps, Fred's comrades, all sergeants, came from all over the US. None of them had gone to college, and some had not completed high school. Fred Martini, at 26, was one of the senior hands. Born and raised in Brooklyn, he was cocky and street wise. Lean and handsome at 5'10" and 160 pounds, he wore his uniform with panache and adopted a jaunty attitude. After the crew's exploits in New York City, Fred was widely hailed as a "ladies man." But although the other sergeants at times still called him "Valentino," his amorous interests were on hold for the duration. It was hardly surprising, given that Great Ashfield was remote, the base was dry, and with missions every day or every other day, there was no time in any case.

Fred served as left waist gunner (LWG) and assistant flight engineer for his crew. He manned a pair of 50-caliber machine guns mounted just aft of the left wing, defending that side of their B-17 bomber. The right waist gunner, Sam Pennell, protected the right side with a second pair of 50-caliber guns. The plane was too narrow for the two men to work back to back, so the guns were staggered, with the left waist gun forward of the right waist gun and the two gunners facing one another. Sam was 5'9" and 145 pounds, hailing from Columbus, Georgia. His wavy, brown hair was closely cropped, framing a narrow face with a sharp chin.

Sam had a friendly disposition and a competent air, and everyone liked him immensely. Although more reserved than Fred, after training, berthing, and flying together for nearly a year, the two had become close friends. At Drew Field, in Florida, they had filled their off days at the beach or in the bars in Tampa, whereas at Great Ashfield, there was little to do other than play cards, shoot pool, or swap stories. Sam was riding on Fred's left. Next to Sam was Ervin Pickrel, the radio operator, from Parma, Idaho. Light-haired and over 6' tall, Erv towered over the other sergeants and took considerable ribbing about it. He was a nice guy who generally kept to himself, seldom joining Fred, Sam, or other airmen on those rare occasions when they went out on the town.

Armando Marsilii, known to his friends as "Mandu," was the only married member of the noncom crew. Mandu, the upper turret gunner and the lead flight engineer, was from Wilmington, Delaware. He was roughly 5'6" and 140 pounds, with thick black hair and dense, bushy eyebrows that often put his eyes in shadow. He had a small, new scar along his right temple, a souvenir from the ditching of the crew's second B-17 in the English Channel a month earlier. Like Erv, Mandu seldom left the base on liberty, spending his free time snoozing, playing cards, or writing letters to his wife.

Felipe E. Musquiz was an enlistee whose family lived in Musquiz, Mexico. Felipe was a short bundle of energy. He had a ready smile, and a slender mustache that he probably thought made him look like Clark Gable. At 5'4", Felipe was the smallest member of the crew, which might have explained how he achieved the singular honor of being the ball turret gunner. This was not only one of the more dangerous positions in the aircrew, but also the most claustrophobic. Although Felipe could climb into the turret on his own, once he was tucked inside, getting back out could be a struggle. Their first B-17, which they had flown from the US to the UK, had been named Crashwagon as a joke. Rather ironically, upon arriving in the UK, they found that their landing gear would not lower,[1] and they were forced to do a belly landing in Langford Lodge, Northern Ireland. Because they had jettisoned the ball turret over Loch Neagh before attempting the landing, the other members of the crew took pleasure in reminding Felipe that they could have left him in the turret when they detached it. As was typical of crew banter, Felipe had a variety of rejoinders like, "Wish you had — I hear Irish girls are terrific."

The tail gunner was Theodore Dubenic, from Chicago. Ted was 5'9" with a stocky build and relatively heavy features as compared to Fred or Sam with whom he often traveled off-base. He availed himself of every opportunity to see the sights when liberty

---

[1] A drive shaft had shattered in the extreme cold of their cruising altitude of 21,000'.

passes were distributed, as he considered it to be stress relief. Only slightly less isolated than the ball turret gunner – with some effort, the tail gunner could crawl forward to reach the waist – from his station, Ted had amazing views of combat operations and potential threats astern as well as the relative positions of the planes in the formation. Information relayed from the tail gunner was often invaluable to the pilot and the aerial gunners whose fields of view were relatively limited.

As they bounced along in the 6x6, the men tried to make sense of their situation. The general consensus was that this was a SNAFU.[2] They had been told that they were out of the mission rotation because they were going to Lead Crew School the next day, and Crashwagon III was in the maintenance hangar being prepared for training operations.

Fred and the other sergeants were pleased to have been selected for Lead Crew School. It was an acknowledgement that they were experienced and their bombardier was proficient. What they didn't know was that it was also an acknowledgment of the high attrition rate in terms of planes and crews. The Army Air Corps was selecting and training experienced crews to lead missions and increase the survival odds for new air crews. It took time to train a bombardier to use the Norden bombsight, a complicated apparatus that factored in air speed, wind direction, and altitude to predict where released bombs would impact the ground. When short-handed, planes could be sent on missions without a bombardier, but under orders to maintain a tight formation and release their bomb load when they saw the lead crew drop theirs.

When the truck pulled up by the entry to the mess hall, Fred, Sam, and the other crewmen clambered down to join the stream of men heading for breakfast. The interior of the mess hall had a capacity of around 400 men. The arriving air crews hastily grabbed trays and went through the chow line collecting their usual breakfasts. The choices included reconstituted powdered eggs, bacon, corn flakes with powdered milk, toast, and black coffee.

Shortly after they were seated, the cluster of six sergeants was visited by their pilot, Lt. Loren E. Jackson. Jackson, 26 years old, was a striking young man who carried himself like a career officer. He had short brown hair, and his athletic frame carried no extra weight. He was from Douglas, Arizona, and had enlisted after graduating from the University of Arizona. At the time, college graduates volunteering for the Army Air Corps were usually assigned to either

---

[2] Situation Normal, All F****d Up.

pilot, navigator, or bombardier training based in part on test results from a Classification Center and in part on the need to fill open positions. Loren had been able to talk his way into pilot training despite some lingering injuries sustained in a severe motorcycle accident several years earlier. It turned out he had a natural aptitude for piloting, and his competent, easy going nature made him a natural leader. Shortly before deploying to the ETO (European Theater of Operations), Loren had married Alice, four years his junior, in a quiet ceremony in St. Petersburg, Florida. His primary goal was completing the requisite thirty missions, going home, and reuniting with Alice. He was all business, and the carefree life of the single enlisted man was the farthest thing from his mind.

Confirming their suspicions, Jackson said that Major Masters had just apologized for waking them. Apparently there had been a screw-up in the paperwork, and the rotation wasn't adjusted when Jackson's crew was assigned to Lead Crew School and the plane pulled for maintenance. They now had two options: they could take the day off and go back to bed, and another crew would be hastily aroused to take their place, or they could go ahead and fly the mission. They had to decide immediately.

Jackson and the rest of the officers felt that since the entire crew was already up and dressed, they should fly the mission. Between flying as reserve or having missions scrubbed, their combat missions weren't accumulating very quickly. They had fewer than one-third of the 30 missions needed to head stateside. Besides, Shaffer needed only one more mission to complete his tour and receive the unofficial but coveted Certificate of Membership in the Lucky Bastard Club, which the Bomber Group awarded to airmen upon completion of their combat tour of duty in the ETO. Getting to the point of completing one more mission was a distant dream for Fred, but he could imagine how disappointed Shaffer would be if they pulled the plug now.

Lt. Gerald Shaffer had been temporarily assigned to replace Lt. Lindquist, their navigator for their first set of combat missions. A small, earnest man, Shaffer had been hospitalized with food poisoning, missing two missions with his previous crew. As a result, when the other guys completed their 30th mission and were rotated home, he had stayed behind. This would be his 30th and final combat mission, and he was anxious to return to his parents in Cochranton, Pennsylvania. They all understood how he felt, and the sergeants quickly agreed with Jackson's plan. He then headed back to the table he shared with the other officers in the flight crew, Lieutenants Ross Blake and Joseph Haught.

Blake, the co-pilot, from Great Neck, New York, was of lighter build than Jackson and about an inch shorter. He was a thoroughly competent and reliable character, and his sense of humor often had the other officers smiling. Haught, the bombardier, was from Grantsville, West Virginia. He had an uncanny knack with the Norden bombsight, and with only nine missions behind him, he was considered to be among the best bombardiers in the 385th. His bombing skill and Jackson's steady leadership were the reasons they had been chosen for Lead Crew School.

At 0345, Fred heard the trucks pulling up outside to shuttle the assembled aircrews to the briefing room. The Jackson crew left the mess hall as a group, the ten men climbing onboard a waiting 6x6 truck in company with another complete aircrew. In convoy, the trucks ran west and then turned north into the area known as the Willow Woods, where they arrived five minutes later. The complex of operational buildings was immediately adjacent to the western end of the runways. The briefing was held in a long building with concrete walls and a steeply pitched wooden roof supported by internal trusses. The hall could seat more than 50 aircrews on bench seats or small, folding wooden chairs. There were windows on either side, blacked out for the night, and a dozen bare light bulbs in reflector sockets dangled from the ceiling. The walls were covered by bulletin boards with notices, weather reports, news articles, and posters of friend/foe plane silhouettes. A pot bellied stove provided heat, although when full, the room tended to become uncomfortably warm. Smoking was permitted, and there were butt cans by the tables. By the time the briefing got underway, the air was heavy and thick with smoke.

At the front of the room was a raised platform set in front of a 12'x12' wall map showing the ETO, which stretched from the North Sea to southern France and from west of Ireland to the eastern edge of the Black Sea. When Fred and the men filed in and took their seats, the map was covered by a black curtain. However, some important information was readily available to the flight crews. A tall blackboard along the wall to the left of the map showed the formation for the day's mission. It was divided into three sections, one for each of three involved squadrons. The term "squadron" in combat was distinct from the four squadrons in the 385th BG. Organizationally, the 385th air crews were assigned to the 548th, 549th, 550th, and 551st Squadrons. In combat, however, a "squadron" was a group of planes flying together in formation.

Of the three squadrons in the mission, one was designated the Low Squadron, one the Lead Squadron, and one the High Squadron, each with 12-13 aircraft. The arrangement was designed to provide maximum protection for the group as a whole through the combined firepower of their 50-caliber guns but still allow each plane to drop its bomb load without striking another airplane in the formation.

Looking closely, Fred saw that planes from the 551st were assigned to the High Squadron, and the YY to the right told him that when the formation assembled in the air, two yellow flares would be fired by the lead plane in that squadron. On the blackboard within each squadron area, a simple T represented each plane, with the pilot's name across the top and the last three digits of the plane's serial number printed to the left of the stem of the T. He looked for Jackson's name and found, to his discomfort, that their plane would fly "Tail End Charlie"— the least well-defended position in the formation.[3]

At 0400, the 38 crews slated for this mission were all accounted for, and when a voice rang out "Attention," the airmen sprang to their feet. A tall man with an aggressive walk and a colonel's wings strode from the entryway along a hastily-cleared path to the platform at the front, where he turned and faced the airmen. This was Colonel Elliott Vandevanter, the leader of Van's Valiants. He was well respected as an officer and as a leader, and his tendency to fly the lead plane on difficult missions had endeared him to the entire bomber group. The colonel was a big man, tall, muscular, and very fit, with an engaging smile that revealed a slight spacing between his front teeth. His uniform was immaculate, the creases like knife edges, and the cut obviously tailored to fit. His only known failing, which the airmen found endearing, was his extreme nervousness when placed in front of an audience.

An aide swept the curtain away, and suddenly the routing and the destination became clear. All missions were hazardous, but those targeting Germany were particularly rough, and there was a general sigh of relief when the crews saw that they were heading to France instead. Col. Vandevanter explained that because the weather over Germany was terrible, the bombing effort would continue to focus on supporting the Allied ground forces in Normandy, and promoting the liberation of France. The situation remained perilous, as the Allies were at most 16 miles from the coast, and east of Carentan the advance had stalled just three miles from the beaches.

Major Jim Lewis, the Operations Officer, and Major McWilliams, the Intelligence Officer, provided the mission details as

---

[3] Planes in the center of the formation had the protection of the guns on all of the planes around them. Planes at the trailing edge were more vulnerable, and a plane flying "Tail End Charlie" in the High Squadron could be attacked from all sides.

Jackson and the other officers took notes. Fred, jangled on coffee, and chain smoking Camel cigarettes, paid scant attention unless the information concerned the location of German fighters or heavy flak concentrations along their route. His ears perked up when he heard that they would have three P-47 fighters as escorts — it was great news, as a fighter escort significantly reduced the threat posed by German fighters. It was not going to be a terribly long mission, which was equally good news. Planes were to be ready to start taking off at 0700, with the last bomber in the air by 0720, and they would be back in time for a late lunch.

There would be 38 planes from the 385th BG on this mission, and their formation would be called Wing 4. Wings left British airspace in a long line called a "bomber stream" with each wing in an assigned position. The High Squadron of Wing 4 would be at 24,000'. The 385th would enter the bomber stream behind the wing from the 94th BG and be ahead of the wing from the 447th BG.[4] Once over France, the bomber stream would break up and the wings would head for their specific targets. Wing 4 would bomb the marshalling yards at Montdidier, approaching from the southwest (downwind) to minimize drift. Montdidier was a major switching center for supplies headed west toward the front lines. The crews were shown aerial views of the target area. This was very useful for the navigators and pilots but of no concern for Fred. But he did look up when Major McWilliams showed a map showing their flight route relative to the estimated positions of German 88mm anti-aircraft batteries. When Fred looked at the map, it didn't seem too bad, as their course would take them south and east of the flagged areas.

Major Lewis always concluded a briefing by synchronizing watches, and in preparation, the men exposed their watches and froze the hands with the second hand at 12. The set time would be at 0430 hours, and with a countdown of "five....four.... three.... two.... one.... hack," nearly 400 watches started ticking in synchrony. Lewis concluded the briefing by reminding the officers to pick up the mission codes and charts on their way out.

From the meeting hall, it was a short walk to the buildings containing the locker rooms and the supply desk. Fred entered the locker room with the crowd and moved toward his assigned locker. He never really enjoyed the prep — when it was done, he felt like a toddler in a snowsuit — but he knew the importance of proper preparation. He would be manning his guns by an open port at

[4] The 94th, 385th, and 447th Bomb Groups formed the 4th Combat Bombardment Wing of the Eighth Air Force.

altitudes where temperatures ranged from -40° to -50°F, and oxygen levels were too low for survival.

Fred stripped down and pulled on his long johns, put his uniform back on, and covered it with a khaki flight suit. He then stepped into a one-piece "bunny suit" that looked like pajamas designed for a giant toddler. Fred loved his bunny suit, even if it wasn't stylish, for when it plugged into the aircraft's power supply, it was as warm as an electric blanket. He sat down on the bench seat by the locker to pull on his boot liners before getting into his heavy, fleecelined leather pants and bomber jacket. He then rigged his emergency oxygen bottle and his survival kit, which held a compass, a silk map, money, and other useful items, including a small medical kit. He rechecked his gear bag to make sure that his flight cap, goggles, oxygen mask, and gloves were there before sitting down to pull on his boots. Fred closed the locker door, slung his gear bag over his shoulder, and worked his way through the crowd toward the exit.

Leaving the locker room, he turned right and walked to the next building to pick up his Mae West inflatable life jacket, his parachute harness, and his parachute — three items that needed inspection and routine maintenance after each mission. Once he had collected them, he returned outside before pulling the Mae West over his head and securing it. He then donned and adjusted his parachute harness. Like most of the airmen, Fred found the groin straps restricted his movement, so he tended to leave them a little loose.

Ready to head for the plane, Fred carried his parachute and gear bag toward the 6x6 trucks that were shuttling air crews to their planes. Partial aircrews gathered on either side of the road, climbing onto a truck only when the crew was complete. It was now around 0515. The sun had yet to rise, but there was certainly sufficient light for Fred to recognize the other members of his aircrew. Although the officers wore flight gear similar to that of the enlisted men, their uniform caps set them apart, and most were carrying leather briefcases containing various mission papers, code books, area maps, personal logs, checklists, and other items. Only when all of the men were present and ready to go could Lt. Jackson give the driver the ID number of the plane they would be boarding, at which point the men boosted their gear up and boarded the truck. Once two air crews were aboard, the truck headed to the airfield.

The truck offloaded the Jackson crew alongside the plane they would use for this mission. Like most of the planes of the 385th BG at this time, it was painted a dull olive drab, although newer planes arriving from the US were a bright, unpainted aluminum.[5] A previous aircrew had named the plane "Junior," and the initial J was used for identification and radio instructions within the squadron. Junior was adorned with nose art showing the name and a skinny yokel in shorts preparing to throw a couple of lit sticks of dynamite.

Like the other planes they had flown, Junior was a B-17G, the newest iteration of the design, and the most heavily armored and armed. It was 75' in length, with a wingspan of 104', and its spindle-shaped fuselage was roughly 9'6" in diameter at the waist. There was little room to spare given that this relatively small volume had to carry the flight control and navigational gear, the generators and cabling, communication lines, hydraulic lines, fire extinguishers, oxygen lines and bottles, tools, radio equipment, and thirteen 50-caliber machine guns (2 chin, 2 cheek, 2 top turret, 1 radio room, 2 ball turret, 2 waist, and 2 tail), plus ammunition, survival gear, parachutes, 10 men, and 6,000-8,000 pounds of bombs.

But as the crew disembarked from the truck, the primary topic of discussion was what to call the plane. After some discussion, the crew decided that they would call this plane Crashwagon III regardless of the name painted on the nose. They were on their third B-17, and other than Marsilii's bump on the head after Crashwagon II ditched in the English Channel on their first combat mission together, the crew had remained unscathed. So there was a general feeling that Crashwagon was a lucky name.

Upon arriving at the plane, the various members of the crew used different hatches to board. Lt. Shaffer climbed up through the nose hatch and received the four officers' briefcases, gear bags, and parachutes as they were hoisted to the hatchway. Lt. Blake followed him into the hatch to stow gear and start his preflight checks inside the plane. Lt. Jackson, in company with Sgt. Marsilii, the lead flight engineer, began their walk-around inspection of the exterior of the airplane after one of the ground crew handed Mandu a copy of the maintenance log on a clipboard. Fred, the assistant flight engineer, took a second copy of the log and climbed onboard the plane through the waist hatch to do the preflight check on the interior. It was a long list, but after nine missions, the process was almost second nature. A quick scan told him that all gear, including guns and ammunition, was stowed securely, that the control cables were tight

---

[5] The green was useful when the major threat was from German fighters, as the silhouette got lost against the ground. When fighter activity dropped, the main threat was flak, and the bare aluminum was harder to spot against the sky. It also saved production time in the paint shed, and the unpainted planes were lighter, which saved fuel.

and without kinks, fire extinguishers in place, the ball turret and upper hatch locked in position, and hand cranks in place and secured.

By the time the inspection process was completed, it was roughly 0540. Jackson and Marsilii left the ground crew behind and climbed onboard through the main entrance door at the waist. Fred met them and summarized the interior inspection before Jackson and Marsilii continued forward through the bulkhead and into the radio room where Sgt. Pickrel was seated at his tiny desk. The radio logbook was stowed in a wall holder above the desk, mounted next to a clipboard containing a list of frequencies and call signs. Most of his time would be spent monitoring rather than broadcasting, as missions were ideally performed under radio silence to avoid giving the Luftwaffe a way to determine their position.

Opening the bulkhead door, the men entered in single file along a narrow catwalk. On either side of the catwalk, bombs weighing from 100 to 500 pounds were shackled to the airframe. The bombs would be part of the plane until the bombardier decided it was time to send them away.

Jackson, stepping through the forward bomb bay door, stepped down the ladder to look forward into the nose area, checking that the navigator and bombardier were in their seats. He then climbed up to the flight deck and took the left-hand seat. Lt. Blake was already seated to his right. Once Jackson was in his command seat, Mandu made himself as comfortable as possible, standing or leaning at his station in the top turret. By then it was approaching 0600, and a member of the ground crew noted on the squadron mission form that the Jackson crew was onboard and accounted for at 0605.

While Jackson and Marsilii were doing the exterior checks, and Fred was inspecting the interior, Lt. Haught had been working through the bombardier checklist. The last step was seeing that the chin and cheek guns were secure and the bands of ammunition had a free run to the guns. Those guns were their only defense against head attacks by Luftwaffe fighters. The nose of early iterations of the B-17 hadn't been equipped with serious armament, and the Germans had taken full advantage of that weakness.

Behind him, Lt. Shaffer had laid out his five mission maps in stacked sequence for the run to target. He marked the route and checkpoints on the maps. He next checked the "G box" – an electronic navigation aid that could be used to triangulate their position – and thereafter, spent time reviewing the sequence of maneuvers and course lines, and inventing various scenarios for complications and solutions en route. He was being particularly meticulous about his preparations for the mission. It would be his last combat run, and he wanted it to go like clockwork.

As the time for takeoff approached, crewmen not otherwise occupied in preflight checks finished dressing. Fred, his part of the checklist completed, accessed his gear bag near the left waist gun. He clipped his oxygen mask onto the side of his leather cap. Although it would not be needed until the plane was approaching 10,000', Fred uncoiled the attached oxygen hose and plugged it into the regulator valve for the ship's oxygen system. The valve was in a box mounted on the hull just above the ammunition box aft of the gun station. Fred plugged in the cable from his headphones and from the microphone in his oxygen mask into the connection box for the ship's intercom system, which was just forward of the oxygen valve. He wrapped a heavy woolen scarf, a gift from his younger sister, Liz, around his neck and tucked it into the jacket, leaving the bailout oxygen hose accessible. His electric gloves, which he snapped onto the electrical leads of the jacket liner, would hang free until the temperature dropped. He would then pull on the wool glove liners that, for the moment, he stuffed in his jacket pockets where he could reach them while the plane was climbing toward cruising altitude. He checked that the flak helmet and the flak vest were accessible near his gun station, and after pushing the empty gear bag against the hull out of the way, he stowed his parachute in the same location, using fixed tie down straps.

It was 0620. On the flight deck, Lts. Jackson and Blake were well along in their preflight check, with Blake reading from the cockpit checklist and Jackson performing the checks. At 0630 the engines were started one by one, each coughing and chuffing until the rpms rose and the vibrations smoothed out. Fred heard them start up and knew that Jackson and Blake would be monitoring the engine gauges and performing operational checks on the engines and generators. He trusted his ears as much as the gauges, and he listened closely for any abnormal sounds or vibrations. They had never flown the plane before, so its faults and idiosyncrasies were unknown. If there were any problems in the air, he and Mandu would be asked for solutions. Fortunately everything sounded good.

Jackson hit the switch to activate his microphone, and said "Pilot to crew: Report." One by one, the men responded, giving their positions. When it was his turn, Fred called out "Left waist, loud and clear." The brakes were then locked and the engines run up to check that the turbos engaged properly. That completed, Blake throttled back, and the plane sat idling comfortably. Fred glanced at his watch – 0645 – and looked across the left wing along the row of parked airplanes. Most of the planes in view were either running at idle or preparing to start, but the first plane of the lead formation was moving onto the perimeter runway. As it turned and taxied toward the northeast end of Runway 24, other planes began to follow, forming a long and continuous line of aircraft. Once the signal was given, the planes would be taking off every 30 seconds and climbing at a prescribed 300' per minute at an airspeed of 150 knots.[6]

Fred knew that Lt. Jackson had to wait for the plane that he was to follow, and he and Sam stood, leaning on their guns as the engines rumbled and the plane jiggled and swayed. When the neighboring plane taxied toward the perimeter roadway, Fred felt the jerk as the ground crew removed the wheel chocks, and heard the pitch and throttle increase as the plane started moving forward. As an aircraft mechanic, Fred had driven planes on the ground countless times, steering by controlling the pitch and throttle of individual engines and deftly working the brakes. When the plane came to a halt, and the engines were again idling, he saw the control cables working back and forth as Jackson gave them a final check while waiting to take off.

At 0700, a green flare was fired from the control tower, and the first plane of the lead group lumbered on its way. At 0720, it was their turn at last, and Fred felt the surge of acceleration as the engines went to full military power, and they rushed down the tarmac. When flight speed was reached, the wheels left the tarmac, and Junior/Crashwagon III joined the line of planes climbing toward their assigned altitudes.

By the time the planes reached 10,000', the air temperature was at 15°F and dropping fast. Fred had already put on his electric gloves, turned on the heater in his bunny suit, secured his oxygen mask, and opened the oxygen delivery valve. With the engines powered up for climbing, the sound was overwhelming — the entire fuselage was vibrating like a stereo speaker with the volume at maximum. It wasn't a comfortable ride, especially for Fred and Sam, exposed to the frigid air blasting through the openings accommodating the barrels of their machine guns.

The line soon started to break up, and the two waist gunners braced themselves as the plane banked and maneuvered into position. Once the formation was complete, the 38 planes, officially designated Wing 4, occupied an airspace that was roughly 500 yards wide, 250 yards long, and 200 yards deep.

It took longer than usual to get into position, and Fred felt some unusual changes in direction. Looking out he could see that

---

[6] Abbreviated kt, a knot is one nautical mile per hour; a nautical mile is roughly 6,000'.

the jogs were needed to avoid passing formations of B-24s.[7] Realizing that the delays had put them several minutes behind schedule, the lead navigator decided to alter the planned course to make up the time. When they arrived at the assembly point, Crashwagon III was at 17,000', and at 0815, Wing 4 joined the bomber stream and headed for occupied France. As they crossed the English Channel, the High Element of the High Group, including Junior/Crashwagon III, reached an altitude of 24,000'.

Conditions onboard were pretty routine. The noise level was deafening due to the roar of the engines and the scream of the wind through various openings in the fuselage. It was, of course, bitterly cold – roughly -40°F – and the gunners had to remember that if their guns jammed, they must ignore the natural tendency to discard the bulky gloves to free the mechanism. If they did not, their hands would instantly freeze to the gun, and severe frostbite would result.[8]

There was little communication of any kind en route. The planes were under radio silence, all intercom traffic was mission related, and conversation was almost impossible unless two heads were close together and both shouted. So each man passed the time his own way. The officers were kept busy by assigned tasks, flying the plane, monitoring instruments, plotting the position, or reviewing target notes.

The enlisted men had less to occupy them. The radioman listened for traffic, but the other sergeants just stood, leaned, or sat by their guns, daydreaming until it was time to start scanning for enemy fighters. Fred passed the time thinking about his life back home in Brooklyn.

---

[7] The B-24s flew faster than B-17s, but they could not fly as high with a full bomb load. As a result, their formations and bomber streams were organized separately. With so many formations in the air at one time, pilots had to stay at high alert to avoid airspace conflicts.

[8] They also had to remember that in combat they must fire only short bursts of a few seconds. Otherwise, despite the extreme cold, the gun barrel would melt, forming a curved banana that would quickly be torn apart by the emerging rounds.

CHAPTER 2

Reverie

⊰ 🙰 ⊱

Frederic Cosmo Martini was born in Brooklyn, New York, on 18 October 1918. His father, Federico Martini, had emigrated to the US in 1897 and became a naturalized citizen in 1904. Federico was a contractor by trade and gradually built a solid reputation as a builder in the Coney Island area. He enthusiastically adopted the conventions of his adopted home, changing his first name to Frederic and, once he had mastered English, refusing ever to speak Italian. In 1915, at the age of 32, he married Mary Rose Ippolito, a beautiful woman 13 years his junior. Their first child, Lucille, was born in 1917. There followed Frederic a year later, Peter in 1920, and Elizabeth in 1923. They had a home large enough to house the family plus an adopted child, Raulin, and Mary Rose's brother, Sam.

Federico was a hard man who used a heavy hand in disciplining his sons, and who left all household tasks, including raising his daughters, to Mary Rose. His business flourished, their house was lavish, they had multiple rental buildings and properties, and in general, the 1920s were boom years. And then it all fell apart.

In April 1929, Mary Rose died in childbirth, and their new son died with her. The market crash followed, and their investment properties were sold or seized one after another. Without Mary Rose, Federico was unable to cope with the family. Peter, who had cerebral palsy, was sent to an institution, and the others were shipped off to a Catholic boarding school in the Adirondacks. When they returned two years later, Lucille, at 14, became the housekeeper, maid, cook, and general manager for the family.

By the time he entered Abraham Lincoln High School, Fred was spending his free time on the street, hanging out. He had disciplinary problems at school, he got into fights, he made friends his father didn't approve of, including Eddie Virgilio (his future brother-in law), and in general, learned things never taught at Catholic schools.

Fred was called Frederic by his parents and his elder sister, Fred by most of his friends and acquaintances, and Freddy by his girlfriends. He wasn't fond of his middle name (Cosmo) and used it only when use of his full name was absolutely necessary. Of course his closest friends and younger siblings knew this and teased him about it. Eddie Virgilio and Peter and Raulin Martini often called him

Coz, whereas his sister Elizabeth preferred Cossie.

In 1934, Fred just couldn't wait any longer to set out on his own, so he left school after year 11. He found the freedom exhilarating, but finding a job was more difficult than he had expected. In the end, he swallowed his pride, and he and Eddie started working for Federico's construction business. Fred had an aptitude for mechanical work, and he soon became involved in maintaining the heavy equipment. He used his earnings to buy flashy clothes and a dead Model A Ford, whose engine he successfully rebuilt and tuned. Having been a regular visitor over the years, he was well known in the night spots of New York City. Fred was a cheerful, charming young man who tipped well, bought drinks for his pals, and dated showgirls.

But in September 1939, Federico died of a heart attack, and the business folded. Fred's mechanical skills enabled him to find a job at a Brooklyn bakery, where he operated the wrapping machine and maintained the other equipment. By the summer of 1941, the bakery job had gotten old. He could see trouble brewing overseas and war on the horizon, and he thought he'd be better off enlisting immediately rather than waiting for a conflict to start. If he was wrong about a war starting he would only have to serve a year before being discharged. If he was right, he'd have extra seniority time, and might be able to have a better job than carrying a rifle on the front lines.

So in August 1941, Fred enlisted in the US Army. He went to basic training at Camp Upton on Long Island. As an enlistee without a college degree, he wasn't officer material, but the army was preparing to mobilize, and they needed Quartermasters to manage the supplies. So Fred was sent to Quartermaster School at Fort Lee, Virginia. When the war started, Fred was sent to Dayton, Ohio, where he went through evasion and escape training as a corporal.[9]

He enjoyed Dayton and its clubs and bars, although it was hardly Brooklyn. But spending the war as a supply clerk held little appeal for him. It sounded awfully dull, and the Army Air Corps, created in 1941, sounded a lot more exciting. So Fred decided to volunteer for air service. When asked why he would do such a crazy thing, leaving a cushy desk job to climb onto a flying target, he had a standard reply: "I heard the food was terrific." He also liked the uniforms, especially the leather jackets. That reasoning made sense to everyone who knew him, for Fred was always hungry, and he was always well dressed.

---

[9] Fred had a good time in Dayton, and partied on leave in Chicago. The back of his notebook from that period has a list of 14 names and addresses; nine of them were young ladies.

Even after a day tearing down machinery, he would leave home for a night on the town with clean hands and nails, and sharply pressed pants.

When his transfer was approved, Fred began his training with a six-week stint at the Aerial Gunnery School at Tyndall Field, Florida. Already rated Expert Marksman, he adapted quickly to compensating for relative motion, and his mechanical skills became apparent as he serviced the guns. His talents were noted, and upon graduation from gunnery school, Fred was ordered to report to Airplane Mechanics School at Keesler Field in Mississippi. He spent the next three months learning to service B-17s and B-24s. After receiving his mechanics certification in the summer of 1943, he was sent to Will Rodgers Field, Oklahoma, for flight training. He was a staff sergeant when, after several months and multiple training flights in both types of airplanes, he was assigned to Drew Field in Tampa, Florida.

Drew Field was one of the regional sites where flight crews bound for the ETO were assembled and trained to work together as a unit. It was there that he met Loren Jackson and the other men who would be part of his aircrew. Fred had a great time in Florida. His sister Betty, who had also enlisted, was undergoing advanced training at a Coast Guard facility in Palm Beach, and Fred could visit her (and hundreds of other young women cloistered on the base) whenever he got leave. Betty, whose nickname was "Liz," was rooming with her friends Anastasia Murphy, called "Murph" or "Sheila," and Betty Hover, who was usually called "Boop" (after the cartoon character Betty Boop). Fred was polite to his sister's friends, and he had a passing flirtation with Sheila, but there were many other girls to chase and, as he put it, "You don't fish too close to the dock."

Fred spent six months at Drew Field, training and flying simulated combat missions with a new flight crew under the command of Lt. Jackson. As often happened, the original flight crew changed while training was underway. Lt. Blake arrived when their original copilot left to become the pilot of another crew, and Sgt. Pickrel replaced the first radioman when he left for another assignment. The crew list finally stabilized, and in late March 1944, the Jackson crew received clearance to depart for the ETO.

The Army needed to replace planes as well as crews lost through combat or accident. As a result, the standard practice was to give new aircrews a new plane to deliver rather than getting them to the UK by other means. After completing the paperwork, Fred and the rest of the crew went by train to Hunter Field, in Savannah, Georgia, to pick up their new ride. The plane was identified only by number 42-102416,[10] and the crew had struggled to come up with a nickname. It was a group effort. Initially, they tried taking the first letters of the crew's first names or last names, but that didn't work, as there were too many consonants and too few vowels. They next tried the first letters of their home states, but the only thing they could spell was Nagid Wimin. Fred rather liked that name, but Jackson vetoed that one because he thought the nose art would be potentially embarrassing. So as a lark, they decided to thumb their noses at fate, and call the plane Crashwagon.

Crashwagon would be one of a number of new B-17s headed overseas in convoy. The routing involved flying in hops to Richmond, DC, Philadelphia, Mitchel Field (outside New York City), Grenier Field (New Hampshire), Goose Bay (Labrador), and Meeks Field (Iceland), before heading for Nutts Corner, an airfield in Northern Ireland. The planes left Hunter Field on 5 April 1944, and all went fine until they got to Mitchel Field.

Other than Blake, who was from Long Island, and Fred, from Brooklyn, none of the crew had been in New York City before. Fred acted as the social director and tour guide. He started with the bar at Jack Dempsey's and ended at dawn on top of the Empire State Building. The next night he got tickets to a movie at Radio City Music Hall, and when it was over, Fred took them on a pub crawl through his favorite night spots. The following day, they went to the plane to fly out with the other crews, but when they arrived, the engines wouldn't start. Jackson immediately reported this to the ground staff. Stuck on the ground, and with nothing better to do, the crew then headed back into the city for another day of adventure, visiting the Statue of Liberty, the Chrysler Building, Yankee Stadium, and finishing with another round of the nightclubs.

When they got back to the base in the wee hours of the morning, there was a message for Jackson to see the maintenance officer ASAP. In a rather aggrieved tone, the maintenance officer told him that he understood how alluring New York City could be, and how much the crew wanted to paint the town red, and that he didn't care one whit if Jackson wanted to delay departure for a few more days. But Jackson had to tell his crew to stop snapping off the stems of the spark plugs, because it was a pain in the neck replacing them. And, he reminded Jackson, 100 B-17s had left Savannah, 99 of them were already in Labrador, and at some point, hard questions would be asked. Fred,

---

[10] The first two digits of the aircraft number (42-) indicate the year funding was approved. The serial number (102416) was issued by the manufacturer. The plane was received by the Air Force on 2 March 1944.

the guilty party, knew that Jackson suspected he was responsible, but when the crew was called together for a heartheart no names were mentioned. Suitably chastened, they were soon on their way again.

On successive days, they made the jumps to Grenier Field, Goose Bay, and then Meeks Field without incident. But on the final leg, as they neared Nutts Corner, their landing gear refused to deploy, and when the hand crank was used to deploy the wheels manually, the handle spun freely. Without landing gear, there was the risk of a crash that would close the airstrip at Nutts Corner, so they were diverted to a secondary field at Langford Lodge. On the way, they diverted over Loch Neagh, into whose waters they dropped Felipe's belly turret. The landing went perfectly, although the hole where the ball turret used to be acted like a potato peeler, and the back of the plane quickly accumulated a long, thick strip of sod. There were no other incidents of note as the plane slid off the runway into the adjacent grassy field. It was a textbook crash — there were no injuries, and damage to the plane was limited to the destruction of the propellers. Without the extra ground clearance provided by landing gear, the props were mangled by impact with the ground.

Fred and the rest of the Jackson crew were sent to Belfast for some R&R. Afterward, they took a ship to Scotland to connect with a train to Boddington, where they received their assignment to the 385th Bomb Group.[11] They arrived at the Great Ashfield airbase on 5 May 1944, and on 9 May they were assigned to the 551st Squadron as air crew MM-37. On arrival, the senior air crews were cordial but a bit reserved, as the odds were stacked against new crews surviving long enough to make friends. Fred was told very bluntly that there was no reason to worry, as in three months it would all be over — by then he would be dead, a POW, or on his way home with 30 missions completed. What they didn't tell him was that the life expectancy of a B-17 was 13-14 missions, and that if those missions involved fighter attacks, the life expectancy of the waist gunner (roughly three minutes of firing time) was the shortest of any crewman. German fighters found it all too easy to knock out defenses on one side of the plane by targeting the guy standing up in the middle of the aircraft.

Before flying combat missions as a group, the crew was split up and assigned to fly two missions as temporary members of more experienced crews. Fred and Sam flew as waist gunners for two missions with Lt. Percival, flying in two different aircraft. The first mission was to bomb Liege, Belgium, and it was a rough baptism.

---

[11] These were also officially called Bombardment Groups, but most airmen used the term Bomb Group.

Fortunately for Fred and Sam, there were few fighters in the air, but flak was heavy, and accurate enough to throw the plane around and punch holes in the fuselage. Fred and Sam found it disconcerting, but the plane tolerated the damage and returned relatively intact with no injuries onboard. Flying in combat was very different from flying practice missions around Florida! On the plus side, they completed a flight that ended with a landing rather than a crash. The second mission was to bomb Kiel, inside Germany,[12] and it was a seven-hour mission with heavy flak and occasional fighters. Once again, the plane returned safely but with numerous holes in the cabin that the ground crew would patch with duct tape before the next mission.

Their two individual training missions completed, the Jackson crew was assigned their first combat mission as a complete crew. For that mission, they were given aircraft 42-39951, formerly called In the Mood. Fred and his colleagues called it Crashwagon II. The mission, number 112 for the 385th BG, targeted the marshalling yards at Chaumont, France. It was not an auspicious start to their combat careers. On the way back to England, they encountered heavy flak. Fred was looking out of his gun port when a burst took out an engine. Fred knew that the required response was to feather the propeller, reducing drag and allowing the remaining engines to keep the plane headed home. But it soon became clear that Jackson was having trouble feathering the prop. It "ran away," spinning uncontrollably. Without lubrication, the hub was soon glowing red hot, and the plane shook so violently that it was difficult for Fred to remain on his feet. He could hear Jackson increase power to the other engines, but the plane started losing altitude, and Fred became concerned about the prop breaking free and spinning through the nose.

Flames were spreading along the wing when Fred realized he could see Dover in the distance. It was too far away, and the waters of the English Channel were approaching rapidly. Jackson must have decided to ditch the plane. Fred and Sam braced themselves and tried to remember the proper sequence for leaving the plane after a water landing.

It was a hard landing, but Jackson controlled it beautifully, and the plane stayed level and afloat for several crucial minutes while the crew climbed out through the top turret and inflated a pair of life rafts. The only injury was sustained by Mandu, who cut his head on the top turret hatch as he left the plane.

Before the plane went down, Erv Pickrel had sent a rough

---

[12] Kiel, a coastal city, was the site of a major U-boat (submarine) base.

position fix to air rescue. The teams ashore were fast and efficient, and a rescue boat from Brighton picked up the crew shortly after they boarded the life rafts. As they headed for shore they watched Crashwagon II sink beneath the waves.

Marsilii was soon patched up and everyone outfitted with dry RAF uniforms, which they were still wearing when they were shuttled back to Great Ashfield the next day. After tedious debriefings by the Public Information Officer, the Supply Officer, the Intelligence Officer, the Operations Officer, and various other authorities, they were released on a three-day pass and headed for the bars of London. Fred got the sergeants more than one round of free drinks telling the story of their harrowing experiences, without mentioning that it had been their first mission.

Fred wrote home regularly. A letter to his sister Lucille, dated 19 May 1944, included:

Lt. Jackson did a wonderful job and all ten of us were fished out of the water by an English naval vessel. The English, both Navy and RAF, can never get enough praise from me for the treatment they gave us and the swell rescue job they do. This crew of ours certainly is running on luck, that is the second crash in a months' time and not one of us has been hurt yet. Let's hope it keeps up. For further details, consult local papers. The story...should have been in the Eagle.[13]

Their next mission was to Hamm, in the Ruhr Valley of Germany. Their plane was 43-97818, which they called Crashwagon III. It was pretty much a "milk run" (easy and uneventful) with light, inaccurate flak and no enemy fighters in sight. Fred was delighted to find that some missions were relatively straightforward. Unfortunately, the next day's mission targeted the same area, and the Germans were ready and waiting. There were enemy fighters galore and heavy flak, and the weather at times was lousy. Flak was so heavy that Fred later joked that they could have put the wheels down and landed on it. After landing, Fred, Mandu, and Jackson did a walk around the plane looking at the damage. They stopped counting after finding more than 200 holes in the aluminum skin. The ground crew chief, TSgt. Joe Zorzoli, later told Fred that they'd also broken a wing support.

They had the next day off to recover, and Fred took the time to write home:

---

[13] The Brooklyn Daily Eagle was the newspaper popular in that Borough of New York City.

The flying here is, to say the least, a bit different and quite a bit rougher on a person than it was in the states, so between missions it is usually sack time, never seem to get enough of it either. The boys send their best and Sam says he sure intends to take you up on that dinner as soon as we get back to the States (oh Happy Day).

After their plane was repaired, they flew a mission to bomb the airfield at Evereux-Chonces, France, followed by one to bomb the harbor facilities at Boulogne. There were few enemy fighters around, and Fred had nothing to shoot at, so he just wedged himself in place, scanning the skies and hoping that his flak vest would do its job if necessary. On the Boulogne run, Fred was startled to see exhaust trails tracking up from the ground, following small missiles that flashed through the formation at blinding speed. It was the first time that the 385th BG had encountered anti-aircraft rockets. They were impressed by the technology but relieved by the inaccuracy — no planes were hit.

At the mission briefing on the morning of 6 June, Fred learned that D-Day, the invasion of France, was underway and that the 385th BG would be tasked with air support for the ground forces. The target for this mission was Falaise, roughly 40 miles south-southwest of the Normandy beaches. En route to that target, cruising at 21,000', Fred was astounded by the size of the assembled fleet and the scale of the landings underway along the Normandy coast. He didn't envy those ground troops one bit, and he hoped that Crashwagon's bomb loads would help those brave guys on the beaches. As Jackson had said before this mission, "They'll need all the help they can get!"

The 7 June mission was their first mission with Lt. Shaffer as navigator. Fred thought he seemed quiet and reserved, and wondered if that was the result of having flown so many combat missions. From the intercom traffic, it was clear to Fred that Shaffer was a top-notch navigator who gave information quickly and precisely. The mission was long — eight hours — with little drama until they were approaching the British coast as darkness fell. While still in formation, they received word over the radio that German fighters were in the area and that the formation should break up and take separate routes back to base.

All of the airbases had doused their lights to avoid giving the Germans clues as to their location, which made accurate landing rather difficult. Jackson relayed word over the intercom that they had just been told they had a Ju-88 (a German night fighter) on their tail, and he was reducing altitude to lessen the chances of attack from below. Fred, searching the night sky for the telltale glow from a fighter engine, or worse yet a string of tracers, suddenly saw a runway passing below him. Jackson, equally alert, saw it as well and decided to set the plane down then and there. There were no runway lights, and landing lights were too risky, so it was a matter of letting the plane drop and hoping for the best. They hit the ground hard enough to knock Fred and Sam off their feet and bounce the plane 25' in the air. The landing was especially exciting for Musquiz, who was in the ball turret trying to locate the Ju-88 and had no warning of the landing.

Crashwagon III had landed at Rattlesden, home of the 447th BG, but it felt good to be on the ground. The next day, 8 June, with the skies clear of enemy fighters, the crew flew back to Great Ashfield. When he got back to the base, Fred wrote to Lucille again, telling her that he appreciated her letters. He added:

> *Damned if I have anything to write about. I haven't been off the Post since I had that three day pass [to London] so that is it as far as my social life. I can't write about the missions as censors would cut it out. So nothing left but to say that I am feeling OK and the crew is still intact and none of us have been hurt. We've been through some mighty damn spots together and now I don't think anything can knock us out. They have raised the lid on the amount of missions we fly so I imagine I'll be in the ETO for some time.*

On 9 June, they flew a short training flight, and on 10 June, they spent six hours on a mission to Germany that was recalled due to bad weather over the intended target. June 11 was spent on high altitude formation flying, part of a training exercise for less experienced crews. In the last 18 days, Fred had flown 12 times, completed seven combat missions, and lost his second airplane. The Jackson crew was considered an experienced member of the 551st Squadron, worthy of assignment to Lead Crew School. At least that was what Fred had thought until Major Masters awakened him for duty that morning.

CHAPTER 3

Combat

-ʝ⊱-

Somewhere around mid-Channel, Fred's reverie was interrupted by an announcement over the intercom that gunners could test-fire their guns to show that they were ready for action. The chatter of the 50-cal machine guns woke everyone up and got them scanning the skies for threats with renewed vigor. The inbound Control Point (CP) was located just west of Le Havre, outside of the range of the heavy flak defenses that guarded that port city. As they continued, Fred could see the entire spread of the Normandy beachhead passing below him, extending to the west. The coastal ocean was still blanketed with ships — more were arriving — and the shore was a mass of vehicles and equipment. Clouds of smoke indicated heavy artillery fire just inland of the beachhead.

After passing the inbound CP, the bomber stream started to fragment. Wing 4, the 385th, turned northeast toward Beauvais while other wings went their separate ways. By 0900, Fred was looking north, toward a small city he knew must be Rouen, when he saw the black puffballs that indicated anti-aircraft fire. Soon Jackson came on the intercom to let the crew know about the flak they were approaching. Fred, along with Mandu, Erv, Sam, and Lts. Haught and Shaffer, struggled into heavy flak jackets and donned armored helmets. Jackson and Blake relied on their armored seats for protection, while Musquiz and Dubenic were protected by armor plating around their gun positions.

The formation lumbered on, maintaining speed, holding its position and hoping for the best. It soon became apparent that most of the flak was exploding a considerable distance below them, and neither Crashwagon III nor the other planes in the Wing were taking damage.

Unfortunately, it was all too good to last. Before the bombers were completely out of range, the flak rose to meet them. Now the explosions were everywhere, dense black clouds appearing and then flashing astern. Over the roar of the engines, Fred could hear a sound like gravel on a tin roof, and small openings appeared in the skin of the plane around him. As eerily silent concussion waves buffeted the plane, it jerked and shook and bounced its way through the sky. Fred hung on for dear life as Lts. Jackson and Blake struggled to stabilize their position in the formation.

Suddenly, a shock jerked the plane up and to the left. The plane began to vibrate, and slewed to the right. As Jackson fought the turn, Fred looked out Sam's gunport, where he could see the #4 propeller winding down. He was relieved to see the prop feathered, stopping its rotation. Although he both could hear and feel Jackson increasing power to the other three engines, it was not enough to maintain their position in the formation. Fred could see that they were being left behind, and making matters worse, they were gradually losing altitude as well.

By 0906, Fred could feel the damaged plane struggling to hold altitude. He knew what their options were, and he wasn't surprised when he heard Jackson order Haught to drop the bomb load. Even with the radio room door to the bomb bay closed, Fred could feel the turbulence created as the bomb doors opened and the raging wind found the interior of the plane. Seconds later, he felt a lurch as the bombs fell away and then the surge as the plane, free of her explosive cargo, gained altitude and speed.

With the plane four tons lighter, Fred thought they would soon catch up to the heavily laden squadron and regain the safety of numbers. But before they could regain their position, the plane entered another zone of heavy flak. As the heavy plumes of smoke erupted around them, the plane was jostled and jolted, knocking everyone around. There was one especially severe shock that slapped the left wing.

That shock got everyone's attention. At the waist, Fred was knocked off his feet, hanging by one hand from the guard of his gun. Blood streamed down the left side of his face, and the left leg of his flight suit was shredded. He had been hit by flak, with one piece passing completely through his left calf. Sam rushed over to see if he could help, but under the circumstances, there was little he could do.

The plane was shaking severely, and the oscillations were getting worse. The strain on the plane was severe, and on either side of the fuselage, the control cables that ran aft suspended between guides were vibrating like tuning forks, each cable a blur. There were more lurches from incoming flak, and more patches of daylight appearing in the airframe. The #2 engine was spinning unevenly, and the wild windmilling was what made the plane shake so violently. And then Fred, fighting to remain conscious, saw the engine burst into flames, the fire spreading rapidly along the left wing, heading toward the fuselage. With the engine in flames and the hydraulic lines ruptured, Fred knew there was no way to control the runaway propeller. He also knew there was no way to put the fire out. Fred had learned in training that engine fire extinguishers had been removed from the design to save weight.

Without any way to suppress the fire, he could envision only two possible scenarios, neither of them encouraging. One was that the propeller shaft would fail and the freed propeller would spin right through the cockpit on its way toward the right wing. The other was that the spreading fire would weaken the wing, ignite the fuel in the wing tank, and then the left wing would collapse. Once either of those scenarios came to pass, it was game over for the aircrew.

Their luck had run out. With only two functional engines, there was no way to gain or even maintain altitude, and with the fire raging, the plane was unlikely to reach the ground intact. None of the crew was surprised to hear the bailout alarm, followed by "Pilot to crew: Abandon ship" over the intercom. The alarm would have been deafening had they been on the ground with the engines off, but under the current circumstances, it was just a new sound in an already noisy environment. Its meaning, however, was unmistakable to everyone onboard.

On the navigator's deck at the front of the plane, Lt. Haught opened the bomb bay doors and then clipped on his parachute. He then opened the hatch in the floor below the flight deck, and left the plane. He was followed moments later by Lt. Shaffer. Lt. Jackson could feel the resistance added by the opening of the nose hatch and the bomb bay doors, but he decided to hang tight for 3-4 minutes to give the crew adequate time to leave the plane. Behind him, Sgts. Marsilii and Pickrel were grabbing their parachutes, and they quickly left the plane via the bomb bay.

At the waist, Sam ditched his flak vest as Fred, fumbling a bit with the straps, dropped his. Running on adrenaline, Fred detached his oxygen hose and the intercom cables from the plane's systems, stuck the hose from the bailout oxygen bottle in his mouth, and opened the valve on the bottle. He then joined Sam at the ball turret, which they noted with alarm had not rotated to bring the access hatch to the top. Either Felipe had not heard the alarm, or he was hurt, or there had been a hydraulic or power failure. In any case, he could probably use a hand extracting himself from the ball turret.

Taking the handles from their brackets on the bulkhead, they manually rotated the ball to bring the access hatch to the top. Opening it, they quickly boosted Musquiz, who was uninjured, out of the enclosure. The three sergeants hastily assisted one another with clipping the parachute packs onto the D-rings on the front of each harness. They then raced aft, to the waist hatch on the starboard side of the fuselage. On the way, Fred could see light through the open tail hatch. It meant that Ted Dubenic, the tail gunner, was already out of the plane, and there was no need to crawl back to check for him.

At first, the waist door would not open, the airframe having twisted, but by slamming their shoulders against the door repeatedly, they finally managed to free it. Thanks to the delay, compounded by exertion, shock, and adrenaline levels, Fred's bailout bottle was already low. At risk of oxygen deprivation as well as shock, Fred dove through the hatch head first, falling into the blue toward a layer of cloud roughly a mile below them. Sam and then Felipe followed a heartbeat later.

Fred, free-falling and only half conscious, felt the bitterly cold wind tearing at his face and the corners of his now useless oxygen mask. By making shifts and adjustments to the positions of his arms and legs, he managed to flip over to his back. Above him, he could see the bright blue sky, and with the wind roaring past and pressing against his back, he felt much more secure. He barely had time to appreciate that sensation before he lost consciousness.

Certain that other members of the crew were already on their way, Jackson held the bucking yoke with his left hand and motioned to Blake to leave the plane. Ross unclipped his harness, pulled his parachute from beneath his seat, and climbed over the central control console. He clipped the parachute on before climbing down to exit via the forward hatchway. Although the official plan was for the pilot and copilot to leave via the bomb bay, the forward hatch was preferred — one was less likely to collide with the belly turret.

As Blake was climbing down, Jackson began his preparations for departure. His parachute was stuffed under his seat, and as he leaned forward, struggling with his harness and air hoses and wiring, his weight shifted forward, pushing the control yoke to the front and sending the plane into a steep dive. He got the parachute out as quickly as possible and hauled back on the yoke to level her out at 16,000'. He had dropped over a mile in the few seconds that it had taken him to access his chute! He glanced at the left wing to see how bad things were, and realized with a shock that the rushing air in their descent had blown the fire out. They might be able to make it home after all!

Jackson hit the intercom to tell any remaining crew members to stay on board, but he got no replies. He set the autopilot momentarily and shifted back to look down and forward to see if Blake had left yet. He was still aboard, sitting on the hatch coaming. Blake stuck his head up, but when Jackson took off his mask and yelled "Stay with the plane!" Ross waved jauntily and dropped through the hatchway. Jackson, totally alone on the plane, returned to his seat, disconnected the autopilot, and started a banking turn to the west to head for home. But within moments the fire restarted with a vengeance, flaring across the wing. At a lower speed and lower altitude, the fire was much better fueled, and it was really raging. "Well," thought Jackson, "now it really is time to go!" Setting the autopilot for the last time, he descended to the forward hatch and dropped toward the ground.

Lt. Haught, the bombardier and the first of the officers to leave the crippled ship, fell well clear before pulling the ripcord to deploy his parachute. Almost immediately, he was startled by the rush of a falling body trailing a tangled, streaming parachute. The free-fall continued before his horrified stare until both airman and parachute were lost in the cloud layer below. Haught was now descending toward the cloud layer at a more stately pace, and he was being steadily blown to the northeast.

Jackson, the last to leave, had hardly opened his parachute before he saw to his dismay that the plane did not appear interested in leaving his side. Like some huge lumbering shark, the plane had gone into a flat spiral, pivoting around the flaming right wing and centering on his approximate position. Three times he watched the plane rush past, once so close that he thought he would be struck head. But each time, it passed with either lateral or vertical separation before its descent accelerated, and it plummeted through the cloud layer toward the ground below.

Long moments later and a considerable distance below, Fred recovered consciousness. He was still on his back, still falling, but with a layer of cloud in view, rather than the sharp blue he remembered from just moments before. Groggily, he flipped himself over and saw to his shock that he was very low, far below the 5000' that he had planned on, and he could see what looked like a church steeple rocketing toward him like a javelin. Frantically, he pulled on the ripcord, and with a jolt, the deploying parachute slowed his descent — at the cost of a mule kick to his private parts, the result of having a slack harness. With the parachute full, the wind pushed him rapidly to the northeast, away from the village and its church.

His parachute was a small, hemispherical canopy known as a "survival chute," and each time it rocked, it would dump air. As a result, Fred descended in a sequence of rock-fall jerk, rock-fall jerk. With the ground now 400-500' feet beneath him, he moved laterally, passing over fields, dirt roads, and then a small crossroads. Ahead, about where he expected to touch down, he saw a cultivated field and a small trail adjacent to a small forest. At the last moment, he attempted to pull the shrouds to keep the chute from rocking and thereby control his landing speed, but to no avail. The parachute dumped air in the moment before landing, and he fell hard, his weight falling on his injured left leg, which promptly collapsed and pitched him face first toward the ground. He hit with a bang, and again the lights went out.

CHAPTER 4

12 June 1944, Peenemünde, Germany

⇥⊟⇤

The office of Baron Wernher Magnus Maximillian von Braun was in House 4, a brick two-story building that was the administrative and engineering headquarters for the Peenemünde research facility. Von Braun was a tall man who in many ways resembled the idealized German male. At 32, he was blond, blue eyed, and very fit, with a commanding presence and an arrogance that was in part a consequence of birth — his father was a Prussian aristocrat who had been the Minister of Agriculture and whose support in the cabinet was instrumental in Hitler's rise to power — and in part the result of his rapid ascent through the academic, political, and scientific ranks. He had arrived at work as usual, wearing one of the custom-tailored business suits he preferred for his day-to-day life in and around Peenemünde. He always wore a prominent Nazi Party lapel pin, but donned his SS[14] uniform only for meetings of the local SS[14] unit and when traveling to outlying rocket assembly and testing sites.[15] When dealing with SS field teams, the uniform was a definite plus, and it encouraged immediate obedience from the general public. But as an SS-Major[16] (*Sturmbannführer*) there were hundreds of SS officers who outranked him and to whom he must defer, whereas as Professor and Technical Director of the Nazi rocket program, he needed to defer only to the Führer and General Dornberger,[17] the head of the Army Ordnance team that employed him.

As technical head of the rocket program, von Braun was

---

[14] The Schutzstaffel was a Nazi paramilitary organization that began as Hitler's personal guard.

[15] Albert Speer was an architect who'd been appointed the Minister of Armaments and War Production after his predecessor, Fritz Todt, a civil engineer, was killed in a plane crash. Todt had been a one-star general (Generalmajor) and Speer was a two-star general (Generalleutnant), but both preferred suits and lapel pins to uniforms. Speer was one of Wernher's staunchest advocates, and Speer's Ministry provided funding for his programs. Speer felt that he and Wernher were intellectual cousins, and they certainly dressed alike.

[16] All SS ranks will be shown in this format because unlike the equivalent Army ranks, they were awarded without comparable military training.

[17] Dornberger was a *Generalmajor*, the German equivalent a US Brigadier General (one star).

responsible for the design office, the five laboratory complexes (materials, ballistics, guidance, fabrication, and testing), as well as budgeting and associated administrative operations. The challenges kept him energized and very, very, busy.

It was 0930, and Wernher was tired from traveling but excited about the days ahead. Two big events were scheduled. The most important, from his perspective, was the test flight of a V-2 rocket equipped with a remote-controlled guidance system intended for use with the new anti-aircraft rockets already being fired (with little success) at enemy bombers. Wernher was in charge of this project, which was code named *Wasserfall* (Waterfall). The V-2 wasn't intended for anti-aircraft use (it was a ballistic missile) but it was big enough to carry all of the communication and testing gear needed to assess the remote control system intended for use in smaller rockets.

Although still referred to by the engineers as the A-4, the missiles headed for mobile launch facilities in Germany and the occupied territories would become widely known as the V-2s, the V designating "Vengeance Weapons" (*Vergeltungswaffen*). The first of the Vengeance weapons would become fully operational the next day, when the V-1 bombardment of England would begin. The jet-propelled flying bombs, developed by the Luftwaffe (German Air Force), were already being loaded onto their launch rails, and a test firing earlier in the morning had already sent one toward an unknown fate in England.[18] The V-1, technically the Fi103, was cheap to construct and available in large numbers. Thousands were either already built or under construction. Each was basically a simple jet engine strapped to a glider frame carrying a 500 pound bomb. It was a cumbersome, slow, primitive, and limited weapon, as compared to Wernher's cherished V-2, but the propaganda value of flights of unmanned, pre-programmed flying bombs raining down on Germany's enemies would be considerable. His direct involvement with V-1 development was limited, because the Luftwaffe ran the program in Peenemünde-West, whereas Wernher's V-2 project was based in Peenemünde-East. Yet the success of any advanced weapon from Peenemünde would bode well for long support for Wernher's projects — as long as they could overcome the logistical hurdles and win the war.

The V-2 rocket to be tested had been shipped from the manufacturing plant at the Mittelwerk. Like the others under construction, the rocket was 46' tall and capable of delivering nearly a ton of explosives to a target roughly 200 miles away. That particular

---

[18] It crashed in the English countryside, well short of London.

unit was painted a dull green camouflage color, and rather than carrying explosives, its payload consisted of radios that would provide onboard telemetry. Some compromises that had been made to improve transmission quality concerned him. For example, the skin of the central section of the rocket had been made of wood rather than sheet metal, and although he had calculated that the wood would be strong enough to tolerate the launch forces, uncertainties remained.

In fact, there were many uncertainties about the V-2 program in general. Primary among them would be whether or not Arthur Rudolph, his friend and former subordinate, had managed to suppress the continuing problems with quality control with the aid of SS-General Hans Kammler. The problems were generally attributed to intentional sabotage by the prison laborers on the assembly line. He was sure that Rudolph and Kammler would do whatever was necessary to overcome the problems, so that the V-2 barrage could begin on schedule.[19]

Wernher had certainly done everything he could to simplify the design and improve quality control on the production line. It had become very clear that he was going to need to visit the V-2 assembly complex, known as the Mittelwerk, every few weeks to oversee the numerous design changes and to check progress and production quality. He had just returned from one of those trips the previous day.

The pressure was intense. By the end of the year, the Führer expected 1,000 V-2s to be slamming into London every month, and von Braun was determined to do everything possible to make that happen. He pushed himself hard, and his staff was treated no differently, driven by a mixture of patriotic exhortations and thinly veiled threats — "I will call the responsible people to account."[20] There was general agreement, however, that Wernher was a superb organizer and leader. He was considerate to his staff, he celebrated and encouraged teamwork, and he rewarded their achievements. If an engineer suggested a technical improvement during a meeting and von Braun overruled it, he would often buy the engineer a drink to smooth the waters. On the other hand, he demanded absolute loyalty. Once he'd made a decision, he expected everyone to follow it without

---

[19] The technicians referred to the rocket as the A-4, but the public and the Nazi propaganda machine called it the V-2. Because the latter name is best know, the rocket will be called the A-4 until mass production efforts started at Peenemünde (June 1943), unless there is a particular need to revert to the technical designation.

[20] Fort Eustis microfilm collection, Roll 41/732, National Air and Space Museum (NASM), Chantilly, Virginia.

question. They were a team, he was in charge, and that was the end of it. He would take the heat if there were setbacks, and he would take full credit for all successes. Both the team and the V-2 were "his."

Wernher thrived on the responsibility and the status it afforded, and he enjoyed being the center of attention. At social events, he entertained the group with his piano skills, and his romantic exploits — such as showing up at parties with two girlfriends — raised eyebrows and stimulated lively gossip. He was charismatic and a gifted speaker, fluent in French and capable in English. He also automatically assumed that he was the smartest guy in the room. That was not an unusual attitude at the upper levels of the Reich — the same could be said about Speer, Himmler, or Göring.

Although Wernher wouldn't say it aloud, he expected everyone else to share that opinion of him. This intellectual arrogance was recognized by those around him, as was his driving ambition and his obsession with rockets.

Wernher's attitude often affected his management style, which caused problems with colleagues who considered him arrogant and self-important. He didn't mind technical disagreements, as long as his decisions were accepted. But he would not tolerate having his decisions challenged. As Technical Director he had no trouble seeing that those who disagreed or displeased him wound up working elsewhere. In 1938, in the early days of V-2 development, he had optimistically promised Walter Dornberger, then an *Oberstleutnant* (lieutenant colonel), that the missile would carry a onepayload more than 550 miles. Dr. Paul Schröder, who was in charge of testing the rocket engine, objected, saying that the engine could at best have a range of 120 miles. Although Schröder was correct, Wernher formally accused him of insubordination. Dornberger defused the situation, but the following year, after yet another heated confrontation (this time over a rocket guidance system that Wernher advocated and Schröder disparaged), Dornberger transferred Schröder to another division, one that didn't report to von Braun.[21]

Wernher was equally ruthless when dealing with subordinates who failed to show adequate enthusiasm. He transferred a group of design engineers to the Mittelwerk when he felt their work was "in no way carried out to my satisfaction and that they in fact passively resisted." The transfer was intended to put them "where these men will have increased supervision" by Arthur Rudolph and the SS.[22] For

---

[21] In combat, the guidance system on the V-2 performed poorly, although the rocket team never knew just how inaccurate it was. Schröder probably felt vindicated when he learned those details after the war.

[22] Fort Eustis microfilm collection, Roll 28/694/a, NASM, Chantilly,

most of his staff, the exhortations were more effective than the threats. After all, the scientists and engineers at Peenemünde were a close-knit group brought together by a shared common vision, the triumph of Germany over its enemies. They felt confident that under Wernher's leadership, the V-2 rocket would make that vision a reality.

All of their considerable talents and creativity were focused on creating a missile that would fulfill that goal. The hours devoted and the design tweaks continuously produced (estimates range from 35,000-65,000 changes in specifications during production) were testimony to their dedication. By June 1944, both sides knew that the Germans could still turn defeat into a stalemate, if not a victory, if their plans for long-range missiles, jet planes, anti-aircraft rockets, and the atomic bomb came to fruition. The technical breakthroughs that made the first three of these advanced weapons possible occurred at Peenemünde, and a lot of the paperwork crossed Wernher's desk.

So, as much as he wanted to go down to the launch site to see how the preparations were going, he would have to leave that to his staff. He sighed — every day was as busy as this one. Wernher turned to the pile of paperwork on his desk, and returned to work. There was a war to win, and he had a job to do.

⊷⊰⊱⊶

Wernher von Braun was born in Prussia in March 1912 to a proudly nationalistic family. He would be an aristocrat, with the title of "Baron." His father, Magnus von Braun, was a prominent attorney who at that time was chief administrator of a province in Prussia. Three years later, he would shift to the Ministry of the Interior in Berlin. In 1920, Magnus became involved in an attempt by right-wing ultra-nationalists to overthrow the Weimar Republic that had been established in Germany after WWI. Initially successful, the coup collapsed after a few days, temporarily scuttling Magnus's political career.

Wernher had an older brother, Sigismund, and a younger brother, Magnus. Sigismund, as the eldest son, was groomed for government work. He was sent to the French Gymnasium in Berlin, the preeminent choice for the children of the German elite. Founded in 1689, it conducted classes in French, rather than German, and its graduates were well suited, if not predestined, for foreign service. Wernher was precocious but unfocused. As a child he learned to play

Virginia.

the piano, and at one stage he wanted to become a composer. In 1925, Wernher was sent to a boarding school in Ettersburg, situated in a converted castle on the outskirts of Weimar. This progressive school was organized on the principles of Hermann Lietz, who felt that classical languages and rote learning were a waste of time. At first Wernher did poorly and seemed uninterested in his classes, which included physics and mathematics. But reading a book by Hermann Oberth, *By Rocket into Planetary Space,* changed the course of his life by stimulating both his imagination and an interest in science and engineering. This coincided with his transfer to the newly opened Hermann Lietz boarding school in Spiekeroog, a sandy island bordering the North Sea. (His brother Magnus, seven years younger than Wernher, would be sent to this school as well, and would later get a masters degree in organic chemistry.)

While at the Lietz school, Wernher's dreams of a music career evaporated, and he became totally fascinated by and fixated on rocketry. Rockets were making news in Germany. Racing drivers were setting speed records by attaching rockets to cars, bicycles, gliders, and sleds. Wernher was so impressed that he bought a pile of fireworks and strapped them to his wagon to see how fast it would go. He spent his last year at Lietz doing independent study and developing mathematical models and formulae relevant to rocketry. He joined the Society for Space Travel (*Verein für Raumschiffahrt VfR*) and got advice from a German science writer and spaceflight advocate, Willy Ley, about how to pursue a career in rocketry.

Wernher graduated from the Lietz school a year early, sitting his final exams in the spring of 1930. He knew he needed an advanced degree in engineering, and the Technical University of Berlin was close to his parents' home (his father Magnus, transgressions forgiven, was again working in the government). Berlin was also the headquarters of the *Vfr;* and Wernher quickly solidified his connection with that group, attending meetings and assisting with the preparation and launching of experimental rockets.

Although Oberth and Ley had formed the nucleus around which the society had formed, the operation was poorly managed and so short of cash that, by the end of 1929, it had stopped publishing a journal. The managerial void was filled by Rudolph Nebel. Nebel was a flamboyant showman who would stretch the truth at a moment's notice if that would achieve his goals. He raised money by giving speeches and publishing right-wing pamphlets that promoted the use of rockets to free Germany from the shackles imposed by greedy and unscrupulous foreigners after WWI. These lectures and handouts, which played upon the nationalistic and xenophobic feelings and frustrations of pre-Nazi Germany, supported the *VfR* and raised enough money to secure a small but dedicated area for rocket design and testing. The area was known as the *Raketenflugplatz* (rocket airfield).

Despite his fundraising success, based in part on the promise of intercontinental ballistic missiles, Nebel's group had trouble building rockets that managed more than a few seconds of flight. That sort of progress would require a much larger commitment of funds and personnel. The promotional work, and Nebel's grand promises, attracted the attention of the Ordnance Department of the Heer (German Army), which provided some funds toward development of a rocket with military potential. Whereas advances in artillery were explicitly prohibited by the Treaty of Versailles that ended WWI, rockets weren't mentioned at all. It was an enticing loophole.

Wernher learned important lessons during his time with the *VfR*. First, he learned about the power of media and the importance of showmanship in fundraising. Wernher's talent for "persuasion" was noticed early. He was often asked to make presentations to potential donors, and from time to time, Nebel took him along on promotional trips. So, his second lesson was that he had a knack for convincing others to fund his rocket work. Third, he learned that funding was only part of the puzzle, and that organization, management, and record keeping were vital to successful work.

Unfortunately, those three insights could not compensate for three essentials that the *Raketenflugplatz* group lacked: (1) There was no development plan. When a rocket failed, everyone went home disappointed, and when they came back, someone would suggest a modification, and they would try again. (2) There was little semblance of discipline. When everything worked and the rocket flew, it was time for a party. In Wernher's view, it was a grand social group but not much of a research team. (3) There was no structure to the organization. They had no test equipment, no schematics, and only sketchy records and opinions about what had worked and what hadn't. It was basically a bootstraps operation chronically short of funds.

In early 1932, shortly before Wernher received his diploma in engineering, he met then-Captain (*Hauptmann*) Walter Dornberger of the Army Ordnance Department, who was visiting the *Raketenflugplatz* to see what was going on. Wernher made a big impression, and Dornberger was struck by the young man's enthusiasm, energy, and organization. He was less than impressed with the rest of the *VfR* operation, however.

Despite their dislike for Nebel's flagrant exaggeration and self-promotion, the Ordnance Department invited Nebel and members of his group, including Wernher, to give a rocket demonstration at the ordnance testing grounds at Kummersdorf, south of Berlin. The demonstration did not go well — the rocket exploded a few seconds after launch.

The failure appeared to confirm Nebel's reputation for inflated claims and unreliable results. In the aftermath, the Army decided that the Ordnance Department would pursue rocket development in-house. With Dornberger's endorsement, the Army lured Wernher away from the Technical University and the *Raketenflugplatz* before he had completed his bachelor's degree. The Army registered him in the graduate school of Friederich-Wilhelm University in Berlin, but his graduate work would be done at Kummersdorf.

In preparation, the Kummersdorf facility was upgraded, adding test stands, new buildings, and testing equipment that could monitor things like thrust generation and fuel consumption. This kind of instrumentation and record keeping was essential for the transition from amateur "try this and see what happens" rocketry to a focused, professional approach to rocket development. Everything about the rocket project and Wernher's role was so secret that even his close friends in the amateur rocket community were unaware of the arrangement.

In 1932, Magnus, Wernher's father, became the Minister of the Interior, a cabinet level position. He was still a right-wing nationalist, and his support was influential in the Nazi takeover of the government. However, he only retained his cabinet position until 1933, when Hitler became chancellor and started filling government positions with long-Nazi loyalists and personal friends.

Almost immediately upon taking office, Hitler began rearming Germany, ignoring the terms of the Versailles Treaty. He also started consolidating his hold on society, establishing Dachau, the first of many concentration camps intended for political and social undesirables. That same year, while in graduate school at Friederich-Wilhelm University, Wernher joined an equestrian unit of the SS. Although Wernher dropped out of the unit after two years, he was kept on their books as inactive until he rejoined in 1940.

Wernher von Braun became Dr. von Braun in 1934, at the age of 22. Although doctorates typically require a thesis presenting original research by the candidate, Wernher's dissertation, classified Top Secret, summarized the work done by an army team that was developing liquid rocket fuels. Wernher was a key member of that team, but although it was a group effort, he was the one who received the degree and the kudos. Although he had made several key design improvements, what most impressed Dornberger (and his superiors) were Wernher's talents for organization and team motivation. It was probably not coincidental that Dornberger received an honorary doctorate in engineering that same year — it was already apparent that the fates of Dornberger and von Braun were intertwined. They were a potent duo. Dornberger, older and politically astute, provided important guidance to his younger colleague, while Wernher's organizational skills and salesmanship helped Dornberger keep the program funded.

Dornberger's rocket program continued to expand as the Nazi government, at the request of Army Ordnance, quietly disbanded or shut down amateur rocket societies and clubs across Germany. Members with useful skills and experience were hired by the Army and brought to Kummersdorf to work under tight security, free from the prying eyes of Germany's enemies. In this way, two influential engineers joined von Braun's "team." The first was Arthur Rudolph, who had built a working rocket engine for the Army on a shoestring budget, and the second was Walter Riedel (nicknamed "Papa"), an older engineer with industrial experience in quality control practices. Both would become valuable and trusted colleagues.

In 1935, Dornberger was promoted to major as his responsibilities increased. At this point, the Kummersdorf group was working on a small rocket designated the A-2 (A meant "aggregate," a term intended to obscure its meaning). There was a move within the Ordnance Department to focus on the A-2 as an artillery alternative, but Wernher was able to convince Dornberger's superiors that the A-2s were too limited and unreliable, and that with further investment, they could have long-range missiles with intercontinental range.

It was clear to von Braun and Dornberger that they faced both a funding problem and a PR problem. Both had to be overcome before the rocket program could advance. Wernher's strategy, reminiscent of Nebel's, was to prepare an elaborate presentation that he delivered to representatives of the Army and the Luftwaffe in June 1935. In it, he proposed the establishment of a joint research facility that would develop long-range liquid-fueled rockets that could be adapted to power advanced aircraft. Development would be done at a special site, housing all equipment and personnel in one highly secure, top secret location. Commercial firms would be excluded and all work would be done in-house presumably under his direction.

The proposal hit all of the right buttons — German missile and aircraft supremacy, total secrecy, and organizational efficiency — and Wernher's delivery was dramatic and convincing. By 1936, funding was secured for the establishment of an Army Rocket Center at Peenemünde. The site was largely Wernher's idea, as it was near a coastal resort town and close to his family's estates. The research complex would sit on the edge of the Baltic Sea, near the mouth of the Peene River in northeastern Germany.

The creation of the Peenemünde facility was a remarkable accomplishment both physically and politically. In terms of relative influence, the Army had the upper hand, as the Luftwaffe had control of a mere 22 acres in the northwest corner of the facility, an area known as Peenemünde-West. The rest of the complex, Peenemünde-East, was controlled by the Army Ordnance Department. It would have eleven launch pads, areas for testing components, and a highly sophisticated wind tunnel for advanced design work. With both the German Army and the Luftwaffe providing funds, no expense was spared, and what emerged over time was largely self-contained and physically insulated from the deprivations and sacrifices made by German citizens elsewhere.

Construction took two years (1936-1938), and much of the heavy labor involved in building Peenemünde was done by slave laborers housed in a squalid mini-concentration camp near the site. In 1937, while construction was still underway, Peenemünde-East was occupied by the ordnance team. Major Dornberger was appointed Director of the Army Rocket Center (Peenemünde-East), with Dr. Wernher von Braun as the Technical Director, responsible for research, budgeting, and missile production. To say that Wernher's ascent had been meteoric was no exaggeration. He had graduated from high school at 18, received his doctorate at 22, and at 25 he was Technical Director at Peenemünde.

By the time war began in 1939, Dornberger had been promoted to Lieutenant Colonel (*Oberstleutnant*), and over 90% of the employees, including Dr. von Braun, were members of the Nazi party.[23] In 1940, Wernher had rejoined the SS as a lieutenant and gained a snappy black uniform to go with his usual dark suits. Over the years, both Dornberger and von Braun would be promoted at regular intervals, and by 12 June 1944, Dornberger would be an army brigadier general and von Braun an SS-major.

Peenemünde was a cloistered community of very social young people who loved to party, and Wernher greatly enjoyed (and was renowned for) cutting a wide swath through the unattached young women. There were also "special entertainments" available to the personnel entrusted with security and labor control. The SS operated a small brothel, probably staffed by "volunteers" from the women's

---

[23] Sigismund joined the Nazi party in October 1937 and Wernher in November 1937. Magnus had joined in 1933 at age 13, as a member of the Hitler Youth.

concentration camp at Ravensbrük. For five reichsmarks ($25 today), an SS officer could get a drink, a cigarette, and a woman. Of course, such a facility posed serious threats to security — nobody could predict what secrets would accidentally be revealed in pillow talk. No record has been found to show how that was handled at Peenemünde, but at SS brothels run for V-2 launch sites in Holland, the women and girls were routinely executed after a month "in service," and a new group brought in. The diversity probably made the business even more attractive to its patrons.

Wernher saw the Führer at a distance in 1933, and again in 1934. Each time, he came away unimpressed. But after personal meetings in 1939 and 1941, he was struck by Hitler's intellect and force of personality, describing him as a colossus and a new Napoleon. Hitler was equally impressed by the young engineer, and Wernher convinced him that the missiles built at Peenemünde could reshape the course of the war. With Hitler behind the program 100%, additional resources became available, but since the collapse of the Russian offensive in December 1941, labor was a serious limiting factor for all of German industry. The solution Propaganda Minister Göbbels announced was "Total War." It required the total commitment of the German population. Established norms of civilized behavior were tossed aside, and the use of POWs (primarily Russian and Polish) and slave laborers from concentration camps became commonplace all across Germany.

Wernher was responsible for budgeting, and he was also a key member of the A-4 Special Committee, tasked with project oversight and the finalization of production deadlines. The promised delivery dates were slipping away, in part because he had too few German technicians to deal with rocket production and assembly. A factory he had visited was using POW labor, with one German technician overseeing groups of skilled slave laborers. The approach was definitely worth considering as a way to maximize the productivity of German technicians. In May 1942, he wrote to Gerhard Degenkolb, the chairman of the A-4 Special Committee, to suggest that fuel-tank construction be done by foreign laborers and POWs.[24] This practice was subsequently adopted by a number of subsidiary production firms.

In April 1943, Wernher authorized his friend and subordinate Arthur Rudolph, head of the Development and Fabrication Laboratory, to visit an aircraft manufacturing facility where civilian employees each had charge of ten skilled slave laborers provided by

---

[24] "Niederschrift uber die dienstreise vom 2.-5.5.42 nach Friederichshafen" RH8/v.1959, BA/MA.

the SS. Rudolph was impressed by what he saw, and he endorsed the approach in a report to von Braun. This led to a detailed proposal to use skilled slave laborers on assembly lines to mass-produce the missiles. In addition to a substantial savings relative to a contracted, salaried workforce — something significant for Wernher, as he was in charge of budgeting — there was also the issue of improved security. Contract laborers had friends outside of Peenemünde with whom they corresponded and visited when on leave. The more contracted workers, the greater the risk of security breaches and leaks. Security would be much easier to manage with a small group of known and trusted technicians supervising prisoners who were completely cut off from the outside world.

Wernher approved the proposal and brought it before the A-4 Special Committee. The committee discussed and approved it, and forwarded it to the SS for action on 2 June 1943. The committee requested 2,200 concentration camp laborers and a suitable number of SS guards for oversight. The intention was to solve a manpower shortage while reducing costs and increasing security — things of critical importance to von Braun. The proposal was quickly approved, and the first 200 skilled laborers for the V-2 assembly line arrived from Buchenwald with their SS guards two weeks later.[25]

One month later, in July 1943, von Braun met with Hitler to narrate a movie showing the launch of a V-2 rocket. Hitler was so enthusiastic about the presentation that he granted von Braun the title of Professor, an unusual accolade for someone just 31 years of age. Hitler also awarded him the War Merit Cross First Class with swords, a German military decoration second only to the Knight's Cross. All of Hitler's inner circle knew Wernher's quirks, including the fact that he took great pride in having his importance and superiority acknowledged. The Third Reich fed his ego a steady diet of honors ("Professor"), awards (War Merit Crosses), and titles like "Technical Director or "Vice President" as they loaded him with responsibility for program after program, and put him on committee after committee, usually as the committee chair. Wernher responded by jumping into each new project with great enthusiasm.

A second group of 600 skilled laborers arrived in early August. The V-2 rockets were assembled in enormous hangar-like buildings, designated Halle F-1 and Halle F-2. Each was 750' long and 750' wide, with lofty ceilings, doors 60' high, and a full-length

---

[25] The Luftwaffe had already requested 500 slave laborers for work on the V-1 and jet engine assembly lines. They had arrived with their SS guards in May and were put to work in Peenemünde-West.

basement. Half of the basement was a sophisticated machine shop, the other half an ersatz barracks. Up to six hundred skilled slave laborers could live in squalor in each basement, working in the machine shop and emerging only for a shift on the assembly line above.

If a Peenemünde employee felt that a prisoner was doing shoddy work or not working to capacity, a word to the SS would see them removed and replaced. General Dornberger, Wernher's confidant and patron, said "I say to you now directly that they are all murderers, thieves, and criminals, and every criminal will always protest that he is innocent."[26] As such, they were not worthy of a second's consideration, and the Peenemünders casually referred to them as "zebras," a reference to their distinctive vertically striped prison uniforms.

All of Wernher's carefully orchestrated plans fell apart on the night of 17-18 August 1943, when the RAF bombed the technical facilities and residences at Peenemünde. This was part of a British campaign code-named "Operation Hydra." Altogether, 1,795 tons of explosives were dropped on the facility. Both assembly halls burned, and the design offices, the women's residence halls, three-quarters of the staff housing, testing facilities, and many of the V-2 launching sites were destroyed. The death toll was 600 slave laborers (including many living in the basements of the assembly halls) and 135 German staff, including several of von Braun's close friends. The bombing was so successful, and the defense such an unmitigated disaster, that the officer in charge of air defenses committed suicide shortly afterward.

Wernher was shocked and distressed by the deaths in his close-knit community. It was a sudden glimpse of the realities of war and the devastation Germany's enemies could and would inflict if they weren't forced to abandon the fight. The war had become immediate and personal, rather than theoretical and remote, and it brought a new intensity to the work underway. The Allies had succeeded in damaging the facility and ending the idyllic lifestyle the Peenemünders had enjoyed, but doing so only increased their determination to rebuild and return the favor in kind.

The Führer had already decided to move important manufacturing operations underground, where they would be protected from air attack, but Peenemünde wasn't originally considered as a candidate because it was supposedly top secret and well defended. Both assumptions were clearly incorrect. A week after the bombing, General Dornberger ordered Wernher to plan the shift of production from Peenemünde to a facility that would be prepared

---

[26] Missiles for the Fatherland, p152 (for complete citation, see Appendix 7).

near Nordhausen, in Thuringia, a mountainous region in central Germany. Although Wernher preferred having everything in one place and under his direct supervision, he was glad to be staying at Peenemünde, as his work could continue without interruption. Several key testing areas and other facilities, like the liquid oxygen plant, had survived the bombing, and the Peenemünders had taken care to avoid obvious repairs or upgrades that might attract attention and additional bombing strikes. So Wernher and the design team stayed in place, while the assembly operations were shifted to an underground factory complex to be called the Mittelwerk because it was near the *mittel* (middle) of Germany. The shift would, however, dramatically complicate his life. Nordhausen was at least 300 miles away, an hour by plane or a day by car.[27]

Wernher chaired a meeting on the transfer of slave laborers from Peenemünde to the new facility at the Mittelwerk on 25 August 1943, and four days later he flew to Nordhausen to inspect the site for the Mittelwerk. He was the first Peenemünder to do so. One reason it had been selected was that extensive tunneling work had been done by a gypsum mining company a decade earlier, and the rock was soft enough that further extension would be relatively straightforward. When Wernher arrived, he found a dirty, dank underground maze that was already full of equipment and fuel storage tanks. There were two parallel tunnels, each roughly a mile in length, interconnected by smaller lateral tunnels like the rungs in a ladder. Railway tracks ran the length of the tunnels, and the facility had long served as a storage depot for oil and gasoline. It was shockingly clear to Wernher that it would be many months before this subterranean complex would be ready to start churning out V-2 rockets. All of the stored tanks and machinery had to be hauled away, the existing tunnels had to be enlarged, and additional cross tunnels had to be added. After all that, the entire complex needed to be wired, plumbed, ventilated, surfaced, and air conditioned.

Preparations to begin the work were already underway. Less than a day before Wernher flew to the Mittelwerk, the first batch of slave laborers arrived from Buchenwald Concentration Camp, located roughly 37 miles to the south. The relative proximity of Buchenwald was critical to the success of the venture and another reason why this site had been selected. SS-General Hans Kammler, who directed the construction effort, was quite familiar with Buchenwald, as he'd been

---

[27] A state-funded, privately operated company called Mittelwerk, Gmbh (*Gesellschaft mit beschränkter Haftung*, the designation of a private company) was established on 21 September 1943, and contracted to produce 12,000 rockets, paid for in advance. This funded the construction work.

responsible for the construction of an adjacent factory, the *Gustloff Werke* (Gustloff Works), that relied on prison labor to build military equipment. He had used slave labor from Buchenwald to build both the Gustloff Works and the railway lines that connected the concentration camp to the nearby city of Weimar.

The construction was managed by Sonderinspektion II, the SS division for labor, materials, and security. One of the officers reviewed the plans with Wernher as he gave a guided tour. When completed, each of the main tunnels would be almost 2 miles long, 46' wide, and 32' high. There would be 47 cross tunnels, each 650' long. Some of these cross tunnels were 100' high to allow completed rockets to be stood upright. The 27 tunnels at the south end would be assigned to V-2 production, and the other tunnels would be used by the Luftwaffe to build V-1s and the engines for Me-262 jet fighters. Raw materials for V-2 assembly would arrive on railroad cars that entered the main tunnel. These would be offloaded and the parts distributed to the cross tunnels, each involved with the assembly of specific components. The finished components would then be fitted together in sequence on railroad cars in the second tunnel. Completed missiles, mounted, secured, and ready for shipment, would emerge from the front of that second tunnel, ready to be delivered to mobile launch sites in Germany and the occupied territories.

Wernher spent five days inspecting the tunnels and discussing the remodeling required, moving past and around the slave laborers from Buchenwald. He returned later in September, in early October, and in late November when construction had been underway for three months. Although pleased by the progress he saw, Wernher was disgusted by the noise, the smell, and the suffocating clouds of dust and debris, and he spent no more time in the tunnels than absolutely necessary. At that point, there were 10,000 slave laborers in the tunnels. This was manual labor at its worst, for no tools were provided because they could be used as weapons. Digging was done by hand after shattering the surfaces with explosive charges. They labored around the clock, the exhausted men sleeping on makeshift pallets or at the sides of the tunnels, with no water or sanitary facilities. The noise was deafening, the air almost unbreathable. There was little food, and no medical care for men injured by heavy equipment and explosives. Dysentery and disease were rampant, and corpses lay by the sides of the tunnels and stacked by the entrance. If asked, Wernher's guide would have told him they were awaiting transport to Buchenwald, for disposal in an industrial-style crematorium.

On 12 November 1943, Wernher wrote to Degenkolb discussing

a shortage of prisoner laborers for critical aspects of production and quality control. He noted that for critical work formerly done by 180 German employees, prison laborers could be introduced at a ratio of 2:1, which would free up 120 employees for other tasks.

After Wernher's inspection visit on 26 November 1943, he suspended missile production work at Peenemünde and had the skilled slave laborers transferred to the tunnels of the Mittelwerk. Employees moving from Peenemünde to supervise production left behind what they would later describe as a paradise, but they got substantial raises, a generous moving allowance, a housing allowance, and many other benefits. Most of the raises were associated with loftier job descriptions and greater responsibility, so they were seen as positive career moves. Once the laborers and supervisors were on site, they began to assemble missiles on a small production line, as at Peenemünde, rather than on the grand scale planned for the Mittelwerk. That massive complex would gradually emerge as the facility was completed. At the moment, tunneling work was continuing, and many of the completed tunnels still needed to be plumbed and wired.

Because he was responsible for final acceptance, Wernher had oversight power for all aspects of design and production, which meant he needed to monitor operations at the Mittelwerk closely. Fortunately, he was on good terms with both Albin Sawatski and Arthur Rudolph. Sawatski, a fanatical Nazi even by SS standards, was in charge of production planning and the design of the assembly lines, whereas Arthur Rudolph, the production manager, had been responsible for missile production at Peenemünde before the bombing raid eliminated that capability.

The quality control division at the Mittelwerk reported directly to von Braun rather than to Sawatski, Rudolph, or Georg Rickhey, the general manager at the Mittelwerk. There were 200 quality control personnel monitoring the assembly lines, and they needed to be kept updated on design changes and specifications, as did Arthur Rudolph, whose office was located at a key position within the underground factory. Von Braun had set up the QC division and written the service manual that specified the treatment of workers who were not performing up to his standards. The QC group was to order the "removal of specialists (foreigners) [from the assembly line] who are not particularly qualified." Nobody could have had any illusions about the fate of a slave laborer fired from the production line. If they were of no value for manual labor, they would be eliminated by execution or starvation.

As technical director, Wernher was still in charge of test firings, design modifications, and specification changes. His travel schedule was chaotic. A typical month included trips to testing grounds in Poland, Reich offices in Berlin, visits to subcontracted engineering firms across Germany, and flights between Peenemünde and the Mittelwerk. He also managed to squeeze in regular inspection visits to potential launch sites in and around Paris, where he was careful to keep his rank and his mission secret from his Parisian girlfriend. And as if all of that travel weren't enough, whenever he returned to his office, he found it awash in a sea of paperwork.

Despite his best efforts, progress was frustratingly slow, and he was behind the eight-ball. Based on his optimistic projections, Dornberger had committed them to producing 900 missiles per month by the end of 1943. As things turned out, only four had been manufactured, none of them operational. As they fell further behind, the pressure on staff and management increased. This did nothing for the condition or treatment of the slave laborers, but more important from Wernher's perspective, it reduced his credibility and put his funding at risk. The main problem was that their prototypes had been works of art, each one individually hand-crafted and flawless. They were now trying to reproduce that quality on an industrial scale, using semi-skilled laborers unfamiliar with the principles and constraints. So he and his design staff were continually searching for ways to simplify and idiot-proof the design. Sabotage was certainly a risk as well, but even small inadvertent mistakes could have fatal consequences during a launch.

Quality control was not the only problem they faced in the first half of 1944, as the A-4 design entered mass production as the V-2. There was also political infighting between the various military departments and government agencies. The rocket program found itself competing with other projects and agencies for ever-scarcer resources. To save weight, major components were built of aluminum, but the supply of aluminum was limited, and the Luftwaffe needed it to build aircraft, especially jet fighters. Fuel in general was a problem, even for trucks and tanks, but fuel for rockets was in even shorter supply. The V-2 burned a mixture of liquid oxygen and ethyl alcohol. Both were hard to source at that point in the war. Each V-2 required roughly 16 tons of liquid fuel for launching (10 tons of alcohol and 6 tons of liquid oxygen) that were mixed and burned in the first 65 seconds of flight. They could stretch alcohol supplies by diluting the alcohol with water to a concentration of 74%, rather than using pure alcohol, but there was no way around the liquid oxygen requirement. Liquid oxygen was difficult to produce, hard to store, and very expensive, and there were not many sources of supply.

Fortunately, the liquid-oxygen plant at Peenemünde had escaped the bombing and was still fully operational, and another plant had been set up at the Mittelwerk.

Wernher had been around Hitler often enough to know that his support could open any door. Everyone in Hitler's inner circle knew this, and as a result, his subordinates were continuously jockeying for his attention and affection. The three men whose maneuvering had the greatest impact on Wernher's projects were Hermann Göring, the Minister of Aviation and President of the German parliament (*Reichstag*), Heinrich Himmler, the Interior Minister, head of the Nazi Party and *Reichsführer* in charge of the civilian police and the various divisions of the SS, and Albert Speer, the Minister of Armaments and War Production, who had streamlined and optimized wartime production through nationalization of industries and the wholesale use of slave labor.[28]

It was a three-way battle for supremacy. Göring was officially Hitler's second in command, but Himmler's influence steadily increased as the Luftwaffe proved unable to conquer the skies over Britain, nor to defend Germany from Allied bombing attacks. But Himmler's SS and Göring's Luftwaffe were both dependent on the funds and materials provided to them by Speer. As resources became scarce, and internal competition for those resources increased, Speer gained tremendous power. Fortunately for Wernher, Speer was an admirer and a firm believer in the power of rocketry, and his ministry provided generous support.

Hitler's enthusiasm and Speer's support of the Army rocket program and the Luftwaffe V-1 and jet projects did not sit well with Himmler, who distrusted the German Army, disliked Speer, and detested Göring. Thus, when the Peenemünde group requested slave laborers from the SS, Himmler took the first steps toward wresting the rocket project, and its associated influence, from the Army. His plan took another step forward when the decision was made to build the Mittelwerk, since the construction was assigned to Sonderinspektion II of the SS.

Himmler next tried to outmaneuver the Army. He invited Wernher to a meeting in late February 1944 to try and convince him to leave his position at Peenemünde to become the director for rocket programs for the SS. Wernher probably wasn't too surprised

---

[28] There were many similarities between Speer and von Braun. Both had attended school in Weimar, and both were extremely smart and politically astute. Speer has been described as a mediocre architect whose main talent was in planning and organization. Dornberger made similar comments about Wernher after the war.

at this, as he was already a ranking SS officer, and without him. the Army program would collapse. Pressed for an answer, he realized that there were tactical reasons to decline the offer. The first was that it would undercut his mentor, General Dornberger, with whom he had worked for the last nine years. Wernher expected loyalty from his team, and he felt equally loyal to Dornberger. The second reason was that given the vagaries of German politics, there were advantages to the current state of affairs. It was better for his rocket program to have both the Army and the SS involved when neither was in a commanding position. That arrangement gave him near autonomy and access to the resources of both. Wernher had always been careful to spread his allegiance around. He had joined the Nazi party, he was employed by the Army, he had received his pilot's certification as a Luftwaffe reservist, and he held a commission from the SS.

Wernher was relieved to find that Himmler listened politely as he declined the offer, and the meeting ended cordially. However, Albert Speer, Wernher's main supporter in the Reich administration, developed a mysterious but serious illness that required hospitalization.[29] Himmler took the opportunity to flex his muscles and attempted to force the issue. Three weeks after his interview with Himmler, Wernher had a visit from the Gestapo (the Nazi Party's secret police), who placed him in "protective custody." The reason given was that he was not serious enough about winning the war through missile production — a claim that, given his work schedule, was hardly credible.[30]

Wernher wasn't particularly intimidated by this turn of events, as he knew the importance of the rocket program, and he knew that he was the only person who could deliver the weapons that both the Army and the SS desperately wanted. His confidence was apparently justified. Speer recovered and returned to work, and Wernher was released from custody and told that it had all been a misunderstanding. When he returned to the office, Wernher was just as paranoid about security, just as obsessed with design enhancements, and just as blunt with his staff as he exhorted them to work harder and faster and longer.

As the Mittelwerk factory neared completion, with proper utilities and air conditioning, off-duty laborers were housed at the newly established Dora Concentration Camp and no longer sleeping

---

[29] He was placed in an SS hospital, and there were rumors that the attending physician was orchestrating his demise. He made a swift recovery following the arrival of his personal physician.

[30] Over time Wernher would tell the tale, often with great embellishment, as proof that he wasn't a "real Nazi."

wherever they could find an open space. These improvements made Wernher's visits relatively pleasant. The scrawny zebras still labored under the stern gazes of their supervisors, but the stench of sewage no longer fouled the air, and there were fewer corpses stacked by the entrance. After four trips in March, he made four more in April, the last one extending into May for an important meeting. At that meeting, held on 2 May 1944, Wernher discussed the major production and quality control problems with Albin Sawitski, General Dornberger, Dora Commandant Otto Förschner, Ernst Steinhoff (a former Peenemünder now a director at the Mittelwerk), George Rickhey (the general manager), SS-General Kammler, Arthur Rudolph, and representatives from major subcontractors. Wernher reviewed the failure rate they were experiencing during testing. Although he had originally estimated that a ratio of one German contract worker for every ten slave laborers would both save money and ensure quality, the results simply hadn't been up to expectations. The production work was simply too difficult for unskilled prison laborers to master. Even skilled German laborers had trouble. The ratio of managers to prisoners, currently 1:4, might need to be 1:2. Sawatski suggested that the SS scour the prison camps and provide them with an additional 1,800 laborers to improve the civilian:slave ratio and to replace those who had died over the previous winter. This proposal got Kammler's full support. Something certainly needed to be done quickly to get V-2 production to the levels that they had optimistically projected years earlier.

However, to be of use on the production line, the additional laborers had to possess mechanical and technical skills. There was a general consensus that Wernher, who had highlighted the issue, would be in the best position to select the additional skilled laborers. They would have to come from the Buchenwald Concentration Camp (*Konzentration Lager Buchenwald*, population roughly 64,000), as the skilled labor pool at the nearby Dora Concentraiton Camp (population approximately 12,000) was very limited. Wernher had put this on his task list, but as of 12 June he hadn't made the necessary arrangements.

CHAPTER 5

Evasion and Capture

-◁▯▷-

12-16 JUNE 1944: CHAUVINCOURT, IN OCCUPIED FRANCE

On the morning of 13 June 1944, Fred awakened, tired and sore, in a small, dark bedroom. The windows were shuttered and the curtains drawn, but there was enough light for him to see his watch. It was late morning. He carefully sat up and swung his legs over the side of the bed, pain flashing from his left leg. He discovered he had a headache, and gingerly touched the heavy bandage that wrapped across his forehead. He knew he wasn't thinking clearly because he felt confused and anxious, and his memories of the preceding day were a jumble. He lay back down, closed his eyes, and tried to make sense of them. He remembered a line from *Alice in Wonderland*, one of his favorite childhood stories: "Begin at the beginning, and go on till you come to the end: then stop."

He could remember the mission through the point where things started going very wrong. He knew he had been hit by flak, had passed out after leaving the plane, and been knocked out in a hard landing. The next thing he remembered was waking up with his flight gear and shoes already off and his uniform pants around his ankles. As he struggled to sit up, he could see that the left leg of his long johns was saturated with blood. Two men were standing over him. The older man was in his 40s and the younger in his 20s. The younger man had Fred's leathers, flight boots, bunny suit, and coveralls in his arms, but appeared to be waiting for further instructions.

The older man, short and slender, with dark hair and a narrow face, introduced himself as Paul Stinkelbout, a local farmer. Paul's father was French, but his mother was English, and he had spent time with his English grandparents. As a result, Paul spoke reasonable English. Although married to an Italian woman, Paul was unsympathetic to the Germans and was sympathetic to the French Resistance. The younger, taller man, Henri Brown, was a friend of Paul's. Henri's father was Victor Brown, and the Brown family were active members of the local resistance network, part of the FFI (French Forces of the Interior).

Paul helped Fred out of his uniform shirt. Before giving it to Henri for disposal, Fred carefully removed his aerial gunner wings and clipped them to his dog tags for safekeeping. Henri moved off into the forest to bury Fred's flight gear. He returned to do the same to the parachute and harness. Paul's immediate concern was to get Fred out of sight before any German patrols arrived on the scene. Fred couldn't stand unassisted. There was a deep gash along the inside of the knee and punctures through the meat of the calf, but the left ankle was the main problem. It had swollen prodigiously and turned an angry purple.

So with Fred's weight on his right shoulder, Paul half-carried, half-walked him over to a small mule-drawn cart that stood by the edge of the field. As Fred clung to the edge of the cart for support, Paul opened the lid and boosted Fred up to the top. Rolling over the lip, Fred fell into the nearly empty tank, landing on his back with a thud. Paul closed the lid. When Henri returned from the woods, the two men led the cart over the rugged, unpaved road. Inside the water cart, the ride was bouncy, damp, and uncomfortable. Fred's injuries were throbbing, and the jolting and bouncing weren't helping a bit. His face felt wet, and with his left hand, he could feel a jagged tear in his scalp. Although the darkness was nearly complete, he wiped what he assumed was blood out of his left eye. He carefully checked his neck, chest, and abdomen, and was relieved to find nothing amiss (he had heard about men having mortal wounds but being unaware of them). His left ankle, calf, and knee were throbbing. He knew how he'd hurt his ankle, but his memories of the flak injuries were hazy, and he had no clear idea of how bad those wounds were. With no way for him to assess any of his injuries while inside the water carrier, he tried to relax and await developments.

After an interminable period (probably less than 30 minutes), the water cart jolted to a halt. They were at the Brown's farmhouse in Chauvincourt, a small village roughly three miles south of the town of Etrepagny, and 30 miles southeast of the city of Rouen.

When the cart stopped, Paul climbed up and lifted the lid, as if checking the water level. He explained that Victor Brown, Henri's father, was the resistance leader for the Chauvincourt-Provement area. Paul couldn't hide Fred at his small farmhouse, but Victor would be able to shelter him and get word to the local resistance chief, Captain Max Raulin in Hacqueville. With luck, Captain Raulin would be able to organize a way for Fred to rejoin the Allies, something that had been done many times in the course of the German occupation.

Paul and Henri left Fred in the cart while they went inside and explained the situation to Victor and Henriette, his wife. The Browns had three children. Henri, 20, and his sister Eda, 22, were well aware of their father's "other job," but Bernard, who was only seven, was kept in the dark because he was a chatterbox and Victor worried about his ability to keep secrets.

When Paul returned, the water cart was moved into the barn. With a struggle and some painful wriggling, Fred was soon out of the water tank, but Paul explained that he had to stay in the barn until after dark. There was too great a risk of his being seen by a German patrol or a collaborationist neighbor. Paul then introduced Fred to Victor, Henriette, and Eda before he took his mule and water cart back to the field.

The Browns spoke little English — Eda knew a few words from a high school class, and that was about it — but they let Fred know that they were going to tend to his wounds. Victor cut away the left leg of Fred's long johns to view the damage there. When the area had been rinsed and wiped, Fred could see that he had a deep cut on the inside of his left knee, and roughly eight inches below the knee, he had a ragged hole right through the calf muscle. Victor looked somewhat relieved that nothing appeared to be trapped within the leg. Henriette and Eda carefully cleaned and bandaged Fred's leg wounds and wrapped his ankle, before cleaning and bandaging his head wound. Henriette had brought a set of clean clothes (Fred was about Henri's size) and the women left the barn while Victor and Henri helped Fred out of his trashed long johns and into his new clothes. When buttoning the shirt, Fred made sure that his dog tags and wings were completely covered.

As darkness fell, and Bernard was tucked into bed, Fred was assisted across the yard, up the stairs, and into a small room on the second floor. It was at the back of the house, with windows that opened overlooking the walled back yard where Eda had earlier hung clothes on a line. His bureau had a small towel, a hand basin, a pitcher of water, and a wooden bucket to serve as a toilet. He would be confined to the room during the day with closed window shutters, to avoid alerting outsiders to the presence of a guest. He would be fed in his room, and allowed outside into the courtyard only after dark, and only if his mobility improved.

It was his first day in France, and he would be spending it in a darkened room. His only identification as an American airman were his dog tags and his gunnery wings. His best guess was that he had come down about 100 miles from Allied lines. If those troops managed to break free, they could be in Chauvincourt within a few days. In that case, all he had to do was avoid being spotted by the Germans and wait for Allied troops to arrive. He hoped it would happen soon.

As the day slowly passed, Fred thought about the guys at the 385th, and wondered how the rest of the Jackson crew had made out. Were they OK? Were they hiding somewhere, as he was, or were they POWs? Perhaps Victor would be able to tell him over the next couple of days.

But Victor had heard nothing about the other men in Fred's aircrew. He did caution Fred that the odds of successfully evading capture were long.[31] The FFI had to contend with German military and SS patrols, the Vichy government's secret police, corrupted regional policemen, the intelligence agents of the Gestapo, the SD (the SS Secret Police), the Abwehr (Army Intelligence), and a network of paid informers and German sympathizers. Fred had been briefed on his probable fate in the event he was captured while evading. The official protocol was that downed airmen were the responsibility of the Luftwaffe, which operated POW camps called stalag lufts. The German Army collected captured soldiers and held them in POW camps called stalags. The SS and associated agencies (the Gestapo, the SD, the SiPo, and others all answering to Himmler)[32] focused on finding spies and saboteurs, who were often executed on the spot.[33]

What Fred didn't know was that after the US entered the war in late 1941, the German attitude toward Allied combatants had become increasingly severe. Hitler was incensed by the bombing of German cities without regard for the resulting civilian casualties — somehow the fact that since 1935 he had funded projects intended to carpet bomb London with exploding rockets did nothing to reduce his sense of outrage. A series of secret decrees were subsequently issued by the Führer, Martin Bormann (head of the Party Chancellery), and Reichsführer Heinrich Himmler (head of the Nazi party and the SS). Allied airmen, even when in uniform, were to be considered *terrorfliegers* (terror fliers) and war criminals. As such, they were not to be protected from retribution by civilians or from summary execution by German military or paramilitary (SS) forces. When captured alive, airmen were to be transferred to Luftwaffe POW camps only if it could be proven that they had not bombed or strafed

---

[31] Between 1941 and the liberation of France in 1944, approximately 22% of downed airmen who survived to reach the ground evaded capture. The ratio for Crashwagon's crew, 2 out of 9, or 22%, was representative. Fred and Sam avoided capture primarily because they waited to open their chutes. Sam landed near St.-Denis-le-Ferment, roughly 7 miles from where Fred touched down.

[32] See Appendix 1 for a glossary of important individuals, terms, and agencies.

[33] See Appendix 2 for a discussion of the German intelligence services looking for downed airmen.

civilians, trains carrying civilians, or German flight crews hanging from parachutes. Lacking such determination, the captives would be subject to civilian "lynch law" or given to one of Himmler's groups to deal with. Local police were specifically prohibited from interfering with these events.

Fred spent three boring days with the Brown family, sheltered in the upstairs bedroom. Over this period, arrangements were made to transfer him to the local FFI (*Forces Françaises de l'Interior*) headquarters in Hacqueville, roughly seven miles away. On 15 June 1944, with Henri on one side and Eda on the other, Fred was assisted over a half-mile of dirt trail to an intersection where he could be picked up by a car. The car was driven by a veterinarian, Dr. Maurice Daviaud (because veterinarians were important to the health of the local livestock, the German military issued them driving passes). Fred was quickly but carefully assisted into the trunk of Dr. Daviaud's car, and transported as cargo. Fred found himself once again placing his fate in unfamiliar hands, hiding alone and uncomfortable in the dark while a complete stranger took him who knows where. He was already tired of life on the run, and there was no end in sight.

JUNE-JULY 1944: OFFICIAL REPORTS

The Germans kept careful records of their successful downing of Allied aircraft, and within 24 hours there was a German military file on the Jackson crew. The file was nearly complete, since most of the crew was accounted for. As was standard practice, it would be updated as additional information became available.

On the American side, a small storm of paperwork was generated when the Jackson crew failed to return from the 12 June mission. The leaders of the Lead, High, and Low Groups prepared after-mission reports, and the High Group report noted the loss of Jackson's plane. In addition, all arriving air crews were debriefed and asked about sightings of downed aircraft. The sightings were combined with the bomber group's Missing Air Crew Report (MACR) and a map showing the approximate location of the crash, and the packet forwarded to the 8th Air Force command headquarters in High Wycombe, England.

After a delay for processing, the information was relayed to the US, and on 30 June 1944, Fred's sister Lucille received a telegram notifying her that her brother was Missing in Action (MIA). This was followed by a letter from the station chaplain at the 385th. Although written on 21 June 1944, the letter did not arrive until after Lucille had received the telegram from the War Office. Shorty thereafter, Lucille received a letter from the War Department confirming the information reported by telegram. After this brief flurry of unwelcome news, Fred's family and friends entered a period of limbo, hoping for the best but fearing the worst. They were not alone — in the August 9th edition of the *Brooklyn Daily Eagle*, Fred's name was one of 22 former Brooklyn residents listed as Missing in Action.

17 JUNE TO 5 AUGUST 1944: HACQUEVILLE AND THE RAULINS

Hacqueville was a small village with fewer than 400 residents. The central focus of the village was its school, an attractive brick building that also served as the residence of the headmaster, Mr. Max Raulin, and his wife Yvonne. Max was a French patriot who had been a decorated lieutenant in WWI and promoted to captain in early 1940. After the fall of France, he continued to be well respected locally, serving as both the headmaster of the school and the mayor of the town. Knowing his dislike of the Germans, Dr. Daviaud had approached Max in 1941 about establishing a resistance operation in Normandy, and the two had begun recruiting among their contacts.

Captain Raulin was of average height (somewhere around 5'7") and stocky, but he had a commanding presence as befit a central figure in the community. His wife, Yvonne, was a lovely and gracious woman, devoted to Max and to her young son Lionel, who was five years old at the time. In his clandestine role as the head of the resistance in that portion of Normandy, Max was responsible for directing and coordinating the activities of the FFI within a 20-mile radius of Hacqueville. He was also in charge of the collection and concealment of downed airmen.[34] In the course of the war, Max, with Yvonne's help, arranged safe haven for 14 American airmen and 18 RAF airmen. Fifteen of those airmen were kept for varying periods within their home. The regional headquarters for the Eure district was in Chartres, where Max reported to Mr. Louis Picourt.

When Fred arrived in Hacqueville, the Raulins were already hosting Staff Sergeant Paul J. Wilson, a gunner on a B-26 from the

---

[34] There were at this time roughly 1,400 men in the FFI active in Normandy, plus innumerable others who either assisted or ignored resistance activities. Lt. Raulin's base in Hacqueville was the hub for the Normandy network, with communication originating from Chartres traveling first to Hacqueville and then on to agents in Ecos, Les Andelys, Puchay, Gisors, Etrepagny, and Lyons-le-Forêt.

574th Squadron of the 391st BG. His plane had been shot down on a 27 May 1944 mission to bomb a railroad bridge northeast of Paris. As luck would have it, his parachute delivered him to Hacqueville, where he was quickly picked up and stashed away.

Fred and Paul spent the next six weeks with the Raulins, eating all their midday meals as an extended family. Late each day, they were shuffled to the nearby church and placed in the care of Mme. Simone Carpentier, another member of the FFI. Simone, known in town as "Tati," was 42 years old, unmarried, and the caretaker of the church and the adjacent home of the pastor, who had recently died. Paul and Fred had dinner there, but slept inside the church because it had a special hiding place within the ceiling that could be used if German patrols came to town. There was also a more devious hiding place at the top of the church bell tower — a crawlspace above the small platform from which the bell was suspended. The hideaway was virtually invisible from below.

Fred spent his first few days in the Raulin's kitchen getting a crash course in French while identity documents were prepared. He loved children, and spent hours playing with Lionel, something that endeared him to the family and especially to little Lionel. It also did wonders for Fred's growing command of French. Once he was sufficiently proficient in the basics, he became involved in passing messages among FFI families in the town, traveling by bicycle. His identity papers identified him as the local parish priest. This was not a particularly difficult role for him, as he had been raised Roman Catholic and attended Catholic primary and high schools. He therefore knew various Latin phrases that could add to his cover story. Simone provided the proper garb from the wardrobe of the recently deceased cleric. Moving along the narrow, unpaved roads through the village, he sometimes rode one-handed, keeping the other free to issue a *Deus tecum* or *Deus vobiscum* as he rode along. His trips often took him to the home of the local butcher, Louis Lesoeur, or to Jacqueline Robert, a local shopkeeper.

Although the FFI had initially planned a general uprising for 14 July, the plan was changed due to the continued failure of the Allies to shatter the German lines and break free into Normandy. (The new plan, ultimately successful, was to cache the weapons until that breakout occurred and then harass the retreating German units from all sides.) Each evening, the group listened to the BBC radio, waiting for a code phrase such as "grandmother loves chocolate" that would indicate that an arms drop would be made that night. If the drop was made near Lyons-le-Forêt, roughly 25 miles away, FFI members from that area would pick up the materials, cache some of them, and move the rest through the network for dispersal. Sometimes an air drop included caged carrier pigeons that would be transported to Hacqueville. Max would then prepare a message reporting significant regional events or specific requests. When released, the birds would (with luck) carry the missive to London.[35]

On 8 July 1944, Fred and Paul met Flight Engineer Alexander MacPherson of the 207th Squadron of the RAF. His Lancaster bomber had been shot down, and he landed undetected on the outskirts of Hacqueville. He was the only surviving member of his crew, which led Fred to worry about the fate of his friends on Crashwagon III. Max had no information — he knew where other airmen were being sheltered, and who sheltered them, but not their identities. That information was kept secret.

The airmen had worries of their own, however. In many ways, the last months of the German occupation of France were particularly dangerous and stressful for both the French populace in general and the FFI in particular. Hitler had established the *Nacht und Nebel* (Night and Fog) policy in December 1941. His decree mandated the death penalty for anyone in the occupied territories who either injured military personnel, destroyed equipment or supplies, or otherwise interfered with German military operations, or reduced military capabilities. In 1942, he advocated the shooting of 100-150 French civilians for every German killed by resistance activities. In early 1944, he added orders to burn the associated houses or entire communities. These instructions were usually carried out by units of the SS.

Fred had heard of the SS, but knew little about the organization or its various divisions now operating in occupied France. As the days turned into weeks, Max filled him in. The SS was a paramilitary group of fanatical volunteers who had become infamous for atrocities against French civilians. Roughly half of the SS divisions in the field were manned by Germans, and the rest by French, Polish, Hungarian, Dutch, Belgian, and Russian volunteers. Max didn't have exact numbers, but he said that the SS troops seemed to be far outnumbered by the Army troops.[36] Both groups, however, aggressively pursued the FFI and searched villages for downed Allied airmen.

The French Resistance also had to contend with intelligence services, spies, and traitors working for or with the Gestapo, the SD,

---

[35] This was risky because the Germans sometimes dashed to a supply drop, swapping London's pigeons for their own before the FFI got there.

[36] In 1944, the SS had one million troops, and the German Army had twelve million.

and the Abwehr. What infuriated Max the most was the Milice (the security police of the Vichy French government), as it consisted entirely of traitors working to imprison or kill fellow Frenchmen.

When Fred first arrived in Hacqueville, Army patrols were sweeping the area at irregular intervals. The troops could be recognized by their gray-green wool uniforms, dark-green collars and shoulder straps, and a swastika on the right breast. Over the period Fred was in town, SS units began to sweep through the community looking for real or perceived threats against the German occupying forces.[37] Although the uniforms of SS troops were similar, their lapels were decorated with twin silver "SS" lightning bolts, and the swastika was placed on the left sleeve. Often more distinctive at a distance, their hats bore silver "skull and crossbones" badges. By early July, everyone had heard rumors of SS barbarity and the razing of entire towns. The SS patrols became even more aggressive and frequent after the failed attempt to assassinate Hitler on 20 July 1944.[38] Convinced that the Army leadership was potentially disloyal and the Luftwaffe ineffective, Hitler became increasingly reliant on Himmler, whose power and influence grew rapidly.[39] Unaware of the intricacies of German politics, all Fred, Paul, and Alex knew was that they found themselves spending more and more time hiding in the ceiling, the church bell tower, or the crawlspace above the bell while the village was searched by roving patrols.

Through it all, Max remained convinced that the best strategy was for the airmen to stay in Hacqueville and await the arrival of the Allies, which he felt was imminent. Fred was OK with this approach, but Paul and Alex grew increasingly restive. The resulting dissension in part reflected the fact that the three men had very different backgrounds, perspectives, and temperaments. Fred was raised in Brooklyn and relatively street-wise. In Brooklyn, he and Eddie Virgilio had learned when to fight and when to run, and how to read the odds. Paul came from a small rural community approximately ten miles west of Manchester, New Hampshire. He was a good guy, but

---

[37] On 17 June 1944, Hitler ordered that any uniformed British personnel parachuting into France were to be executed.

[38] One of the organizational changes made at that time was that the Abwehr would thereafter report to the SS, rather than the Army. Another was an order issued on 22 July 1944 stating that Allied military personnel captured out of uniform were to be executed as commandos.

[39] All traces of legality and due process were suspended inside Germany, and the SS detained and executed more than 5,000 German civilians considered either to be insufficiently committed to the Nazi agenda or to pose a potential security risk.

the unforgiving world he found himself in was totally unfamiliar. Fred liked Paul, and felt as if he needed to counsel him at times. Privately, the Raulins and Tati referred to Paul with great fondness as a "dear boy" or a "sweet child," and remarked about how anxious he was to return to his wife at home. Alex was more of a firebrand and sometimes hard for Fred to take. He was almost a caricature of a British aristocrat — a bit overbearing, condescending to Yanks, and dismissive of the Germans. He also had a rather low opinion of the French, when none were in the room. That really annoyed Fred. One day, Alex's temper caused a serious problem when an SS patrol was heading for the church. Part way up the stairs to the steeple, Alex had his fill of hiding and quite loudly started talking about shooting it out with the stupid, bloody Germans and getting it over with. Fred, with Paul's help, had been able to muzzle and physically restrain him. They were never totally forgiven, and the discord among the airmen, as well as Alex's general attitude, did not especially endear Alex to the Raulins.

The dynamic at the Raulin's began to shift as the men became more familiar with Jean Jacques, a trusted member of the FFI network. Jean was based in Paris, but he was a regular visitor to Hacqueville. Jean was 5'7", very slender (bordering on scrawny), and had short light-brown hair, and pale-gray eyes. He also had a distinctive gold filling in a front tooth that flashed when he smiled. He dressed well, spoke excellent English, and his relaxed attitude tended to put people at ease. Jean's visits were welcomed by the airmen, as they provided a break in the daily routine and an opportunity to converse freely in English. He arrived in his own car, which was in itself cause for comment. Although Dr. Daviaud had a car and a driving pass, few other local FFI members were so fortunate.

Jean sometimes showed up alone, but at other times he brought his girlfriend, Collette Orsini. Collette was in her twenties and a very attractive redhead, and the young airmen were a bit envious of Jean. Collette had met Jean through the FFI network. Her parents were involved in the Comet Line, an underground network that shifted evaders from Paris across the southern mountains and into neutral Spain. Collette's family had facilitated the escape of two Allied airmen before she had been introduced to Jean. Although the fact wasn't shared with the airmen, Collette was married, but not happily, and her husband was not living in Paris.

After almost two months in hiding, Fred was feeling frustrated at the confinement. The Allied front line still hadn't broken through the stubborn German defenses, and nobody could predict how long that stalemate would last. Between the German atrocities and the increased frequency of SS patrols, he worried not only about his own safety, but that his presence threatened the whole community. Max steadfastly maintained that they should take no chances, stay put, and await the arrival of Allied ground forces — there were reports that the Allied forces were starting to advance. But Jean felt differently. He assured the airmen that the contacts he had in Paris would make it very easy for them to return to Allied control either by plane from a private aerodrome or overland through Spain. He said that he had escorted more than a dozen airmen to safety in the last month alone, and that they were probably already flying missions against the Nazis. That information made the airmen wonder if it wasn't their patriotic duty to make the attempt. When asked about this, Max confirmed the fact that Jean had in the past used his vehicle to transport FFI members and/or Allied airmen to various destinations, including Paris. All three airmen had been advised in evasion training classes that if they were shot down but avoided capture, Paris would offer their best chance of repatriation. Everything seemed to be pointing them in that direction.

5-15 AUGUST 1944: PARIS

By early August, the airmen had decided to leave Hacqueville over Max's strenuous objections. Fred, although less enthusiastic than Paul and Alex, felt that they should stick together and go as a group. So, early on the morning of 5 August, the three airmen, dressed as French peasants, climbed into the backseat of Jean's car and headed for Paris. The 50-mile ride was uneventful. The men spoke quietly as the countryside rolled past under cloudy skies.

They arrived in Paris in the late morning and were taken to the lobby of the Piccadilly Hotel on Rue Jean-Baptiste Pigalle, where they were introduced to Louis Gianoni. Louis was the proprietor of the adjacent lounge, Le Prélude. He was much older than the airmen — 35 at least — and built like a bull. He had a round head that was balding on top, and the frames of thick tortoise-shell glasses extended into a fringe of dark hair. He looked as Italian as his name suggested, and Fred could easily imagine him working for the Mafia in Brooklyn. The airmen were instructed to have a seat and a drink in Le Prélude while Jean made further arrangements.

After nearly an hour had passed, Jean returned and told them that another car, driven by "Henri," whose identity would be verified by Louis, would pick them up and take them either to an aerodrome or to a spot where they could easily cross to Allied lines. Jean then left the three airmen seated in a corner with a bottle of wine and varying degrees of impatience and excitement. It was almost overwhelming to think that their long period of clandestine existence would soon be over.

After 30 minutes or so, Louis came to their table to report that Henri was waiting in a car parked outside of the hotel. On emerging, the men found a four-door sedan idling at the curb and a tall, well dressed gentleman climbing out of the front passenger seat. After introducing himself as Henri in heavily accented English, he opened the rear door and told them to slide inside and to get down as low as possible so that they would not be seen. Once everyone was onboard and suitably pretzeled out of sight, the car pulled away from the curb. The driver, a large, heavyset man with a dour expression, gave them a glance but said nothing to the airmen.

For a few minutes, the men rode in silence as the car worked its way across the city. The airmen huddled near the floor, bouncing against one another as the car stopped and started, took corners, and rumbled over cobblestone streets. Then the car suddenly swerved, turning into an alley and jerking to a halt. As Fred raised his head, he saw they had entered an open courtyard. At this point, Henri turned toward the backseat with a large pistol in his hand and said to Fred, this time in perfect English, "We are members of the Security Police, and you are now under arrest." They had been delivered to the Gestapo headquarters at 84 Avenue Foch.

As the stunned airmen sat up and looked outside, they saw uniformed SS guards armed with machine guns surrounding the vehicle. It was obvious that they had no options but to surrender. One by one, the guards dragged the men out of the car, clubbing them to the ground before dragging them up the stairs and into the building. Fred was roughly searched and his personal items removed — including his dog tags — before being dumped into a small windowless room, hardly larger than a closet, on the fifth floor. After an interminable period, the guards returned and escorted him to a small office to undergo his first interrogation.

The interview room held an imposing desk that faced a single chair. A tall, slender man in a dark suit sat behind the desk, and he stared hard at Fred as he was led in and slammed down into the seat. The two guards remained in the room, one standing on each side of the chair. Fred immediately stood at attention, saying "Frederic C. Martini, staff sergeant, US Army number 32163997," but his interrogator was dismissive. "You are a spy, a saboteur, traveling out of uniform, and you will be shot." When Fred responded that his dog tags proved his identity, he was told that spies often removed the dog tags from dead soldiers to embellish their cover stories.

The interrogator demanded the names of those who had

helped him evade capture, but Fred just repeated his name, rank, and serial number. As the exchange took place, the interrogator picked up a manila envelope that contained Fred's confiscated possessions and dumped them on the desktop. He started sorting through the items but froze when he reached Fred's dog tags. Grabbing the tags, he stormed around the desk and shook them in Fred's face, pointing not to the tags themselves but to the gunner's wings Fred had attached to the chain for safekeeping. He seemed enraged and almost speechless. He spit in Fred's face and started slapping him, saying "United States Motor Corps" over and over.

Fred, unable to restrain himself, said "No, sir, United States Army Air Force Air Corps, not Motor Corps" whereupon the German hit him so hard that his feet left the floor and Fred went down hard. From the floor, Fred managed to croak out "Air Corps" one more time before he got a boot in the face. "You are worse than a spy, you are a *terrorflieger*, a butcher, a killer of women and children! You should have been hung, not brought to be shot." The interrogator was now kicking him repeatedly in the side and in the head. By the time he tired of the exercise, Fred was unconscious and badly bruised, within an area marked by streams of blood and the broken remnants of two teeth. The guards then dragged him away to recover in his tiny room.

When he regained consciousness, Fred was stunned and in pain. His jaw was aching and he knew that he had lost a couple of teeth. His ribs were almost as painful, and the first time he tried to stand, a shaft of pain from the right side of his abdomen froze him in position until he worked up the nerve to continue. Thirty minutes or so later, he was breathing a bit easier when the guards came and escorted him to another room where a uniformed SS officer told him to fill out a fake "Red Cross form" that was designed to extract useful intelligence about air operations. Fred took the form and wrote down his name, rank, and serial number, crossing out the rest. When he handed it back, the SS officer glanced at it in disgust before crumpling it up and tossing it in the trash. He told Fred it didn't really matter, as they would be burying him in a week or two anyway.

Fred was then assisted downstairs into the courtyard, where he found himself in company with Alex MacPherson, Paul Wilson, and several other men he didn't recognize. An SS officer addressed them, saying (1) they were all spies and terror fliers, and as such not covered by the Geneva Conventions, (2) a French magistrate had authorized their execution, and (3) they were now to be transported to another facility for further interrogation before the sentences were carried out.

A large, black panel truck entered the courtyard. The back of the truck was divided into what looked like animal cages, and pairs of airmen were handcuffed together and thrown into the cages. The man handcuffed to Fred introduced himself as Lt. "JD" Coffman from the 489th BG.[40] Fred, with slight slurring, managed to identify himself and his outfit before the truck jerked into motion and talking became difficult to impossible. Over the next half hour, they rode to the southern suburbs of Paris, where the truck came to a halt in front of a long single-storey brick building with a high-peaked entryway.

FRESNES PRISON

As he and JD emerged from the van, Fred could see that there were heavy, vertical iron bars across each window. A walkway extended from the street to tall double doors, and as they were dragged from their cages, the men could see into an interior courtyard with additional buildings extending into the distance. A concrete wall roughly 20' high extended to either side for at least one block, ending at guard towers marking the corners of the compound.

The airmen stood at the entry to Fresnes Prison, built 40 years earlier and the largest prison in France.[41] After France surrendered to the Germans, the SS took over the operation of the prison. They used it primarily to house members of the French Resistance and captured British spies, with areas set aside for executions as well as interrogations. Those surviving a stay in Fresnes Prison were usually deported to Germany to work in forced labor camps or prison factories. Still in handcuffs, Fred, JD, and the other airmen were led through the prison gates and herded to an administrative station. Their names and arrival times were noted and the handcuffs removed before they were stripped, searched, and their personal effects confiscated. The airmen were then led deeper into the complex to the cell block.

Fred was led along a long, central hallway from which three pairs of side corridors branched at right angles. The interior was harshly lit by hanging floodlights as there were few openings to the exterior other than the barred windows found in some of the cells. The

---

[40] Lt. Coffman, another airman sheltered by Max Raulin's resistance network, was lured to Paris by promises of a flight to England. He too was delivered to the Gestapo on 5 August 1944.

[41] It became the second largest after completion of the Fleury-Merogis Prison in 1968.

Gestapo had taken advantage of this layout to organize Fresnes Prison into three major divisions. Division 1 was for German prisoners, Division 2 was where spies, British Special Operations Executive (SOE) agents, and saboteurs were held,[42] and Division 3 was reserved for male and female political prisoners, most of them French. Fred and the other airmen were led to Division 3, the two side corridors at the far end of the long central hallway.

Fred looked along each of the side corridors as he passed them, and they all looked identical to the one he found himself entering. Cells were stacked four stories high, with the doors on the upper levels opening onto elevated walkways. Suspended catwalks connected the walkways on either side of each level. Although Fred didn't have time to count them, there were roughly 400 cells in each division. Not all of the cells were of identical size, but none were spacious. At the time the airmen arrived, Fresnes prison held approximately 3,000 prisoners. As the airmen entered Division 3, it was dark, smelly, and noisy — Fred could hear cries and moans (mostly in French) echoing along the gloomy corridor.

The men climbed two sets of stairs. Fred, who was having some difficulty keeping pace due to the persistent pain in his side, was shoved into the first small cell available and the door locked behind him. The other airmen continued varying distances along the walkway before being directed into other cells, some already occupied.

Fred found himself in a concrete and stone enclosure approximately 12' x 6' with a single, frosted window high on the exterior wall. The window was nailed shut, and steel bars could be seen on the other side of the glass. There were small ventilation ducts opening high on either wall. Very little air flowed through them, but they did interconnect the cells along the corridor and would provide a potential means of communication. A straw mat on a metal frame bolted to the wall took the place of a bed. The room also contained a toilet with neither seat nor lid, a wooden table bolted to the floor, and a rickety, wooden chair. There was no sink and no faucet. A small cup and a wooden bowl, both empty, sat on the table. The walls were grimy and unpainted, lit by a naked lightbulb dangling from the ceiling. There was no light switch in the cell. The heavy door that sealed him in had a small viewing window and a slot through which he hoped food would pass. He was very hungry.

He sat at the table and gazed around in despair. What was this

---

[42] SOE agents parachuted into enemy territory as undercover agents. Only a few Allied airmen, generally those who had been held and interrogated for long periods, were kept in Division 2.

place? They surely knew he was an aviator, that they were all aviators, so why were they here and not heading to a POW camp? His glance went to the bare floor, and for a brief instant, he thought it odd that previous prisoners had used so much pepper that it spilled everywhere. But then some of the grains disappeared, reappearing elsewhere, and he realized that these were fleas rather than pepper grains — the floor was alive with them. He pulled his feet up onto the chair, but it was too late. He could feel the vermin moving along his legs, and the first bites at his ankles were already itching fiercely.

Outside the cell and echoing from the ventilation ducts, he could hear a steady babble of voices, mostly in French but a few in English, often American English. Through the verbal exchanges he overheard, Fred learned that he was in a Gestapoprison, housed with a mix of other airmen and members of the French Resistance. Nobody knew what fate awaited them, but each day, prisoners were selected for removal to a place of interrogation and sometimes execution

Late that evening, with the light still on, Fred found it impossible to stay awake. Against his better judgment, he left the chair for the "bed" hoping to get a night of recuperative slumber. Instead, he found that the bedding was infested not only with fleas but with lice, and the most he could manage were periods of fitful dozing separated by frantic scratching, or exploring sleeves or seams to find and crush offending vermin.

Each morning at 0630, a guard using a cart with a distinctive squeaky wheel stopped by the door and opened the inspection port. Fred passed out his cup, to have it returned half-filled with a liquid that looked like a cross between tea and coffee (made primarily with acorns). Lunch was delivered sometime around noon, and Fred passed both the bowl and the cup through the door slot. When returned, the bowl contained a watery, potato-based soup, and the cup another round of ersatz coffee. He also received a chunk of hard, dark bread. With his jaw still tender and aching, the soup was ideal, and he found that he could deal with the bread as well if he first soaked it in either the soup or the fake coffee. But it was hardly a filling meal, and when he finished, he found he was almost as hungry as he had been before the meal started. And those were the high points of his day, other than another half-cup of coffee that arrived around 1500. This particular hotel had no dinner service.

His mornings were marked by bursts of gunfire from the courtyard below, where executions were being carried out. The airmen were clustered in cells on the third and fourth floor, and each day, he listened for news and comments relayed from cell to cell. In that way, he learned bits and pieces about the progress of the Allies and heard other airmen speculate about their fate. Some feared they were to be executed, whereas others felt they would be removed to a POW camp. Fred could also hear the sobs and moans of French prisoners, and sometimes Allied airmen, returning from Gestapo interrogation sessions.

Fortunately, he was only taken from his cell once, a few days after he had arrived. An armed guard beat heavily on the door and shouted "*Raus!*" Upon emerging, Fred was taken downstairs and along the corridor to a room holding a rather dapper Luftwaffe officer in an immaculate, blue-gray uniform. Fred stood at attention and again related his name, rank, and serial number. The officer, who spoke excellent English, responded quite equably, simply posing a question about hatch operation to verify his claim to being a B-17 crewmember. Fred could not see any possible military use for this information — they had plenty of wrecked aircraft to look at — so he answered the question but gave no further information on follow-up questions about his unit or his mission. The Luftwaffe officer made a few notes on his clipboard and then signaled the guard to take Fred back to his cell. Perhaps it was good luck, or perhaps it was because he had already been severely beaten by the Gestapo before arriving at Fresnes Prison, but this was his only interrogation, and he spent the rest of his time in solitary confinement. From listening to conversations called between cells, he realized that he was one of a lucky few, for many other airmen had been severely beaten.[43]

In the second week of August, distant rumblings were heard, and soon the entire prison population knew that the Allied artillery was nearing the city. Speculation ran wild over what the German response would be. Ominously, there was a noticeable increase in gunfire from the courtyard area, and word was passed that the SS guards were executing prisoners. On 12 August, thirty members of the FFI were executed by machine guns. Fred heard the roar of the guns, the moans, and the individual coup-de grace shots, in his dreams thereafter.[44]

---

[43] Among the US airmen, Sgt. Donald Leslie lost two front teeth, Sgt. Leo Grenon was severely beaten, and Sgt. Charles Roberson lost hearing on one side. RCAF Flight Lieutenant (F/L) Art Kinnis had his right eardrum ruptured; among the RAF airmen, Flight Lieutenant (F/L) Tommy Blackham, struck across the throat with a baton, had difficulty speaking and swallowing, F/L Stan Booker had been beaten repeatedly, and Flying Officer (F/O) Philip Hemmens, who had a broken arm, was left in chronic pain with a makeshift splint.

[44] The dead included Suzanne Spaak, who was killed for saving Jewish children from deportation to German concentration camps.

Early on the morning of 15 August, the airmen knew something unusual was happening, as they could hear trucks and shouted orders as well as the clear sounds of an ongoing artillery exchange. Word was soon passed that the prison was being evacuated, although opinions differed on their fate. "Breakfast" never arrived, and at around 1000 (Fred's watch had of course been confiscated), SS guards were on the walkways, opening cell doors and ordering everyone into the corridor. The prisoners were herded in a crush along the walkway, down the stairs, and along the corridor until they reached the open area just inside the prison entryway. There followed a period where the prisoners waited for something to happen. Although adjacent cells had exchanged names, no one had an idea of how many airmen were held in the prison. Fred took the time to see if he recognized anyone. He soon spotted Sam Pennell in the mob, and worked his way through the crowd to reach him. It felt like the reunion of two brothers, and Paul Wilson soon joined them. Such reunions were not unusual, and many other airmen found comrades they hadn't seen since bailing out of their crippled aircraft.

It was a hot, still August day, and everyone was soon perspiring freely. The heat only added thirst to the discomfort caused by hunger and maltreatment. All of the airmen looked worse for wear. There were vivid facial bruises, black eyes, torn scalps, and odd postures resulting from unseen injuries. The men were also still wearing the clothing they arrived in days or weeks or even months before, and they had neither bathed nor shaved while confined. They stood packed together in the atrium, each man hoping that the delay meant they were awaiting evacuation, rather than execution. At that point, Fred would have welcomed evacuation, as he felt certain that conditions anywhere else would be more hospitable. Neither Fred nor any of the other airmen would have believed that they would soon wish they could return to Fresnes Prison.

CHAPTER 6

Striving for the Fatherland

⊰⊱

On 13 June 1944, Wernher attended the launching of the modified V-2, both to see how it worked and because he always enjoyed watching his rockets take off. The launch preparations went without a hitch. The rocket was brought to the stand, placed in position, and then fueled with great care — the combination of ethyl alcohol and liquid oxygen was explosive to say the least. The launch itself had gone perfectly, the rocket leaping skyward with a deafening roar on a plume of fire. As it ascended, an engineer with a joystick made small, deliberate changes in the flight path, operating servomotors by radio control. By the time the rocket was out of sight and out of control range, the test was viewed as a complete success.

At that point, the rocket was left to its own devices, and they had expected it to complete its flight arc and impact somewhere well out to sea. However, that wasn't how things worked out. Thanks to a slight trajectory change inadvertently made during the test phase, the rocket headed for neutral Sweden rather than the empty North Atlantic. Fortunately for the Swedes, the stresses on the descent proved too much for the structural modifications made to the rocket, and it broke apart before it reached the ground. The Swedish government was furious, and Berlin called Dornberger, demanding an explanation. Such things roll downhill, and Wernher knew he would have to shoulder much of the blame. He didn't think it would be a major problem — thank goodness it hadn't killed any Swedish citizens — and he doubted anything useful could be learned from the debris field.[45]

For the rest of June and into July, Wernher continued to travel to the Mittelwerk to monitor production and to Blizna, Poland, where mobile launch crews were being trained and test launches conducted. The tests weren't going well at all. Only 40% of the V-2s launched were reaching the ground, the rest disintegrating in the upper atmosphere or on descent.

The accuracy of the surviving rockets was nowhere near

---

[45] The British obtained pieces of the rocket and were distressed to say the least. They estimated the rocket could carry an explosive load eight times greater than its actual capacity. It made them take Hitler's "German wonder weapon" threat much more seriously.

satisfactory either. When Wernher attended a test, he would stand in the center of the target — he felt confident that, under the circumstances, that was the safest place to be. The rockets that managed to complete their flight path typically impacted several miles away. He was in position, watching the sky and waiting for a missile to descend, when he realized that he could see one coming right at him. All he could do was drop to the ground and hope for the best. The rocket struck perhaps a hundred yards away, the force of the resulting explosion blowing him into a ditch. He had learned how it felt to be on the receiving end of one of his creations. What a story he had to tell!

From the test results, the design team was finally able to sort out what was causing the air bursts. The primary problem turned out to be the lack of insulation between the shell of the missile, which air friction heated to over 900 F, and the underlying liquid-oxygen tank. When the tank wall overheated and failed, the rocket exploded. The solution involved adding insulation and a reinforcing ring, modifications that had to be incorporated into the production and assembly lines at the Mittelwerk.

Few V-2s could be produced at the Mittelwerk in June or July, since there was no use building them until the problems causing rocket failure were solved. And Germany's enemies weren't making it easy. On 18 July, hundreds of American B-17s bombed Peenemünde and damaged Test Stand VII, where V-2s were launched. Fifty Peenemünders were killed in that raid, and the only luck they had was that the attack came before the next rocket scheduled for testing had been moved into position.

Two days later, the German government was thrown into turmoil by the unsuccessful attempt on Hitler's life. Both the Army and the Luftwaffe fell from grace, as conspirators were identified in their ranks. Himmler, charged with the protection of the Führer and the Nazi Party, henceforth operated with few restraints. Wernher found himself spending more and more time dealing with SS personnel and regulations at Peenemünde. But despite the increased paperwork, he finally managed to schedule his trip to Buchenwald after one of his regular visits to the Mittelwerk.[46] The trip to the concentration camp was unusually productive, and he had found Commandant Pister very accommodating. With Pister's help he at least temporarily solved the shortage of skilled labor. Within a week of his visit, 636 skilled laborers were shipped to the Mittelwerk, and more would follow. He was not

---

[46] This visit was thought to have been on 24 July 1944. Because he went by car, there is no flight log to determine an exact date.

sure whether or not he could rely on Pister to select the best possible workers from the available pool. If not, he would have to return to Buchenwald periodically.

On that trip, Wernher was able to combine business with pleasure by taking the opportunity to visit his old high school at Ettersburg, relatively close to Buchenwald. He had fond memories of the school where he had first pursued his fascination with rocketry, and it was his last chance to do something other than work. He hadn't returned to Paris recently, and with the enemy approaching the city, he wouldn't be going anytime soon. Moving ahead, there would be no time for distractions — combat launches of the V-2 rockets would begin in early September.

Shortly after he returned to Peenemünde, a second US bombing raid smashed the main hangar and damaged both Wernher's office building and the laboratory wings. It was another close call, and it reminded him to stretch his schedule to give more time to the Wasserfall anti-aircraft rocket program.

The SS was in charge of the physical facility and security at the Mittelwerk and the labor force at Dora, and they operated the V-2 testing facilities and the mobile launchers that were being distributed ahead of the first combat launches. That was the main reason Wernher made it a point to wear his SS uniform when visiting the testing, launching, and training facilities. The only aspects of missile production that the SS did not yet control were the design, manufacturing, and quality control of the rockets, which Wernher handled, and operational control of the mobile launch vehicles, which would, at least for the moment, continue to be operated by Army Ordinance rather than the SS (over Himmler's strenuous objections).

Wernher had seen the preliminary plans that would dramatically increase the production of V-1 and V-2 rockets, jet engines, and other advanced weapons. Seven large underground factories were envisioned, centered in the area northwest of Nordhausen and interconnected by railways. It was called the Bauvorhaben X Project, and the facilities were referred to as B1, B2, etc, the numbers referring to their construction priority. When completed, 45,000 additional slave laborers would be provided by the SS. One of the factories was already operational, producing turbines for the V-2s assembled at the Mittelwerk,. It had been excavated by slave laborers from the Dora Concentration Camp and its Ellrich sub-camp. The increased production would be welcome, and if done fast enough, it could reshape the war. Unfortunately, the more factories involved in V-2 production, the greater the competition for Wernher's time, as he had to be sure that quality control was adequate and the components as near perfect as humanly possible.

As evidenced by these expansive plans, Albert Speer continued to provide encouragement and support. Speer was also concerned that Himmler was inching closer to taking total control over the rocket program and shifting the balance of power in the Reich. In early August, he had attempted to thwart Himmler's machinations by nationalizing the Peenemünde facility and reorganizing it under the Reich Armaments Ministry as Elektromechanischewerk (EW), GmbH. As a nationalized corporation, EW would have top priority for materials in short supply, such as aluminum and liquid oxygen. From that time onward, Wernher would no longer be technical director of an army research facility. He would be a senior vice president of a major corporation. The change in title had no real impact on his duties and responsibilities, but it made it easier for him to deal with the sometimes conflicting demands of the army and the SS.

On 15 August, Wernher prepared a letter to be sent to Herr Director A. Sawatski, Mittelwerk, Ltd. It read, in part:

> DEAR MR. SAWATSKI,
> DURING MY LAST VISIT TO THE MITTELWERK, YOU
> SUGGESTED UTLILIZING THE SKILLED TECHNICAL
> BACKGROUND OF VARIOUS PRISONERS BOTH AT THE
> MITTELWERK AND IN BUCHENWALD IN ORDER TO
> ACCOMPLISH ADDITIONAL DEVELOPMENT WORK AS WELL AS
> TO CONSTRUCT SAMPLE DEVICES . . . . I IMMEDIATELY ACTED
> ON YOUR SUGGESTION AND WENT WITH DR. SIMON TO FIND
> A FEW OTHER SUITABLE PRISONERS IN BUCHENWALD AND
> THEN, ACCORDING TO YOUR SUGGESTION, ARRANGED WITH
> STANDARTENFÜHRER[47] PISTER FOR THEIR TRANSFER TO THE
> MITTELWERK . . . .
> WITH BEST WISHES AND
> HEIL HITLER!
> SINCERELY,
> B [WERNHER VON BRAUN][48]

Shifts at the Mittelwerk were working around the clock, but despite a reduced laborer:manager ratio, there were still production problems caused by unfamiliarity with Wernher's design changes. The SS was convinced that other failures were the result of deliberate sabotage,

---

[47] An SS rank comparable to a Colonel in the German Army.
[48] Fort Eustis microfilm collection, Roll 28/694, NASM, Chantilly, Virginia.

and SS guards had taken to hanging suspected saboteurs from the construction cranes outside Arthur Rudolph's office as a warning to the prisoner workforce. Wernher received copies of the labor reports that tracked the number of laborers and the losses to death or injury. The losses had declined after the peak in March 1944, when the manual construction phase ended, but under the pressure for increased production, the death rates were climbing once again.

Wernher had no control over sabotage, and his only involvement in punishment, other than a few minor incidents on the assembly line, was through his insistence that laborers be replaced if they were incapable of meeting his quality control standards. What happened to incompetent *häftlinge* (prisoners) was none of his concern. He did have complete control over the design, and he continued to demand small modifications and improvements that he hoped would simplify assembly. These tweaks brought him into constant contact with both Albin Sawatski and Arthur Rudolph. To keep him in the loop, Wernher was cc'd on all correspondence and reports related to missile production.

Wernher sometimes felt he was a victim of his own success — his dramatic, charismatic, and flamboyant presentations had convinced Hitler and Speer that a massive V-2 bombardment would change the course of the war, and now they would accept nothing less. Although Wernher remained confident that he could deliver on his promises, given enough time and materials, it was still a struggle. He was certainly committed to that effort, and he and his engineering staff were driving themselves hard, putting in long hours every day of the week to overcome the logistical and financial hurdles. As Dornberger continually reminded them, this was Total War, and their work could save Germany from another humiliating defeat.

A year earlier, Wernher had tried to get additional funding to build the A-10, a three-stage rocket that could reach the east coast of the US and strike Boston, New York, and Washington DC. Surely, if rockets started to rain down on both London and New York, Germany could demand an armistice on the western front and turn its full attention to the eastern front and Germany's real enemy, the Soviet Union. But for once, he had failed to convince Hitler, who wanted all of the available resources devoted to producing V-2s. Although he was still disappointed that the A-10 concept hadn't been seen as a stroke of genius, he now returned to the preliminary designs. The third stage of the A-10 resembled a V-2 with stubby winglets on each side. Adding those winglets would potentially double its range. enabling them to continue the barrage of London even if Germany was forced to abandon France and the low countries. He made some notes, and decided to call the new iteration the A-4b.

CHAPTER 7

Transport

—◁◈▷—

15-20 AUGUST 1944

At Fresnes Prison, most of the captured airmen were held in the upper floors in the last portion of Division 3 to be evacuated.[49] When all of the Allied airmen to be evacuated were assembled, trucks and buses carried them to the northeastern edge of Paris. It was almost an hour before the 18-mile trip ended with their unloading at the trainyard of the Gare de Pantin. They were offloaded near the end of a string of boxcars. Passenger cars near the front of the train, roughly 1,500' away, contained members of the puppet Vichy or Laval governments, German military officers, counterintelligence agents, and collaborators who felt it was time to leave Paris and never look back. Every other boxcar in the chain held prisoners, with the car in between reserved for a dozen guards and their equipment and personal gear.

The prisoner convoy was under the command of SS officers, but many of the guards were wearing different uniforms from those at the prison. These were Gestapo agents, hardened by service on the Russian front. There were also regular Waffen-SS troops providing additional security and leaving Paris on the same train.

The boxcars were small (10' x 25') and marked "40 hommes ou 8 chevaux" (40 men or 8 horses). In practice, each car was loaded with 70-90 prisoners. The boxcars had a steel frame and steel corners, but the floors and walls were rough planks, set parallel to the long axis of the train. The roof was a curved piece of corrugated iron. Behind the train was a tail of barbed wire netting. This was intended to prevent any prisoner trying to escape by dropping from a boxcar onto the tracks and waiting for the train to move past.

The station yard was chaotic. The guards needed to control and organize 2,453 prisoners. This involved verifying that all who had left Fresnes Prison had arrived at the train station, and recording who

---

[49] For unknown reasons, roughly 500 prisoners, including some captured airmen, were left at Fresnes Prison. They expected to be executed, but they were ultimately abandoned when the last of the SS guards fled Paris ahead of the Allies.

boarded each boxcar. Nerves were on edge, in part because of the heat and in part because they knew that it was their last chance to escape Paris. The clock was ticking. While the guards dealt with crowd control and paperwork, members of the French Red Cross moved through the throng with lemonade and aspirin.

All of the women from the prison were taken to the last five boxcars.[50] The airmen, mixed in with French prisoners, were loaded into the three boxcars in front of the women. Each car contained two five-gallon buckets, one filled with water and the other empty, presumably for use as a toilet. Fred saw an airman from the Fresnes group bull his way through the throng to confront an SS officer. Fred's first thought was that the guy was a force to be reckoned with. He was tall and rugged looking, and from the look of his nose he had been in a few brawls. He looked both determined and totally committed to his course of action. At attention before the officer, he loudly protested that the airmen were military prisoners, and under the Geneva Conventions they should be treated as POWs and not cattle. The response was curt and direct: an elbow to the face and an escort back to the cattle car. Fred saw that although he left the confrontation bloody, his bearing was unchanged, and he showed no signs of either discouragement or disappointment.

After giving their names to one of the guards with a clipboard, Fred, Sam, and Paul were each given a chunk of dark bread with a dollop of margarine on it and a small tin of horsemeat. They were directed into the last of the three boxcars, along with 25 other airmen[51] and 63 French prisoners. A few of the prisoners had managed to secure Red Cross parcels from harried volunteers who were attempting to help. The small packages, intended for one person, contained a few biscuits, jam, margarine, some sugar, and a can of sardines. Each parcel was shared among six or more prisoners.

The only ventilation for the prisoners came through 2'x1' openings that were guarded with a zig-zag network of barbed wire. There were four openings on each side of the train, but only two were left open. The other two were covered by steel shutters, locked in

---

[50] There were 546 women loaded onto the train, and 370 of them would survive the war. The male prisoners fared much worse, with a survival rate below 30%.

[51] Fred Martini, Paul Wilson, Sam Pennell, Ray Perry, Harry Bastable, Leon Grenon, Bill Gibson, Dave High, Tommy Hodgson, James Prudhum, Joseph Sonshine, Ian Robb, Robert Mills, Les Whellum, Splinter Adolph Spierenburg, Ralph Taylor, Roy Allen, James Harvie, Merle Larson, Daniel McLaughlin, Joe Moser, Michael Petrich, Charles Roberson, Joel Stevenson, Fred Vinecome, and James Zeiser.

position. By the time the car was fully loaded and the sliding door closed and secured, it was 1400, and between the sun beating down on the steel roof and the severe overcrowding, conditions inside the car were almost unbearable. It was stiflingly hot, there was no way to sit down, and getting to the toilet pail or to the freshbucket was so difficult as to be almost impossible except for men within a few feet of them. Many of the French prisoners and several of the airmen had contracted dysentery at Fresnes Prison, and all were still in the clothing they had worn at the time of arrest. It was clear that personal hygiene was a thing of the past, and the smell was at first overpowering.

All that day, the men stood and waited and wondered what would become of them. What with the heat and the crowding, everyone in the boxcar had a short fuse. There was pushing and shoving and angry words exchanged, often caused by a prisoner whose uncontrolled urination or noisy defecation fouled his neighbors. The situation was complicated by language, as the airmen were scattered within the crowded boxcar. Ralph Taylor, an American sergeant, was near a young Frenchman who spoke reasonable English. Together they worked out a plan to organize the car, and gradually, with a lot of wriggling and jostling, the airmen shifted so as to occupy one end of the boxcar. This did nothing to ease the overcrowding, but it made it possible to avoid miscommunication, and gave an opportunity for conversations that would help pass the time.

At first, Fred and Sam had plenty to talk about. Sam told the story of his time with the FFI. He had been sheltered for two months at Saint-Denis-le-Ferment, roughly nine miles from Hacqueville but in a different administrative sector. Jean Jacques had the same siren call in that sector, and on 7 August 1944, Sam, along with three RAF airmen (Flight Sergeants Leonard Barham, Eric Davis and Frank Salt) took a ride with Jean and a red-haired who sounded a lot like Collette. They soon found themselves in the clutches of the Gestapo. Fred and Paul spoke of their time with the Raulins, hiding in the church steeple, and the ride to Paris with Jean Jacques. Those around them chimed in, overhearing the conversation as it proceeded. It soon became evident that of the group in the boxcar, many had fallen victim to the same traitor.

Crammed into the boxcars, the prisoners waited through the long afternoon in the stifling heat. Thirst, smells, cramps, hunger, and anxiety all took their toll. Fred overheard a conversation among Red Cross personnel that suggested the long delay was the result of a French Railway Workers strike, which was an attempt to prevent the departure of the prisoner train. It took the increasingly frantic Germans ten hours to find both a locomotive and a crew they could force to drive it, ten precious hours during which the Allied forces moved ever closer and the FFI became emboldened. The train finally started to move shortly after midnight, and by then it was overcast and raining. This lowered the temperature outside, but with such limited ventilation, it did little to improve conditions for the prisoners. The sound of artillery was now very near, and flares could be seen in the night sky through the small ventilation ports. The airmen were on the last train to leave Paris before its liberation on 25 August 1944.

That first night and on subsequent nights, Fred and other prisoners struggled to find positions where sleep was at least theoretically possible. In Fred's overcrowded boxcar, people around the edges tried to sleep leaning against the walls, while those in the interior took turns sleeping while crouched or sitting, wedged among their comrades, in 30-minute shifts. Over time, everyone became dehydrated, malnourished, and severely sleep deprived.

Near dawn, the train stopped while groups of guards started painting red crosses on the tops of the boxcars to deter air attacks. This effort had barely started before the train was strafed by a passing fighter. The plane made only one pass and caused no damage to the train or the tracks, although debris struck the sides of the boxcars. It was Fred's second time under air attack (the first was at Great Ashfield), and he found it even more unnerving to be attacked by an American fighter. He knew how good those guys were at blowing things up, and he had no interest in dying by friendly fire. The incident seemed to motivate the SS management, however, and the train started moving almost immediately thereafter.

With all of the stopping and starting, progress was slow, and the FFI was doing what they could to make it slower still. There was occasional sniper fire and sometimes firefights, but to Fred's disappointment, the German response — stopping the train and sending out heavily armed SS teams in sweeping movements — outgunned and outmatched the attacking parties.

Late that morning, the train faced a more concerted ambush. After passing Luzancy, the train had to cross a loop in the Marne River. This involved crossing a bridge, driving through a long tunnel, and emerging to cross a second bridge. The train station that serviced Nanteuil-sur-Marne and Saacy-sur-Marne was located just beyond the second bridge. As the locomotive emerged from the tunnel toward the second bridge, it came under heavy fire. In response, the train ground to a halt and then backed to safety inside the tunnel. While the engine idled, the SS troops geared up and left the tunnel to battle the FFI forces. It was nearly three hours before the attackers were driven off and the SS force returned to the train.

In the interim, the idling locomotive was generating dense clouds of exhaust that soon filled the tunnel, forming a cloud layer that over time extended lower and lower. The airmen were at first in the dark, and later within the exhaust cloud. It was thick, suffocating smoke that made it difficult to breathe. Fred was jammed against his fellow prisoners, and there was no way to get his head below the cloud bank. He tried to make a facemask by pulling his shirt up to cover his nose and mouth. It helped a little, but he was still coughing and fighting for air. There was general panic, and Fred heard someone say that the prolonged stop was intentional, and they were being executed. Despair was setting in by the time the train once again jerked into motion and began backing out of the tunnel. As Fred's boxcar was near the end of the train, the air coming through the ventilation holes began to freshen almost at once.

The train stopped once the locomotive had emerged from the tunnel. Word soon reached the airmen, by relay from the prisoner cars ahead, that the railway bridge at the other end of the tunnel had been bombed. Their train had apparently reached the end of the line.

After formulating a plan, the guards emptied Fred's boxcar and selected hostages who would be killed immediately if anyone attempted to escape. Fred and the rest of the men from the boxcar were marched to the front of the train, where the passengers and guests had piled their luggage, and the German SS officers their records and equipment. Ahead, Fred could see the ruined bridge, and in the distance, on the other side, sat a second freight train. Although useless for motorized vehicles, enough of the bridge structure remained to allow careful foot traffic, and the prisoners were assigned to carry the baggage across the bridge and pile it near the front of the waiting train. Back and forth they went through the long afternoon.

When all of the baggage had been transferred, the guards counted the prisoners, verifying that there had been no escapes. Fred and the rest were allowed to relieve themselves and have a drink at the river before they were loaded like pack mules with the food, ammunition, grenades, and other military and personal gear of the guards. Emptied water and waste buckets were taken as well. Fred could see the same thing happening all along the train. The prisoners from each boxcar were being loaded with gear while a small number (usually six or seven) were under close guard. The guarded prisoners were hostages, to be killed if anyone from that boxcar resisted or attempted to escape.

Like the other men, Fred and Sam, already fatigued from multiple trips across the bridge, had sacks on their backs and duffel bags in their hands. Fred saw a young airman with an obviously broken arm being beaten by a surly guard for not carrying a full load. The airman, in pain, could do nothing to defend himself. Suddenly, the distinctive older airman, clearly a senior officer, stepped in. Looming over the surprised guard, he moved the injured airman, who he called Mr. Hemmens,[52] to the side. He then protested to an SS officer, who was standing nearby, that this was a wounded prisoner of war, not a draft horse. There was no further beating. Hemmens was given a small bundle of straw, intended for the boxcar floor, that he could carry in one hand. Many of the airmen saw the incident and were impressed by it. Word soon spread that Hemmens' defender was Squadron Leader Philip Lamason of the Royal NZ Air Force.

No attempt was made to drive more than 2,000 heavily laden prisoners across the damaged bridge. Instead, a long slow procession walked south around the hill through which the tunnel extended. Any stragglers were dealt with harshly with clubs and kicks. Fred saw Lamason step up to the plate yet again, protesting the treatment and the use of POWs as hostages and baggage carriers. But this time he was thwarted by a burly *SS-Scharführer* (staff sergeant) who kept Lamason from "bothering" an officer, by clubbing him to the ground. Lamason was kicked repeatedly, hauled to his feet, and shoved back into the line.

The marching prisoners followed the sweeping curve of the river until the ground leveled out, and followed the edge of the river as it turned to the north. They soon took a road heading east, marching through a small village where the occupants attempted to pass apples and other treats to the prisoners over the strenuous and sometimes violent objections of the SS guards.

After another three miles, they crossed the Marne River on an elevated roadway leading into the town of Saacy. As in the smaller village they had passed through, the townspeople did their best to assist them by tossing bits of fruit or bread to the prisoners. Once through the village, the procession turned north and continued for another mile to the train station at Nanteuil- s u r - Marne.

It was late afternoon, and the prisoners were exhausted. The guards and SS officers were tired, nervous about possible FFI attacks, and heavily armed. It was a bad combination. Somehow, French Red Cross workers had learned about the train, and they tried to distribute

---

[52] Flight Officer Philip D. Hemmens, bombardier on a Lancaster bomber, 49 Squadron RAF.

sandwiches and lemonade to the prisoners. The Germans made it extremely difficult, blocking their access and shoving them out of the way. By the time Fred and Sam had arrived, the opportunity for either food or drink had almost passed.

As the duo approached the boxcar, a pregnant volunteer working with the Red Cross saw them and started in their direction. An SS officer called to her, ordering her to stop and give him the lemonade she was carrying. When she ignored him and tried to walk past, he pulled his pistol, pressed it to her chest, and fired, killing her on the spot. Guards dragged her body off the platform as if she were a sack of potatoes. The airmen turned to each other in mute distress. Confronted with such stark violence, Fred could only wonder "What kind of people were they dealing with? What consideration could they expect from officers with so little concern for human life and common decency?"

The train loading began again, with the prisoners being stuffed into the filthy boxcars. Fred saw Lamason protesting to a guard about the condition of the boxcar he was to be loaded into. Three times he was clubbed to the ground, and three times he got back up and protested, after which he was forced into Fred's boxcar at gunpoint. Several other airmen boarded as well.[53] One of them questioned the stationmaster as he passed by and was told that they would be leaving the train in Frankfurt. The information, quickly relayed from boxcar to boxcar, made sense because Frankfurt was near Dulag Luft, the Luftwaffe processing center for captured airmen and a relay station to POW camps. This was welcome news — at least they could look forward to being treated like military men rather than spies or criminals. Fred had been told that conditions in POW camps weren't too bad. Prisoners got fed and clothed, received Red Cross packages, and could send and receive mail from home.

But for the moment, things were looking grim. Their new train had been passing through Nanteuil - Saarcy, the local station servicing the two villages of Nanteuil-sur-Marne, a few hundred yards away on the opposite (north) side of the river, and Saarcy-sur-Marne, a half-mile away but on the same (south) side. When it arrived at the station, the train had been carrying cattle. The animals had been hastily removed in preparation for the arrival of the SS and their prisoners, and the stench radiating from the boxcars was palpable.

Before boarding the boxcars, they were ordered to relieve themselves at the sides of the tracks. Men and women alike had no

---

[53] Additions were Lamason, Watmough, Patrick Scullion, James A. Smith, Les Head, Earl Watson, and Charles Hoffman.

choice but to do as instructed, or either hold it in for an unknown length of time or foul the interior of their boxcar, much to the amusement of the laughing guards. Fred, his mind still struggling to deal with the shock of witnessing the Frenchwoman's brutal murder, climbed into the car without saying a word. Sam and the rest followed, equally somber.

As before, each boxcar was equipped with a bucket for water and one for waste. Late in the loading process, Leo Grenon and Les Whellum, two men from Fred's boxcar, were assigned to fill the water buckets at the river before the train departed. That was the first and last time that the water buckets were refilled on the entire trip.

The new boxcars differed from the old ones in two respects. First, the floors had a thin layer of straw mixed with manure from the recently departed occupants. Second, because cows are not escape artists, the ventilation holes were not secured by strands of barbed wire. So as the prisoners were counted and loaded into a boxcar, one man was pulled aside and given a claw hammer, some nails, and a small spool of barbed wire, and ordered to secure the windows. The process was carefully monitored and the tools recovered after the job was done. But in Fred's boxcar, with the chaotic boarding process underway, the Frenchman assigned to barbed-wire duty was able to lean down and pull the nails from one end of two floor planks before returning the hammer to the waiting guard.

It was evening before the train was ready to depart, with boxcars locked, searchlights manned, and guards warily trying to look in all directions. By midnight, 24 hours after leaving Paris, the prisoner train had managed to cover just over 45 miles.

Just after midnight on 17 August, Fred became aware that something was going on. The French prisoners had managed to pry up the two loosened boards. They planned to attempt an escape the next time the train slowed on an upgrade or accelerated from a stop. Nobody knew whether or not a barbed-wire tail had been affixed to the last car, so the plan was to drop to the tracks and roll between the wheels to cover in the brush or down the embankment. The Frenchmen setting up the escape would go first, followed by Allied officers, as they were considered to be the most valuable to the war effort. Fred, as a noncom, was near the end of the list.

The train progressed slowly, not only because its inherent speed was unimpressive but because it stopped every hour or so, to let the SS guards check for signs of escape attempts. The train also stopped when fired upon, which happened often, as the FFI was determined to stop the prison train from crossing the border into Germany.

After a routine stop, as the guards clambered onboard, Fred

heard the excited chatter as two Frenchmen dropped through the floor to the tracks below. After the next stop, another pair left, and as the train slowed for a climb, the last of the Frenchmen went out, followed by the first two Allied officers.[54] But suddenly, the train screeched to a halt, shots were fired, and guards sounded the alarm. The escape had been discovered. The boards were hastily pushed back into position as the guards closest to each boxcar began using their flashlights to search the walls and floors for anything out of place. Unfortunately, in their haste to replace the planks, one of them had hung up on its neighbor, creating a gap that was all too easy to spot from below.

The guards were furious. The doors were opened, and under the guns of the guards the occupants were ordered out of the boxcar, counted, and names ticked off the master list. The water and waste buckets were taken from the boxcar, and the men were stripped and returned to the boxcar naked. This was not the end of the incident, as the guards said that there would be more punishment in the morning. The men stood within the car for an interminable period until the search for escapees ended and the train again got underway. In the long night hours, the men talked about what their fate might be. They decided that if they were to be executed, they would rush the guns and the guards and hope for a miracle, rather than stand and wait to be slaughtered.

Shortly after dawn on the morning of 17 August, the train stopped and the boxcar doors were opened. Splinter Spierenburg, a Dutch RAF officer who could understand German, acted as translator. He told the men that 35 of them were to be executed for attempting to escape. Fred was one of the men selected for the fatal punishment. After he and the others were removed from the boxcar, they faced an arc formed by guards with machine guns at the ready. Although naked and unarmed, Fred and the others were ready to rush the guards if they heard the guns racked into firing position. There was a long pause while the men stood, hearts racing. Spierenburg then relayed the order for the men to turn around and face the boxcars, which they did rather reluctantly. After another agonizing pause, a heavily accented voice called in clear English, "Take a leak!" The SS officer in charge had decided not to shoot them after all. He told

---

[54] The first airman to use the escape hatch was Flight Officer Joel M. Stevenson, a Canadian airman whose Lancaster bomber was downed on 5 July 1944, and who was captured on 14 July in company with five other airmen. Stevenson was to be followed by Dave High, Roy Allen, and others, but High was the only airman other than Stevenson to make it out of the boxcar.

Spierenburg that he felt the men had learned their lesson, but he assured them that any further escape attempts would result in the deaths of all of the prisoners in the boxcar.

The naked airmen climbed back into the boxcar, and the train began rolling. It had gone only twelve miles when, on the outskirts of Dormans, it was ambushed by the FFI in another attempt to stop the train. The attempt, like the others, was unsuccessful. The SS drove off the attackers, and the guards, using prisoner labor, were soon able to repair the minor damage to the train tracks. When the repairs were done and the prisoners were back in their boxcars, Spierenburg related that the guards were reminding everyone that any attempts to escape would be dealt with harshly. It was almost noon, and the Germans knew that they had to pick up the pace. After 36 hours, the train was only 60 miles from Paris.

The men learned the fate of only one of the escapees. Dave High was recaptured, beaten with rubber-wrapped batons until he was a mass of livid bruises, and returned to the boxcar later that day. It was several more days before he could drink, breathe, or move a limb without pain, and he said very little to anyone.

At a security stop in the early afternoon, a young French boy about 17 years of age put his hand on the lip of one of the ventilation holes to pull himself up and peer out. Fred, leaning against the forward wall of the boxcar, saw him and thought nothing of it. But outside, one of the SS guards, perhaps still smarting from the embarrassment of an escape from that car, saw movement at the opening and shot into the boxcar. The bullet slammed across the back of the boy's hand, opening the skin and breaking the bones before continuing into the car, where it grazed Bill Gibson's forehead near his right eye.

Fred stood by as Harry Bastable, who had some medical training, quickly assessed the damage. With the bones broken and the open wound bleeding, the boy needed professional attention and treatment. So when the guards opened the car door and, via Spierenburg, asked if anyone was injured, Bastable called out, and the French lad was assisted to the doorway. After climbing down, the boy, cradling his injured hand, was asked by an SS officer if he was English. When he responded that he was French, the officer motioned that he should descend the low embankment to where a small stream ran alongside the tracks.

As the boy turned and started hesitantly walking downslope on the sharp cinders, the officer made a gesture to the nearest guard, who shot the boy in the back. Two other shots followed before the officer pulled his Luger, walked down the slope to where the boy lay, and put a round into the back of his head. Stunned, Fred watched as Leo

Grenon and Andrew Rowe were ordered out of the boxcar, given shovels, and told to bury the body. They were given so little time to do it that, when ordered back into the boxcar, the boy's hands and feet were still visible, projecting from an uneven pile of cinders. Fred now had a very clear picture of the value the SS placed on life, and their willingness to use lethal force without hesitation. He would be relieved when they were transferred to Luftwaffe control at Frankfurt.

The train continued eastward. No additional rations had been provided in an organized fashion since the train left Paris more than two days before, and the prisoners were both famished and dehydrated. A few hours after the death of the French boy, driven by a combination of sleep deprivation, stress, dehydration, and hunger, James Prudham, who had been leaning against Fred, toppled to the floor of the boxcar and went into convulsions. When Spierenburg called to the SS guards for assistance, the request was ignored. Nothing could be done other than physically restraining him to prevent injury to himself or others until the seizure passed. Fred was relieved when the seizures stopped and Prudham seemed to be sleeping quietly.

The train arrived in the town of Bar-le-Duc late that night. The French Red Cross was ready for the arrival and did their best to pass drinks and food parcels to the occupants, although time was limited and the demand far exceeded the supply. Only a few parcels made it into the boxcar, but everything arriving was shared. Fred got a couple of crackers and a small slice of cheese. It seemed just enough to whet his appetite, but he was grateful for it. After this brief pause, the train proceeded in a series of fits and starts, despite all that diplomacy and force of arms could do to prevent it. By the time the train reached Nancy near noon on 18 August, Fred could tell that the guards were on edge, as they were firing their machine guns to clear people from walkways and overpasses.

The third day in the boxcars was uneventful. Beaten down by fatigue and deprivation, Fred began to wonder if he would survive the transport. The only good news he heard that day was that at the Nancy station, the Red Cross had managed to remove one more woman from the train, and that two other women had somehow managed to escape. The Germans had apparently underestimated the determination and abilities of the female prisoners.

Late on August 18th, the train stopped for several hours in Strasbourg, where Fred saw that the Red Cross had peaches and tins of meat ready for distribution to those fortunate enough to be able to reach around the barbed wire and claim them. Fred was at the far corner of the boxcar, so he wasn't one of the lucky ones — there were too few to share among so many prisoners. By now, conditions inside the boxcars were virtually indescribable: filth, fleas, lice, dysentery, thirst, and hunger; swollen ankles from standing for days; sweltering by day and shivering, naked, at night. Fred was in a haze of exhaustion and despair. It had been days since anyone around him had thought of, let alone spoken of, making an escape attempt.

That night, the train crossed the Rhine River and entered Germany, and on the morning of 19 August, the train was running parallel with the Rhine. The German guards seemed more relaxed, and they were no longer shooting at anything that moved. There were still security stops, but at intervals, individual boxcars were opened and the prisoners allowed to relieve themselves by the tracks.

As the train rumbled through small German towns, Fred saw signs of Allied air strikes, but the intervening rural areas looked calm and normal, as if the war was underway in some remote location, rather than approaching at a rapid pace. But he was totally unprepared for what greeted them at the stop in Frankfurt. When the boxcar doors were opened and Fred climbed down to be counted for the nth time, the city lay in ruins as far as he could see. The sight brought home in graphic terms the devastating power of the Army Air Corps.

Frankfurt was the stop Fred had been eagerly awaiting, as the airmen expected to be taken off the train and delivered to Dulag Luft for POW processing. Fred's spirits lifted further as his clothing was returned, along with a full water bucket and an empty waste pail. Their treatment was already improving! Fred waited anxiously as he heard boxcars uncoupling and shifting. With his head at the wall, he could see that the five cars behind theirs, the ones holding female prisoners, were being shuttled onto a siding. It was exciting — clearly their turn would come next. But he waited in vain, and when the guard cars at the end of the train were brought up and coupled onto his boxcar, Fred's optimism evaporated, to be replaced by despondency. Fred felt terribly disappointed and lost, and he could tell that he wasn't alone in that regard. His exchanges with Sam, Paul, and the other airmen all centered around uncertainties. Who knew they were on the train? Where were they being taken, and what would become of them? If they were executed, would their families ever learn what happened to them, or would they lie in shallow unmarked graves like the young Frenchman?

At noon the next day, after another hungry, thirsty, anxious, and sleepless night, the train arrived at Weimar station, where it was shunted onto a branch line that ran northwest into low, heavily forested hills. It was around 1400 when the train shuddered to a stop and the locomotive shut down in an isolated train yard. One hundred sixty-nine airmen had been loaded into the boxcars in Paris, and at journey's end the train held 82 Americans (USAAF), 49 British (RAF), 26 Canadians (RCAF), 9 Australians (RAAF), and two New Zealanders (RNZAF). Only one airman (Joel Stevenson, RCAF) had escaped en route.

Prisoners by the ventilation ports were still trying to make sense of their surroundings when Fred heard Spierenburg, who was listening at the door, tell them they had arrived at Buchenwald Concentration Camp (*Konzentration Lager Buchenwald* or *KLB*).[55]

---

[55] See Appendix 3 for a list of the airmen delivered to Buchenwald.

CHAPTER 8

Arrival in Buchenwald

⊰⊱⊱

The airmen were in the boxcars at the tail end of the train, but because it had backed into the station, they were among the first to be offloaded. While awaiting his fate, Fred could hear factory noises (the diesel sounds associated with heavy equipment), shouted orders, cries, thuds, and occasional shots. The breeze through the ports brought them smells of dust, oil, and a cloying smoke reminiscent of badly burned barbecue beef. Although a change from the humid, fetid atmosphere of the boxcar was welcomed, the overall impression brought by the "fresh" breeze was ominous.

When the boxcar door slid open, and the exhausted and apprehensive airmen left the boxcar, uniformed SS guards armed with short batons shouted "*Raus!*" and "*Mach schnell!*" Other guards were barely restraining huge German shepherds that were snarling and snapping as they attempted to reach the prisoners. Behind them stood still more guards armed with rifles or machine pistols. These guards wore different uniforms from the guards on the train. There was a skull and crossbones at the right collar rather than the lightning bolts Fred had seen on other SS troops.

The airmen started moving slowly, their ankles and feet swollen and their joints stiff after five days packed together. As Fred moved to the doorway and clambered to the ground, he was disoriented by the noise, the dogs, the shouted commands. Blows from the clubs or rifle butts of the SS guards steered him past the tail of the train, which had stopped at the end of a short off-shoot of the main railway line. Across other tracks, he could see a tall, conspicuously electrified fence, strung between tall wooden guard towers. On the other side of the fence was some sort of commercial building or factory. There were SS guards aplenty, but they were far outnumbered by figures in what looked like vertically striped pajamas, many of them doing heavy construction work. It certainly didn't seem like a POW camp.

Under the continual pressure of the guards, the men were pressed into a moving column roughly the width of ten men. Although the column tended to bunch up at times as men at the outer edges of the column tried to escape the clubs of the guards or the teeth of the dogs, the guards kept them moving forward. The procession soon turned right, away from the isolated factory complex, and proceeded between a row of two-storey buildings on Fred's left and a much larger complex whose dimensions he could not estimate. What was clear was that the facility was designed to be secure. The boundary consisted of a double fence 13' high. The inner fence was heavy barbed wire with icons indicating it was electrified, and the outer fence was a dense meshwork of barbed wire. Between the two were coils of heavy barbed wire, forming chest-high spirals that by themselves would be almost impenetrable. There were multiple guard towers 50' tall at 650' intervals along the fencing, and secondary guardposts as well, all of them manned and equipped with machine guns.

The prisoners were herded even more closely together as they approached an opening in the fencing. Fred thought it seemed uncomfortably similar to the way cattle entered an abattoir. The guards were using clubs and fists to keep the men moving and to ensure there were no stragglers. The dogs now formed a line on either side at the entry, and the panicking prisoners pushed and shoved to get to the center. Men on the edges were nipped or bitten, to the delight and amusement of the guards.

Fred fell to his knees, trapped in a melee, and with a lunge, one of the dogs tore a small chunk from the top of his left ear. He thought he was lucky only to lose the top edge of that ear, rather than the whole thing. Fred recoiled from the snarling animal, got back to his feet, and moved on with blood trickling down his neck. Ahead he saw a Canadian airman, Ralph McLenaghan, who was using a walking stick to support an ankle broken on landing. As he approached the gateway, he was beaten to the ground and his stick taken away. There would obviously be neither mercy nor aid forthcoming.

As he entered the compound, the first building Fred saw was on his left. It was a low brick building with an outsized smokestack, partially screened by a brick wall. The smokestack was belching a thick black smoke, and a heavy ash fell on the prisoners. It was accompanied by the cloying burned smell that they had first noticed in the boxcar. One of the SS guards pointed to the building and called out in passable English that the chimney was the only way any of them were going to leave Buchenwald. A moment of confusion preceded the chilling realization that it was a crematorium. That explained both the greasy ash and the awful smell.[56]

As Fred moved forward, the new arrivals were watched in silence by a number of resident prisoners who looked like caricatures of human beings. They were gaunt and haggard, with empty eyes and

---

[56] The crematorium could dispose of 400 bodies every 10 hours.

blank faces. Some called out to the airmen, but they were too far away to be heard and understood over the barking of the dogs and the bellowing of the guards. Making the environment even noisier, classical music of some kind was playing from distant speakers. That music would be with them continuously during every daylight hour, the same few selections played over and over and over.[57]

From the entry point, the dazed and intimidated airmen walked along a barbed wire fence-line that isolated one corner of the concentration camp. From the equipment, sounds, and activity, it looked to be another factory staffed by prisoners, although it was tiny by comparison with the one by the train yard.

Their destination soon became apparent. It was a small set of buildings directly opposite the center of the enclosed factory complex. There were approximately 200 French prisoners ahead of them and an unknown number in the line behind them. Every 20-30 minutes, a batch of around 40 prisoners was taken from the head of the line and escorted into a low brick building. What happened to them after that was a mystery.

Although it was 1630, the sun was still high and the day still uncomfortably warm. With their prisoners inside the main camp, the guards relaxed enough to allow the men to squat or sit on the bare ground as they waited. Fred sat by the curb wishing he had something to eat, or at least a cigarette. Some of the Canadian airmen who had spoken with the French prisoners reported that Buchenwald was well known to the FFI as a slave labor camp. Its reputation was dire — those who were shipped there were never seen again. Fred could hardly believe it. Everything about the place seemed so foreign, so unreal to him. But then he remembered how callously the SS had executed the French boy and the pregnant woman at the train station.

At the far end of a low building, Fred could see an enormous oak tree towering over the adjacent structures. It was the only tree in sight, and he wistfully thought about how cool it would be under the branches. It all seemed like a strange dream.[58]

By 1800, the air was cooler, and Fred was approaching the head of the line. A number of SS officers were in attendance, standing by the entry to a brick building to the right of the roadway. Lamason

---

[57] One of the selections was used in the soundtrack of the 1953 Disney movie The Living Desert. Fred left the room (or the house) when that movie was on TV, although he didn't explain why until decades later.

[58] The tree was called the Goethe Oak because the poet Johann Wolfgang von Goethe supposedly sat under its limbs while writing a famous poem. The tree was preserved when the surrounding forest was cleared in 1937 to build the Buchenwald concentration camp.

quickly identified the ranking officer, and when close enough, accompanied by Dutch Spierenburg, he pushed his way through the prison stream to speak with him. Before beginning, Lamason surprised the Germans by snapping to attention. He spoke in precise tones, pausing for translation, and Fred strained to hear him. He told the officer that he was Squadron Leader Philip Lamason of the Royal New Zealand Air Force, and that the men with him were captured military personnel. He said that their presence at Buchenwald must be a mistake, as under the Geneva Conventions, they should be at a POW camp and treated with the appropriate courtesies. He then demanded to be taken to see the camp commandant.

The man he was addressing listened politely as Dutch translated. He then replied that he was *SS-Hauptsturmführer* (Captain) Hans Schmidt, the Deputy Commander of Buchenwald and the legal officer for the camp. Schmidt, who was shorter than Lamason, was in his mid-40s. He had fair hair and wore dark-framed glasses. After a pause while he made a show of consulting the paperwork from the transport, he told Lamason, through Spierenburg, that the airmen had been listed as police prisoners (common criminals) rather than military prisoners, and if a mistake had been made, it would no doubt be corrected. But until that happened, they would be held at Buchenwald. Lamason was then dismissed and ordered to rejoin the others.

The airmen soon began moving into the building to face their future, whatever it might be. When the men formed a single line, there was a lot of mixing and shuffling. Fred was separated from Sam and Paul. Sam ending up ten places ahead in the line, Paul two places behind.

When his turn came, Fred stepped up to a long table, signed the Buchenwald entry book, and was given his official number, KLB 78299. In this way, he became officially registered as a prisoner at Buchenwald. A prisoner-clerk with a black armband handed him a pencil and a file card to fill in. The card, in German, had spaces for all kinds of personal information, and even without speaking German, Fred could tell what *Mutter* and *Vater* meant.

Fred left the card blank, but across the bottom, he wrote S/Sgt Frederic Martini USAAF 32163997. He handed the card to the clerk who, when he saw it was incomplete, tried to give it back. When Fred refused to accept it, the clerk shook his head with resignation — Fred was not the first airman to be unwilling to provide information — and wrote *weitere Angaben verweigert'* (further information refused) on the file card. He then motioned Fred to move along, hoping for better luck with the next man in line. Several of the airmen were so exhausted and dispirited that they went ahead and filled out the cards.

The card Fred filled out was not the only file kept in his name, as there were others intended to record infractions, assignments to work details, and so forth. The most important card in his file — in every airman's Buchenwald file — was one they never saw. It was bright orange, and it bore his name, prisoner number, State/Country of origin, and **Dikal** in large block letters Dikal was an acronym for *Darf in kein anderes Lager* (may not be sent to another camp). At Himmler's direction, the airmen were not to be transferred. As the guard had intimated, their intended fate was departure via the smokestack of the crematorium.

At the next station, Fred was handed a hanger, and by gestures told to put his clothes on the hanger and to put his shoes and the contents of his pockets on the desk. Fred pulled out a handful of French francs from his pants. The clerk carefully counted the bills and coins, entered the amount on a clipboard, and then placed the confiscated funds in a manila envelope. His shoes were put in a box, and his clothing was thoroughly searched before being tagged and stored. He was then handed a metal disc with a stamped number as a receipt.

Naked, Fred and the other airmen entered a large room where Polish prisoners in the now familiar striped pajamas awaited with electric sheers in their hands. When it was his turn, Fred sat on a stool while all of his body hair other than his eyebrows was removed. The prisoner did his job with mechanical motions, paying no attention to Fred's cries as he cut into his scalp. The mute barber remained totally focused on his task, his expression intense, unflinching. He seemed less man than machine.

After the fleecing, Fred was directed to a second station where prisoners with pads on poles dunked the pads in a foul-smelling liquid and proceeded to wipe it over every exposed millimeter of Fred's body. The vapors were pungent and it produced shockingly severe pain when applied to Fred's private parts, the cleft between his buttocks, and the ragged edge of his ear. It felt like a thousand bee stings.

The men were then hustled down a corridor to a second building with a large shower room. When water came out of the pipes, there was a general sigh of relief. Even with a mere scrap of soap, it felt good to wash off at least some of the accumulated filth and the residue of whatever disinfectant he'd been doused with. Fred hadn't had a change of clothing or a bath in more than two weeks. He had a few moments to dry himself, sharing threadbare scraps of towels with the men around him, before he was hustled out of the showers. Upon emerging, there was a brief and cursory medical inspection. Several of the airmen were so obviously ill that they were declared temporarily unfit for work.

Fred was next sent to a counter where he received a vertically striped shirt and a pair of matching striped pants, each marked KL in black block letters. The stripes might once have been blue on a white background, but everything was now a faded, grimy, gray color. Fred was also given a striped Dixie-cup hat. His shirt and pants were both too big for him, and the hat was too small. Some of the airmen got a striped overshirt as well, but Fred wasn't so lucky. Nobody was given either shoes or what passed in the camp for blankets.

Once everyone had been clothed and dressed, each man was photographed holding a card with his name and prisoner number. The airmen were then led outside where a group of thirty SS guards were waiting. Once everyone was accounted for, the guards herded the airmen into lines five abreast and led them into the camp. Progress was hesitant, as their bare feet were tender. The ground was dark and stony, without grass or even weeds, and everything was coated with a dusting of grime and a heavy layer of black ash. Only the clubs of the guards provided the motivation that kept the line moving.

Fred could now see that the camp consisted of row after row of one or two storey green wooden buildings that looked to be shoddily constructed barracks.[59] Prisoners were everywhere, most of them just as listless and skeletal as the ones they had seen on arrival. As the guards approached, all of the prisoners in the area took off their caps and stood at attention. Although there were SS guards at the perimeter of Buchenwald patrolling the fence-line and manning the towers and gun stations, their guards seemed to be the only SS personnel moving among the prisoners at the moment.

Fred was stunned by the condition of the prisoners they passed. They were incredibly scrawny. Some were blind, others lame, and many had open wounds and skin sores. It was impossible to guess their ages — 16 or 60? Their glazed eyes had shrunken into their skulls. Some stood in small groups, and others lay slumped by the roadside or against the barracks, and it was hard to tell if they were dead or alive. As the airmen passed by, some of the moving skeletons called to them in French, asking for information about who they were and where they were from. They seemed surprised and excited when they learned the new arrivals were Allied airmen, and hobbled off to

---

[59] In August 1944, the official prison population was approximately 82,000. That total included approximately 35,000 prisoners working in various satellite labor camps scattered around the area.

spread the news. As the group turned to the right, Fred counted nine rows of barracks buildings — the camp seemed to go on and on.

The dirt roadway they were on led to a gate in a secondary enclosure bounded by a double set of barbed wire fencing, similar but lower than the fences around the camp as a whole. As they approached, on their right was a large stone building, Block 50, surrounded by its own double fence. Someone in the group — Fred wasn't sure who — said that the sign indicated that this was an SS medical research facility. Nobody wanted to think about what that might mean.

The SS guards led the airmen through a double gate in the secondary enclosure, which was guarded by prisoners with black armbands on their right sleeves. The airmen were now in a smaller prison compound that was, in essence, a camp within a camp. Spierenburg, who had been conversing with one of the prisoner-guards, passed the word that they had arrived at the Little Camp, or *Kleines Lager*. Little Camp was used to hold new arrivals who might have contagious illnesses, special prisoners, and those about to be shipped to other destinations.[60] It was not clear which group the airmen were in.

The true size of Little Camp was not apparent, because it contained multiple buildings of varying size, and the area was subdivided by interior fencing. This fencing impeded free movement, limiting passage to a few gateways that could be monitored and controlled. As the airmen entered Little Camp, they were heading north. The building immediately to their left was Block 56, and the section closest to the gate was used for the quarters and "office" of the trusty, or *Kapo*,[61] designated as the camp leader (*Lager Ältester*). The stench in this portion of the compound was terrible. The worst odors seemed to be coming from the building parallel to Block 56, which was identified as Block 61.

The kapo in charge of Little Camp was Jakob Kindinger, a tall German (6'2"), who carried a stout wooden club that the airmen would find he used on other prisoners at the slightest provocation. As a trusty, he had a black armband on his right sleeve. When he emerged from his "office," he spoke with the SS guards briefly before they turned and left the compound. Kindinger and several prisoner-guards then escorted the airmen along a dirt road that led west, with low wooden buildings on either side.

---

[60] At this time, the most likely destinations were (1) the camp crematorium, (2) one of the extermination camps such as Auschwitz, or (3) the Mittelwerk.

[61] German nouns are capitalized and will be shown in italics on introduction. Terms used frequently, such as kapo, will thereafter appear in normal font.

The road they were on almost immediately crossed a second, smaller road that ran north-south. Turning right, the airmen passed through a gate in an internal fence and entering a fenced enclosure that contained three barracks buildings as well as other, smaller structures. Like everywhere else they had been at Buchenwald, the area was densely packed with prisoners. Some stood, some strolled, some squatted, and some lay on the ground, but all those nearby watched the new arrivals and their guards very closely. They were now in the quarantine area of Little Camp, where new arrivals spent days, weeks, or months awaiting final decisions on their fate.

The quarantine section was located near yet another internal fence-line that separated the barracks area from an area of open ground that contained five large tents. Other prisoners were milling around in the open area, but they kept well away from the new arrivals and their SS escort.[62] It was inhospitable ground, some of it covered in cobblestones and the rest consisting of bare stony ground dusted with lime powder. There was no cover of any kind, other than a couple of scrawny trees at the far side of the enclosure, which offered little protection from the elements. To the east, beyond the fencing, they could see the factory complex they had passed on their way to arrival processing. It looked a few hundred yards away.

Kindinger was an old hand, having been imprisoned in Buchenwald for years, and he received better treatment in exchange for maintaining order and keeping other prisoners under control. Because he knew that the new arrivals were military personnel, he went out of his way to be very accommodating. He was aware that their goodwill could be valuable in terms of his status in the camp, and if the Allies ever triumphed, his survival when the camp was liberated. With one of his assistants translating, Kindinger directed the airmen to an open area by the fence to the east of the barracks buildings. There were already prisoners squatting and sitting in that area, but they soon moved on, albeit under duress. The airmen would have sole possession of this area, which they called the Rock Pile.

Before leaving the airmen to their own devices, Kindinger cautioned them that they could leave the quarantine area, but to stay within Little Camp. Several times each day, a roll-call or *Appell*, would be held, and attendance was mandatory. They should at all times avoid approaching an SS guard without specific orders to do so. The guards would shoot anyone who approached unexpectedly. And if

---

[62] In August 1944, 13,000 new prisoners arrived in Little Camp. The number continued to increase, and Little Camp was expanded with additional barracks in December 1944.

approached by a guard, they were to stand at attention and doff their caps. Failure to do so would risk being beaten or perhaps even executed.

Without the guards, there was no clear organization, and small groups were free to wander around. Fred, Sam, and a few others went exploring. Their goal was to explore the compound and get their bearings. Farther to the east, past the fence-line, was the factory complex located inside the boundary fencing of the main camp. On the other side of the western fence-line of Little Camp was a barn-like building. It had what appeared to be patriotic movie posters on the side, so perhaps it was a theatre. To the right of that building was an isolated enclosure containing a large tent with its sides lowered. To his surprise, Fred saw a young woman standing between the fencing and the tent, gazing toward Little Camp with a face devoid of expression. Beyond the enclosed tent was a roadway that ran roughly north-south On the other side of the road were tents and ramshackle wooden huts, and a large stone building that they would later learn was the SS hospital.

They walked back the way they had come, strolling to the south, past the ends of two large barracks buildings that looked like horse stables. Through the open doors of these buildings, Fred could see prisoners lying on stacked shelves five layers high, like goods stored in a warehouse. He couldn't imagine how many men could be crammed into each 150' x 32' building when packed like that.[63]

As they approached a third barracks building, Block 59, the fence jogged west, parallel to the side of the cinema. They now had the fence on their right and Block 58 on their left. It was slow going, because there were prisoners everywhere. The barracks were full, the roadside was filled with men squatting or sitting, and Fred thought that some looked like they'd never move again. Many of those still walking moved slowly, with glazed eyes and a shambling gait, but a significant number were alert enough to recognize the airmen as new arrivals. They were continually being asked for news of the war, for their backgrounds, and sometimes for help.

Suddenly, Fred realized they were in a cul de sac, with one of the interior fences blocking their path. They turned around and retraced their steps, this time continuing east until they reached the path they had used to enter the quarantine section of Little Camp. To the right of the entrance was a low stone building, which he now realized must be

---

[63] These barracks routinely contained 750-1,000 prisoners, and sometimes more were crammed in. The numbering system for the barracks in this area changed when Little Camp expanded. At the time, the blocks Fred passed would have been 63 and 62.

the latrine, or *Abort*, for this section. A small pile of corpses was stacked just outside the entrance. The ones at the bottom were swollen and decomposing, whereas the ones at the top looked relatively fresh.

While Fred stood speechless, struck by the implications of this scene, two French prisoners showed up pulling a small wooden cart. After taking the freshest corpses off the top of the pile and setting them aside, they loaded the rest onto the cart. Fred, whose French was passable, approached the workers and learned that they spent their days doing rounds of the camp, collecting corpses, and delivering them to the crematorium. They could only fit a half-dozen or so bodies on the cart at each stop, so they always took the oldest and left the rest for another day.

The toilet was nearly as distressing as the corpse pile. It consisted of an open, concrete-lined pit, with a plank running along either side as a seat. With care, a prisoner could balance on the plank while defecating. The seating capacity was 15, and the planks were filled with a waiting line that ran outside. The smell was nauseating, and the air was filled with the buzzing of the flies that swarmed over the dead bodies, the foul ground, and the open cess pit.

There were no washbasins or even water troughs in the area. An upright pipe and faucet stood at one end of the latrine. A weak trickle of water was coming out, but as they watched, it slowed to a halt. The people using the latrine ignored it completely. That was very bad news. There was no water at the Rock Pile, and Fred knew that many of the airmen had been stricken with dysentery before they left Fresnes Prison. Without a reliable source of clean fresh water, they would all be sick in a matter of days. So one of their first priorities would have to be figuring out a way to collect whatever water was available and make it drinkable — even if that meant using the occasional weak trickle at the latrine.

They next turned to the south and passed through the interior fence-line to reach the main roadway within Little Camp. This dirt street started at a gate to the north-south road they had seen earlier. It ran east for perhaps 1,000' with buildings on either side. Even with the crowd milling around, they could walk its entire length in ten minutes. Block 51, on the south side of the roadway near the western entry gate, was opposite Block 57. The boundary fence separating Little Camp from the main camp started along the south side of Block 51, but beyond it Fred could see a stone building enclosed by a double fence, with gates opening both to Little Camp and to the main camp. It was identified as Block 46. Fred wondered what went on there that would require such elaborate defenses and isolation from the rest of the camp.

From passing French prisoners, Fred learned they were on the *Boulevard des Invalides* (street of invalids) so called because it passed barracks used (1) for isolating tuberculosis cases (Block 53), (2) for a primitive infirmary (Block 54), (3) for prisoners weakened to the point of immobility (a portion of Block 56), and (4) for prisoners dying of severe dysentery (Block 61). That, Fred thought, explained the foul smell that lingered like a fog over that portion of Little Camp. The prisoners were too sick and weak to do anything other than lie in their own filth and wait for death to claim them.

As they walked back, passing the gate to the quarantine area, Fred could see that the small latrine within the quarantine area was continuous with the much larger latrine in the main portion of Little Camp. It had larger, deeper cess pits and seated many more prisoners, as it was the main toilet for prisoners in the Little Camp. It was not comforting to see that the pile of corpses near the entry was considerably larger than the one inside the quarantine area. They decided not to walk all the way to the end of Block 56 and 61. As soon as the smell became overpowering, they retraced their steps, returning to the Rock Pile to see if anything significant had happened in their absence.

The other airmen were standing around, talking quietly. Small clusters formed where men from the same aircrew, such as Fred and Sam, formed a nucleus that expanded to include contacts made while evading the Nazis.[64] It was not uncommon for more than one member of an aircrew to be sheltered by the FFI and travel together thereafter. Airmen from several squadrons and bomb groups reconnected, comparing notes and finding friends in common. Fred and Sam found five other airmen from the 385th BG, and it was the largest number from any single unit. Each network was gradually expanding through contacts made in Fresnes Prison and during the boxcar ride to Germany. Somehow it helped to be among familiar people.

At around 2100, several trusty prisoners entered the compound carrying large pots that contained a thin broth. There was no meat in it and only a few wisps of unidentifiable plant material. They were also given several loaves of heavy black bread. Two of Kindinger's minions distributed tin cups and wooden bowls, nowhere near enough to go around, and the airmen were starving, dispirited, and exhausted.

---

[64] The group included 86 airmen who had been collected from 28 downed bombers. Seven were from a single B-24 from the 489th BG. At the other end of the spectrum, eight airmen were the sole survivors of their bomber's aircrew.

When the meager meal arrived, it triggered a chaotic free-for all, with each hungry, thirsty airman desperate to get whatever he could. There was a lot of pushing and shoving, and some angry words were exchanged. Fortunately, everyone was too tired to do more than threaten violence. When all was said and done, Fred was fortunate enough to get a small chunk of the dark bread, which he wolfed down despite his sore jaw. His conclusion was that it was almost inedible. Sam and Paul managed to get a chunk of bread and a bowl with some broth, which they shared.[65] Other airmen made the mistake of refusing the meal, spitting out the broth after tasting it. Some airmen saved their unappetizing bread, thinking that it might taste better when they were even hungrier, but a few discarded their bread in disgust. All were amazed to see fights break out among the other prisoners in the compound over possession of these discarded scraps.[66]

At twilight, it was clear that the airmen would not have shelter for the night, so the men spread out in search of places to sleep on the stony ground. The night was relatively cool, but not cold. There was little that could be done to improve their berthing situation, but where large or sharp rocks could be dug out they did so, and those without overshirts ("jackets") or blankets made pillows out of pebbles and leaf litter. Stretching out on the ground, the exhausted airmen were soon sound asleep.

---

[65] The recipe for the broth involved boiling 25 pounds of meat (of indeterminate origin) in 260 gallons of water. Assuming equal distribution and a serving of one quart per prisoner, each man would receive one-third ounce of meat, roughly two level teaspoons. The only variations in their diet were an occasional dollop of margarine for the bread, a small piece of sausage every other day, and either jam or honey (not both) once a week.

[66] The official recipe for this bread, called *Schwartzbrot*, was 50% grain, 20% sliced sugar beets, 20% sawdust, and 10% minced leaves and straw.

CHAPTER 9

Adjustment

◆═┨┠═◆

The First Week in Buchenwald

THE SECOND DAY

Shortly after midnight, a group of young gypsies who lived in Barrack 58 swarmed over the sleeping airmen, stealing anything that they could find. Jackets serving as pillows, hats, cached scraps of uneaten bread, food bowls — it was all fair game. The airmen, muddled by exhaustion, could do little to defend their meager possessions. It was a wake-up call in several respects, and Fred realized that in this environment, when dealing with other prisoners, there were no rules except those you could enforce. Despite their exhaustion, few of the airmen were able to return to sleep.

At 0515, Kindinger and his assistants were moving through Little Camp, rousing the prisoners. Shortly thereafter, four of the airmen, all sergeants, were selected and sent under guard to the camp kitchen. When they returned carrying small tubs, the airmen had their first chance to enjoy morning "coffee," a thin, warm liquid flavored by passing boiling water through crushed acorns.[67] The trusties gave the men some spare cups, which the airmen politely shared among themselves. In retrospect the chaos of the previous evening was embarrassing.

As dawn was breaking, Fred saw Lamason moving among the airmen, asking them to gather around so he could talk to everyone at once. There were 168 Allied airmen, so the process took some time, but eventually they were all seated within earshot. He started by acknowledging that they were in a bad spot and had no idea what the Jerries intended to do with them. But he reminded the airmen that they were military men and not criminals, and the distinction should be made abundantly clear to the Germans. He added that he was shocked by the free-for all that developed when food was provided the previous night. Those who act like animals will be viewed as animals, and as no different from common criminals. No further lapses in

---

[67] Airmen were sent to collect food or drink each day at 0530, 1100, and 1630.

judgement would be tolerated.

During the night, Lamason continued, he had discussed their situation with the other officers. As the senior officer, he was taking command moving forward, seconded by Captain Merle Larson, representing the US Air Corps, and Flight Lieutenant Thomas Blackham, representing the RAF. This morning, the airmen would be divided up into 17 squads of 8-10 airmen, with each group a potential aircrew in the event they were able to develop a viable escape plan. He reminded everyone that they were near a major city serviced by airfields.

From now on, when traveling together, they would march in military formation. Food distribution would be done squad by squad, and squads would be assigned to guard duty on a rotating basis. This would prevent further pilfering by other prisoners.

Lamason reminded them to avoid antagonizing the SS, and to avoid going anywhere alone, not even to the abort. Even in groups, they should be cautious, especially when outside of Little Camp. They had yet to understand the camp rules, and prisoners were often shot for breaking them. They were a force of 168 airmen, and every one was important. Finally, he said that nobody should try to escape independently. If and when they escaped, it would be together.

Fred felt like a great weight had been lifted off of his shoulders. Suddenly there was clear organization, a survival plan, and even the tantalizing possibility of eventual escape. He wondered how the groups would be set up, and hoped he'd be assigned to the same team as Sam.[68] That line of thought was interrupted by the call, *"Raus! Appell! Mach schnell!"* The airmen quickly got to their feet, but rather than rushing en masse toward the call, they formed lines and marched as a group to a position opposite the entry to their subsection of Little Camp. The other prisoners who had spent the night in the open hastened to form their own lines under the eyes of the *Lager altester*. Fred was not surprised by the sight of prisoners being assisted or even carried to the *Appellplatz* (roll-call square). He was, however, amazed and horrified to see that there were pairs of prisoners carrying corpses. The dead as well as the living apparently had to be counted.

As a group of SS guards entered the compound, the command

---

[68] There was no record of the squad assignments. If the members of related units were kept together, Fred's squad would have included sergeants Sam Pennell, John Hanson, Arthur Pacha, Leo Reynolds, and William J. Williams, and Lt. William Powell from the 385th BG, and Sgt. Ray Wojnicz and Lt. Russ Hilding from the 447th BG. All were from the 4th Combat Bombardment Wing.

"Mützen ab!" (Hats off!) was given, and the prisoners removed their hats and stood at attention. With their clubs and their clipboards, the guards moved along the lines of assembled prisoners, doing their tallies. The first counting was relatively desultory, and after only an hour and a half, the SS guards left the compound, and Kindinger gave the command *"Mützen auf!"* (Hats on!). The bodies of the dead were carried off to stack by the abort, and the rest of the prisoners dispersed. The airmen remained together, and the next couple of hours were spent forming the squads and making plans.

Fred's squad members spent the rest of the morning exchanging background information and discussing their situation. Escape looked difficult if not impossible, but they could take steps to address things like security and communication. Lamason had said that airmen who were fluent in other languages should talk to other prisoners and see what they could learn about camp organization, and whether it was possible to scrounge additional clothing, shoes, blankets, cups, and other essentials. Fred, whose French was the best of the group, was asked to do what he could.

At 1100, sergeants from another squad were sent to collect buckets of warm "soup" and the usual dark bread. Fred thought the watery soup contained grass, although there was an oily skin at the surface. Near the bottom of the bowl he found the source of the oil — a small, greasy bit of meat burrowed by maggots. The maggots were distasteful, but Fred was so hungry that he ate them anyway. Some of the airmen rejected the maggots at first, although over time, they would come to accept them as a matter of course. For dessert, as a special treat, Fred received a small, moldy, sprouting, raw potato.

The airmen had yet to solve the clean water problem. Although it was only their second day at Buchenwald, more and more of the airmen, Fred included, were experiencing stomach cramps and diarrhea. He found himself periodically looking for a partner for a trip to the abort. Although necessary, it could hardly have been more unpleasant. Dysentery was near-universal, often so severe that a prisoner's bowels let loose prematurely, soiling his uniform and splattering the surrounding ground. The constant arrival and departure from the abort had churned the already damp soil into a swamp of fetid goo that squished up between Fred's toes and glued itself to his bare feet. He tried his best not to dwell on the sensation nor its potential health consequences.

Fred had just come back from one of those trips when the call came for appell. This time things went smoothly. Fred's group quickly formed up, and the squads marched in formation to their position in the assembly. This time the SS guards who entered Little

Camp were led by *SS-Rottenführer* (a corporal designated squad leader) Hans Hoffman. Hoffman, in his early 40s, was short (5'4"), heavyset, and armed with a stout club. His uniform was black, rather than gray-green, which indicated that he wasn't German but an SS volunteer. He had a dark complexion, and an unpleasant and violent personality. He had not seen the airmen before, so he gave them special attention, moving down the lines and scrutinizing each individual. The airmen, used to stern inspections, remained motionless and held their gaze fixed on infinity. Hoffman was just starting to inspect one of the British squads when he drew his Luger and struck one of the airmen, opening a gash in his temple.[69] He then turned, furious, to Kindinger, waving the pistol and giving him an earful. Kindinger, through a translator, relayed that the man had been standing at attention with his hands clenched, and to the Germans, clenched hands were a blatant sign of disrespect, potentially indicating hidden contraband or even a weapon.

Other airmen received lesser abuse — cuffs, pokes and whacks — as Hoffman moved through the lines, but he eventually moved on to the other prisoners in the assembly. Under his vicious scrutiny, the appell was longer than usual, and by 2000 the men had been standing for almost three hours.

When the counting was finally completed and the assembly was dismissed, Fred and many others rushed to wait in the long lines at the abort. Afterward, he tried to find a comfortable position to get a few hours of sleep before it was his turn to stand watch. It had been a long day, but with a plan in place, he felt much better about their chances of survival.

THE THIRD DAY

The next morning was very similar to the first: early arousal, ersatz coffee, and morning appell. Hoffman did not return, and appell was quickly concluded. Shortly after the dead had been dragged off to add to the pile, a handcart arrived to take bodies to the crematorium. It had been two days since the last pickup, so once again, the badly decomposing corpses were removed and the remainder left to ripen in the sun.

Although the airmen were still hungry, the general mood was upbeat. They now had organization and a guarded home base, uncomfortable though it might be. People were talking quietly about

---

[69] The airman was Lt. Robert Mills of the Royal Australian Air Force.

what they would do after the war. One of the officers suggested planning reunions where they could reminisce and swap stories nobody else would believe. They decided to call it the KLB Club, rather than the Buchenwald Club, and Ralph Taylor designed a logo on a scrap of paper. Men from each national group were designated as club leaders: Blackham, Taylor, Mutter, Jackson, and Chapman for the British; Prudham, Kinnis, Harvie, Watson, and Hodgson for the Canadians; Powell and Brown for the Americans; and Johnston for the Australians and New Zealanders. Brown told Fred's squad all about the plans that afternoon, and Fred got his first look at Taylor's logo. Brown said that meetings were planned at five-year intervals, and that they'd gone so far as to decide what to charge for annual dues, although for the moment, IOUs would be accepted.

At the evening appell, SS-Corporal Hoffman returned with his squad, and another airman received an education in the proper way to stand at attention. What Fred found most disconcerting was that there was absolutely no warning given. One moment Hoffman was strolling along seemingly at ease, and the next he was striking out in a rage. Shortly afterward, Fred had a glimpse of the brutal enthusiasm Hoffman brought to his work. A young, Polish prisoner suffering from dysentery had asked the guard for permission to go to the abort. As usual, permission was denied. In the hour that followed, the lad soiled himself, and when Hoffman saw this, he took a baton and beat the boy to the ground, kicking him repeatedly after he was unconscious. Throughout the process, he was shouting that prisoners were worthless animals, unfit to survive.[70] After the guards had left and the assembly was dismissed, the young prisoner's friends carried him away. Several days later, Fred heard that he had died from his injuries.

THE FOURTH DAY

The next day was quiet in Little Camp, the appells proceeding slowly but without the presence of Hoffman. After morning appell, an SS officer came to escort Lamason to a meeting with the camp

---

[70] One of the keys to the survival of the airmen was their diversity of background. Many were first-generation Americans who had learned another language from their parents. Ed Ritter spoke Polish and could understand German, Frank Vratney spoke Czech, Dutch Spierenburg spoke Dutch and German, Bernard Scharf spoke German, and in addition to the Canadian airmen fluent in French, every airman who had spent months with the FFI could get by in that language.

commandant, *SS-Oberführer* (Colonel) Hermann Pister. On his return to Little Camp, Lamason told the officers that he had gotten an audience but not much else — their future was still a mystery. Fred was sorry to hear that, but he wasn't too surprised. Even if their presence was a mistake, he found it unlikely anyone in the SS would admit it.

The previous night had been noticeably cooler, and Fred's squad was delegated to comb the grounds for scraps of paper, wood, leaves, and anything else that would burn. If they could get a fire going, they could boil drinking water and toast their bread, which could only help the flavor. It would also be a source of heat if the nights grew even colder, as they were sure to do.

That day, August 23rd, the airmen had many visitors. Fred saw representatives from the various nationalities and factions within the camp as a whole. All sought out Squadron Leader Lamason to get news and forge some form of an alliance, both against the Germans and against other factions. It was clear that the internal politics of Buchenwald was complex.

Fred spoke with several French civilians who had been part of the resistance. They were looking for protection from the Communists, who assigned fellow prisoners to work details outside of the camp. Many of those assigned to such work details, which were known as *kommandos*, did not return. Ed Ritter, a B-24 airman Fred had gotten to know, spoke with several Polish Communists who wanted an alliance against the Germans, thinking that additional men with military combat experience would ensure the success of an uprising. Their enthusiasm was dampened somewhat to find that some of the airmen were officers, rather than members of the proletariat, but compromise was part of life in Buchenwald. Fred and Ed passed these entreaties along to their officers, but the senior officers had decided to be congenial to all parties, but not to commit to any particular faction. This tactic had unexpected benefits. In an attempt to provide incentives for an alliance, several blankets and a number of additional bowls and cups were given to the airmen. Instead of having no blanket at all, Fred and Sam would be sharing a threadbare covering.

Around the time the afternoon "coffee" was to arrive, Fred saw the guards speaking with two prisoners outside Little Camp. After a time, they were allowed through the gate, and once within the compound, they headed directly for the airmen. Fred assumed they were representatives from yet another faction within the prison. But as they approached, he realized that they were speaking English, and they sounded very British. One of them asked to speak with their commanding officer. Lamason stepped forward and introduced himself, whereupon the visitor said he was Kenneth Dodkin, and his colleague was Christopher Burney. They were the leaders of a group of 37 British SOE[71] agents who had been captured by the Gestapo, transported to Buchenwald, and assigned to Block 17. Although it was technically an isolation barracks, the rules were not rigidly enforced by the kapos assigned as guards. The three men went off for a private meeting. Afterward, Lamason briefed the officers, and the officers relayed the information to their squads.

With the arrival of the airmen, there were 205 Allied military personnel in Buchenwald. If they could obtain arms, they would be a force to be reckoned with, especially when backed by volunteers from the French, Communist, and other factions in the camp. The basic plan was to break out of Buchenwald and head southwest through the surrounding forest to reach a small Luftwaffe airfield called Nohra, five or six miles away. The Nohra base was said to be lightly staffed, and if the airmen could seize one or more planes, they could use them to escape Germany. However, they would first need to obtain weapons and figure out how to escape the confines of Little Camp and the more heavily secured main camp. But to Fred, those were mere details. There was no way these goons were going to keep them in this hell hole.[72]

THE FIFTH DAY

The next morning, 24 August, began like the others, with an early arousal followed by the bizarre coffee surrogate. Despite its curious flavor, Fred, Sam, and Ed were glad to have some, as they had been part of the late shift guarding the airmen's portion of the compound. Just after the midday appell, the men heard a faint rumbling sound that gradually increased in volume. Fred, who could diagnose sick or healthy engines by their sound, told the rest of his squad that those were B-17s. [73] Before long, the engineers from other squadrons were agreeing, and soon they could see formations of planes approaching

---

[71] The Special Operations Executive sent undercover agents behind enemy lines to conduct espionage and sabotage, and to coordinate Allied efforts with those of the FFI.

[72] See Appendix 4 for a discussion of Lamason, the Special Operations Executive (SOE), and plans to escape Buchenwald.

[73] The 8th Air Force sent 129 bombers from the 401st, 351st, and 457th Bomb Groups on this mission. These bombers released approximately 300 tons of bombs. One-half were 1000-pound high-explosives and the rest were 500-pound incendiaries.

from the southwest.

The men were interested and excited, but not concerned, because their first thought was that this was a bombing run targeting industrial areas to the northeast. When the air raid sirens started wailing, they decided the target must be Weimar. Excitement finally turned to alarm when they saw the first of several marker flares falling from the lead aircraft in the formation. Buchenwald was the target! The airmen looked around and realized that there was no cover and no means of digging a trench for shelter. So they stood and watched as first the lead plane and then those that followed opened their bomb bay doors and dropped their bomb loads.

When the bombs actually started descending, it was abundantly clear that they were going to land very close to their position, and with no other options the men threw themselves to the ground and covered their heads with their arms. After a brief pause that seemed like an eternity, the first bombs landed. The sound was deafening, the ground shaking violently as rocks, timber, shards of steel, and debris of all kinds rained around them. Tremendous explosions followed, some from the bombs and others from within the buildings of the adjacent factory, and the men were bounced around on the rocks like rag dolls. Screams of pain and fear were lost amidst the roaring of the fires and the concussions of the explosions.

The bombing was relentless. The first wave of bombers dropped 1,000-pound high-explosive bombs in a swath that ran right across the *Gustloff Werke*, the large factory complex by the railway yard,[74] and continued across the administration buildings and through the SS housing area. The planes that followed dropped firebombs along a trail that started at the Gustloff Works and extended across the *Deutsche-Ausrustungs Werke* (German Armaments Works), the small factory complex inside the camp.[75] Because the latter was a munitions plant, the firebombs triggered a chain reaction that sounded like the end of the world.

Little Camp had been out of the direct path of the bombing, but the open area where the airmen were lying was relatively close to the munitions facility, and when it blew, they felt like the ground was trying to throw them into the sky. Shrapnel whistled over the airmen as they hugged the dirt. Fortunately, only one airman was injured by

---

[74] The *Gustloff Werke* (Gustloff Works) manufactured rifles, pistols, and — most critical at this stage in the war — gyroscopes that were part of the guidance systems for the V-1 and V-2 rockets.

[75] The *Deutsche-Ausrustungs-Werke*, or DAW, was a munitions plant and small arms manufacturer.

flying debris.[76]

The smoke blotted out the sun, flaming debris filled the air, primary and secondary fires raged and roared, prisoners in the main camp were screaming and running, and Fred could hear shots being fired as frightened guards, fearing an uprising, shot anyone approaching them. The last few planes in the formation flew lower than the others, dropping propaganda leaflets that fluttered down across the camp like confetti.

In the aftermath, as the planes headed off, Fred stood and took stock of the situation. Although none of the highexplosives landed outside of the factory area, firebombs had drifted into the prisoner areas, setting fire to several barracks as well as the disinfection station where the airmen had been processed on arrival. Good riddance, he thought.

A party of SS guards entered Little Camp, shouting for the *terrorfliegers* to line up. Lamason and the other officers gave the word, and Fred hastened to join his squad as they assembled at attention. He steeled himself for the possibility that they were to be shot in revenge for the bombing. Well, at least he'd seen the Germans given a beating. But rather than shoot them, the guards escorted them into the main camp. They were taken to the area known as the *Appellplatz* (roll-call square), where the prisoners in the main camp area were counted each day. It was a large open area with a Nazi flag on a flagpole and a narrow band of staging that ran parallel to the fencing.

The appellplatz was adjacent to the main entrance to Buchenwald, and Fred could see the ornate iron gate at the entry, which stood open, adorned with welded block letters saying *Jedem das Seine*. Spierenburg and Scharf translated this as "You get what you deserve." Fred thought that under the circumstances, the phrase had ominous implications. Before the gate was a clock tower with a large Nazi flag hanging from it. Teams of SS guards with machine guns were watching them from platforms at roof level. By gestures and blows, the men were ordered to remove their hats and stand at attention while they were counted yet again.

Lamason was pulled aside, out of earshot, to receive instructions. On returning, he spoke to the squad leaders, and Fred learned that the teams were being sent to assist the guards in fighting the fires that threatened to spread further, and if possible, rescue victims from the rubble. Some squads went to the burning barracks and administrative

---

[76] Flight Sergeant Frank Salt, 35 Sq RAF, had a small piece of shrapnel in his shoulder. He was taken to the camp hospital, but the medical staff was too overloaded to deal with a "minor" injury, so he was returned to Little Camp, where fellow airmen removed the fragment.

buildings, but Fred's squad was assigned to the German Armaments Works. In the distance, beyond the train yard, Fred could see the Gustloff Works burning furiously. The immediate concern, however, was to save the camp itself.

It was tough going. Fred was barefoot, and the ground was strewn with debris, shards of metal, shattered rocks, still-smouldering pieces of wood, and chunks of broken glass. His tender feet — he'd only been barefoot for a few days — were soon bleeding from multiple cuts and scrapes. When he reached the factory, it was a pile of rubble with small fires burning. The immediate priorities were to fight fires, clear rubble, and rescue trapped prisoners. So despite the smoke and the heat and the injuries to his feet, Fred did his best, working with Sam to move debris, and beat out small fires with scraps of cloth wrapped around their hands.

The SS guards were distracted, and there were too few to keep track of what every prisoner was doing — the main thing was that work was being done. Once Fred realized that, he passed the word to his squad members to keep their eyes peeled for small items of potential use. Fred found a few coins, scraps of cloth, several bullets (probably for a pistol), and what looked like the trigger assembly from an M-1 carbine, although he doubted the Germans used that particular rifle. He secreted these treasures in his pockets and rolled into his waistband.

With blisters on his hands, and painful, bleeding feet, Fred wanted nothing more than to sit down and rest. But there were still survivors trapped in the debris, and he couldn't ignore their cries. So he pushed on, clearing wreckage and carrying the injured and the dead from the shells of still-burning buildings. The gruesome work continued until the light failed.

At the end of the long day, the airmen were rounded up and returned to the appellplatz. It was an eerie scene in the flickering light of the fires that still raged unchecked on the other side of the train yard. Off in the direction of the laundry, Fred could see a vertical column of flames that could only be the oak tree he had admired on that strange first day. It was burning like a beacon. Through the clouds of passing smoke, he could see wounded prisoners everywhere, and dead bodies scattered around them. Fred had lost count of the number of dead and injured prisoners he'd seen in the rubble of the German Armaments Works. Some had been wounded in the bombing, whereas others had been shot, probably for trying to leave their station in the air raid. Tired, filthy, hungry, thirsty, and soaked in rapidly cooling sweat, the airmen were led back to Little Camp. The water system was inoperative, so there wasn't even a trickle of water at the abort. Fred was saddened to realize that there would probably be no coffee the next morning. It might be terrible stuff, but it was better than nothing.

Once back at the Rock Pile, the squad leaders assessed the condition of their men. Nobody in Fred's squad had been badly injured, but Fred and several others had second-degree burns, and cuts and bruises on their feet. The scavenged items were collected for use by the group, although Fred held onto the scrap of cloth as he had already used it to bandage his deepest cut. The coins could be used for bartering with the other prisoner groups for blankets, cigarettes, or perhaps even shoes. Fred received kudos for recovering the rifle part and ammunition.

The squad leaders met with the senior officers while Fred and the other noncoms mingled and compared notes and experiences. When the officers returned, Fred was told that finding loose ammunition and parts for rifles and pistols was now a top priority. With luck, they would eventually be able to scrounge the parts needed to assemble their own weapons. One of the leaders of the Communist prisoners had had the same idea, and the two groups had agreed to cooperate. Living on the Rock Pile the airmen had no place to cache weapons, but the Communists had the run of the camp at large. So they would receive, stockpile, and assemble the components.

THE SIXTH DAY

Early the next morning, the airmen were rounded up by SS-Corporal Hoffman and his men, and again marched under guard to the main camp appellplatz. As Fred had feared, there would be no coffee today. On arrival, the airmen were counted and then groups were assigned to continue assisting in the cleanup and repair of the camp. One of the German guards commented that the airmen had been chosen for this work because it was clear that they understood order and discipline, qualities that were unusual within the general prison population.

They worked through the day. Late in the morning, men were sent to the kitchen to get soup, which they carried to the various work teams. Although they were still technically under the eyes of SS guards, now that the fires were out and any survivors removed from the rubble, quick work was no longer essential, and the guards paid less attention. A few of the airmen, including Fred, Sam, and the others assigned to the factory complex, found that they could reduce the damage to their feet by carrying things out of the ruins along a carefully selected path, then surreptitiously carrying them back. This process, which could be repeated indefinitely, kept them looking busy but didn't help the German recovery efforts at all. Moving back and forth, they could scan the surrounding area very carefully for any items of potential use.

Again the long day ended with a return to the square and a quick counting, after which they were escorted back to their "home" in Little Camp. When the SS guards left, the airmen again gathered together to compare notes and share any treasures they had managed to collect during the day. More cloth had been secured, and large pieces were turned in to be used as bandages or foot protection. Small bits and pieces of cloth too small to be of other use were kept by those who found them, for use in lieu of toilet paper.

Fred had obtained several scraps that he thought would last a day, or perhaps two, given the diarrhea and cramps he was experiencing. He hated going to the abort, knowing that on every trip his bleeding, aching feet would be immersed in the horrid, stinking goo that surrounded the facility. He didn't want to begin thinking about what diseases and infections could result. Of course, most of the other airmen were in the same predicament, all trying to put the trip off as long as possible, but when one broke down and announced he was heading that way, there were always several others who agreed to join him.

Something else was going on, and the senior officers seemed agitated. Finally, Lamason pulled the men together to explain. Speaking in low tones, he said that he had been part of a work detail near the laundry, where the Goethe tree still smoldered. A Dutch kapo, who spoke reasonable English, had them clearing debris by a wooden building near the crematorium. The man, who had been a doctor before his arrest, let the three men into the building for a look at what the Nazi medical staff had been doing. Lamason paused, struggling to find the right words before describing a room filled with atrocities.

There were rows of shrunken heads, a bound book of tattooed human skin, what appeared to have been a healthy young man who had been skinned and preserved for display, isolated organs, stomachs that had somehow been stretched to the bursting point, spinal columns, genital organs with various sexual diseases, hearts ranging from healthy to abnormal to diseased, and death masks taken from prisoners of various personality types. It was bizarre, sickening, and very frightening. Everyone had by now accepted that members of the SS were ruthless, but Lamason's chilling account made Fred realize that the term "ruthless" was inadequate — they were perverted sadists who treated prisoners as curios and experimental animals.

THE SEVENTH DAY

The only real source of relaxation for the airmen was smoking the cigarettes they received as gifts or obtained in exchange for coins or other valuables recovered from the ruins of bombed buildings. While they waited for the evening appell, Fred, Sam, Paul, and Ed were standing by the fence, smoking their precious cigarettes. They were standing in the corner closest to the ruins of the German Armaments Works when they saw two German officers, one of them SS-Captain Schmidt, and an older, heftier officer who, judging by the elaborate uniform, outranked Schmidt.

They were accompanying a tall man in an SS uniform who looked like a Nazi recruiting poster. His immaculate uniform, which looked custom tailored and impeccably pressed, set him apart from the other officers. Watching through the fence-line, the airmen made a few rude comments about how tidy his uniform would be when he got home. Fred was pleased to see that his burnished black boots were already coated with mud and filth.

The Germans were perhaps 50' away when they stopped and talked, Schmidt pointing to various places in the wrecked complex. The airmen were too far away to hear the entire conversation, but it looked like the Germans were discussing the bomb damage to the munitions plant and to the Gustloff Works, from which a tenuous cloud of smoke still lingered above the barracks of the main camp. As he listened, the attention of the SS-major was at first on the ruined factory, but after a time, he seemed to have seen enough. As he turned toward the officers and faced Little Camp, he spied the men standing at ease nearby.

He gave them a careful examination, his gaze sharp. For several long moments he stared directly at Fred, and the inspection made him very uncomfortable. The man then turned to the officers abruptly, interrupting the monologue Schmidt was giving, to speak to the senior officer in the group, who nodded. The three men then turned and walked toward the bombed out factory complex, eventually turning right, toward the train yard, and disappearing from view.

When appell was finally called, the SS guards were accompanied by the camp commandant, SS-Colonel Pister. His presence made the airmen fear the worst, because the rumor mill within the camp had already advised them that the commandant's wife and daughter had been killed in the bombing. Pister was accompanied by the same SS officer Fred had seen earlier, whom he'd been told was an SS-major.

Pister began with a diatribe that his harried translator could barely keep up with. He called the airmen *terrorfliegers*, blaming them for the deaths of civilians and the destruction of his camp. He then paused, calmed himself, and walked toward the airmen, Schmidt at his side. Through his interpreter, Pister asked several airmen what their particular skills were — Could they weld? Could they operate heavy equipment? Were they machinists? — but all he got in return was name, rank, and serial number. In disgust, he turned and stood before Philip Lamason, who was waiting at attention in front of the assembly.

He told Lamason that their work since the bombing raid was appreciated, and said that he had a critical need for skilled labor in a manufacturing facility of extreme importance to the Reich. If Lamason's men agreed to do the required work, their treatment and their living conditions would improve significantly. The location of the facility was not identified — there was certainly no manufacturing to be done around Buchenwald anytime soon — and it was obvious that whatever work was involved, it would further German military interests. So Lamason thanked Commandant Pister for is offer, but explained that he must refuse to allow his men to undertake such work, as under the Geneva Conventions, POWs were not required or permitted to further the war efforts of their captors.

In response, an angry SS-Captain Schmidt whipped out his pistol and thrust it under Lamason's chin. When Lamason, forced onto his toes, remained silent, Fred braced himself for the shot. Schmidt cast a quick glance at Pister, as if to ask whether or not to pull the trigger. Pister let the moment linger and then gave a subtle shake of the head. Schmidt holstered his pistol as Pister expressed his disappointment at that decision and added that perhaps Lamason would have cause to reconsider his position at a later date.[77]

The men were then counted and escorted back to Little Camp, where they were dismissed, appell having already been completed. Apparently, similar questions had been asked of the French prisoners at appell, and in desperation, many had volunteered. The next morning, over 400 French prisoners were loaded onto trucks and headed off to the Mittelwerk, although the airmen knew nothing about their destination.

---

[77] Prisoners not slated for immediate execution were usually held in Little Camp until they had lost 20-30% of their body weight. At that point, when they were much more tractable and much less likely to defy their captors, they were assigned to labor kommandos.

The workload, the inadequate food rations, the hard ground, the fleas and lice, all were taking their toll. Without exception, the men were losing weight, the loss being especially marked among those with dysentery. Every morning, the airmen arose scratching at infected sores, their joints and muscles aching and stiff, their stomachs grumbling with hunger, their feet swollen and tender. Every day saw a few more airmen stricken with dysentery. And then it started raining.

CHAPTER 10

Endurance

-◄⊒⊢►-

THE SECOND WEEK

It was a steady rain. The nighttime temperature was cool, and with no protection from the elements, the men were soon huddled together, shivering. The blanket that Fred and Sam shared did little except slow the flow of water over their bodies. The rain exposed even more rocks at the Rock Pile, and turned the bare ground elsewhere in Little Camp into a quagmire. Each night the temperature dropped further. It was an awful time for anyone with nowhere to run and no way to shield himself from the elements. By day Fred huddled with the rest, gathered around smoky fires. The only positive aspect was that the SS guards, who disliked the weather almost as much as the airmen, called appell only once each day, and the counting went swiftly.

Exposure gradually took its toll. In addition to dysentery, infected cuts and insect bites, Fred developed a chest cold. He wasn't alone — everyone was sniffling and coughing, and there were a few cases of pneumonia. Fred was shivering and cold, his feet were infected and swollen, the wounds becoming deep ulcerations. The dysentery was unrelenting, and the itching from flea bites and scabies was driving him crazy. But what bothered him most was not his wracking cough, but that each cough triggered one of the sharp, stabbing abdominal pains that he was having at random intervals, day and night. Even so, he considered himself better off than some of the others. Lt. Beck, an officer with one of the other American squads, became weak and listless. Fred heard that Hemmens had had his arm re-broken by a whack from a guard's baton, and he had developed a high fever.

Efforts to clear rubble and recover equipment had been suspended for the moment, so Fred had plenty of time to think about how miserable he felt and how much he missed Brooklyn. To combat depression, the officers sent their squads out several times each day to look for anything that would keep the fires going. In Fred's opinion, those fires were all that made their situation tolerable — he could toast his bread and light cigarettes, and at night they provided an illusion of warmth. He made multiple circuits of their small world each day, moving beneath the eaves of block buildings when the wind direction made that beneficial.

The work parties soon resumed. By now the airmen were a known quantity within the confines of Little Camp, and as word spread through the prison grapevine that they were reliable, kapos started arriving to take groups of airmen on kommandos working in and around the camp. The airmen on the labor details returned exhausted, but they invariably brought new information that helped Fred piece together a clearer picture of what went on in the camp at large. And sometimes they brought additional rounds of ammunition or weapons parts that slowly added to their stockpile.

After his arrival processing, Fred associated black armbands with a position of authority. But since then, he learned that prisoners were categorized into discrete types, and each had a place in the prisoner hierarchy. The category of each prisoner was indicated by a badge sewn onto his right sleeve near the shoulder. A red triangle, point downward, indicated a political prisoner. A plain red triangle was worn only by German political prisoners, otherwise there was a letter within the red triangle indicating the nationality of the prisoner — F for French, S for Spanish, and so forth. Apparently now that the airmen were ranging farther afield, proper labeling was required, and the airmen were given red triangles to sew onto their sleeves. Fred's was marked A for American.

Green triangles were worn by convicts. Although most of the prisoners at Buchenwald were either Reds or Greens, there were many other categories and nuances. Roughly 300 German Communists (red triangles) were currently in positions of authority. The Reds had life-and death power over other prisoner groups because they usually decided who went on the kommandos with the highest death rates, and who got transferred to one of the 75 satellite camps of Buchenwald. The Communists were not partial to the democratic French, and over the last year, places with high death rates (like the Mittelwerk) received a disproportionate number of French civilians. Prisoners who returned from such postings were either too weak to survive or already dead. In either case they soon "went up the chimney."

Early in the first week of September, approximately 250 French civilians who had been living in the open area outside of the Rock Pile were collected and led out of the compound for transport to a remote labor camp.[78] Then on 3 September, while a misty rain was falling, Fred watched as the young gypsies from Block 58 were rounded up

---

[78] They were taken to Dora Concentration Camp, a sub-camp of Buchenwald that housed laborers for the Mittelwerk.

and taken away. At appell that evening, Kindinger told the assembled airmen that they could leave the Rock Pile and move into the newly opened space in Block 58. Fred heard Lamason ask what had become of the gypsies. Kindinger's reply was that the only thing that mattered was that they weren't coming back. So after appell, Fred collected his meager belongings — a small cup, a wooden bowl, several cigarettes, and a few scraps of cloth — and hobbled off to shelter after two weeks in the open.

The barracks was definitely an improvement, but it was still barely habitable. A wooden framework supporting four tiers of shelving ran along the walls, the tiers vertically separated by roughly two feet. Each individual shelf was six feet long and four feet wide, and there were dozens of shelves in each tier, filling almost the entire width and length of the room. Bedding, where present, consisted of filthy straw stuffed in worn burlap bags.

There was an open area in the center of the building. Within this space, there were long wooden tables with bench seats, like elongated picnic tables, and toward the front of the room, the area from which the gypsies had been expelled, was a potbellied wood stove. Although small, the stove could be used to heat soup, toast bread, and if kept alight, generate heat at night. Although no longer exposed in the yard, airmen continued to stand guard at night, and those on duty monitored the stove at the same time. The first things burned that night were the mattresses, which were disgusting, fetid, and infested with fleas, ticks, and mites.

The barracks was still frightfully overcrowded — 750 prisoners were jammed into a space appropriate for perhaps 150. The empty shelves were allocated by squad, with four men to a shelf. When Fred climbed in, he realized that there was no way to lie face-up or face-down. He had to lie on his side, and the others had to do the same. If he wanted to turn over, everyone else had to shift to allow it. But the thing Fred disliked most was having to get in and out of his shelf during the night to use the abort. Except for those on the bottom shelf, it meant climbing down or climbing up shelves packed with sleeping airmen. After a trip to the abort, anyone climbing slapped feet coated with wet, stinking goo across the limbs, bodies, or faces of sleeping comrades. Fred, on the second level, could usually avoid tracking across those on the bottom tier. But those on the racks above invariably stepped on someone on their way down and back. The only solution was to change shelf positions at regular intervals. The top tier took the most effort to reach, but nobody ever stepped on your face. Even without the mess imported from the abort, there was filth in abundance within the overcrowded barracks, and the entire building was infested with rats, fleas, and lice. It was an ideal breeding ground for disease. Other prisoners were dying each day, and the bodies dragged to appell for counting before they were left by the abort for eventual pickup.

While they were settling into the barracks and for a long time thereafter, the bomb damage continued to draw curious dignitaries, military officers, and government officials. Fred heard that Lamason and Larson had seen the uniformed chief of the Weimar Police walking in the appellplatz with his entourage, and decided on the spur of the moment to confront him. They marched in front of the officer, a tall, heavyset man in his mid-40s, made a precise turn and snapped out crisp salutes. Lamason quickly explained that there were 168 allied airmen being held at Buchenwald illegally, in violation of the Geneva Conventions, and asked him to intervene on their behalf. Through another officer who acted as his translator, the chief said that he had heard rumors about the airmen, and that their situation was being investigated. To Fred, that assurance was much more encouraging than promises made by Schmidt or Pister.

A few days after they moved into the barracks, Fred and the others were ordered to assemble in the small appellplatz of Little Camp. Once the men had assembled, SS guards entered the compound escorting an SS officer, accompanied by uniformed assistants and prison laborers. The airmen were then ordered to remove their shirts.

It was heavily overcast, but fortunately not raining as the men stood in the cold wind. Two of the laborers walked slowly down the line. The first had a small cloth pad on a short wooden handle. At each airman, he dipped the cloth in a bucket carried by the second prisoner, and painted an X across the man's chest. The X was a bright yellow-orange but unlike their original swabbing, it was painless.

The SS officer[79] followed close behind, carrying a stainless steel syringe that was probably intended for veterinary use. It was quite large (roughly 300 ml) and attached to a stout hypodermic needle that was probably 18-gauge. When abreast of an airman, he stopped, turned, and pushed the needle into the left side of the chest, close to the sternum. When fully inserted, he injected a portion of the contents of the syringe. The needle was then withdrawn, and the officer shifted to the next airman in line.

When the syringe was empty, the officer handed it to an SS assistant who refilled it from a large container, whereupon the process

---

[79] Probably SS-Major Erwin Ding-Schuler, who performed many medical experiments on prisoners.

was repeated. It was difficult to stand there in formation, knowing what was coming, but Fred didn't see that he had any other options. When the shot was given, it burned briefly but then faded to a dull ache. Once all of the airmen had received their injections, the SS team left Little Camp, and the assembly dispersed. Speculation ran wild over what they had received, but the airmen never learned what they had been given.

In his first week in the barracks, Fred met several of the SOE agents who had been picked up in France and delivered to Buchenwald only a week before the airmen arrived. There were 37 of them housed in Barracks 17, located a short distance away from Little Camp. Over time, most of the SOE agents visited Little Camp to spend time with the airmen, swapping stories and making friends. Fred enjoyed meeting them, and thought they would have been much easier to get along with in close quarters than Alex had been.

That week, Fred also learned what had become of the young gypsies when Kolchat Salazar, an English speaking prisoner who worked in the crematorium, began visiting Little Camp. Salazar, who said he was from California, reported that the gypsies had been executed at the firing range, and that their bodies were now stacked outside the crematorium. There was, Kolchat told them, an execution detail that operated in the basement of the crematorium. Kolchat's job was to remove the clothing from bodies and extract any teeth that were gold-crowned or had gold fillings. The gold was melted down and added to the Reich's coffers. He also checked the skin for any tattoos that might make interesting additions to the anatomy museum.

This was done in a satellite building, called the pathology lab, where death certificates were signed by the SS doctor on duty. The death certificates were often filled out without a glance at the corpse. "Shot while trying to escape" or "By order of the RSHA"[80] were often listed as the cause of death. In a few instances, an SS doctor took the heads off the prisoners for preservation. In such cases, the doctor filled out a special form indicating what had been done, and Salazar had to ensure that the form accompanied the body to the crematorium. Everything, no matter how bizarre, had to be documented. He had been at this job for over a year, but he still found it difficult to believe. Fred was simply flabbergasted. He had never imagined that inhumanity could be so obsessively organized and bureaucratic.

---

[80] *Reichssicherheitshauptamt*, the Reich Main Security Office, run by Reichsführer Heinrich Himmler.

On Sunday afternoons, kommandos were suspended, and the prisoners had their only really uplifting moments. At that time, the Buchenwald prisoner symphony gathered to perform in the appellplatz, with the music broadcast through the speakers in the camp. Fred welcomed the change in the music that played over the loudspeakers every other day. The music never changed and never paused, except when announcements were made. He had learned to associate that music with pain, abuse, and hard labor. It was wonderful to have it stop and be replaced by live music that was always new. He had never been a big fan of classical music, but he found himself deeply moved by the soaring melodies.

It was a brief window into life outside of what he had come to consider as hell on earth. There were dead bodies by the aborts, outside the hospitals, and by the barracks entrances; they arrived by the truckload from satellite camps, by wagon from the stone quarry, and by handfrom just about anywhere in the camp. The abused prisoners were immersed in violence and surrounded by death. The crematorium was running each and every day, and on calm days, the thick smoke belching from the smokestack blanketed the sodden camp like a shroud. What more would Hell offer? A barb-tailed Satan might be missing, but surely the SS men could fill the role of demons.

THE THIRD WEEK

Fred's dysentery was wearing him down. Several times each day he hobbled on his bandaged, bloody feet to the abort. As more and more prisoners in the quarantine section of Little Camp were similarly afflicted, the lines grew and the waiting time extended. One morning when it was particularly long and the internal pressures acute, Fred decided to use the larger abort in the main portion of Little Camp. He easily talked his way out of "his" compound, and rushed to the nearby abort, and found an empty place at the far corner.

With a sigh of relief that was more like a groan, he balanced his posterior on the beam and let it go. As his wastes splattered down into the pit, he heard splashes and sensed movement below him. Startled, he glanced down to see a young man, his face slathered with waste, shifting away from Fred to crouch at the side of the tank. When Fred opened his mouth to call out, the man raised his right hand above the muck and put his finger across his lips, as if to say SSSHHH. Fred glanced around, but the prisoners seated nearby were staring straight ahead, clearly avoiding any glances in his direction. Curious, Fred leaned forward as if straining to defecate, and asked the man in French what he was doing and if he needed help.

No help was needed or possible. The man was hiding from a kommando working at the stone quarry. The kapo at the quarry and the guard, *SS-Oberscharführer* (Sergeant) Baier, had singled him out for special treatment, kicking, punching, and clubbing him at every opportunity. He had seen this before — one or two prisoners were selected, abused repeatedly, and then executed while "trying to escape." It was generally assumed that this was done to get the "killing bonus" (extra pay, sausages, liquor, and sometimes a Red Cross package) that would be split between the guard and the kapo.

He was sure that if he went to the quarry one more time, he would never return, so instead of heading off with the others that afternoon, he had snuck away. He had hidden in the cess pit ever since, out of sight from the entrance. At nightfall, when the abort was relatively empty and he'd be easily spotted from the entrance, he planned to hide among the pile of corpses. His tale told, the young man then asked Fred where he was from, and how he got to Buchenwald. Fred found it rather surreal to have a friendly, rational, otherwise normal conversation with a guy immersed in fetid goo.

When Fred left, he promised to return the next day and talk further. But when he returned, there was no sign of his new acquaintance. He strolled casually around the tank, surreptitiously looking for him, but to no avail. His activities did not go unnoticed, and one of the other prisoners approached Fred and asked with a wry look if he'd lost something. Interrupting Fred's stammered reply, the man explained that late the previous afternoon, SS guards had entered Little Camp searching for a prisoner missing from his kommando. When they found him hiding in the abort, two of the guards took boards and pushed the man below the surface until he drowned. The guards were laughing the whole time. The body had yet to surface. Seeing Fred's astonishment and dismay, the man merely shrugged and said that it had happened before.

On 13 September, Fred's squad had the job of retrieving the morning coffee. At 0630, a team that included Fred, Sam, and two others left Little Camp and headed to the kitchen. They were almost to the entrance when they were approached by a burly SS sergeant with a kapo in tow. The airmen, by now well trained, immediately stopped, whipped off their caps, and stood at attention, their eyes lowered. The guard circled the group once, then asked in passable English if he was correct, that they were terrorfliegers from Little Camp. On getting the response he expected, he ordered Fred and Sam to leave the detail and come with him on a special duty.

Fred and Sam recognized him as the guard who had told the

arriving airmen that the way out was through the smokestack.[81] Following the guard with some trepidation, their unease increased when they realized that they were heading to the crematorium.

They were led along the brick wall, and entered the courtyard through a gate at the front of the building. As they entered, the first thing they saw was a tall pile of corpses to their left, stacked like cordwood near a side door to the main building. More bodies were piled on a corpse cart. Their minds were still wrestling with the implications of that pile as they were led to the side of the building, down a set of concrete steps, and through a door into the basement.

The guard walked ahead, but Fred and Sam stood frozen in place until they were pushed into the room by the kapo who was following them. They were standing in a small, open portion of the basement (the rest of the basement housed the crematorium furnaces). The room had unusually high ceilings. Two or three feet below the ceiling, 48 L-shaped hooks jutted out of the white plaster walls. But the stark decor was not the focus of their attention. What transfixed them was the sight of the bodies of prisoners dangling from many of those hooks. The room stank, and there were puddles of urine and dribbles of feces beneath many of the bodies.

In a daze, Fred did a quick count almost automatically, and realized that there were more than a dozen dangling bodies. They were hung by double loops, one around their neck and the other around a wall hook. Some of the loops were made of slender cords, others from heavy wire. The faces of the dead, grossly distorted and discolored, bore agonized expressions. Their hands were bound behind them, now pressed against the walls by their sagging body weight.

There was an SS officer in the room as well as a second SS guard and two green triangle prisoners (German criminals) who worked in the basement. The SS sergeant who had fetched them ordered them to each grab a leg of the closest body and lift it. As they complied, he used a short pole to slip the upper loop off the wall hook. After the body had been lowered to the floor, the SS officer, presumably a doctor, checked for a pulse while the guard removed the strangulation loop from the neck.

With Fred and Sam as one team and the two German prisoners as another, they repeated the process several times. The SS doctor moved between the prisoner teams, checking each body. If there was a stubborn sign of life, a crunching blow to the head from a wooden

---

[81] This was probably SS-Sergeant Hermann Helbig, who also worked at Block 99, where Russian POWs were executed.

club wielded by a guard solved the problem.

Fred tried to blank his mind, tried not to think about what he was doing each time he wrapped his arms around a wet, cool, stinking thigh and pushed upward so that the loop could be freed. Each time he went through the motions, he felt the backs of his hands and arms scraping against sharp irregularities in the grimy plaster walls, but he simply ignored the sensation. His attention was more on the need to lift the weight and ignore the stabbing abdominal pain that would accompany the effort.

It wasn't until the fourth body was being lowered to the floor that Fred noticed that the bound hands were bloody and the fingers raw. Glancing back at the wall, he saw bloody streaks a foot or so below eye level. The next time, as he and Sam were directed to the next dangling body, his detachment failed, and as he grabbed the prisoner's thigh and began to lift, his eyes focused on the irregularities in the plaster that had been scratching his hands and forearms. Over a band at least a foot wide, the wall was carpeted with the broken pieces of fingernails torn from the hands of struggling prisoners as they slowly strangled. There were hundreds of these fragments below each hook, thousands in the room. How many deaths, how much agony, how much evil could one room contain?

The scale was overwhelming, and Fred was consumed by horror and loathing. He paused in mid-lift, leaning against the wall, his heart racing. Sam, uncertain as to what was happening, paused as well, with anxious glances at the guards. Fred, realizing the danger he was in, returned to the job at hand, but his mind was still reeling. By the time they lowered the last of the executed prisoners to the cold concrete floor, he was fighting back the dry heaves, much to the amusement of the guards. Fred knew even then that he'd be seeing that wall and the fingernails of countless unknown victims in his waking and sleeping moments for the rest of his life.

When the doctor left the basement, the two prisoner teams carried the bodies across the basement to an open steel elevator, like an enormous dumb-waiter. When the bodies were loaded, they pulled on the ropes to the pulley system that lifted the corpses to the ground floor, where they would be unloaded by other prisoners.

At last the job was done. The SS sergeant, smirking at Fred's obvious discomfort, explained that he had wanted them to understand that this was what spies and *terrorfliegers* deserved, and that their turn was coming. He then ordered the kapo to escort them back to Little Camp, with the promise that he would be seeing them again very soon.

When they rejoined their squad, they were peppered with

questions, but neither man was in the mood to talk. Fred just shook his head, and Sam mumbled something about telling them later. Fred went off and sat by himself, trying to absorb what had happened and what it meant. He had been raised as a Roman Catholic. He was never as devout as his sisters, who had wanted to be nuns until they discovered boys, but he had gone to church regularly. He had fervently prayed several times since being shot down — for his family, for his friends, and for his own future. Looking back over the last month, he saw all too clearly that prayers from Buchenwald weren't answered. He would never pray again.

Within a few hours, all of the airmen knew about the executions as Salazar, the prisoner working in the pathology lab, passed the word that many of the SOE agents had been escorted to the crematorium and executed in the strangling room. The execution order had come directly from Reichsführer Himmler's office in Berlin.

THE FOURTH WEEK

On 17 September, at the end of his fourth week at Buchenwald, Fred saw the SS medical party approaching Little Camp. Fred, Sam, and many others were out in the open, and Fred was too exhausted to run. But many of the other airmen immediately scattered, and when Kindinger ordered an assembly, fewer than half of the airmen could be located. Fred stood midway along the first row of airmen, with Sam to his immediate left and Charles Roberson two spaces farther down the line. The SS doctor seemed annoyed that so few airmen had assembled. He spoke angrily to Kindinger, and his movements were abrupt.

Before reaching Fred, he broke the hypodermic needle when he missed the intended spot and buried the tip in the airman's sternum. Cursing, he used a pair of pliers provided by an aide to extract the broken tip, remove the base of the needle, and screw on a replacement. He repeated the procedure, successfully this time, and moved on down the line.

Whether it was general inattention or some other factor, the doctor missed his mark again, slamming the needle into the edge of Fred's sternum. Trying a different strategy, he first smacked his hand hard enough to drive the needle through the sternum. Once it was inserted far enough, he gave the injection before attempting to retrieve the needle by rotating and wiggling it while the orderlies braced Fred. The strategy failed — the hypodermic needle bent and broke just above the skin surface. With a pair of pliers, the doctor was able to extract the needle remnant from Fred's chest. But when he removed the base of the needle from the syringe, he was told that they had run out of spare hypodermic needles. Shaking his head in disgust, the doctor marched off in a huff, and the ordeal was over.

After the men were dismissed, Fred, aching and sore and a bit nervous about the whole experience, was treated as a hero. Sam kidded him that he must have intentionally broken the needle to spare Sam and the rest from receiving doses of the mystery drug. Fred found the banter raised his spirits, reminding him of his days with the Jackson crew.

Outside of Little Camp, just past the cinema building, was a large tent enclosed by an electric fence. Fred had heard that it was the SS brothel, and every once in a while he would wander over by the fence, hoping to get a glimpse of a woman. One morning, he was dismayed to see the body of an obviously pregnant woman dangling from the electrified fence. Later in the day, prisoners passing by told the airmen that she had committed suicide rather than have yet another baby taken away and killed. The guards left her body there for several days, perhaps as a warning to the other women.

THE FIFTH WEEK

On 20 September, midway through their fifth week, the airmen were called together, marched out of Little Camp, and taken to the processing area for their first shower. When his turn came, Fred was given 3-4 minutes to rinse in tepid water, with neither soap nor towel. After removing the last traces of the orange X on his chest, he no longer felt like a marked man. His head was then shaved before the airmen were taken back to Block 58.

Later in the day, Fred was hanging around the open area, smoking a cigarette, when he saw SS guards and a senior SS officer escorting a pair of high-ranking Luftwaffe officers along the northern fence-line. They were heading toward the German Armaments Works. One of the officers was tall and almost regal in his bearing, and his gray uniform was adorned with countless ribbons and medals that Fred didn't recognize. In addition to the ribbons, he wore an Iron Cross around his neck. This was obviously a person of importance and potential influence. While the SS officer spoke at length and pointed out details of the bombed factories, the Luftwaffe officer's eyes were scanning the compound.

After a quick consultation with Lt. Powell, the closest officer, Sgt. Bernie Scharf marched to the closest point on the inner fence-line, snapped to attention, and saluted, calling out a request, in German, to speak with the Luftwaffe officer. The SS officer attempted to move the party along, but the Luftwaffe officer curtly dismissed these efforts, and moved to the fence-line opposite Scharf.

The Luftwaffe officer was Major Hannes Trautloft. In the exchange that followed, Powell, with Scharf translating, reported that there were 168 Allied POWs being held at Buchenwald in violation of the Geneva Conventions. When asked for additional specifics, he gave the names of Lt. Powell, Captain Larson, and Squadron Leader Lamason. The Luftwaffe officer listened carefully, jotting some notes on a pocket notebook pulled from his uniform jacket. He promised Scharf that he would check out their story, and if true, he would do what he could to secure their transfer to a POW camp.[82]

Since their arrival, the Gestapo had been taking one or two airmen aside for interrogation at random intervals. Late in the week it was Fred's turn. It was an odd session — for some reason they wanted information about his family and Brooklyn. As usual he refused to give any information other than name and serial number, and as usual, this resulted in assorted slaps and punches. As he stood at the end of the session, one of the guards clubbed him in the right side, and the pain it produced was staggering.

THE SIXTH WEEK

Fred could feel himself losing a little ground each day. He had a chronic head cold, dysentery was taking a toll, and he itched constantly from fleas, lice, and scabies. He had large pus-filled abscesses on the soles of his feet and at his ankles, and he hobbled to the abort and to the daily appell. Among the other airmen, it was Hemmens who was in the worst shape. He had double pneumonia, rheumatic fever, and blood poisoning, and he was so malnourished and debilitated that his broken arm wasn't healing. Philip D. Hemmens died early on the morning of 27 September, after 38 days in Buchenwald. He was only 20 years old, and he had been treated like a younger brother by most of the other airmen. Fred had admired his pluck — he had survived the broken and re-broken arm, beatings from guards, and harsh treatment, without flinching or

---

[82] This was politically challenging. Trautloft was engaged to a woman who was part-Jewish, and if the SS focused attention on him there would be terrible consequences. So he took the matter to his superiors, which led to a meeting among senior Luftwaffe officers, including Hermann Göring.

complaining.

THE SEVENTH WEEK

The weather continued to deteriorate. Another half-inch of rain fell on 1 October, and temperatures dropped. The high temperature on October 2nd was 46°F. Around that time, the person Fred thought of as "The Movie Star Major" returned, and several hundred additional skilled "volunteers" were collected from Little Camp. Although they would have welcomed better living conditions, Fred and the other airmen loathed the Germans and would never willingly assist them. Earlier that day, he had seen 300 Jews arrive in Little Camp after being shipped by boxcar from a kommando at a salt mine.

The men, ages 15-65, were exhausted and malnourished, no longer fit for heavy labor. They had been given no food or water during the three days they stood packed together in the boxcars. When they moved past, Fred saw the blank, glazed expressions of people with neither strength nor hope. When they were marched back to the boxcars a day or two later, everyone knew that the men were headed for execution, but they looked just as listless and unconcerned. Fred discussed his observations with Sam and the other noncoms in the squad. They decided that if they knew they were going to be executed they would not go passively. Better to rush the guards hoping that someone would get a weapon and take a few of the Germans with him.

How much good Fred would be in that effort was an open question, as he was now in serious trouble. He had lost at least 30 pounds, roughly 20% of his body weight. Several teeth had fallen out, lost to pyorrhea (gum disease) and malnutrition, and his feet were swollen and badly infected. There was blood in his urine, his remaining teeth felt loose, and his flak wounds, which had healed months earlier, were reopening.[83] He was severely sleep-deprived but afraid to fall asleep because his dreams were so terrible. He considered simply giving up and waiting for the end, but he refused to give the Germans that satisfaction. He would fight them every step of the way and hang on until the bitter end, if for no other reason than to spite the Nazi bastards. No matter the cost, he would survive for his family in Brooklyn and for his friends in Hacqueville, and he vowed that somehow he would settle the score for his betrayal.

---

[83] These problems, common among the airmen, were related to malnourishment and vitamin C deficiency.

It helped a little to know that many of the other men had similar problems. Snoring and coughing were common at night, but so was whimpering, moaning, and silent crying. What created a crisis for Fred was the pain that had started at his last interrogation and grown to become a gnawing beast tearing at his insides. He'd had episodes of abdominal pain in the past, but nothing like the agony he was experiencing.

By that evening, Fred had developed a high fever. Several days later, the pain was so intense that Sam had to help him out of his bench and prop him up at appell. However, when SS-Corporal Hoffman spied weakness, he gave Fred a jab with his baton that dropped him like a stone. After a farewell boot in the side, Hoffman ordered Kindinger to deliver Fred to the hospital tent. On a cot in the tent, nothing was done except to take his temperature every hour. While his nervous buddies could visit, they could do nothing, and they watched helplessly as Fred became delirious.

There was general consensus among the prisoner orderlies that Fred had acute appendicitis and needed immediate surgery, but there was no operating theater, and neither surgical instruments nor anesthetics were available. A transfer to the SS hospital would have only one result — execution by lethal injection.[84]

Dr. Balachowski, the prisoner-physician assigned to Block 46, told Sam the situation was hopeless, but an Indian prisoner with limited medical knowledge (he'd trained as a pharmacist) advocated surgery. In preparation, he made a scalpel by carefully shaping and sharpening a discarded spoon. Nobody was very enthusiastic about Fred's prospects for survival, and Fred, delirious, was in no condition to make a decision. For Fred, it was all a blur, and his memories of Balachowski, Sam, Paul, Ed, and the Indian orderly ran together, with sentence fragments in a mixture of German, French, and English.

That evening after appell, Ed Ritter was visiting when Fred's eyes opened and he groggily asked where he was. Delighted, Ed told him that he was in the hospital tent with appendicitis. When the orderly came for the hourly temperature check, he found that the fever had broken. Fred, weak as a kitten but no longer in acute pain, was soon able to sit up and eat a few small chunks of bread soaked in soup broth. The next day, rather than undergoing field surgery with a sharpened spoon, Fred was escorted back to Block 58, where he was warmly welcomed — nobody had expected him to survive.

---

[84] Sick airmen were kept in the medical tent, in Block 54, or occasionally in Block 46. Sixty to eighty of the airmen were sick enough to require "hospitalization" while at Buchenwald.

There was more good news. At long last, the airmen were given shoes, flat wooden sandals with cloth straps that size fits all. They took some getting used to, but they offered much better foot protection than pieces of boards or strips of cloth. The shoes were welcome, but they had arrived far too late for most of the airmen who, like Fred, had badly infected feet and swollen legs.

THE EIGHTH WEEK

The week of 8 October was cold, gray, and miserable, matching the moods of the airmen. No one, not even the officers, talked about escape plans. Instead, they spoke of survival or said nothing at all.[85] Fred needed no coaching as he was already committed to hanging on. He hobbled to the abort, to appell, and on work details. When several teeth fell into his hand after a prolonged coughing spell, he just shook his head in disgust and tossed them aside. He swore to himself that the only way the Germans were going to defeat him was to shoot him.

Midweek, SS-Corporal Hoffman and a platoon of SS guards entered the compound and ordered Kindinger to assemble the airmen. The 155 airmen — 12 were in the hospital tent, too sick to move — were marched out of Little Camp and taken to the cinema block, where a decorated, senior Luftwaffe officer was waiting for them.

When the airmen were present and accounted for, he introduced himself as an officer from Dulag Luft, the processing center for POW airmen. He said that the Luftwaffe had lost track of the airmen when Paris was evacuated, and it had taken this long to locate them. He apologized for the delay, promising to return as soon as suitable transport had been arranged for their transfer to a Luftwaffe POW camp. The relief in the room was palpable, and the march back to Block 58 seemed shorter and easier.

Lamason remained uneasy. He knew about the DIKAL classification, and also knew that their execution orders were on file in the camp office. All it would take would be a phone call from the RSHA giving the final authorization, and they would be scheduled for immediate execution. Lamason gathered that there was no love

---

[85] Things were bad enough that Lamason considered gathering up the cached weapons and making a potentially suicidal escape attempt while some of his men could still stand and fight. But the Communists felt that with the SOE agents dead and the airmen all but incapacitated, there was no reason to give them any weapons.

lost between the SS and the Luftwaffe, and the simplest way for the SS to avoid a political tug-of over their fate would be to kill them before the Luftwaffe arrived to remove them. That did seem to be the plan, as he soon received word that "the call" had been received and their execution scheduled for Tuesday, October 24th.

THE NINTH WEEK

While the airmen waited in anticipation, life and death in Buchenwald continued as ever. On 16 October, punishment was administered to three Polish prisoners. The three had escaped from an outside work kommando. With no idea of where to go in central Germany, they were soon recaptured. They were brought back to Buchenwald after five days, but they were either caught at different times, or two of them had bribes or other bargaining chips, as only one was executed.[86] The sentences were carried out at appell, in front of the assembled ranks of prisoners, and the proceedings were broadcast over the speakers.

Fred, in the main camp on a kitchen assignment, watched the events unfold. A chained prisoner was escorted from the cell block, and SS-Sergeant Werner Warnstedt took him to the gallows. After the execution, the other prisoners were led out and stretched across the whipping table where the 25 lashes were administered. It was all done with little apparent emotion, and in near-total silence. The Poles offered no resistance, the SS guards showed a cold detachment, and the assembled witnesses — all 25,000 of them — stood quietly at attention with their hats off, waiting for the proceedings to end. Fred realized that he no longer seethed with outrage at the brutality around him. It was just another day at the office for the staff and prisoners at Buchenwald. With bodies stacked like cord wood throughout the camp, why make a fuss over a single death?

Although Hemmens had so far been the only casualty among the airmen, Fred knew that all of them were on thin ice. He had no idea how much more weight he could lose — he hardly recognized his own body. Everyone had lost considerable weight, but the high

---

[86] The standard policy was that an escaping prisoner recaptured after less than three days on the run would be publicly whipped. A prisoner at large for more than three days was to be executed, because it was assumed that the only way he could have survived that long would have been to steal food, and theft was a capital crime.

fever and appendicitis had hit him hard.[87] A dozen airmen were in the hospital tent, their fates uncertain. Fred was determined to hang on as long as possible, but he still worried that the Luftwaffe transfer might come too late.

Fortunately, the Luftwaffe knew that the airmen were in dire straits, and the planning was expedited. Two days later, the airmen were collected and returned to the cinema block for another meeting with the officer from Dulag Luft. He informed them that transport had been arranged, and that they would be leaving Buchenwald the next day. One detail needed to be taken care of before this could happen, however. All of the airmen would need to fill out the Red Cross cards that his aides were distributing. Anyone who did not fill out his card would not be considered a bona fide POW, and would be left behind. The officer and his aides then left the room.

The discussion that followed was long and at times quite heated. Lamason began by saying that the information requested on the cards would for all practical purposes be worthless intelligence — whatever the men could recall would be so far out of date that it would probably mislead the Germans rather than help them. But he then said that although he would not fault anyone for filling out one of these cards, he intended to provide only his name, rank, and serial number, as required by the Geneva Conventions. Others in the room were much less forgiving, angrily denouncing anyone who filled out a card as a cowardly traitor. Fred stayed out of the discussion, as he had already decided that he would give the Germans no more information than Lamason would.

When the Luftwaffe officer returned hours later, from the 155 airmen in the hall, he collected 118 "completed" cards, although many of those cards contained deliberate errors and misstatements, and others had only minimal information. There were 37 airmen who had simply refused to fill out the forms, and those men were advised to consider their situation further.

The next morning, coffee was delivered, and the airmen — all 155 of them, even those who had refused to complete the forms — were taken to the processing room. There they surrendered their metal discs in exchange for their clothing and shoes. There was some grumbling when they found that other personal effects, such as watches or rings, would not be returned, but the general mood remained upbeat.

Fred could hardly believe how good it felt to strip off his striped

---

[87] The airmen lost on average 35-40% of their body weight while in Little Camp.

suit and don the dirty, smelly, civilian clothes he had worn on the train from Paris. He was equally glad to lose the hard wooden sandals, although his swollen, infected feet protested at being forced into covered shoes. Although he welcomed the prospect of imminent salvation, Fred was worried about the airmen they would be leaving behind, but Lamason had been assured that those men would follow as soon as they were fit to travel.

The airmen ready to leave Buchenwald were taken outside where they were assembled and counted. It was raining and cold — not yet 50°F — and a layer of smoke from the crematorium hung over the camp beneath the low clouds, but those details probably escaped them. When the counting was completed, the airmen marched, escorted by 30 SS guards, past the crematorium and on to the train yard, following the route taken when they had arrived.

It was the morning of 19 October 1944, and Fred had survived 61 days in Buchenwald, losing an average of one pound of body weight per day. He emerged as a pared down version of his former self, leaving youth, optimism, faith, and all illusions about human nature behind in the dust and the greasy ashes.

CHAPTER 11

Stalag Luft III

-◆᠊᠍᠊᠍◆-

TRANSPORT AND ARRIVAL

At the Buchenwald train station, after being counted one last time, Fred was loaded into a boxcar by guards wearing Luftwaffe uniforms. It was a relief to be in the custody of military personnel whose uniform insignia did not include silver skulls. Several Red Cross parcels were handed out for the men to share. It was the first food parcel Fred had seen since his August boxcar ride. His opinion as to the quality of the contents had gone up considerably over the interim.

The boxcars were not overcrowded — only 35-40 men per car — so Fred could sit down or even lie down and sleep. But it was too cold for that. There was no heat in the cars, and his clothes were soaked from walking in the rain. Once the train started moving, a wet wind blew in through the ventilation openings, chilling him further. It was a long day and an even longer night, with the men huddled together for warmth.

The train ran northeast from Weimar through Neustadt and Jena, then continued on through Gera, Dresden, Gorlitz, and finally to Sagan [postwar Zagan], Poland. The trip, which took two days to complete, was largely uneventful. The guards seemed relaxed, and they seemed startled and a bit confused every time Fred or another airman tensed at their approach or flinched when they made sudden moves. When the train finally stopped at a siding and the doors were opened, Fred had a terrifying flashback to his arrival at Buchenwald, and he half-expected to be greeted by angry SS guards and snarling dogs. But the scene before him was quiet and orderly. They were at Sagan station, an imposing building with a clocktower that looked like it belonged in a fairy tale.

Slowly, the men climbed down from the boxcars, their limbs aching and their strength limited. The weather had warmed a bit, but it was still overcast and gray. There was a bit of confusion and delay as they were organized into ragged columns. They were then escorted away from the station along a main road that led to a smaller, unpaved road that went through a dense forest, the pine trees crowding in from either side. For anyone else, it would have been a simple stroll, but it was slow going for the starved airmen, and an endurance test for Fred. After a half-mile or so, the road swung to the right and entered an area cleared of vegetation. Ahead, Fred could see the corner of a barbed wire enclosure consisting of double fences strung between sturdy guard towers. The airmen turned left and went through the main gate, which had a particularly prominent tower, behind which a huge Nazi flag fluttered in the wind.

The plaque at the gate informed Fred that they were entering Stalag Luft III.[88] He could see that it was a large facility, but only later would he learn that it covered nearly 60 acres and was subdivided into five separate compounds.

Arrival processing was done in the *Vorlager* ("before-camp"), a fenced enclosure near the road. The vorlager contained the administration offices, a POW prison, a bath house, a small hospital building, and various outbuildings for storing food and other supplies. The men were taken into the administration building in batches. While Fred was being processed, one of the prisoners in the adjacent Center Compound took a few grainy black and white photos of the Buchenwald airmen with a clandestine camera.

Inside the administration building, Fred was given a complete set of clean clothing, including hightop shoes and a warm winter "great coat," plus a towel and even a toothbrush. Compared to Buchenwald, Stalag Luft III was the lap of luxury. He was next taken to the shower block, where he took a long hot shower with plenty of fragrant Camay soap. After he was deloused, he was given the OK to don his new uniform. It felt so good to be clean, dry, and warm, that Fred could hardly believe he wasn't dreaming.

For their part, the Luftwaffe staff were taken aback by the shocking physical condition of these prisoners, who had ulcerated sores all over their bodies. Fred looked like a walking skeleton. But what they found more disconcerting was that every time a uniformed guard approached, Fred would reflexively cower and then freeze, his eyes on the ground. As a group, the new arrivals acted like dogs that had been starved and beaten to break their spirits. It was embarrassing for the staff to witness what those SS fanatics had done to them.

Once dressed in his new clothes, Fred's photo was taken for a POW ID card. The photo was printed on the spot, and the ID card filled out with personal information, camp identification number, and

---

[88] This prison camp, built and staffed by the Luftwaffe, was originally intended to hold Allied air officers, although it now held officers, non-commissioned airmen, and a few POWs from other services. In the fall of 1944, there were 12,774 POWs at Stalag Luft III. Of that number, 6,387 were Americans; 5,869 officers and 518 NCOs.

barracks assignment. He was also given a square metal ID tag on a chain, to be worn like dog tags, before being sent outside to wait for the rest of the group to complete processing. As he compared notes with other airmen, he realized that they were being split up. The camp was near capacity, and the new arrivals were randomly assigned to compounds that were generally organized by nationality.

After being part of a cohesive group for so long, the impending separation came as a bit of a shock. Fred was dismayed to learn that Sam was assigned to a different compound.[89] Fred, Ed Ritter, Paul Wilson, and 22 other sergeants[90] were assigned to South Compound, where the proportion of American noncoms was greatest. It was expected that they would serve as orderlies to the officers, and do manual labor as required.[91] Fred joined the cluster of men headed for South Compound, and with a loose escort of Luftwaffe guards, they left the vorlager through the main gate.

They turned left and walked along the main road, with the forest 150' to their right and a complex of buildings to their left. Fred could tell that the buildings were not part of the camp — there were no guards or fences. They were in fact the buildings of the German lager, where the Luftwaffe guards and staff resided. As they reached the end of that complex, they turned left onto a small access road that divided the camp.

Fred then had the German lager to his left and the coiled wire fencing of North Compound to his right. North Compound looked relatively clean and tidy, especially as compared to Buchenwald, and Fred was relieved to find that he could see no bodies stacked around the buildings. But could it mean that the Luftwaffe was more efficient at cleanup than the SS? There was plenty of dust in the air, but no ash, and no stench of corruption. Yet Fred remained apprehensive. He looked for a crematorium, or any building with a suspicious smokestack, but he didn't see one. The general appearance of the entire camp was stark, as if the vegetation had been stripped away, leaving only the bare, dry ground. Fred thought it looked like the surface of the moon.

---

[89] The Geneva Conventions require that whenever possible, prisoners should be grouped by service and nationality. By this point in the war that policy was recognized but the rule wasn't absolute. Due to overcrowding, prisoners were sometimes assigned to a compound on a space- available basis.

[90] Sgts. Bowen, Coats, Friel, Heimerman, Horrigan, Johnson, Ludwig, O'Masters, Pacha, Paxton, Pelletier, Reynolds, Richey, Roberson, Scharf, Scott, Shearer, Suddock, Vallee, Watson, Williams, and Zeiser.

[91] Under the Geneva Conventions, officers could not be assigned to forced labor details, but noncoms had no such protection.

As Fred continued along the fence-line, he passed several guard towers, each with mounted machine guns and floodlights capable of sweeping a large area. The barricade fence consisted of heavy spools of barbed wire strung along posts between these towers. Ahead, they could see a spot where the fence turned toward them, and at the inner corner of that angle was another gate and guardhouse. The guards turned off the road and led them through the double gate and into South Compound. Fred experienced a surge of panic when he saw that the guards at the gate were holding the leashes of large German shepherds. The dogs looked much like those at Buchenwald, and they had the same attitude. They stood at the limits of their leashes, fully alert, watching every move of the prisoners as they walked by. The guards took no notice as the entire group of airmen recoiled and then crowded together to get as far from the dogs as possible.

When they entered the compound, the group was met by a small group of USAAF officers and NCOs who escorted them along a well-worn track toward another elaborate entry gate. As they cleared the gateway, the Buchenwald airmen walked through a gauntlet of curious onlookers.

It was a standing joke among the prisoners in Stalag Luft III that new arrivals in South Compound were always shocked at the hungry, disheveled, and unmilitary appearance of the long prisoners. That was hardly the case with this particular batch of arriving airmen — Fred and his colleagues were amazed at how clean and healthy the POWs looked. It had been two months since Fred had seen fellow prisoners who weren't walking skeletons. Fred could feel everyone staring at him as he walked past.[92]

As at Buchenwald, the perimeter of the compound was marked by a wooden rail 33' from the double fencing. Fred knew what would happen if anyone stepped over that rail. The perimeter just inside the rail was worn flat by heavy foot-traffic. The path, known as the circuit, was a popular walking route that the POWs used to keep in shape.

Fred's group soon turned right and continued to a supply station where Fred received a cup, a bowl, and a knifefork spoon set with embossed swastikas on the handles. Properly equipped, they were then taken to the cookhouse where their fellow POWs had been busy getting some hot coffee and hot soup ready for them. They were all starving, and the soup was considerably tastier and richer than the

---

[92] A POW who saw them arrive later said, "They were on the verge of pneumonia and were actually starved. They were in a dazed condition and looked like they didn't care if they lived or died."

watery soup they had been given at Buchenwald.

ORIENTATION

Word had spread quickly that the new arrivals looked like they could use a good feed, and the soup was followed by a full meal that had been hastily created from donations provided by POWs who had stashed items from Red Cross parcels. Fred was tired and listless, and when he tried to eat real food, he became full almost immediately. It would clearly be a while before his shrunken stomach would adapt to the prospect of larger daily portions. Their fellow POWs also provided vitamin pills galore, as the new guys looked like they needed them.

As the men finished their meals, they were shown the latrine, which was an enclosed trench with seating for 15, before being escorted to another building to pick up a sheet, two thin blankets, a mattress cover filled with wood shavings,[93] a small towel, and a pillow stuffed with straw. They were then taken to their assigned barracks.

There were 14 barracks in South Compound. Space was at a premium, so the sergeants were scattered across the compound. Groups of five were sent to barracks 125 and 124, groups of four went to barracks 127 and 132, a group of three was directed to barracks 133, and pairs were sent to barracks 130 and 131.

Fred was in a group of four. He, Ed Ritter, Stan Paxton, and Roy Horrigan were assigned to barracks 127. They found the barracks and entered to find a long central corridor with bunkrooms on either side. There were fifteen large rooms and a few smaller ones. Senior officers and clergy got the small single or double rooms, which were near the entry doors, while junior officers and enlisted personnel were assigned to the larger bunk rooms. Fred, Ed, and Stan went to Room 5 and Roy to room 15. Their room was designed to hold up to 15 men, with berthing in wooden bunks stacked three-high. Fred was delighted that he would not have to share the bunk with three other POWs!

Fred, Ed, and Stan found empty bunks and set their mattresses and pillows on them. Then they walked through the barracks to sort out what was where. Near the entrance was a small bathroom with two toilets for use at night, when the grounds outside were off limits and patrolled by sentry dogs running loose. The thought of encountering

---

[93] Simple mattresses of this kind were called palliasses.

those dogs in the dark made Fred's blood run cold. There was also a separate washroom with multiple sinks, and a small kitchen area with a coal stove that provided heat as well as a cooking surface.

As they were nosing around, other men who happened to be in the building politely said hello, and introduced themselves. The introductions were wary, and the mood reserved. There were rumors that Gestapo and Abwehr agents were posing as airmen to infiltrate POW camps, gather intelligence, and foil escape attempts. New arrivals were never fully trusted until they were either vouched for by someone already in the camp or cleared by the officers who conducted arrival interviews.

While they were looking at the barracks kitchen, they were given a brief overview of how meals worked. The Germans provided only a bare minimum, giving each man a loaf of bread, 4-8 oz. of ersatz margarine, 2 turnips, and 4 oz. of sauerkraut per week. When available, each POW also got three potatoes per day, and intermittently the barracks might receive 2-3 pounds of horsemeat each week. Even on a good week, this was far below what was necessary to sustain the prisoners, and their nutrition relied on the food parcels packaged and shipped by the International Red Cross. The Germans warehoused parcels from the Swiss, American, and British Red Cross. The American parcels were considered to be the best, as they contained both chocolate and instant coffee.

Each Red Cross parcel was designed to sustain a single prisoner for one week. Thousands of the parcels were shipped to the Germans, but they doled them out sparingly. The stated goal was an allocation of 1,928 calories per day per man, roughly 200 calories below what an average young man with a sedentary lifestyle would require. The attitudes and policies of their German captors had changed after a mass escape attempt earlier that year. Food tins were punctured before the parcels were distributed, to prevent storage as escape supplies, and the boxes and empty cans had to be returned before new boxes were distributed. Because Allied air strikes interrupted supply lines, by the time the Buchenwald airmen arrived, the rations had been cut in half, and each Red Cross parcel had to last two men a week.

Appell was called late in the day. With some trepidation and occasional physical support, Fred joined the stream of prisoners headed to the appellplatz, located near the cookhouse. It was a very different experience than what he had come to expect. The rows of airmen formed a large square around the perimeter of the grounds, facing inward, while the guards performed their count. Try as he might, Fred could not keep from cringing away from the guards as they approached to do the counting. By the time they had passed, his heart was racing, his palms were sweating, and his legs were quivering. Fortunately, the entire operation seldom lasted more than an hour unless the count was off.[94] When appell was done, Fred headed directly back to his bunk and fell into an exhausted sleep.

Fred's slumber was brief, for he was awakened in the pre-dawn hours by vague memories of a nightmare and a stabbing pain in his lower abdomen. The pain continued, and he became feverish and disoriented, unable to climb out of bed. Ed Ritter, who had seen Fred in a similar state at Buchenwald, went to an officer for help. To signal a medical emergency, a red light outside the barracks was turned on to summon a guard. After a quick consult at the barracks block, Fred was transported by stretcher to the medical room at the north end of the cookhouse. The room was staffed by Capt. Heston C. Daniel, with Lts. Luther Cox and "BJ" Lovin assisting. It was basically a first aid clinic. Serious illnesses could theoretically be transferred to the main hospital, but that facility was grossly overcrowded and undermanned. The preliminary diagnosis made on Fred's arrival was acute appendicitis, but the camp aid station was not equipped for major surgery. So while the staff worked out the mechanics of transfer to the main hospital, often a lengthy and difficult process, Fred was given painkillers and his condition monitored. At the same time, he was given a physical exam, and his infected insect bites and the ulcers on his feet were treated with a salve containing sulfonamides.

By the end of Fred's second day in the clinic, the pain was lessening, and on the third day, Fred was able to sit up and take some soup. That day, he was interviewed by Lt. Ewell McCright, who had been directed by Lieutenant Colonel (LtC.)[95] A. P. Clark to keep a secret journal for South Compound. In his journal, McCright recorded information about each new arrival to the compound. He carefully recorded each airman's name, rank, serial number, home address, birth date, blood type, religion, military unit, POW number, date shot down, injuries sustained, where and how captured, serial number of plane, and where held prior to arrival at Stalag Luft III. By writing clear but almost microscopic letters, he fit all this information into four small ledgers that he could conceal easily. The information was considered Top Secret, and McCright interviewed individual airmen privately. Fred was the eighth of the Buchenwald

---

[94] This could reflect an escape attempt, but typically it was caused by prisoners tricking the guards for a laugh.

[95] The abbreviations used for military ranks are those used in WWII. Today Clark's rank would be indicated as Lt. Col. or LTCOL

airmen to be interviewed by Lt. McCright.

Because the crisis had passed, the request for Fred's hospital transfer was canceled, and he returned to barracks 127 the next day. By the time Fred returned to his barracks room, things were more relaxed, as Ed and Stan had been cleared by the security panel chaired by LtC. Clark. Clark, who had been struck by the appearance of the new arrivals, wanted to get first hand information on their experiences. Fred had his session that afternoon. He provided the basic information and then answered specific questions about his capture, the boxcar ride from Paris, and Buchenwald.

As he answered the questions, Fred became increasingly agitated, and his heart was pounding. At one point, he thought he saw one of the officers glance at another with a skeptical expression, and Fred was suddenly furious, coming partway out of his seat. Trembling with rage, he demanded to know if they thought he was making his story up. LtC. Clark assured him that they were taking him seriously, but that what he was describing was so bizarre and disconnected from their POW experiences that it was difficult to accept. His face flushed, Fred took some deep breaths and settled back into his chair.

LtC. Clark then cautioned Fred against telling other POWs about his experiences in Buchenwald in any detail. Relations with the Germans were very strained, and the POWs were near the boiling point. Following the "Great Escape" months earlier, the Gestapo had executed 50 recaptured RAF prisoners from North Compound.[96] The prisoners at Stalag Luft III were furious, and the guards cracked down, fearing an uprising. If Fred's experiences became widely known, nothing good would come of it. If the stories were believed, things could quickly get out of hand. Clark instructed the other members of the interview team to be equally careful, and he told no one other than Colonel Charles "Rojo" Goodrich, the Senior American Officer (SAO) in South Compound.[97]

---

[96] On the night of 24-25 March 1944, 76 POWs from North Compound made it into the forest before their tunnel opening was discovered. The 50 airmen recaptured by the Gestapo were executed on Hitler's orders. Their ashes were returned to the camp, and the POWs permitted to build a memorial to them in North Compound.

[97] LtC. Clark prepared a report that summarized the information obtained from the sergeants and sewed it into the lining of his coat for safekeeping. It reached the authorities in late April 1945. However, on 7 November 1944, S/L Philip Lamason, held in North Compound, gave a lengthy report to the Swiss Delegation during a periodic camp inspection. As a result, detailed information concerning the Buchenwald airmen reached the Allies three

Fred had a lot to think about when he returned to his barracks. Ultimately he decided that he would not discuss anything about Buchenwald with anyone who had not been there. When he broached the subject with Ed Ritter and Stan Paxton, he found that they had come to the same conclusion independently.

SETTLING IN

Donated vitamin pills were combined with food from the emergency caches of his fellow prisoners and distributed to any of the airmen who, like Fred, were having trouble regaining their strength. For the first week, Fred was too weak to eat more than a token amount. It was as if the relief of his deliverance had used the last of his energy reserves.

Each day, Fred worked on stretching his stomach and taking larger portions of the "real food" served at mealtimes. Fortunately, the kitchen produced large batches of what was known as "Green Death Soup" four times each week, which he found easy to keep down. After a month of determined effort, he could eat everything on his plate, at which point his weight slowly started to climb. One of the camp rules he had learned was that wasting food was considered a serious crime. Fred thought that was pretty funny — the idea that any Buchenwald airman would waste even a scrap of food was ludicrous.

As the days passed, Fred and the other Buchenwald airmen settled into the daily routine of life in Stalag Luft III. A list of the new arrivals, their home towns, and their barracks assignments had been posted on the bulletin board at the cookhouse, so that any friends already in South Compound would know they were nearby. The men in Fred's room were from all over the US, but Fred was the only New Yorker. There were, however, four other New Yorkers among the 131 men in his barracks. One of them, Capt. John Grunow in Room 1, was from Brooklyn. Grunow, still not certain of Fred's bona fides, asked a few questions about the city that only residents could answer — what stores were on which corners, who played what position for the Dodgers, and where Fred liked to hang out. Fred rattled off the answers with ease, and that led to an exchange of war stories about neighborhood characters, showgirls, and wild parties. After that, everyone accepted Fred as genuine.

With the help of his new comrades, Fred soon learned the local

---

weeks after their transfer to SL III.

vocabulary: a "Kriegie" was a POW, a "goon" was a guard, a "canary" was a hidden radio, a "goonbox" was a guard tower, a "goonskin" was a German uniform, a "ferret" wore blue coveralls and probed the ground with long rods (searching for tunnels), the "cooler" was the punishment block of cells, and a "purge" was an arriving batch of new prisoners. He also learned that each day, a Kriegie was posted near the main gate as "duty pilot" to note the movements of the guards, who were counted as they entered and later as they left. If the numbers didn't balance, there was a German sneaking around somewhere. When a goon came around a barracks, the first person to see him would call "Tally Ho" to let everyone know about it. Eventually, goons with a sense of humor would call "Tally Ho" themselves, as a way to say hello.

With escape attempts on hold, the airmen had a lot of extra time on their hands. Some spent their time reading novels or nonfiction, while others took classes that used textbooks from the camp library, taught by POWs with specialized training. There were long, meandering discussions about food and women — the hungrier the men became, the briefer the conversations about women and the more elaborate the discussions about food. There were church services on Sunday, and the Red Cross and YMCA had supplied each compound with enough instruments to form bands that played at the services and in the theaters during musical productions. There was a continual effort on the part of the officers and men to keep morale up and to stay upbeat. Yet none of it seemed to mean much to Fred, who felt isolated from the goings on around him. He wished Sam had been assigned to South Compound, and he wondered how he was doing, wherever he was. It was a real shame that the compounds were totally isolated from one another.

There was a lot of card playing, mostly poker and bridge, accompanied by discussions about back pay, sports, and aircraft. There were arguments over the best heavy bomber — B-24 or B-17? [98] There was incessant banter between bomber crews and fighter pilots. Fred liked to play cards, and he would join in the chatter, especially if other Buchenwald airmen were in the group. Fred's favorite story was about an exchange that took place while he was at Great Ashfield. A fighter from a base nearby had flown over the 385th to drop a big bag of manure on the runway near the planes of the 551st Squadron. In return, the 385th had sent a plane to do a bombing

---

[98] The twin-engine B-26 wasn't in contention — it lacked the range, bomb load, and altitude of its larger brethren — and South Compound held only two (Don Shearer and Paul J. Wilson) of nine Buchenwald airmen who flew the B-26.

run over the fighter base, but rather than dropping a larger load of manure, which was probably anticipated — ground crews scattered as the plane approached — they dropped an elaborate document that read, "We regret to inform you that your commanding officer fell out of his airplane to his death on our airfield yesterday. We share your grief and await the arrival of your representative to claim the body." The story was so popular, and so often repeated, that one of the POWs illustrated it as a comic strip.

The POWs played outdoor sports, but none of the Buchenwald airmen had recovered enough to participate before early November, when severe weather put an end to such pursuits. For days at a time, temperatures were below freezing, and it snowed almost every day. None of the men had heavy enough clothing to stay outside for long, and the daily appell tested Fred's endurance as well as his patience. To conserve the supply of coal, the barracks were unheated during daylight hours. The stoves were used only for cooking and to reduce the nighttime chill in the barracks. Fred spent a lot of time on his bunk, wrapped in blankets, catching brief naps, and wishing he could just sleep until the war was over.

He was still terribly sleep deprived, but he had pretty much given up on getting a good night's sleep. The cold and the nightmares, plus abdominal cramps and pains that struck with no warning, kept jolting him awake. On 2 November, his attempts to sleep were interrupted by air raid sirens and the sound of approaching bombers. There were no air raid shelters, and no slit trenches to hide in, so the men huddled in the room, as a target roughly five miles away was demolished by the RAF. The anxious prisoners could hear anti-aircraft fire and smell smoke, but there was no damage to the camp and no injuries to POWs.

Fred continued to avoid discussing Buchenwald with anyone who hadn't been there. The few times he loosened his guard and, under prodding, tried to describe what Buchenwald was like, the response was disbelief and derisive jokes. It was clear to Fred that his perspective was so different that he might as well be from another planet. So he spent much of his time with Ed, Stan, Roy, Paul, and others with whom he could talk freely.

None of the Buchenwald airmen were doing particularly well at Stalag Luft III. The restricted rations weren't sufficient to rebuild their strength, and each had lingering medical concerns. Fred's vermin bites and ulcerated feet had largely healed, but his mouth still ached, and he was missing 13 teeth. The hard black German bread was unkind even to healthy teeth, and Fred learned early on that when he gnawed on a hard chunk, he could feel his remaining teeth shifting in place.

The only indoor activity Fred was enthusiastic about was writing letters home and waiting (and waiting, and waiting) for a reply. Kriegies could send four postcards and three letters each month. All outgoing and incoming mail was heavily censored. Fred's first letter home, sent in early November, did not reach Brooklyn until late January. It read:

> *Dear Lu,*
>
> *Hello again. How are you and everyone at home? It's been a long time since you've heard about me but now everything is OK. Sam and I were finally taken prisoner and are now in a prisoner of war camp and in good health. Please get in touch with the Red Cross and find out what types of packages and how much you can send and send the limit in food, candy, and tobacco. I don't remember Betty's address and since we are limited in our letters I'll just keep writing to you. The setup here isn't bad at all and there is nothing to worry about as far as I am concerned. Give my love to all and I'll write as often as I can.*
> *Love to all, Fred*

Fred got no response to his letter, nor did he receive any of the parcels from home that sometimes arrived for other Kriegies. He did get the news each day when summaries were narrated by runners, who relayed information from one barracks to the next. The episodic arrival of news from Britain helped them better assess the war news posted on bulletin boards by the Germans, which largely consisted of glowing accounts of Nazi victories.

On 10 November, the news grapevine that operated within Stalag Luft III reported that Lt. Robert A. Burke, assigned to North Compound, had died in the hospital from untreated pneumonia. He had been sick with a fever and a severe cough for ten weeks before admission. Although he had repeatedly pleaded to be taken to the hospital, the Germans had refused. Instead of hospitalizing him, they sent aspirin and cough syrup to his barracks. It was not the first time that neglect had killed a sick airman, and one had died under similar circumstances earlier in the year.

Later in the month, the grapevine brought the news that the Buchenwald airmen left behind in the hospital tent had finally arrived at Stalag Luft III, and that they were being distributed to North and Center Compounds.[99] Shortly thereafter, Fred heard that a fellow

---

[99] H. Bastable, J. Sonshine, E. Carter-Edwards, T. Malcolm, R. Allen, H. Hunter, E. Vincent, R. Ward, W. Bauder, and J. McClanahan arrived at Stalag

American, Lt. Beck, had died in the medical tent on the same day the main group had left Buchenwald. Fred's nightmares that night were even worse than usual. It so easily could have been him.

It had become brutally cold, and frostbite was now a hazard at appell. In response, Fred wrapped cloths around his feet, stuffed them in his shoes, and then wrapped cloths around his shoes as well. Although roughly one-third of the airmen suffered frostbite injuries of one kind or another in late November and early December, Fred was not among them. On 4 December, the weather warmed, and while outside, Fred caught glimpses of a formal ceremony underway in North Compound, where a memorial was dedicated to the airmen executed by the Gestapo following the March escape.

The canaries were reporting that the Russians were advancing across Poland, so the liberation of Stalag Luft III was a real possibility. The news stimulated a lively discussion of what it could mean — whether the Germans would stay and fight, evacuate the camp, or execute the POWs. In expectation of an evacuation, Fred started leaving the barracks to do laps around the perimeter. He knew how weak he had become, and he wanted to strengthen his legs.

Soon thoughts were focused on Christmas. Any remaining hordes of food or spices were tapped in preparation for a grand dinner, and the arrival of some Christmas Red Cross parcels helped immeasurably. On Christmas Eve, the theater held a performance of Handel's *Messiah*, followed by Christmas carols sung by POWs together with the guards and prison staff attending the festivities. After the men left the theater and the compound was locked down, one of the secreted radios broadcast a Christmas message from the POWs to their families in the US. The message was received, recorded, relayed to the US, and rebroadcast on Christmas day by radio stations scattered across the country.

The excitement of Christmas temporarily overshadowed the news reports concerning the continued advance of Nazi forces at the Ardennes, in what would become known as the Battle of the Bulge. That news was followed by reports of the massacre of over 100 US troops by SS units after the Americans had surrendered. The POWs were outraged, and some of the Luftwaffe guards expressed their dismay that fellow Germans would perform such a dishonorable act. Neither Fred nor any of the other Buchenwald airmen were surprised at all.

Fred had accepted the general view among the POWs that the war was in its final stages, and that between the American and

---

Luft III on 28 November 1944.

British forces to the West and the Russians to the East, Germany's defeat was only a matter of time — months at most, and perhaps just a few weeks. Suddenly that optimism seemed unfounded. The Germans were trying to sweep behind the Allied troops to cut their supply lines. If the effort succeeded, the encircled forces would have to choose between annihilation and surrender. That could lead to a lengthy stalemate, or even an armistice that left the Nazis in power, validated their control of occupied territory, and left Hitler free to pursue his genocidal goals while rebuilding the Wehrmacht for another attempt at world domination.

This was not a prospect that made for a happy new year. Of course, it was out of Fred's hands — all he could do was sit tight, fret, and hope for the best. If he hadn't already had trouble sleeping, the thought of concentration camps like Buchenwald being established on Long Island would certainly have kept him up at night.

CHRISTMAS ON THE HOME FRONT

As Christmas approached, the mood stateside was more optimistic than it had been in quite a while. The families of the surviving Buchenwald airmen knew that their loved ones were alive, which was a vast improvement over being MIA. The news had reached them less than a month earlier. However, the families had been busily corresponding for almost two months, after the army released the names and addresses of the Jackson crew to their families in October. On receiving the addresses, Lucille immediately began writing to them to see if any had heard news of Fred.

On 6 November, Lucille received a letter from Mrs. Pennell, Sam Pennell's mother, asking her to stay in touch and let her know if any news was received about Sam. In this way she learned that Sam, like Fred, was MIA. Two days later (8 November), she heard from Ted Dubenic's mother, who reported that Ted was at Stalag Luft 4, adding, "He wrote me some time ago and told me of his Buddy, your brother. Ted likes him very much." Mrs. Dubenic also spoke of her concerns about her other son, who was somewhere in the Pacific on an LST.[100] That same day, Lucille heard from Armando Marsilii's wife, reporting that he was at Stalag Luft 4 with Ted, and doing OK. She also commented that Fred and Mandu were good friends. The next day, 9 November, Lucille got a letter from Mrs. Shaffer, Gerald's

---

[100] Landing Ship, Tank: a large vessel with a ramp at the bow, intended to carry troops and tanks and deliver them ashore for combat operations.

mother, hoping for good news that would never arrive.

On 11 November, Lucille got a letter from Loren Jackson's mother, reporting that Loren, Joseph Haught, and Ross Blake were together in Stalag Luft III. She said that Loren had written and said that one member of the crew had been killed, but censors had blacked out the name.[101] On 13 November, Lucille heard from Ervin Pickrel's mother, reporting that Erv was fine and in the same POW camp as Ted and Mandu. A letter from Ross Blake's mother followed, saying that she had been sending mail and packages to Stalag Luft III for months but had yet to receive a response or acknowledgement. But she hoped Fred and the other men were OK, and reminded Lucille that the plane had not exploded, and that multiple parachutes were seen, so hope remained. When Lucille put the puzzle pieces together, she found that of the ten men in the Jackson crew, three were apparently at Stalag Luft III, three were at Stalag Luft IV, and four remained unaccounted for: Martini, Pennell, Shaffer, and Musquiz. One of the four was dead, but which one?

Lucille dutifully replied to each of these letters. On 14 November, Mandu's wife responded with an aside that said much about Fred's personality, at least in the period before 12 June 1944.

> *The night before they shipped out of Drew Field, Mandu and I had dinner out. We met Fred and a few of the other boys. While I was dancing with Fred he told me not to worry about Mandu, that he would take care of him for me. He also said "Oh don't worry we'll get in our 30 missions and be home in one month."*
> *PS — Chin Up!*

Lucille waited on tenterhooks until, on 9 December, she received a telegram from the War Department stating that her brother was a prisoner of war. It was the best Christmas present she could ask for, and she was crying with relief when she called her sister Betty to give her the news.

On 26 December, Lucille received a letter from Joseph Haught's mother, thanking her for her Christmas card and asking if she had heard the Christmas message sent over the radio from the prisoners at Stalag Luft III (she had not). The next day, she received a letter from Mrs. Pennell saying that she was using the labels provided by the War Department to ship parcels containing six cartons of cigarettes, toiletries, socks, handkerchiefs, and other

---

[101] Loren and the others were in Center Compound of Stalag Luft III, and unaware that Fred was in South Compound.

sundries. She added "Sam mentioned Fred in several of his letters and how well he liked him." So Fred must surely be among friends, but as yet, she had received no word from him. While she waited for a letter, she wrote to Fred each week using the address provided by the War Department. After a long delay, all of those letters were returned marked Undeliverable.

CHAPTER 12

Vengeance

AUGUST - DECEMBER 1944

Wernher Von Braun continued to do his best to drive his various projects forward while the Allies did *their* best to make his life difficult. On 25 August 1944, the day after the devastating B-17 raid on the Buchenwald factories, Peenemünde was struck by a third, even larger bombing raid, putting Test Stand VII out of action for six weeks. Over that period, all test firings had to be done in Blizna, Poland. The site was 620 miles away, which meant Wernher wasted a day in travel each way. It was inconvenient and frustrating to say the least. Making August even more stressful, as the Allies pushed them out of France, they risked losing the French factory (Brown, Bouvarie, and Cie) that produced servomotors for their rockets. At a hastily convened meeting, they found a solution — the French civilian workers would be arrested, enslaved, and shipped to the Mittelwerk with their equipment.

For a time, the V-2 program had competed with the Luftwaffe for funding, as the Führer was impressed with the results of the massed V-1 bombardment of London. But as Himmler, through SS-General Kammler and his SS units, assumed greater and greater control of the V-2 program, resources became much easier to obtain. By early September, Kammler had sent mobile launch teams staffed by thousands of SS troops into Holland and western Germany to prepare for the V-2 offensive. Group North, in Holland, would target London, and Group South, in the Rhineland, would strike Paris and other continental targets. But the first day of the V-2 rocket barrage, 6 September 1944, had not gone as planned. The two rockets fired by Group South both crashed on liftoff or shortly thereafter. Fortunately, successful launches on 8 September struck London (from Group North) and Paris (from Group South). News of the London strike was particularly welcome, as the Peenemünders were still smarting over the British bombing in August 1943.[102]

---

[102] Although decades later von Braun said that he regretted the use of his rockets as weapons, others spoke of champagne toasts and bold talk of his team saving the Fatherland.

General Dornberger was reassigned and relocated from Peenemünde to a new headquarters in Bad Sachsa. He would henceforth be the Army Commissioner for Special Tasks (*Beauftragter zur besonderen Verwendung Heer*), with primary responsibility for mobile V-2 launch equipment, sites, and staff training. The mobile launchers that had been developed under General Dornberger were working as planned, and it took only about 30 minutes to set the rocket onto a launch platform, which could be as small as 70 square feet. The liquid oxygen was delivered by a tanker truck and the missile fueled as quickly as possible, since every minute of delay reduced the range of the weapon due to evaporation of this critical ingredient. Because the launch area was so small and the preparation time so short, camouflage-painted missiles could be fired from small roads passing through forested land with little fear of detection by Allied air patrols. There was a steep learning curve for the SS teams tasked with preparing and launching the missiles, and many of von Braun's trips were to run training sessions for launch crews in Bavaria and Poland.

Wernher was struggling to maintain control of his far-flung operations. He sent his younger brother, Magnus, a chemical engineer, to the Mittelwerk, where he would supervise the assembly of the control units for the steering vanes. The goal was to give him another trustworthy window into operations at the factory. Wernher was simply too busy to be there often enough to be sanguine about quality control. Roughly two dozen completed V-2s were leaving the Mittelwerk each day by rail, and he wanted every one to be perfect. He had hoped that the redesign work done in June and July would drastically reduce the failure rate, but judging by the news from Group South, there was still room for improvement.

Dornberger's reassignment had for all intents and purposes left Wernher von Braun in charge of Peenemünde-East. Despite the increased workload, von Braun's schedule still put him on the road much of the time. He had a regular circuit, traveling overland, rather than by plane, to avoid Allied fighters. He visited launch sites in Blizna (Poland) or Oetzal (Bavaria), took the test results back to Peenemünde, reviewed design modifications, and then delivered the revisions to Albin Sawatski, Arthur Rudolph, and the Quality Control team at the Mittelwerk.

Both quality control and factory output had improved, but they appeared to have reached the limits of the production system. The production target for the Mittelwerk was 1,000 rockets per month, but their output was unlikely to exceed the current 600-700 units per month despite running 24-hour shifts and pushing the staff to their limits. Although output might be increased by taking over areas of the

Mittelwerk being used by the Luftwaffe for jet engine and V-1 production, such a move would be politically difficult, and in any case they would still be faced with labor, material, and fuel shortages. The failure rate remained disconcertingly high, despite the many design changes von Braun's team had made to date. Reports of sabotage continued to reach him, but Sawatski had assured him that it was a problem that Rudolph and the SS would deal with decisively.

He continued to work on the Wasserfall project whenever possible, and the July and August air raids provided incentive to get the anti-aircraft rockets operational. Problems remained with steering and guidance, but it was only a matter of time before they solved them. The question was, would they have enough time? In September, he had presented a proposal that might buy them more time. The idea was to put mobile V-2 launchers in submersible cannisters and tow them across the Atlantic by U-boats. Once in position, the cannisters would surface, to launch rockets targeting major US cities. Preliminary testing had already been completed, and the project was given the green light to continue development.

Morale and motivation was a concern for staff working long hours and juggling multiple complex projects. Funds were tight, so bonuses weren't an option, but Wernher gave rewards, citations, and medals to key personnel. Unless he could keep everyone focused and productive, the Fatherland would be in serious trouble. The only way to secure a just peace was to show that Germany possessed a suite of weapons against which Allied forces had no defense.

By October, there were daily launches targeting London, with additional strikes on Antwerp and Paris. V-2 production had stabilized at just over 600 units per month, and at the same time, Wernher had managed to keep Wasserfall, the anti-aircraft rocket project, advancing rapidly. Innovations adapted from the preliminary A-10 design were underway, designed to increase the range of the V-2 so that even if German forces retreated further, it would still be possible to strike important Allied targets like London. Wernher still maintained that given sufficient time and resources, New York City was within reach, if not with the A-10 then using submarine-towed V-2 launchers. A prototype towable launcher was already being constructed at Stettin, with the goal of having the project operational by March 1945.

On 9 December, Walter Dornberger and Hans Kammler were guests of honor in Schloss Varlar, a grand stone castle in the forest near Osterwick, Germany. The festivities were hosted by Albert Speer, who had spent the day with them visiting V-2 launch sites. In preparation, the SS had set up mobile V-2 launchers in the forested land around the castle. At predetermined points in the evening program of events, the lights in the dining hall were turned out so that the guests could marvel at the thundering roar and brilliant light show that accompanied a rocket's lift-off. Hitler was delighted with the progress of the V-2 program, and on Hitler's orders, Speer awarded Dornberger the Knights Cross of the War Merit Cross with Swords, the highest honor Nazi Germany could bestow. It was awarded only in cases of extreme bravery in combat or heroic military leadership.

Dornberger was not the only designated recipient. Wernher von Braun and Albin Sawatski had also been designated as recipients, but their schedules made it impossible for them to attend the ceremony. Wernher and Albin would receive their awards at a second celebration held in Peenemünde on 16 December 1944. It was a gala event with everyone in uniform or dressed in their finest, in a lavish display of Nazi power and influence. The recognition given to Dornberger, Sawatski, and von Braun acknowledged the importance of the entire rocket team to the war effort.

Wernher wore his finest suit, and Dornberger, seated at his side, was in full uniform with his medals on display. There were illustrated place cards for the festive dinner. These cards were passed around at the dinner table so that everyone could have a good laugh. Wernher's showed him cooking his usual eggs and bacon breakfast with reflected sunlight, while Dornberger's had him shooting a stag at point-blank range. The card for Albin Sawatski showed slave laborers pulling his car out of a ditch, and the card for Georg Rickhey, the general manager for the Mittelwerk, depicted bent slaves hauling a V-2 out of a tunnel while Georg, in his usual pinstriped suit, looked on proudly. This was the only acknowledgment of the slave laborers who made their triumphs and awards possible — as sources of levity rather than concern.

The mood was ebullient, and it promised to be the most festive Christmas season in recent memory for Wernher von Braun. His list of titles already included Vice President, *SS-Sturmbannführer* Baron, Doctor, and Professor, and the newspapers were reporting that V-2 attacks were wreaking havoc and demoralizing the British. But the accolades just kept coming. This would be Wernher's second War Merit Cross, but there were several different grades, and the Knight's Cross with Swords was the most prestigious. Only 118 were ever awarded, and Wernher was beaming with pride as the official photographer took photos throughout the dinner and the ceremony that followed.

All at the party knew that a major offensive had begun earlier that day. It was a sudden and massive attack designed to give the Allies a defeat so disastrous that they would accept an armistice under Germany's terms. Army and SS troops had already broken through the Allied lines at the Ardennes Forest, and what the Allied forces would call the Battle of the Bulge was off to a great start, from the German perspective. The plan was for German forces to sweep around to the west of the Allied front lines to seize the port of Antwerp. Hundreds of thousands of Allied troops would be encircled, trapped, and forced to surrender. The V-2 rockets launches over the last ten days had prepared the way for the Nazi advance.

Wernher was in his element, shaking hands and accepting lavish praise and congratulations. His funding was secure, the V-2s were flying, and Germany's enemies were in retreat. It seemed like Hitler would once again mastermind a stunning victory. Toasts were made far into the night as the radio reports continued to bring only good news. It was a moment to savor, and the rocket team enjoyed it immensely. While they celebrated, a V-2 struck the Rex Cinema in Antwerp. It killed 567 people and injured hundreds more, making it the deadliest V-2 strike of the war.

Wernher was well aware that the aftermath of the Normandy invasion had been a serious setback for Germany. He had already reviewed plans to relocate his team to an underground facility in central Germany if the Russian forces got too close. But that was only one possible future. Germany had lost the last war, but with superior weapons, there was still time to win this one.

Wernher was proud of his team and of their role in saving the Fatherland. Engineering teams with softer hearts or flagging faith in the Reich might have slacked off, but the Peenemünders hadn't complained when he increased their work hours and drove them seven days a week. Key team members were nominated for the War Service Cross. Foreign newspaper articles and photographs of the devastation produced by V-2s striking England and Holland were prominently displayed in the offices and hallways, along with cartoons showing their muscular missiles as national heroes. The Peenemünders were an isolated community that had continued to perform while enduring massive bombing attacks, supply shortages, and production setbacks. They reacted like a medieval city under siege, hunkering down and doing their best.

There was still a shortage of skilled labor on the assembly line. The round-the clock 12-hour shifts burned through laborers relatively quickly, and replacements were continually being supplied by Dora's satellite camps and by Buchenwald, as per his agreement with Commandant Pister. A close eye was kept on Little Camp, as other concentration camps routed their excess prisoners through

Buchenwald for evaluation. The labor reports from Rudolph's office indicated that after a decline in the death rate over the summer, it was again climbing. This was troubling, as training a new worker slowed the production line. However, given the poor rations, executions for shoddy workmanship or sabotage, and the merciless work schedules, there was little to be done about it. Total War came at a high cost.

The festive Christmas mood at Peenemünde continued through the week following the awards ceremony. Wernher heard nothing but good news about the advance of Nazi ground forces, the surrender of Allied troops, and how the offensive had completely surprised the Allies. When he joined the other Peenemünders to sing Christmas carols, he sang with confidence and optimism. He knew that by the end of December, more than 1,500 V-2s would have struck London and Antwerp, with additional launches targeting Liege, Paris, Lille, Ipswich, and other population centers. Between that rain of fire and the hammer blows of the Ardennes offensive, the British and Americans would surely welcome an armistice on Germany's terms.

CHAPTER 13

Into the Storm

As the somber new year receded into the past, Fred continued his daily routine, chatting with Ed and Stan, writing letters that were never answered, playing cards, and trying to keep warm. As he regained some strength, he started taking turns in the kitchen and helping with light chores around the barracks. Keeping busy helped take his mind off of how incredibly hungry he was. At the start of the New Year, rations had been further reduced — Fred received sixth of a Red Cross parcel each week, and any potatoes provided by the Germans were mushy and rotten. At mealtimes, everyone contributed from their meager supplies, and when Fred took his turn as a cook, it was a struggle to make a palatable meal.

The POWs had started to worry that if the Russians approached, the German High Command might order their execution. The daily discussions in the barracks usually focused on food, recipes, and girls (in that order), but now included various "what if" scenarios. This was a subject Fred felt strongly about, so strongly that he overcame his usual reticence. He said there was only one thing to be done if they found themselves facing execution: they should scatter and rush the guards. If even one person could get his hands on a weapon, it would provide a chance to exact some payback, if not clear a path for an escape. There was no way he was going to go meekly, like a lamb to the slaughter. It was a convincing argument, and there was general agreement that it was the best they could do. Meanwhile, as rumors continued to circulate about the advance of Russian troops, Fred continued to brave the cold each day to do a few laps on the perimeter circuit. He hoped it would be useful in an evacuation, but it would also help if everyone had to charge the guards because an execution seemed imminent.

Each evening, the men in the barracks gathered in the kitchen as word was passed from the canaries concerning the status of the war. In early January, Fred learned that the German offensive had stalled.[103] This was great news, but it was followed by even better news — the German troops had begun a steady retreat that rapidly

---

[103] The Nazi forces had advanced so rapidly that they outran their limited supply lines. The original plan had been to capture and plunder Allied supply depots, but resistance at those depots was much stronger than anticipated.

progressed to a rout. Fred's main concern now was how the news (if repeated by the Nazi media) would be received by the camp administration.

Rumors about an evacuation were circulating, and everyone was preparing just in case the rumors proved to be true. Fred extended his perimeter circuits to improve his conditioning, and at times, he was part of a crowd. He was told to keep his personal items stowed so he could move out on short notice, but he really had nothing other than his dogtags and his metal Kriegie badge. On his daily walks, he kept his eyes peeled for scraps of cloth, loose plain papers, or newspapers that could be stuffed in pockets, down his pant legs, or inside his jacket to add insulation. If they had to march, it was certainly going to be cold. He saw other POWs building wagon-sleds from small planks and wooden boxes, to make it easier to bring food and medical supplies.

Fred, good with his hands, helped with some of these projects. He was surprised to see hidden food, money, radios, film, cameras, tools, fake and real IDs, maps, and so forth retrieved from hiding places all over the camp. Some of the stuff had been buried in now-frozen ground, and that explained why concerned POWs were building small fires in odd locations, not for warmth but to thaw the surface below.

All these steps were taken very cautiously to avoid alerting or alarming the camp administration, since nobody knew how they would react if they saw the POWs preparing to leave. They might think there was a mass escape planned, and an overreaction would be potentially dangerous.

On 18 January 45, with the Russian frontline troops less than 50 miles away, Fred wrote:

> *Dear Lu,*
> *I am still anxiously awaiting the arrival of your first letter. It is about eight months since I last heard from you and this waiting to hear whether you are all OK and what is going on is really rough. There is no limit to the amount of letters we can receive so I'll be expecting plenty of mail when they start coming. There is nothing to say from this end except that I am well and with the work I am doing the time is passing as quickly as it can be expected to in a place like this. . . .*
> *Give my love to all and don't you or Betty forget about those letters.*
> *Fred*

But Fred never did receive a reply. By the time the first of Lucille's letters reached Poland, he was long gone.

On 20 January, Fred started hearing the sound of artillery from the advancing Russian forces. Orders came to check that the POWs had at least the recommended minimum supplies: two D-bars, 1/4 lb of cheese, 1/2 lb of oatmeal, half a loaf of bread, and some sugar. Cans of margarine, although heavy, were also recommended both for nutritional value and as a salve to prevent chapping of the lips and other exposed areas of the face.

Yet other aspects of camp life continued as ever, including the planning and rehearsal of a new show at the theater. At 2130 on the night of 27 January 1944, Fred was sitting near the back row of the theatre while the play *You Can't Take it With You* was being performed before a packed house. Without warning, Col. Goodrich suddenly stopped the program, walked onto the stage, and reported that the goons had just given South Compound 30 minutes to prepare for departure. They were to assemble at the front gate.

Pandemonium ensued.

Fred, Ed, and Stan rushed back to the barracks. Fred stripped the blankets from his bed and put on a second layer of clothing, packing the sleeves and legs with newspaper and wrapping cloths around his doubled socks and then around his shoes, as if he were bandaging sprained ankles. A pillowcase would serve as a makeshift pack.

Before heading for the assembly point, the airmen were told to go through the warehouse that stored Red Cross parcels and take whatever they could carry. Fred stuffed every pocket of every layer of clothing with food and helped others load their primitive sleds. He tucked bits of chocolate and loose cigarettes between his layered shirts, and ate the cookies and chocolates he had no place to store. He followed the lead of some of the other POWs, smearing butter over exposed areas of his face to provide additional protection from the elements. Figuring that it couldn't hurt, he also ate as much butter as he could stand, scooping it out of the opened can with his fingers.[104]

Fires were started in the compounds. The POWs burned anything of potential value to the Germans, and the Germans burned anything of potential value to the Russians. Fred could see the flickering lights of a big fire in North Compound through the falling snow as he headed for the main gate.[105] As far as he could tell, neither

---

[104] Officers stashed intelligence documents and other records on their persons or in packages that could be concealed on a sled. Lt. Ewell McCright tied an extra pair of pants around his neck and tucked his POW ledgers within them. These ledgers, which survived the war, are a priceless record of the POW history of South Compound.

[105] In North Compound, it was Block 104, where the tunnel for the Great Escape originated, that burned to the ground.

the Germans nor the POWs were making any attempt to contain the blaze.

What with all of the confusion, there was zero chance that South Compound would be ready to leave in 30 minutes. By the time Fred got to the front gate, weighed down with supplies, it was closer to 2300. He stood in the assembled crowd, stomping his feet and swinging his arms to fight the cold. Snow was no longer falling, but the temperature had dropped further.

Finally, the gates were opened and the order given to move out. It felt good to get moving, even if he didn't know where they were bound. In the initial burst of excitement, some of the POWs got a little carried away and started singing songs (*Off We Go, Into the Wild Blue Yonder* being a local favorite) as they marched, four abreast, along the main road in the darkness. They were treating the evacuation as a lark, assuming that things could only get better, wherever they wound up. Neither Fred nor Ed, who had joined him, felt like singing along. Because Stalag Luft III had been a big improvement over Buchenwald, they knew what the other POWs did not — their destination could be considerably worse.

Fred was part of a ragged column of prisoners. There was empty road in front of them — South Compound had been the first to leave Stalag Luft III — so those near the front, guided by flashlights, had to break through the accumulated snow and those further back, like Fred, had to deal with an uneven surface in total darkness. On either side, armed guards marched with the POWs. A few rows behind Fred, the column ended. Glancing back, he could see a pair of guard dogs and a horse-drawn wagon. The dogs made him nervous, so he quickened his pace, moving a bit farther from the rear.

In the frozen darkness, Fred marched in his own isolated and frosty world. There was no use trying to talk — it was too cold and the wind too strong. Besides, he had to concentrate on keeping on his feet. The makeshift sleds in the line ahead had started falling apart, leaving planks and runners and boxes of food that had to be avoided. He also had to move around men who were trying to scavenge valuable supplies from the wreckage. Fred had to stay alert and pay attention, shifting and maneuvering his way along. Everyone else faced the same challenge, and the pace of advance slowed to a crawl.[106] Fred could hardly believe how cold it was.

---

[106] It took over eight hours to evacuate all of the compounds. Men started leaving South Compound at 2300; North Compound at 0100; West compound at roughly 0200; Center Compound around 0300, and East Compound at 0600 on 28 January. Of the approximately 12,000 POWs held at Stalag Luft III, roughly 500 POWs were left behind for the Russians to deal

The minimum temperature that night was recorded as 7°F, and there were snow flurries and gusty, westerly winds that blew the snow into his face and any exposed openings or seams in his clothing. He had to lean into that biting wind with his packed pillowcase in his arms. After a few hours, it became simply a battle of endurance. Fred could no longer hear the jangling of the horse-drawn wagon behind him,[107] but he knew that the dogs were back there, and the knowledge goaded him on. Every thirty minutes or so, the column paused for a break. At one stop, loaves of bread that had been on the wagon were handed out. Fred took one and tried to eat it, but it was frozen, so he stashed it in his already unwieldy pillowcase pack.

Fred and Ed Ritter lost track of Stan in the darkness. Struggling to keep up, they had slowly but inexorably drifted toward the rear of the column. Frost formed on their exposed hair, on their eyebrows, and on the stubble of their beards. Ice caked on Fred's feet, which had become numb with the cold. He found it even harder to walk through broken snow crust and snow drifts when he could no longer feel his ankles or his feet — his legs might as well have had bricks attached to them. He was continually stumbling and catching himself.

The breaks lasted ten minutes. Whenever one was called, Fred, Ed, and others nearby would collapse in a heap by the side of the road. By the first break, the singing and joking had stopped. For the next few breaks, they had griped about the marching and tried to start small fires to warm themselves. After that, the breaks, like the marching, were silent. Fred, who had neither sung nor joked, remained focused on keeping the pace and not falling behind. He had no idea what would happen to those unable to continue, but he assumed that stragglers would either be shot or left to die of exposure.[108]

As the march continued and men tired, they began jettisoning cargo. The first indication Fred had of this was when he stumbled over a jumbo can of margarine. Soon the snow-covered roadway was littered with debris. The marching continued all night. In the morning, the level of chaos increased as local residents took to the roads desperate to escape the Russians, whose artillery could be

---

with, as they were either too sick or too weak to move.

[107] The horse could no longer pull the heavily laden wagon in the bitter cold, so most of the bread was distributed to the POWs. Prisoners unable to continue were loaded into the near empty wagon for brief periods to recover their strength.

[108] The guards at the rear collected those unable to continue and loaded them onto empty wagons. There is disagreement over the casualty count during the march, but it was probably very low.

heard clearly. In the cold, crisp air, it was impossible to tell just how close the Russians were, but they were certainly close enough to panic the local population.

Fred was pushed to the side by panicked civilians, and the whole column was sometimes forced off the road by horseheading west toward Germany, or truckloads of Army and SS troops headed east into Poland to slow the Russian advance. After getting off the road, it was sometimes a struggle to get back onto it, as the snow was deeper off the edge of the roadway. The breaks were welcome, but as the men were completely exhausted, many fell asleep immediately and were difficult to awaken. Fred and Ed watched one another. If Fred fell asleep, Ed was to wake him, and vice versa. Whether he had dozed or not, Fred always had to force himself to get upright, back on the road, and back into march mode.

Fred saw men fall by the wayside, collapsing from exhaustion, but he had no energy left to help strangers. He hoped that friends or passersby would get them back on their feet. It took all of his strength to avoid joining them. As the afternoon wore on and the snow started falling again, an elderly Luftwaffe guard was marching nearby. Whenever Ed asked him how much farther they had to go, the answer was always three more kilometers.

Visibility was reduced by the blowing snow, and Fred's world shrank to the few feet immediately in front of him. He was marching simply because he was marching. He had no idea where he was going and no clear idea of where he had been. His feet were remote, inert blocks that he steered with his legs.[109] He had lost touch with his nose and his ears as well. Both were frostbitten, as were exposed areas of his wrists and fingers.

Fred fall asleep at least once while marching, going down like a puppet with cut strings, but Ed prodded, cajoled, and ultimately hoisted him back onto his feet so they could continue with the others. His pillowcase was gone, probably lost or stripped away in Ed's battle to get him moving again. No matter, he was too tired to think about eating anyway.

He marched on through the snow, leaning into the wind as he passed through towns and villages. He saw farmhouses, many abandoned with the doors left open. He heard other men talking, but could make no sense of the words. Others were moaning, or he was — it was hard to tell the difference. The sound made by the passing column was soft but eerie, like the mournful wails of the damned.

---

[109] This spared him the pain that he otherwise would have experienced from the blisters and raw, chafed areas on his feet.

Fred ignored the rushing civilians. He just kept his head down and plodded through the broken snow. All he thought about was staying awake and taking the next step. At 1400, after marching steadily for 14 hours, barns were located, and the men were allowed to take shelter for several hours.[110] The barn was unheated, but Fred found a place in the hay near a cow he thought might radiate some warmth. He caught about three hours of sleep before word passed that the farmer who lived there had brought some hot water, so they could make coffee if they had the fixings in their packs. A fire was started outside, and POWs who had taken their shoes off before sleeping had to use it to thaw their shoes before they could pull them back on. Fred opened a small tin of margarine and smeared it on his cracked lips as a balm, smearing the rest on his thawed shoes as waterproofing. Although he tried massaging his lower legs, they remained numb with the cold. He and Ed compared notes on how lousy they felt. They were parched and their voices ragged. Fred chewed some snow, which helped assuage his thirst.

By 1800, it was dark, and the temperature, below freezing all day, was dropping. The men were roused to their feet and sent back into the wind. Fred saw the same German guard Ed had spoken to earlier abandon his rifle, leaving it in the snow. If anybody was going to try to escape, that guard couldn't care less. It had become a battle for survival for all concerned, and it was all Fred could do to keep marching, let alone come up with a viable escape plan.

It wasn't hilly country, but every time the road climbed even by a degree, the column slowed to a crawl. It was just as well — the pace of a crawl was about Fred's top speed. A front came through, causing rapid changes in the weather: first snow, then rain, then hail. On Fred went, stumbling and staggering and sliding, numb with the cold and fatigue, until shortly after 0200 on 29 January, he crossed an icy bridge and entered the German town of Muskau. Fred had been on the road for more than 27 hours and had covered 37 miles.[111]

Once within the town, the column stopped, and Fred stood with the others, waiting for instructions. It was an agonizing wait,

---

[110] This was in the small town of Gross Selten. The POWs were there only because the German officer at the lead got confused and took the wrong road at Priebus.

[111] When evacuating POW camps, the Germans routinely ignored Article 7 of the Geneva Conventions, which prohibited forcing prisoners to march more than 12.5 miles per day. Col. Goodrich estimated that 15% of the men (an estimated 300 POWs) from South Compound arriving at Muskau could not walk without assistance. Sixty prisoners were left in Muskau, too sick and weak to continue.

without even the heat of exertion to fight the cold. He did not know how long he could endure the cold and the exhaustion. He was dizzy, swaying on his feet and barely regaining his balance each time he fell asleep. Finally, at 0400, he was directed to a large factory building with tall smokestacks. It was a glass factory, and when Fred and Ed reached the entrance and stumbled through the door, they walked into a wall of hot, dry air produced by the blast furnaces. It was like a blow from a giant feather pillow.

Ahead of them, men were spreading out and flopping to the floor, too exhausted even to discard their now excessive layers of clothing. Fred managed to shrug off the blanket wrapped around his shoulders and remove his second layer of clothing, laying them out, to the extent possible in the crowd, in hopes that they might dry in the heat of the furnace. He then sank into an exhausted sleep that for once was so deep that no nightmares could touch him.[112]

When Fred awoke, the factory was a hive of activity. There was running water, so those with sufficient energy and motivation were able to wash themselves. Others were using the heat of the furnaces to cook food, and POWs on the second floor found a kitchen area. There was something for everyone. Some of the food provided came from the pockets or sleds of the airmen, but to their surprise, they also received gifts of food from the local residents who took pity on them.

Fred ate what he could, helping himself to soup at every opportunity, for it was warm and easy to chew. He remained in the blissful warmth of the factory all through the day and then had another night of rest before they got the word that it was time to leave, to make room for the arrival of the POWs from West Compound.[113]

At 1100 on 31 January, Fred was marching with the rest toward the west, leaving Muskau behind. The road was still congested by vehicles and by people on foot, some of them leading livestock. As before, the traffic was either going their way (civilians) or opposing

---

[112] The medics in the group were kept busy — 1,500 blisters were dressed. Thus far there had been an average weight loss of 10-20 pounds per POW on the march; Fred's weight would have been roughly 100 pounds.

[113] Each of the camps had taken a slightly different route and some had different destinations. American prisoners from South and Center Compounds were destined to Stalag VIIA, but those from West Compound went to Stalag XIIID, near Nürnberg. British prisoners from North and East Compounds primarily went to Marlag-Milag, a large camp near Tarmstedt, although some from East Compound wound up at Stalag Luft IIIA, near Luckenwalde. The reasons for this distribution are unknown.

them (military personnel). Fred saw civilians digging trenches and makeshift barricades that might slow the inexorable advance of the Russians and buy their families extra time to reach safety. The workers were men of all ages, from boys hardly past puberty to old men barely able to wield a shovel.

The temperatures were high enough that the snow was melting and the surface of the dirt road had thawed. Any sleds that had survived were abandoned, and the contents either carried or eaten. Fred's original treasure trove of supplies had dwindled to a few bits of chocolate and a handful of cigarettes. His outer clothes were still slightly damp, but his inner layer was dry, at least initially, and his mood had brightened considerably. His feet, however, were still not back to normal despite the hours spent in the warm factory and the bandaging of the scrapes, sores, and blisters. Curiously, while the surface of his feet were completely numb, it felt like there were burning coals buried deep under the skin. Every step was painful, and the layer of cold, wet mud that accumulated around his cloth-wrapped shoes did nothing to cool the interior fires.

In the early afternoon, progress slowed as large numbers of airmen were stricken with diarrhea from eating from contaminated cans. Fred passed hundreds of men squatting by the roadside — privacy was a forgotten luxury. At around 1400, Fred was offered meat, bread, and margarine, but his arms were full, and after eight hours of marching, he was more tired than hungry.

After 12 hours of marching along a main roadway, Fred saw a sign identifying the town of Graustein. The POWs were directed to an unheated barn where they would spend the night crowded together for warmth. Some of the men squeezed into chicken coops, but Fred slept on the ground. At dawn, Ed helped Fred to his feet yet again, to join the column as it continued westward.

Word had reached Fred that they were marching to Spremberg, but he had no idea how far away that was nor how long it would take to reach it. To his great relief, it was relatively close, and they arrived at the town around 1130 on 1 February. Their destination was a large Army training base for tank units. Railway lines ran into the base, and there were tanks parked on flatbed cars with young, nervous crews standing by.

The column entered an open area and formed an assembly. Fred and Ed waiting in one of the rows as the POWs were counted by their German escorts. It was boring and extremely uncomfortable, as the process took hours, and they were standing in slushy mud. Finally the counting was done, and Fred and Ed were sent to a heated garage where they were given hot soup.

The welcome respite was short-lived. By late afternoon, Fred was on the move once again, marching two miles though the town to the railroad station, where a chain of boxcars awaited. Fred thought they looked all too familiar. He waited in the cold breeze, trying to keep warm, while livestock were unloaded to make space for POWs. At 1830, Fred climbed into a boxcar with 50 other POWs. It was overcrowded, but not as badly as Fred's trip from Paris to Buchenwald.[114] Fred and Ed, among the first to board their boxcar, sat with legs outstretched. Other men stood or crouched, while a few stood leaning against the wall. The boxcars had solid walls with very small ventilation openings, and as soon as the doors were closed and locked, the air became foul. The waste bucket filled almost immediately, forcing the men to relieve themselves in corners or on batches of straw on the floors. At that point, Fred and Ed decided it was time to stand. The air initially carried the stench of manure, but attacks of dysentery and bouts of vomiting soon added to the general miasma. At some point, Fred found that he'd adapted to the environment, and he no longer noticed the smell.

Fred and the rest spent two days and three nights in that filthy, overcrowded boxcar. The water bucket was soon empty, and everyone became very thirsty. Fred was allowed to leave the boxcar to stretch and relieve himself only twice, once in Chemnitz and a second time in Regensburg. At each stop, he was able to get a drink and a small chunk of bread. Well before dawn on 4 February 1945, the train pulled into Moosburg, roughly 30 miles outside of Munich. The men closest to the doors beat on them, pleading to be let out, but the guards refused. They remained packed in the locked boxcars for the rest of the night.

---

[114] At the train, the men from South Compound were joined by 200 POWs from West Compound who had taken a different route to Spremberg.

CHAPTER 14

Stalag VIIA

-=][=-

Shortly after dawn on 4 February 1945, the boxcars at Moosburg were opened, and the weary men helped one another climb down onto the tracks. Slowly, the prisoners moved onto the adjacent dirt road that ran between the train tracks and a tall guard fence and formed a marching column. It was a gray day. A chill, misty fog covered the flat and open ground.

Fred marched down the road from the train station, eventually arriving at the main gate of the prison camp. A prominent placard announced that this was *Kriegsgefangenen-Mannschafts Stammlagger VIIA* ("POW-crew main camp," abbreviated as Stalag VIIA).[115] A wide road ran through the center of the camp, and ahead he could see a tall, four-storey wooden watchtower unlike any he had seen at Stalag Luft III. Beyond that, he could see fences separated by continuous coils of barbed wire. Their destination was a small, fenced compound at the northwest corner of the camp, where processing and initial medical checks were performed. All of the staff Fred could see wore gray-green uniforms, which indicated to Fred that the camp was run by the German Army rather than the Luftwaffe. At least it wasn't run by the SS.

Fred was searched as he entered, and what little he had was returned. He then stood with Ed and the rest in the drizzling rain within an open area that smelled of rot and waste. A POW in an adjacent compound, who had watched their arrival with interest, called out "Welcome to the Snake Pit." Fred couldn't tell if that was the name of the place they were standing or the camp in general, but "Snake Pit" didn't seem like much of an improvement over "Rock Pile." The compound they were in had a long slit-trench latrine and four large buildings. Guards escorted small batches of men to one of the buildings for processing. When it was Fred's turn, he found that processing began with delousing (a dusting of insecticide powder) and a warm shower. After showering, he was given back his uniform,

---

[115] At this stage of the war, Stalag VIIA had become the primary collecting point for evacuees from POW camps in what had been the German-occupied territories. On 25 January 1945, before the arrival of the men from Stalag Luft III, the prisoner population was estimated to be 77,249. It had been designed to hold a maximum of 12,000 POWs.

smelling of insecticide, and was sent back to a building that was completely empty. There was no furniture, no water, no food, no stove, and a dirty, cold concrete floor. He soon realized that it was also infested with voracious fleas and lice.

Fred and the other airmen spent four long days in that building, cold, damp, and miserable. There wasn't enough floor space for everyone to lie down at once, so while Fred awaited his turn for floor space, he looked for an open corner. When one was available, he wedged himself in and caught a few moments of sleep. Fred put off visits to the uncovered slit-trench latrine as long as possible, as using it in the cold rain was an awful experience. A single, outside faucet was the only water supply, and he drank from it fully expecting the dysentery that followed. He had no other options.

After this period in limbo, Fred was assigned to a barracks in the main compound. Probably for clerical convenience, men who had roomed together at Stalag Luft III were kept together in groups called "combines." Fred's combine was put in a relatively small area for enlisted men that was connected to the compound designated for British and American officers.[116] The barracks was a long, rectangular, wooden building, approximately 150' x 50', with stucco exterior walls and barred windows. An entrance at each end led to a central hallway with triple-decker wooden bunks on either side. The hallways met at a common room in the center of the building, where Fred found a few tables and a water faucet with a hand pump. There was no sink, no toilet, and no stove in the building.

Back in the US, a barracks like that would have held 120 men, but Fred thought there might be as many as 400 men in his building. Bunks were in short supply — if one was empty when you were ready to sleep, you could grab it. Each had a burlap mattress stuffed with straw, as well as a thriving population of lice and fleas. Fred was soon covered in bites, itching and scratching constantly, just like the other men in the barracks. Men slept on the floor, in chairs, and on tables. Fred never figured out if that was because they hadn't been assigned a bunk, or if they were trying to get away from the associated vermin.

The POWs in this camp weren't paranoid about Gestapo spies, and although they grumbled a bit over the increase in numbers, Fred's barracks mates were congenial. They told him that the most important rule was to stay in the barracks from 0900-0930 and 2100-2130 each day, and to return to the barracks during an air raid. Fred soon

---

[116] To the west of this compound was a much larger compound that held POWs from Greece, Serbia, Poland, Italy, France, and Britain. Russian officers and Russian enlisted men had their own, separate, compounds in the southern portion of the camp.

learned that the Germans were serious about the rules — an Army private with severe dysentery who left the barracks to get to the latrine during an air raid was shot and killed.

There was very little to eat, even less than the worst days at Stalag Luft III. The POWs were almost totally reliant on Red Cross parcels. The allocation of parcels, cut in half the previous September, was steadily decreasing as Allied air strikes cut transportation lines, destroyed bridges, and blew trains and tracks to smithereens. With no stove in the barracks, Ed, Fred, and Stan, all in the same combine, built fires outside to provide warmth, heat water, and cook whatever they could scrounge. There was no firewood in the camp, so they burned bed slats, planks from the walls and ceilings, table legs, shingles pilfered from outbuildings, and anything else they could get their hands on. The guards were too few and too distracted to prevent the repurposing of camp property.

Under the terms of the Geneva Conventions, officers could not be used for work details, but those protections did not extend to NCOs and enlisted men. From mid-February through mid-April, Fred and others in his combine found themselves on such details with depressing regularity.[117] Each morning before dawn, guards with barely controlled dogs entered the compound and collected them for work kommandos that each required from 10-30 men. The guards stood outside the door and called for the men to join them. If the response was inadequate or too slow, the dogs were sent in to drive the men out. Fred, unwilling to face the dogs, always emerged promptly. By 0500 each morning, he was marching to the train station to be crammed into boxcars for a one-hour ride to Landshut or, more often, a two-hour ride to Munich.

There were no markings on the cars to indicate that they contained POWs, and Fred's train was occasionally strafed by Allied fighters. Several POWs were wounded or killed in these attacks, and although Fred escaped injury, each attack left him shaking, his heart pounding. He could not bear the thought that after all of the misery he'd endured, he might be killed by friendly fire. Oh, how he hated the sight of boxcars!

Fred could stand and walk, but it wasn't comfortable. After 30 minutes standing in a swaying boxcar, the fires inside his feet were burning. By the time he was let out of the boxcar, every step was painful. He did his best, but he moved slowly when crossing uneven ground, because he had to decide where to place his numb feet. The

---

[117] As of 10 February, an estimated 3,314 British/Commonwealth POWs and 1,784 American POWs were assigned to work details.

ill-tempered guards were already furious and frustrated by the continuous bombing and strafing runs by Allied planes, angry with the Luftwaffe for not defending them, and terrified by the prospect that Germany could lose another war. They vented their frustrations on their charges, clubbing Fred for not walking fast enough, or poking him with a bayonet to keep him moving. He was also cuffed for not working hard enough, for insubordinate looks, and for various other offenses. He had to mutely accept it all, with his head lowered and his eyes on the ground, just as he'd been taught at Buchenwald.

Lethal force was used at the slightest provocation. While on a labor detail, a guard approached a POW working next to Fred. The guard had his hand open and extended, as if to shake hands. When the prisoner turned toward the guard, he was shot through the trunk with a small-caliber palm gun. Fred was splattered with blood as a hole exploded through the man's back. As far as Fred could tell this was an experiment to test an easily concealed palm gun. The guard was clearly unhappy that the collapsed prisoner was still alive. He shook his head, pulled his Luger, and finished the man with a bullet in the forehead. He then sauntered off without a glance at Fred, who stood frozen on the spot.

Fred spent the hours until nightfall clearing rubble and bomb debris. He worried most about the guards, but the work itself was hazardous. The risk of detonating unexploded ordinance was a constant threat. Fred saw several POWs killed that way.

There were other worries as well. On one kommando, two men working nearby clearing rubble were killed by a German civilian armed with a pitchfork. The guards paid little attention, and did not intervene. When Allied fighters or bombers attacked the city, Fred was forced to remain in the open and to keep working rather than seek shelter — anyone running for cover was shot. He worked throughout the day, usually with no food or water provided. Fred came to hate and fear the Army guards almost as much as he had the SS guards at Buchenwald. Forced to stand in the open during a bombing, he rejoiced at the damage done by the bombs. He only hoped that any bombs that fell on him would blow up his guards, too. Fred spent each of these days in a constant state of nervous anxiety, watching the guards, watching for murderous civilians, watching the skies for fighters or bombers, all the while staying alert for unexploded bombs covered by shifting rubble. At the end of each day, bruised and beaten, hobbling on his burning feet, Fred was marched back to the boxcars for the return to the stalag, arriving at the barracks around 2200. It was a horrifying commute.

When he got back to the barracks, Fred still had to find

something to eat and drink before seeking a place to sleep. In late February and early March, this was very difficult, as no Red Cross parcels were delivered, and the camp was on starvation rations. Things got a little better after that, but it was never enough.[118] When no bunks were open, Fred slept on straw scattered on the floor of the barracks or outside in a makeshift shelter, shivering in the cold, infested by fleas and lice, haunted by nightmares, and dreading the day to come. Fred felt like he was slowly fading away. Something had to change, or he wouldn't make it through this.

Fred found that he could avoid the labor kommandos by hiding before the roundup and spending the day slowly carrying small items — a straw mattress, a chair, or anything else light and portable — from one place to another within the compound. When he reached a good out-of-the-way spot, he would find a place to sit and rest his feet before carrying them back again. Ed and Stan caught on, and soon they had a little work party organized. Fred acted as the leader, which meant he no longer had to carry anything, which was much easier on his feet. The trick was to always look serious and busy, much as they had done when working in the rubble of the Gustloff Works. Any guard that noticed them would automatically assume that they were working under orders. Fred had come up with the idea after hearing about two POWs who escaped using a pencil, a small notebook, and a long measuring tape. One man would stop and hold one end of the tape while the other moved along the curb, calling out measurements that were dutifully recorded. The men had been ignored by the guards as they carefully measured their way along the curb, through the gate, and down the road to freedom.

The main problem Fred faced was that he had no alarm clock, and if they weren't up, out, and hidden by 0500, they would find themselves shuffling off to Munich or Landshut. It was a tremendous incentive for him to develop an internal clock.[119] In the moments before sleep, he wondered how Eddie and Lucille were doing, and if anybody knew where he was. The camp was so disorganized and so overcrowded that he hadn't found a way to send letters home, and he no longer expected to receive any mail. He was resigned to the fact that he would only know how everyone was doing after the war ended. He just wished the Nazi bastards would give up sooner rather than later.

Spring came early, and the thawing ground turned into a

---

[118] The Swiss delegation provided marked freight cars for delivering food to the camp, but the allocation per prisoner averaged only 1,000 calories per day, less than half of what was needed.

[119] For the rest of his life, Fred could always guess the time with uncanny accuracy.

shallow sea of mud. As German forces continued to retreat, additional POW camps were emptied and the prisoners sent to Stalag VIIA. The camp population grew to an estimated 120,000 POWs, and things became more crowded and chaotic than ever before. There was no room in the overcrowded barracks, so POWs were housed in grubby tents or left to fend for themselves in lean-tos cobbled together from scrounged boards, pieces of roofing, and other debris. An estimated 90 percent of the POWs had dysentery, and the latrines, which needed a pumpout every two or three days, frequently overflowed.

Fred was pulled into local kommandos sent outside the camp to gather firewood. He figured that the camp administrators must have realized, rather belatedly, that the POWs were disassembling the camp for cooking and heating fuel. Fred was also recruited to help excavate deep trenches between and around the barracks buildings. The guards told the officers in the barracks that the trenches were for protection during air raids, but Fred didn't believe that for a moment. The trenches made him very nervous, as he'd seen them used as mass graves when the Buchenwald crematorium was overloaded. Apparently LtC. Clark was equally suspicious, for word soon spread through the barracks that they should prepare for the worst. Each man was to remove a bed slat and shave it into a makeshift dagger that could be hidden in their clothing. If the Germans tried to line them up by the trenches, they would face a mass attack from the entire prison population. Fred heartily approved. If they were going down, they would go down swinging.

The camp had a small library. Fred dropped by one day and grabbed a couple of small softcover booklets. One was an illustrated book of heroic Luftwaffe songs, and the other an educational volume called *The Germany Book*. He found that the latter provided a good look at the propaganda that was part of the foundation of the Third Reich. He was particularly bemused by the following passage:

THE DICTATED PEACE OF VERSAILLES LEFT GERMANY MUTILATED AND CRIPPLED, AND WITHOUT THE MEANS OF MAINTAINING A LIFE OF ITS OWN. BUT THE SEEDS OF A NEW BEGINNING WERE ALREADY SOWN. THE GREAT BATTLE FOR SURVIVAL WHICH THE GERMANS HAD WAGED DURING THE WAR HAD CONFIRMED AND STRENGTHENED THEM IN THE DESIRE FOR UNITY. ADOLF HITLER BECAME THE SYMBOL AND THE INSTRUMENT OF THIS DESIRE. . . . THE CUTTING-UP OF THE GERMAN PEOPLE, WHICH HAD BEEN DICTATED AT VERSAILLES, WAS REVERSED. THE

SUDETENLAND (1938), BOHEMIA AND MORAVIA (1939), MEMEL (1939), DANZIG (1939), EUPEN-MALMEDY (1940), LUXEMBURG (1940), AND ALSACE-LORRAINE (1940) WERE JOINED AGAIN TO THE REICH; THE DESIRE OF THE DIMINISHED STATE OF AUSTRIA FOR REUNION WITH THE REICH WAS FULFILLED AS EARLY AS 1938.

THE GERMAN GOVERNMENT NEVER LEFT ANY DOUBT AS TO ITS PACIFIC INTENTIONS. . . . THE NEW GERMAN SOCIAL STATE WAS TOO BUSY WITH INTERNAL REFORMS TO HAVE MORE THAN ONE AIM FOR ITS FOREIGN POLICY: THE SECURING OF PEACE FOR A LONG PERIOD. NONAGGRESSION PACTS WITH NEIGHBOURING STATES, MAGNANIMOUS PROPOSALS FOR DISARMAMENT AND CONSTRUCTIVE SUGGESTIONS FOR THE MAINTENANCE OF PEACE PROVED THE SINCERITY OF THIS AIM. NEVERTHELESS, CERTAIN CIRCLES ABROAD AGITATED AGAINST THE PEACEFULLY WORKING REICH UNTIL WAR FLARED UP. SINCE THEN GERMANY HAS BEEN FIGHTING FOR ITS SOCIAL ACHIEVEMENTS, FOR ITS INDEPENDENCE AND ITS NATIONAL EXISTENCE.

Fred thought so highly of the educational content of this work that he wrote all over it. Around the Table of Contents, he wrote an abbreviated timeline of his experiences, under the heading *A Tale of Woe in the ETO*. Inside of the front and the back covers, he recorded the names and home addresses of men in his combine. The list of names was a mixture of men from Buchenwald, men from Stalag Luft III, and men from Stalag VIIA.[120] There were many other men for whom he really wished he had contact information, but finding a particular individual in a mass of over 100,000 hungry and frustrated men was almost impossible. So he settled for those in his immediate

---

[120] The men were Russ McMains (IA), Ambrose G. King, Jr. (NY), Edward Lahiff (OR), Joseph Kennedy (VT), John T. Ryan (NY), Warren E. Tupper (MA), Chastin Bowen* (CA), Ernest Greer (OK), Merle A. Troup (PA), Roy Jos. Horrigan* (LA), Nelson C. Clairmont (NY), Bernard Scharf* (MN), James Zeiser* (OH), Michael A. Petrich* (CA), George Friedman (NY), Carl Peterson (MN), Ben Tennant (WV), Frank Sullivan (IL), Albert "Gunner" Griffre (NY), Ervin Roberts (MI), Floyd Green (DC), Charles "Chuck" Arnold (PA), Stanley K. Paxton* (CA), Gilbert R. Lish (ID), John H. Hawk (KS), James F. Gillett (IA), Robert E. Honig* (IA), Harold Barchman (IA), Perry L Curtis (MI), Dwayne Blackman (IA), Raymond B. Orogco (CA), George Friedman (NY) and Ledford A. Walling (SC). Those with asterisks were fellow Buchenwald airmen.

area.

Fred had grown used to Allied fighters flashing overhead on their way to strafe targets around Moosburg and in the Munich suburbs. Oddly enough, they never bothered him when he was in the POW camp, whereas they terrified him when he was on a kommando in Munich. In early April, on one of the rare days he overslept, he was in Munich once again, clearing debris at the Munich train station when a staggering number of B-17s rumbled overhead, dropping their bomb loads on the city. Fred had nowhere to hide and simply hugged the ground and hoped for the best while the entire city bounced and shook around him. It seemed like the end of the world.

Stalag VIIA was more chaotic than ever. Thousands of additional POWs had arrived, and the camp was awash with prisoners. There was debris and rubbish everywhere, and although it was late when he returned from Munich, there were POWs squatting by makeshift fires, while others slept on tarps spread on the ground.

On 13 April, Fred was stunned to hear that President Roosevelt had died. It infuriated him that the camp guards were celebrating his death. For some reason, the Germans thought that Roosevelt was equally detested by the Allied military, and they started putting up posters in English imploring POWs to let bygones be bygones and to take up arms with the Germans against the advancing Russian hordes. If Fred hadn't been so tired and hungry, he would have been amused. The Germans had to be getting desperate and delusional! He wasn't sure what that meant, but he hoped it meant the war was almost over.

Things were definitely changing. The internal structure of the camp seemed to be breaking down under the press of additional prisoners. Fences between compounds were disappearing, and the guards weren't doing anything to replace them. The guards seemed really unsettled when, within a week after Roosevelt's death, the daily bombing runs suddenly stopped. The Germans feared the worst, and a guard offered to help Fred escape if he could accompany him to America. The guard certainly didn't want to stay in the camp any longer — it was a filthy, reeking, overcrowded mass of near-starved prisoners living in squalor. There were too many to feed, and it was becoming clear that there were too few guards to maintain control as the prisoners grew increasingly restive.

Word was spread that LtC. Clark had ordered the men to prepare to evacuate the camp, and that they would be marching south in a few days. But nothing came of it, and Fred stayed put.[121]

___

[121] Unbeknownst to the camp administration, a deal brokered by the Swiss

Everyone in the camp, guards and prisoners alike, seemed to be holding their breath. When Fred awakened on the morning of 29 April, he could hear tanks and other armored vehicles approaching, but he didn't know if the equipment was American or German. Guns were firing in the distance.

At around 0800, he was startled to see SS troops entering the camp. Fearing the worst, he moved to a position where he could see what they were up to. To his surprise, they were grabbing the guards and pushing them toward the gate. The guards were refusing to go. Surprise turned to amazement when the SS troops responded by shooting the Army guards and throwing grenades into their barracks. The guards assumed defensive positions and returned fire, and a small battle ensued. It ended when the SS personnel rushed back out of the camp. Fred had no idea where they were going, but it was a relief to see them leave.

At 0945, Fred could hear machine guns firing and see fighter planes approaching. Two fighters strafed the camp, blowing apart a guard tower. As they made another run, Fred dove into a nearby slit trench while bullets zinged around the camp. Fred, determined not to die as an accidental casualty, used his hands to make the slit trench a little deeper. When the planes moved off, Fred emerged to the sound of approaching tanks. When they came into view, and he saw the white US Army symbols, he felt a tremendous rush of relief. After a brief pause, a tank rolled forward and flattened the main gate. Jeeps then entered and stopped before a small contingent of unarmed guards and senior camp administrators. After an informal surrender, the German guards waited patiently while guards from other areas of the camp joined them, tossing their weapons in a pile, and waiting for instructions. The guards were soon loaded into trucks and taken away. Fred hoped they would enjoy their POW experience as much as he had.

The tanks and jeeps moved forward, the tanks mowing down the gates between the compounds as rejoicing prisoners poured out of the barracks and ran to meet them. It was pandemonium. Men were cheering, shouting, and crying, all at the same time. The noise peaked when the American flag was raised on the Moosburg flagpole, and again when it was raised on the camp flagstaff.

---

had been struck between the Allies and Germany. Under the terms of the agreement, no further POW movements would be ordered. In return, liberated POWs would not be returned to active military service. LtC. Clark heard about the agreement in a BBC radio broadcast. When ordered to evacuate, he refused, advising the guards to check with their superiors. The assembly order was not mentioned again.

Fred was caught up in the general mood, pressed into the surging mass of men who were enthusiastically cheering their liberators. The long ordeal was finally over, and in many ways, it seemed unreal. His emotions seemed beyond his control. He was elated at being liberated, then angry at the Germans, then worried about the future. Sure, he had survived, but how could he ever explain any of this to Lucille, Betty, or anyone else in his family? And how could he leave Europe without knowing who had betrayed him and what had happened to his French "family," the Raulins?

Looking out over the sea of prisoners toward the entrance, he realized that the front gate had been repaired, but it was closed, and American guards were posted. Fred found that disconcerting. When, exactly, were they going to leave this hell-hole?

CHAPTER 15

A Strategic Retreat

⊰∃⊱

As the German breakout into Allied territories stalled, Hitler and Speer decided that winning the war, or at least negotiating a favorable armistice, would now depend on their "secret weapons" programs such as the V-2, jet aircraft, and anti-aircraft rockets. Himmler continued to maneuver for increased control over these programs, highlighting his abilities to increase efficiency and provide security, while Göring's influence continued to wane as the Luftwaffe proved unable to stop Allied air strikes. So in early 1945, a number of organizational changes were made.

On 15 January 1945, Speer nationalized all aspects of rocket production and placed them under the control of a team known as Working Staff Dornberger, with General Dornberger as chairman. Two weeks later, SS-General Kammler was given control of military and civilian projects for the Luftwaffe. Dornberger was appointed as Kammler's deputy, and Working Staff Dornberger would report to the SS rather than the Army. To consolidate control over all aspects of production, all key manufacturing work would henceforth be done in the Nordhausen/Mittelwerk area of central Germany.

In the second half of January, everyone at Peenemünde knew that the Russians were coming. The front line was only 30 miles away, and if German defenses collapsed, Peenemünde would quickly be overrun. Wernher felt that the obvious solution was to pack up and move to a more protected location, such as the Nordhausen area where Dornberger was already based. But when he brought this up at a staff meeting, the local Army commander and the head of the Gestapo at Peenemünde were outraged, all but accusing him of cowardice. They had been adamant that the engineers must stay in place and on task to the bitter end. Any further discussion of leaving Peenemünde would be considered treasonous. Wernher thought this was just bluster, but he soon learned how serious they were. When Gestapo spies heard several of his engineers talking about abandoning Peenemünde, their bodies were hung around the facility with signs around their necks. The signs warned that leaving your post was not an option.

Wernher thought a stand the last policy was ludicrous. His team was responsible for producing the weapons Germany needed to defeat its enemies, and they needed time and focus to do that. How could they succeed if the Gestapo kept hanging his engineers? They were doing the Russians' work for them. Things were clearly getting out of hand, but it would not be safe to discuss potential solutions anywhere on the property — security was too tight and the Gestapo had ears everywhere. So he quietly passed the word to key personnel that there would be a clandestine meeting at the Inselhof Hotel in Zinnowitz, a seaside community 12 miles southeast of Peenemünde. Key deputies attended: Ernst Steinhoff, Eberhard Rees, Ernst Stuhlinger, and Werner Gengelback, with Wernher's secretary, Dorette Kerstein, present to take notes. Just getting to the meeting was difficult and potentially dangerous, and they had to leave separately with impeccable alibis.

Wernher chaired the meeting as usual and discussed the problem in blunt terms. The Fatherland was fighting for its life, and their projects could turn the tide of the war. But the Army and the Gestapo were making it impossible for them to reach their goals. The Russians were on their way, but they couldn't leave. He had only been able to come up with three alternatives.

The first option was to obey orders, sit tight, and wait for the Russians to arrive and execute or imprison them. If that happened, Germany would lose its best hope for victory, and the Russians would gain equipment and records they could use to conquer the western world. The second option was to find a way to convince somebody in higher authority, like Speer, that they should be relocated for the good of the Reich. The only other option he could see was to surrender en masse to the Allies before the Russians got there. Wernher thought the Americans would be the best choice, as none of V-2 missiles had been launched against US targets. Everyone agreed that the first option was unacceptable, the second unlikely, and the third logical but impractical. The only enemy forces nearby were Russian, and even if American forces had been close, any attempt to contact them would soon be detected by the Gestapo, and they would all be shot as deserters. It was a very depressing meeting, as no solutions were found to their dilemma.

While the core team evaluated their options should Germany's forces continue to give ground, design and testing continued at Peenemünde. On 24 January, they launched an A-4b equipped with wings as well as the standard tail fins. This launch was related to three of the projects Wernher was juggling simultaneously. First and foremost, it would verify that the design modification would increase the tactical range of the V-2 — something that would permit the bombardment of London to continue, even if the Russians occupied

Peenemünde. Second, if successful, the design could form the basis for a manned rocket plane capable of launching air air or air ground missiles that the Luftwaffe was already testing. Third, the A-4b was originally intended to be the first stage of the multi-stage A-10 intercontinental missile that the Peenemünde group called "the New York Rocket." After 1942, when Hitler became enamored of the rocket program, he had a massive launch bunker built in France for A-10 rockets that would target the east coast of the US. Unfortunately, Wernher's team had become bogged down in the V-2 design modifications, impeding progress on the A-10. The project was still worth pursuing — if the V-2s did their job, he would have the time to push the A-10 to completion. He was delighted when the launch and trajectory went exactly as planned, and although one of the wings peeled away on reentering the upper atmosphere — some structural improvements would be needed to handle those forces — he considered the test to be a resounding success.

Wernher still hadn't solved the problem of how to avoid the approaching Russians, and everyone remained anxious about the future. But then he received orders to attend a committee meeting with SS-General Kammler on 29-30 January at the Mittelwerk to discuss the advanced weapons projects. Wernher attended as Technical Director of Elektromechanischewerk (EW) GmbH,[122] head of the Committee for Final Acceptance in the A-4 Special Committee, and head of the Quality Control Group for manufacturing at the Mittelwerk. Because he was uncertain as to how the meeting with Kammler would go, he wore his full *SS-Sturmbannführer* uniform with the Knight's Cross around his neck.

At the meeting, he was surprised to learn that his authority and responsibilities were expanding further. Kammler commended his work to date and appointed him Technical Director of the newly created Central Construction Development Cooperative at Mittelbau (CCDC-Mittelbau). The CCDC would coordinate the activities of the approximately 30 firms involved in producing the components for advanced weapons. Wernher was flattered and gratified — this was a great honor, placing him in a key position and giving him much more authority. He would be responsible not only for overseeing the assembly and testing of V-2s, including the A-4b, but also the submarine-mobile launching system, the V-1 flying bomb, the Taifun anti-aircraft rocket, the Orkun airair rocket, and the Wasserfall guided missile. These were to be produced at newly constructed underground facilities, part of the Bauvorhaben X complex.

---

[122] The privatized corporation at Peenemünde, established in August 1944.

The very best news of all soon followed: Wernher was ordered to shift all remaining EW GmbH operations from Peenemünde to Bleicherode, a small community conveniently close to the Mittelwerk and the new satellite facilities. Bleicherode, which was 248 miles from Peenemünde, would henceforth be the epicenter of CCDC-Mittelbau. This was far from the front lines — Russian or American — and safely in the heart of Germany.

When he returned to Peenemünde, his world was considerably brighter, and he started making plans to relocate his staff and equipment. When they got wind of this, the Army commander and the Gestapo chief stormed into his office demanding an explanation and making dire threats. Wernher called Kammler's office, and later that day (1 February 1945), a terse directive from SS-General Kammler confirmed Wernher's authority and told the Army and Gestapo to get out of his way.

On 3 February, Wernher held the final planning meeting with his deputies. There were 4,325 staff at Peenemünde involved with missile design, production, and testing. He considered roughly 1,200 of them nonessential, and he would leave them behind to destroy records and equipment before they fell to the Russians. Using his newfound authority, backed by SS-General Kammler's clout, Wernher arranged to have a train waiting at the station and a truck convoy ready to roll as soon as the rest of the staff were ready to leave.

The next two weeks were occupied packing up the important documents, which went into color-coded Official passes were printed in large quantities because SS roadblocks and security checks were everywhere, and Wernher wanted nothing to slow their departure — he wanted to get away from the Russians as quickly as possible. As ordered, the passes were to authorize the passage of personnel and equipment for BZBV, because *Beauftragter zur besonderen Verwendung Heer* (Commissioner for Special Duties Army) was General Dornberger's official title.

Due to an error at the printer, the papers arrived filled out, stamped, and officially approved in the name of VZBV. When he saw the error, Wernher felt a moment of panic — there was no time to get corrected paperwork through the pipeline. But on reflection, he realized that it didn't really matter. After all, BZBV was a secret organization that a lowly SS officer at a road block would never have heard of, so the difference between BZBV and VZBV was meaningless as long as the paperwork was in order. He quickly made up an alternative definition that sounded convincing — *Vorhaben zur besonderen Verwendung* (Project for Special Disposition) — and had all of the crates prominently labeled VZBV to match the clearance documentation.

When the first train departed, it carried 525 key members of the rocket team, their families, and boxcars filled with documents. To make sure they moved quickly through security checks, Wernher wore his SS uniform and his Knights Cross, and pulled rank as needed. The train was headed to the village of Bleicherode, close to the opulent ski resort community of Bad Sachsa where General Dornberger's headquarters was located. Bleicherode was also close to the Mittelwerk and to the newer underground facilities of the Bauvorhaben X complex; all were within a 25-mile radius.

The 360 miles between Peenemünde and Bleicherode passed without incident, although progress was probably slower than anyone would have liked. Once in Bleicherode, Wernher took over the luxurious home of a Jewish factory owner who had prudently opted to leave Germany in 1933, around the time that Hitler rose to power. Wernher's new headquarters, the former administration building for a mining company, was only 12.5 miles from the Mittelwerk.

A total of 264 V-2s were launched from Peenemünde. The last two headed for London on 19 February 1945. Eight days later, Wernher returned to Peenemünde for the last time, to brief the staff who had yet to move as to what awaited them. Some would be assigned to the test sites set up for each of the projects he was responsible for, while others would work at the Mittelwerk, overseeing production, or in Bleicherode assisting with design improvements. The nonessential employees were already aware of their responsibilities. When the Russians occupied the complex, they would find the staff gone, the paperwork burned, and the launch pads demolished.

The Mittelwerk was now a major facility in every sense of the term. There were 2,000 civilian workers overseeing thousands of slave laborers who worked 12-hour shifts day and night. There were over 40,000 concentration camp prisoners in Dora and its satellite labor camps. The best known of these satellite camps were Lager Ellrich, Lager Harzungen, and Lager Rottleberode, but there were 35 other labor camps linked to Dora, providing laborers for the SS construction units involved in the expansion of the Bauvorhaben complex.

The Dora/Nordhausen camp was now functionally two concentration camps, one housing and supplying slave laborers for the Mittelwerk and the other warehousing exhausted workers incapable of further work or workers rejected as incompetent or unmotivated by the civilian overseers. The warehousing operation was just that — no medical services or support were provided, food was minimal, and the death rate unusually high, even by Dora standards.

Wernher kept track of such details in his role as Director of CCDC-Mittelbau. The Bleicherode operation was complex, involving both design and production of multiple weapons systems, and he communicated regularly with Sawatski, Rudolph, and Rickhey at the Mittelwerk, with Dornberger at his HQ, with Kammler's office, and with Sonderinspektion II, the SS division that provided materials and slave labor. He was constantly on the go, driving himself to his limits, visiting subcontractors, dealing with technical issues, approving design changes, attending test firings, and managing quality control. At every stop, he encouraged team members to work harder and longer and more efficiently.

On 3 March, Wernher circulated a detailed memo outlining his plans for reorganizing and redistributing the production of V-1s, jet engines, and Wasserfall, and for increasing the number of V-2 test sites. The plan coordinated the efforts of 30 corporations with a combined workforce of 7,000, and would require many thousands of additional slave laborers for the construction or enhancement of underground facilities.

Work on the remodeling of two calcium mines near Bleicherode was well underway. But it wasn't proceeding fast enough for Wernher. He decided that the original plan had to be modified to suit the realities of the war. Rather than wait for the new facilities to be completed, they would make immediate use of what was available. As Wernher stated in his memo:

> FACED WITH THE CURRENT REQUIREMENT TO RESUME DEVELOPMENT WITHIN THE LEAST POSSIBLE TIME, WAITING FOR THE UNDERGROUND WORK PLACES TO BE COMPLETED IS NOT PRACTICAL. IN ORDER TO QUICKLY RESUME DEVELOPMENTAL WORK, IT IS NECESSARY TO MOVE INTO EXISTING ABOVE-GROUND FACILITIES, INSOFAR AS NEW FACILITIES ARE NOT PLENTIFUL. IT SHOULD BE CONSIDERED THAT A LARGE PORTION OF THE WORK (FOR EXAMPLE CONSTRUCTION OFFICES AND ADMINISTRATION, ETC.) SHALL REMAIN FOR DURATION ABOVE GROUND.[123]

Wernher knew that his plans would succeed only if sufficient laborers could be provided by the SS. In the memo circulated to important figures in the SS, the CCDC, and the Mittelwerk, he requested immediate authorization for the construction of 150,000

---

[123] Fort Eustis microfilm collection, Roll 40, NASM, Chantilly, Virginia.

square feet of additional barracks space, with the notation that additional requests were pending.

On 12 March 1945, Wernher left Bleicherode at 0200 in a chauffeured car. He was heading to Berlin for a morning meeting about the new laboratory that he planned to set up in the Mittelwerk. Although the space had already been created through the relocations ordered in his memo of 3 March, he needed funds for the laboratory. He also needed approval to get a significant number of unskilled laborers from the Dora concentration camp for excavation and construction work.

A chase car followed behind. Sometime before dawn, Wernher's driver either fell asleep or lost control, and the car went off the road and down a steep embankment. Von Braun dragged himself clear and then got the driver out of the vehicle before passing out. He awakened in the hospital with a broken arm. He spent the next two days in a hospital bed, frustrated, bored out of his wits, and itching to get back to work, before he could browbeat the staff into releasing him. When he left, his left arm was in a heavy plaster cast. He immediately returned to work, visiting launch sites, testing facilities, and the production lines at the Mittelwerk.

Wernher found that conditions at the Mittelwerk had deteriorated and that the laborers looked worn and tired. The failure rate for operational V-2 launches had been greatly reduced, but there remained evidence that some of the failures were the result of deliberate sabotage — faulty welds, improperly torqued fittings, subtly misaligned tail fins, and so forth. There were more SS guards in the assembly halls than he had seen on previous visits. Rudolph told him that many of the laborers had been transferred from a concentration camp called Auschwitz.[124]

Between the death rate in the warehousing area, the executions at Dora and the Mittelwerk, and the death rate among the unskilled labor force, the Dora crematorium could not keep pace. Bodies piled up outside the tunnel entrances, waiting to be dumped into open trenches where they could be burned. Wernher tried not to look at the piles too closely, nor at the trenches by the roadside. He found the news from the front lines almost as grim. After the collapse of the Ardennes offensive, the Reich had been losing ground, and the

---

[124] The number of executions for suspected sabotage increased when the SS guards from Auschwitz arrived. Many of the executions were performed at the production facility in the area just outside of Arthur Rudolph's office; it was Rudolph who signed the papers authorizing their execution. An estimated 300 skilled laborers were executed for sabotage on the factory floor in March 1945.

process was accelerating. Dornberger's reports indicated that the mobile V-2 launchers were moving farther and farther from their targets, and there had been no time to convert the production lines to handle the A-4b. The last V-2 rocket to reach England, launched on 27 March 1945, missed London and landed in Kent.

During the campaign, 1,300 V-2 missiles had been fired at London. Of that number, 518 hit that target and the rest struck outlying areas. The death toll in the UK was 2,700. Another 1,265 V-2s struck Antwerp, at a cost of 3,565 lives. To produce those weapons, an estimated 20,000 prisoners from the Dora camps died while working at the Mittelwerk and related facilities of the Bauvorhaben X complex. Thus the V-2 had the singular distinction of killing roughly four times as many people during production as it did in combat.

On 3 April, SS-General Kammler ordered all key members of the rocket group, including Wernher and his team at Bleicherode and Working Staff Dornberger at Bad Sachsa, to relocate to the Messerschmitt jet aircraft design center in Oberammergau, a small village at the foothills of the Bavarian Alps. There they were to become part of Kammler's official staff. Over the next two days, Wernher learned that Hitler had promoted SS-General Kammler to *SS-Obergruppenführer* [125] the highest commissioned rank in the SS. He was put in charge of all jet aircraft and airfields. For all practical purposes, from now on, Göring would be reporting to Himmler. Wernher wasn't surprised that Himmler had finally won that political battle — he was certainly deft at political maneuvering. It wouldn't affect him at all, given that he was already managing the super-weapons programs for the SS and reporting directly to Kammler.

While ferreting out these details, Wernher was thinking about his longterm future. He knew that the war was nearly over and that the Reich was on its last legs. There was no question that it was time to leave Bleicherode behind, and Oberammergau, 400 miles from Nordhausen, was suitably far away. American tanks were only twelve miles south of his office, and he didn't want to be anywhere near Mittelbau or Dora when those facilities were overrun. He shuddered to think what the Americans would think about the condition of the workers. If he was to lead a group to Oberammergau, who should he take? What should they bring with them? What should be left behind for the Americans to find? What steps could he take to ensure that he would emerge unscathed when the war ended?

---

[125] The equivalent of a three-star general in the Army.

Once he came up with a plan, he lost no time setting it in motion. All of the equipment at the Mittelwerk would be abandoned, but they would take the gear from the Bleicherode facility. The key engineering documents and paperwork would be hidden in a secret location from which they could be retrieved at some later date. If Hitler worked some miracle, they could be retrieved. If the war ended as he feared it would, that cache would be his bargaining chip or insurance policy as needed. All nonessential paperwork would be burned.

Wernher called in his technical assistant, Dieter Huzel, who had replaced Magnus von Braun when Magnus was sent to the Mittelwerk. He told Dieter to begin collecting and crating the documents, and that he would be responsible for hiding them in a suitable location once one was selected. The next day, 7 April 1945, Wernher arranged for Bernhard Tessmann to assist Dieter, along with a truck and an Army corporal with eight men to do the heavy lifting. As to a location for the cache, he suggested that Dieter contact the local mining businesses for information concerning suitably remote and abandoned tunnels.

Oberammergau was the location of the Alpine Redoubt, an imposing and dignified name for an old army base. With the Allies continuing to advance, 400 members of his team headed to Oberammergau by train, accompanied by 100 uniformed SD guards. Wernher left by car the same day (7 April 1945) in convoy with 20 truckloads of gear. Dieter Huzel, Bernhard Tessmann, and their soldiers quietly drove their truck in another direction, loaded down with 14 tons of top secret documents. They were going to store the crates in an abandoned mining tunnel near the village of Doernten.

As soon as he arrived in Oberammergau, Wernher was called to a meeting with SS-General Kammler at the Hotel Alios Lang. When he got there, Kammler was otherwise occupied, preparing for an urgent trip, and one of his deputies, SS-Major Kummer, had been placed in charge. Kummer had no idea why von Braun had been called in, but Wernher took the opportunity to ask permission to disperse key members of his team into the surrounding communities, using the vehicles in his convoy. Such a move, he explained, would increase security and decrease the possibility that an air strike would kill the entire team. Kummer seemed unconvinced until Allied fighters made several strafing runs over the compound, whereupon Wernher received permission to proceed.

While Wernher was deciding who to take and working out the logistics, Huzel and Tessmann returned and reported the success of their mission. Since they knew the location of the hidden paperwork cache, Wernher took them with him on 15 April, when he shifted from Oberammergau to the town of Weilheim, closer to Munich. It was a very small group that slipped away — just Wernher, Huzel, Tessmann, Wernher's brother Magnus, and a few others.

CHAPTER 16

Revelations

◆❧❦◆

NORDHAUSEN

American troops liberated the Dora Concentration Camp on 11 April 1945. It was the first slave labor camp to be liberated by the US Army, and the officers leading the troops had difficulty believing what they found. The SS had been given orders to kill all of the prisoners before leaving, but they had lacked the time and equipment to obey. Most of the prisoners had been marched, trucked, or taken away by boxcar, to be killed elsewhere. The prisoners left behind were either near death or otherwise incapacitated by injury or disease.

It was a sight that left the soldiers stunned, sickened, and speechless. There were scattered bodies, mounds of corpses, and trenches filled with bodies. The sense of horror only grew as they approached the Mittelwerk. There were 6,000 bodies stuffed in the trenches on either side of the roadway leading into the tunnels. The stench was appalling. Many of the bodies showed signs of repeated, severe beatings. The condition of the few surviving prisoners found in the tunnels defied description — skeletons dressed in rags, often unable to stand or even sit up. Later the same day, US troops liberated Buchenwald, finding conditions equally horrific.

The liberating troops would be haunted by what they witnessed at Dora, Buchenwald, and other concentration camps. But the technical discoveries at the Mittelwerk provoked a very different reaction within the US intelligence community. By 1944, the Joint Chiefs of Staff had become deeply concerned, if not outright spooked, by the German technological advances their spies were hearing about. Late that year, the intelligence was confirmed as anti-aircraft rockets, jet aircraft, flying bombs, and rockets that flew too fast to detect and counter made their combat debuts. Equally unsettling were the rumors about weapons yet to be brought online, such as intercontinental rockets, super-artillery capable of shooting more than a hundred miles, and — most chilling of all — atomic bombs that could be carried by those rockets and flying bombs.

The pre-D day plans to seize intelligence on these weapons to further the war against the Nazis and the Japanese had been reassessed and enhanced. There were now multiple teams assigned to specific intelligence programs under the direction of the Combined Intelligence Objectives Subcommittee (CIOS). That group included representatives of the US War Department, Army, Navy, State Department, Office of Strategic Services (OSS), Office of Research and Development, and Foreign Economic Administration, plus the UK Foreign Office, Admiralty, Air Ministry, and other ministries concerned with the funding and production of war-related materials.

The CIOS set up intelligence teams embedded in special military units known as T-Forces or Tiger Teams. The T-Force units were responsible for capturing and interrogating Nazi scientists, and seizing scientific paperwork and equipment. The teams contained a mix of specialists, each with an assignment and an agenda. For example, Project Alsos personnel worked to assess Nazi progress on the atomic bomb. Chemical Warfare Service teams looked for research data on poison gas, nerve gas, poisoned bullets, and biological weapons. Aeronautical teams searched for design documents, engineering and manufacturing details, and test equipment associated with rocketand jet-powered aircraft. Chemical engineering teams looked for data on synthetic fuels, synthetic rubber, and glass with special properties. Teams had physicians looking into Nazi medical advances that had military applications, and reporting atrocities that would be the subject of discussion at the Nuremberg War Crimes Trials. And last but not least, there were teams tasked to secure launchers, rockets, testing and manufacturing equipment, and to locate and interrogate the engineers and scientists responsible for the related programs. These teams reported to the Army Ordnance Department, under the command of Colonel Holger Toftoy.

T-Forces accompanied ground troops at the front lines, often in the company of Special War Crimes Investigation Units who debriefed repatriated US military personnel and collected evidence of war crimes as POW camps and concentration camps were liberated. William Donovan, head of the OSS, was thinking more expansively. On 1 December 1944, Donovan asked President Roosevelt for permission to bring certain SS intelligence officers into the US after the war ended. In his 18 December response, Roosevelt categorically ruled that out, saying:

> WE MAY EXPECT THAT THE NUMBER OF GERMANS WHO ARE ANXIOUS TO SAVE THEIR SKINS AND PROPERTY WILL RAPIDLY INCREASE. AMONG THEM MAY BE SOME WHO SHOULD PROPERLY BE TRIED FOR WAR CRIMES OR AT LEAST ARRESTED

At the time Roosevelt sent that letter, the Battle of the Bulge was still raging and the outcome uncertain, but by 25 January 1945, the German offensive had collapsed. The T-Force teams then pushed farther into Europe, hunting for Nazi scientific knowledge and wondering "Where are the Nazi scientists at the top of the T-Force wish lists?" and "What should we do with them after we capture and interrogate them?"

While the liberating troops were dealing with the survivors of Dora and Buchenwald, a T-Force team and a war crimes investigation unit were dispatched to Nordhausen. Two of Col. Toftoy's subordinates, Major James Hamill and Major Robert Staver, were ordered to gather technical intelligence on the Nazi rocket program, while Major Herschel Auerbach of the Command Judge Advocate[127] (CJA) looked for evidence of war crimes.

For Hamill and Staver, Christmas arrived early. All of the heavy equipment, the machinery for manufacturing and assembly, and the testing facilities were intact and undamaged. There were vast rooms filled with the parts needed to build V-2 rockets, V-1 flying bombs, jet planes, and anti-aircraft rockets. There were also — to their great joy — fully assembled V-2 rockets ready for transport and launching. Although they found no paperwork other than charred scraps in 55-gallon burn barrels, they had intact rockets and all of the assembly components in hand. The main problem they faced was that Nordhausen and its environs would be part of the Russian sector after the war ended, and there were agreements in place not to destroy any potentially useful hardware prior to turnover. Time was short if they were to pack up and ship out everything of value, find any surviving paperwork of importance, and locate and interrogate the engineers who had designed such advanced weapons.

At first it was thought that there was little overlap between Auerbach's team, collecting information on the deaths of Dora prisoners, and the Ordnance team working on missiles and advanced technologies. But it became apparent that the two investigations were completely intertwined when Dora survivors told of the abuses at the hands of administrators, engineers, and production managers at the Mittelwerk.

The technical director of the Mittelwerk, Albin Sawatski, featured

---

[126] Record Group 226, National Archives and Records Administration, College Park, Maryland.

[127] The CJA is part of the Judge Advocate General Corps. A CJA is assigned to each Army command.

prominently in those reports, and he was being held in custody by the Army. Sawatski was quite talkative, providing information about the organization and staff of the underground factory. He spoke of Georg Rickhey, the general manager, and Arthur Rudolph, the production director, and said that Rudolph was the person who set the work hours for the prisoners. But Arthur Rudolph was nowhere to be found, as he was off in Weilheim with the others in von Braun's core group.

WEILHEIM TO OBERJOCH

The rocket group was blissfully unaware of the chaos in their wake. In fact, none of the turmoil being experienced elsewhere in Germany managed to filter through the Alps to affect the resort community that sheltered what remained of the rocket team. Life was settled and peaceful in the resort community, and the rocketeers had nothing to do. Wernher had been told that because his arm wasn't healing properly, it should be rebroken and reset. He decided that this was as good a time as any, so he checked into a private hospital in Sonthofen, 30 miles away, for the operation.

Wernher spent three days in traction after the surgery. His physician expected him to stay longer, but Dornberger sent an ambulance to retrieve him, because the town and hospital would soon be captured by Allied forces. The doctor scrambled around and managed to set up an enormous, cumbersome plaster cast with a bracing strut to the waist to immobilize the arm and shoulder. Once the arm was secured, Wernher was taken to Oberjoch, where he took up residence in the Haus Ingeburg, a three-storey luxury hotel near a cleft in the mountains then known as Adolf Hitler Pass. His associates from Weilheim were already there, as were many of the other engineers who had been moved from Nordhausen. General Dornberger and 150 of his soldiers were there as well.

It was a grand setting, and the hotel had a large liquor and wine reserve that many of the men enjoyed. Sometime over this strangely celebratory period, and unknown to Wernher, Huzel and Tessmann mentioned their "special mission" to Karl Otto Fleischer, an Army business manager who had been part of Dornberger's staff since the Peenemünde days. Whether done out of bravado or boozy comradery, it would prove to be a costly indiscretion.

There had been quite a pruning from the heady days in early 1943, when over 6,000 of the Nazi intellectual elite were living and working together at Peenemünde. Half that number had left

Peenemünde for Nordhausen and Bleicherode, only around 400 of that subset were shifted to Oberammergau, and just 150 were now safe in Oberjoch with Wernher von Braun and Walter Dornberger. But this small residual contingent of Peenemünders ended the month of April 1945 enjoying the quiet and idyllic life at their mountain resort. Von Braun, Dornberger, and the others sat around the patio enjoying drinks, talking, laughing, making grandiose future plans, and admiring stunning views of the Alps, while the Russians took Berlin.

PLANNING FOR THE FUTURE

When the news of Hitler's suicide[128] reached him, Wernher knew that the war was essentially over. Over the previous week, he had gone over the situation with Dornberger and the rest of the team, and they had agreed that surrendering to the Americans would be their best option. The consensus was that the Americans had been pulled into the conflict through their support of the British, not because of any historic animosity to the German people. Once they knew the value of Wernher's team, Dornberger was confident that he could write his own ticket. But they would have to be careful not to reveal too much, for the more technical information they gave the Americans, the less leverage they would have to secure the best possible deal. Their involvement in the Mittelwerk and the use of slave labor might be problematic, but that facility was hundreds of miles away, and he and Dornberger felt confident that any records linking them to that facility had been either burned or buried. As long as everyone sang the same song, their history was what they said it was, no more and no less. Although Dornberger would make decisions concerning negotiations with the Americans, Wernher would be the one to negotiate, because he was much more effective at promoting their services.

When it was time to put their plans in motion, American forces were less than three miles down the road, just on the other side of the Adolf Hitler Pass. Dornberger didn't think it prudent to surprise front line troops by suddenly arriving in a car convoy, as the pickets might be nervous and trigger-happy. So after some discussion, they decided to send an emissary to arrange for their surrender. Magnus von Braun was selected because he spoke the best English. He also looked young for his age (25), and in civilian clothes, he could pass as an inoffensive schoolboy.

---

[128] Hitler shot himself on 30 April 1945 after killing his new bride, Eva Braun.

On the morning of 2 May, Magnus tied a white handkerchief to the handle of a bicycle and pedaled down the hill to the American lines at Schattwald. He was stopped by a sentry, PFC Frederick Schneikert, of the 44th Infantry. Magnus imperiously demanded to be taken to see General Eisenhower, but he had to settle for the Schneikert's superior officer. When Magnus explained that he was there to arrange the surrender of Wernher von Braun and the V-2 rocket team, he was placed under guard and driven to the counterintelligence headquarters in Reutte for interrogation. The interrogating officer could scarcely believe what he was hearing — it sounded too good to be true. There were teams all over Germany looking for these guys. Although he had some reservations, he gave Magnus a safe conduct pass that would cover the entire group. Magnus was taken back to his bicycle, and he pedaled back up the hill toward the mountain pass while the intelligence team wondered what they were getting themselves into.

That afternoon, with light sleet falling, seven key members of the rocket team prepared to leave the hotel. All were dressed in their best civilian clothing. There would be no uniforms worn, as they wanted to be seen as intellectual scientists, not soldiers. The party consisted of the two von Brauns, Dornberger, Axster, Tessmann, Huzel, and Lindenberg. They loaded three cars for the trip. Wernher was anxious to get the preliminaries over with so they could start the negotiation. Everyone was confident of a warm reception, and the trunks of the cars were filled with liquor and wine bottles taken from the hotel cellars. It was obviously not a typical surrender. As light faded, the group climbed into the loaded cars and headed toward the pass, reaching the American lines just after dark. Once cleared to enter, Wernher and company were given a hot meal and directed to quarters nearby, where they spent the night.

There were still 150 team members at Oberjoch, awaiting instructions from Dornberger before surrendering. The 300 members of the rocket group still in Oberammergau had scattered, finding refuge in homes and resorts in the area. Those who had remained in the Nordhausen area were hiding as well, hoping both to avoid capture and to avoid being connected to the Mittelwerk and Dora.

The news that the rocket team had surrendered was widely distributed, and the next morning there was a press conference and photo shoot. Wernher, who was near the top of the T-Force "want list" was the center of attention. As he had anticipated, he was treated like a celebrity. He was at his congenial best, smiling, laughing and joking, sharing stories with American soldiers, and acting as the spokesman for the group. The photographs taken that morning show a relaxed and congenial get-together, with the Germans looking happy and rested, and the American soldiers looking exhausted. Not all of the witnesses approved of the celebratory atmosphere. One soldier complained that von Braun acted like a visiting congressman rather than a POW, and another couldn't decide whether he was a genius or full of malarkey. Dornberger stayed out of the limelight, letting Wernher handle the PR work. Lt. Stewart, a member of the T-Force team, later remarked that Dornberger was extremely reserved and reticent, but Dr. von Braun was the life of the party. Speaking to the reporters, Wernher took all of the credit for "his" V-2 program, and boldly claimed that if he had had two more years, Germany would have won the war by launching 200 V-2s per day and striking targets with pinpoint accuracy.

After a short wait, Wernher, Dornberger, and the others were escorted to a luxurious resort, the Hotel Bahnhof, overlooking the site of the 1936 Winter Olympics in Garmisch-Partenkirchen. The generally festive atmosphere continued, and the German supplies of alcohol were dwindling fast. Wernher knew that interrogations would follow, but he wasn't particularly concerned. His reception demonstrated that the Americans clearly knew how important he was. All that was left was to work out an agreement that met his expectations. For the moment, he would simply enjoy the attention and do what he could to shape the news reports of their surrender.

Before the social atmosphere faded, arrangements were made to collect the rest of Wernher's core group from Oberjoch and Oberammergau. While that operation proceeded, interrogators arrived from all over the European Theatre — from the Navy, the Army Air Corps, Army Intelligence (G-2), and British Intelligence, all members of the Combined Intelligence Objectives Subcommittee (CIOS). When Lt. Stewart, the officer in charge of the interrogation program, cabled his superiors about the situation, he was ordered to determine if any of the men who had surrendered were Nazis. He responded that he really didn't think that mattered. What mattered was what they knew, and what they could do for the US military to hasten the end of the war against Japan.

On 7 May, Admiral Karl Dönitz, acting head of the Third Reich, authorized the unconditional surrender of Germany, and the war in Europe was officially over. For the rocket team, this was probably old news and of little interest. Their primary concern was navigating their way through the interrogation phase and emerging with a bright future.

Part 2: Peace, Politics, and Injustice

—◁▷—

A government by secrecy benefits no one. It injures the people it seeks to serve; it damages its own integrity and operation. It breeds distrust, dampens the fervor of its citizens and mocks their loyalty.

SENATOR RUSSELL B. LONG

Nothing is covered up. We have nothing to conceal. The barbarous treatment these people received in the German concentration camps is almost unbelievable. . . . I think people ought to know about such things. It explains something of my attitude toward the German war criminal. I believe he must be punished, and I will hold out for that forever.

GEN. DWIGHT DAVID EISENHOWER

CHAPTER 17

The Long Way Home

⊰ᗡᗧ⊱

On 1 May 1945, the news reached Stalag VIIA that Hitler was dead and the Third Reich was collapsing. There was jubilation at the camp as word was spread — it was clear that the war in Europe was ending. Fred was relieved to hear it. Soon he could go home! But precisely when remained an open question. There were standing orders that no one was to leave the camp, due to concern about rogue SS groups, snipers, and civilian reprisals against Allied military personnel. Fred knew all about the latter problem from first-hand experience. But he still wasn't happy about being locked up by his own guys. And although they were no longer in German custody, food distribution to 130,000 prisoners remained a logistical nightmare. He was still extremely hungry, and there was a lot of grumbling from the POWs, and he heard that some prisoners were sneaking through the fence-line to search for food.[129]

Conditions were appalling and rapidly deteriorating. French, Russian, Polish, and Ukrainian prisoners left the camp and returned with liquor, after wreaking havoc in the town and abusing any women they could find. Drunken brawls occurred, and looting soon spread throughout the camp. The lawless atmosphere added to the general misery caused by hunger and overcrowding. At this point, at least 90% of the prisoners (including Fred) had dysentery, and the lines at the latrines seemed endless. Those unwilling or unable to wait in line squatted wherever they could find a space, adding to the general stench that hung over the camp like a low cloud. Fred found that he could ignore it, except when a gust of wind brought a tantalizing reminder of what fresh air was like.

Several noteworthy things happened over the next week. First, General Patton, commander of the US Third Army, rode a jeep into the camp for a brief visit. He walked around a bit, visited the war crimes investigation unit set up in one of the barracks, said a few words that Fred couldn't hear, and then rode off again. Second, Red Cross trucks arrived and food became more plentiful, although it still took a long time to distribute the rations. The third bit of news was that French POWs, many of whom had been in captivity for years,

---

[129] Lt. Loren Jackson, Fred's pilot, was one of them. He went to a 3rd Army kitchen and collected sacks of food that they dragged back into SL VIIA.

were at the top of the priority list for evacuation, ahead of the American POWs. Fred wondered aloud how long that would take, but nobody had any idea.

In the end, Fred was held in the camp for a week. Many of the men wandered around the camp, looking for friends in the crowd and collecting souvenirs to take home with them (Nazi flags were a popular item). Fred stuck relatively close to the barracks, as his feet were still bothering him, but several members of his crew came by, including Loren Jackson and, on another occasion, Sam Pennell. Loren and Fred agreed to meet in New York City after they got home, but Sam and Fred immediately started hanging around together, catching up.

One of the other men from his combine was in a small mob that broke into the headquarters office for the camp and "liberated" the identity cards for prisoners whom they knew. In this way Fred obtained his Kriegie ID card with the photo taken at SL III.

Shortly after liberation, a war crimes unit set up shop in the alcove of one of the barracks, under a placard that said War Crimes Investigating Team 6824. This team, under Major Sullivan, collected information and depositions from prisoners regarding treatment in violation of the Geneva Conventions. There were many such teams in the ETO, reporting to the Judge Advocate General of the US Army.

Early in the process, the call went out for the Buchenwald airmen, as both intelligence and war crimes personnel had been alerted to their situation by Lamason's report and by the supplemental report provided by LtC. Clark. Fred spent most of a morning in a rickety chair answering questions from the War Crimes team about his experiences. He found them very difficult to talk about, and he was sweating and fidgeting. His answers were brief and sometimes abrupt or halting. Nevertheless, he was told that the OSS wanted to talk to him as well, but that this might not happen before he left the camp. Fred was then handed off to the Military Intelligence Service (MIS), who had their own questions. Fred was told that his name would be mentioned in their report, although he was not warned that it would be decades before he saw a copy.

Germany surrendered unconditionally on 7 May 1945, and the next day, American POWs started leaving Stalag VIIA. Fred and the other Buchenwald airmen had priority status, but he still had to endure a long wait in line for delousing before climbing into a 6x6 for a ride to a local airfield. Once there, he sat in the shade for several hours awaiting an open seat on a cargo plane. But it was worth the wait, as Fred eventually climbed on and strapped in for the flight. He wasn't clear on precisely where he was headed, but that didn't bother him at all.

He was taken first to Fliegerhorst Salzwedel in northern Germany, where Fred and the other Buchenwald airmen showered, were deloused for the second time, and received a change of clothing. Fred then had a medical exam to determine whether or not he required immediate hospitalization, but aspirin was the only treatment provided for the pain in his feet. Other than his feet, Fred's main problem appeared to be malnutrition, so he was flown to what was essentially a holding facility where he could be given extra calories and his physical condition monitored while he was processed for transport to the US. There were several such facilities operating in the ETO at the time, and Fred was sent to one used by recovered airmen. It was called Camp Lucky Strike.[130]

Camp Lucky Strike was located near the Normandy coast, roughly 25 miles northeast of the French port city of Le Havre. Tents of varying size were set in multiple rows all around the central, cleared portion of a large field. People were everywhere, and it reminded Fred of Stalag VIIA in that respect. But everyone seemed to be in high spirits and ready to welcome the newcomers.

Liberated POWs were called RAMPs, which was an acronym for Recovered Allied Military Personnel. The camp was filled with them, all waiting for a ride to the US. On arrival, Fred was directed to a Red Cross station, where he was given a cursory physical review. Because he was obviously malnourished and more than 30% underweight, he was held there for 48 hours while the nursing staff gave him glasses of eggnog, which they said would prepare his shrunken stomach for regular food. Fred had weighed 155 pounds when he was shot down, roughly 100 pounds when he arrived at Stalag Luft III, and only 115 pounds when he reached Camp Lucky Strike. His belly had retreated to the point where he could place a board across the front of his pelvis, and it wouldn't touch his abdomen.

After two days bunking in one of the Red Cross tents and drinking four to six big glasses of eggnog each day, Fred was really looking forward to some regular food. Even with teeth missing and aching gums, he wanted something to chew on. At long last he was released and sent to headquarters for formal arrival processing.

Headquarters consisted of three or four quonset huts much like the barracks buildings at Great Ashfield, plus a shabby wooden building with a placard reading "RAMP Camp Headquarters." The surrounding area was filled with enormous barracks tents. When Fred

---

[130] The tent cities were called cigarette camps, and named after the tobacco companies that shipped free cigarettes to US military personnel.

reported and gave his name and serial number, he found that his name must've been flagged, because he was pulled aside and taken to an interview room set aside for the OSS. He spent much of the day in that office, answering detailed questions about his experiences.

Particular focus was placed on his time at Buchenwald, the medical experiments, and the attempts to make the airmen do skilled factory work. Once again, Fred found it difficult to talk about what he had seen and done, and at several points, the interviewer paused to give him time to regain his composure. When the ordeal was over, Fred went to the main office where, after another wait in line, a harried sergeant filled out the official arrival paperwork. Only the top of the form was completed, because Fred had already been interviewed by the OSS. Across the bottom of the form, the clerk wrote "OSS" and "CJA" (Command Judge Advocate, which handled war crimes) and crossed out the section of the form intended for the POW's history while in captivity.

There were hundreds of thousands of troops heading home, and only so many transports. So a complicated priority system was used to determine who left and in what order. Other than high-ranking officers and special cases of interest to the government, nobody went by plane. Fred was told he would be going home on a ship, either a "liberty ship," a repurposed Navy vessel, or a commandeered liner or freighter. Things were too chaotic for anyone to know when Fred's turn would come, so he was told to scan the bulletin boards each day to look for his name on the passenger list for an upcoming departure.

Fred next went to the supply section, where a Lt. Wilson of the Quartermasters Corps gave him clean clothing and $300 of his accumulated back pay. He left the counter heavily laden, with a belt and cap, a set of underwear, two handkerchiefs, a woolen coat, dog tags, boots, uniform shirt and pants, hand and bath towels, a wool blanket, a can of meat, a canteen with cup and lid, a set of cutlery, and a duffel bag to carry them in. Fred was assigned a barracks tent and a bunk, and he spent the next hour finding it and settling in. The tent was relatively close to the HQ, so it would be easy to check the bulletins boards where the departure lists were posted.

With his gear in his tent, Fred sat on the bunk for a few minutes working up the energy to move again. He then grabbed a towel and a change of clothes and went to find the showers. There was quite a line, but the sergeants in charge kept the men moving. After showering and changing into his new clothes, he retraced his path through the maze of tents until he got "home." He was completely exhausted, so he lay down on the bunk to take a rest and elevate his aching feet. It certainly felt strange to be at loose ends, safe, clean, and with a wad of cash in his pocket.

He tried to rest, but couldn't sleep. Fred knew he wasn't in the best of shape — he was still tired and hungry, and walking was painful. He was jumpy as hell. Any sudden movement made him flinch, and at a loud noise he automatically dove for cover. He wasn't alone — every time a plane flew low over the camp, men dove under bunks or tables — but that didn't help any. He also didn't enjoy sleeping, because his dreams were often terrible, leaving him bathed in sweat with his heart pounding. And whenever he wasn't busy doing something else that occupied his mind, he started worrying about what might have happened to the Raulins. Had the Gestapo arrested them? Was Lionel OK? Without warning, the worry became rage directed toward the traitor responsible. It got him back on his feet, pacing back and forth. He was supposed to go home, but how could he do that without knowing if the Raulins had survived? He would feel like a lazy and selfish coward. But what could he do?

The consensus among the airmen at Buchenwald had been that Jean Jacques was the prime candidate, but Fred knew for certain that at least two of the people he'd met — Louis, who'd arranged things at the Hotel Piccadilly, and Henri who'd delivered him to the Gestapo — were definitely part of the plan, and he knew where Louis worked in Paris. OK, that meant the trail would start in Paris. Of course, that meant leaving Camp Lucky Strike, but was that even possible?

Mealtimes took forever because the lines were long and the portions small. Fred had been told to eat five small meals per day rather than a few huge servings. So when the chow line was operating, Fred grabbed his plate, waited in line, got served, and then hobbled to the end of the line to eat while waiting for a refill. Nobody minded, and he repeated the process as long as the kitchen was serving.

After the evening food service was over, while seated at the long table surrounded by other RAMPs, Fred listened to the chatter and asked some questions. He learned that many of the RAMPS were taking their back pay and heading to Paris to spend it. It was possible to get a liberty pass, but it could take days to jump through the hoops involved. So, many of the enlisted men were simply taking advantage of the generally chaotic situation at Camp Lucky Strike and slipping away.[131] The RAMPs who left without proper papers would technically be AWOL (absent without leave), but the chances of

---

[131] The security policies were pretty slack, as nobody thought the French posed a threat. The main problem was discouraging the young girls who were flocking to the cigarette camps in search of parties and easy money.

being caught were slim, and the chances of serious punishment were even slimmer. Of course, if your name came up on a passenger list while you were out partying, you'd get your ears pinned back when you returned to the base, and you would have to wait for another space to open up. But the allure of Paris, where the liberation party atmosphere persisted, was too great to resist.

Fred found this information quite enlightening, and the next day, he discussed the situation with Ed, Sam and some other friends who had arrived on the transport with him. He was circumspect about it, even though he trusted them. If he decided to take off, he didn't want to leave anyone else holding the bag. To his amazement, they seemed to have put the past behind them. They were focusing on getting home and doing their best to forget everything that had happened. "Let the French sort it out" was their motto. But after all that had happened to him, Fred just couldn't do that.

Once Fred decided to leave, things happened quickly. He needed to get a few things for the trip, so he went in search of the canteen, where he got some additional toiletries and purchased a small B&W camera. That evening, he arranged his kit bag, his personal gear and a change of clothes under his berth in readiness for departure, before lying down and setting his mental alarm clock. In the predawn hours of 10 May, Fred snapped awake and stuffed his gear into his pillowcase, which would serve as a tote bag. Leaving the tent, he strolled out into the cool night air, taking care to move quietly. The fewer people who were aware of his departure the better.

Fred had a stroke of luck on his way out of the camp. An MP had fallen asleep with his holstered .45 slung on its belt over the back of a chair. Very quietly, hardly daring to breathe, Fred moved in far enough that he could slide the .45 out of its holster before backing out of the guard shack. Once clear, he gave a sigh of relief and popped the pistol into his pillowcase where it wouldn't be noticed. He left Camp Lucky Strike, departing through a wooded area and curving around to intersect the road a mile or so away. His feet were killing him, so he sat down and rested while dawn passed and the sun climbed in the sky. As traffic started to increase on the roadway, he stood and hitched a ride. He was now on his way to Paris, 140 miles to the southeast. Although the roads weren't in great repair, and military vehicles clogged some segments and intersections, Fred made it to Paris that evening.

His first stop was the Hotel Piccadilly, where he booked a room for the night. When he asked if Louis was around, he got a curt "no" and a very strange look, but no additional information. Well, he hadn't thought it would be that simple. He was exhausted, as the adrenaline rush associated with going AWOL had long since faded away, so he took his room key and went up to his room for the night.

The next morning, after having breakfast in the lobby, he grabbed his camera and headed into the street. The bar affiliated with the hotel, Le Prélude, was closed until the afternoon, so he decided to take the morning to sightsee and take his mind off the situation. He walked north up Rue Pigalle to the Boulevard de Clichy, where he caught a taxi that took him eastbound for a mile or so to the Arc de Triomphe. The cab did two circuits of the Arc while Fred took snapshots with his camera. Then on a whim, he had the cab go past 84 Avenue Foch, where he had been delivered to the Gestapo and interrogated. It was now flying the French flag rather than Nazi colors, but he was uncomfortable just seeing the building, so he decided not to take photos of the place.

In the early afternoon, Fred had the taxi let him out near a restaurant the driver recommended. He had a leisurely lunch and enjoyed several glasses of wine. The weather was mild, and it was pleasant to be watching everyone around him without worrying about being noticed. The Parisians in general seemed busy and happy and relieved that the war was over and life could start getting back to normal. There was still a ways to go, however. There were few cars other than taxis or military vehicles, as petrol was still in short supply, and the selections in stores were limited. But hey, the war was over and France was free, so things could have been worse.

An hour or two later, Fred flagged another taxi and headed back to the hotel. He went next door to Le Prélude and had a drink at the bar, chatting with the bartender. There were few customers, so they talked amiably and at some length about nothing in particular. Fred then brought up the subject of Louis, but after an awkward pause, the bartender said he'd been working there since last September and he had never met him.

Fred hung out in the bar for several hours. As it got busier, a number of military men showed up, either on leave or AWOL like Fred, often with women on their arms. It was clear to Fred that the hotel was in a red-light district where activities were limited only by imagination and finances. Fred sat at the tables and swapped stories, but his mind was elsewhere, and after buying a last round of drinks, he excused himself and went up to his hotel room for the night. It was his first night in a bona fide homestyle bed since leaving Hacqueville ten months earlier, and between the comfortable mattress and the alcohol he had consumed, he slept soundly and without nightmares.

It was late morning before Fred went down for breakfast, and he was still on his first cup of strong coffee when a well-dressed man entered the hotel and strolled to the front desk. After a brief conversation with the receptionist, he headed for Fred and, without waiting for an invitation, took a seat at his table.

Introducing himself as a detective in the French police, he asked Fred who he was and why he was in Paris. Fred gave a plausible answer — a former POW on liberty, in search of nightlife — but the detective brushed that aside. As he carefully examined Fred's identification papers, he asked why Fred was so interested in the whereabouts of Mr. Louis Gianoni.

Fred thought it best to tell an edited version of the truth: that he had been betrayed to the Gestapo by Louis and an associate called Henri, and that Fred wanted to discuss it with them. He didn't mention the .45 in his pocket or his plans for those men once he found them. As Fred related his experiences at Gestapo HQ and Fresnes Prison, and the boxcars on 15 August, the mood changed palpably. The detective became quite congenial, and expressed his sympathies for what Fred had been through. He told Fred that he was sorry to report that his trip to Paris had been in vain. Louis Gianoni had indeed been a collaborator with the SD. The day after Fred left Paris by train, Louis was involved in an operation to round up a group of FFI personnel. Things didn't work out as smoothly as planned, and in the resulting firefight, Louis was killed. Few tears were shed.

As to Henri, his real name was Maurice Grapin. He had attempted to switch sides and celebrate the liberation of Paris, but he had been arrested and jailed. When Fred asked about Jean Jacques, he was told that, as he had expected, Jean Jacques was another SD agent. He had been one of the German's top undercover agents in Paris, and his real name was Jacques Desoubrie. Jacques had fled Paris ahead of the Allies and was rumored to be somewhere in Germany. The French, British, and Americans were looking for him, but so far he hadn't turned up.[132] Several other SD agents were being hunted, and a few spoke excellent English — good enough to impersonate American or Canadian soldiers on leave. That was the main reason the police had an interest in anyone trying to contact Louis.

The conversation ended with a warning to Fred that he should leave such matters to the police rather than try to have "discussions" with men like Grapin or Desoubrie. His tone indicated that he was well aware of what kind of a discussion Fred had in mind. After the detective left, Fred sat at the table eating a slow breakfast and

---

[132] He was ultimately betrayed by his wife in 1949 and executed by firing squad. His last words were "Heil Hitler."

pondering his next move. This was obviously a dead end, and he wouldn't be surprised if the police weren't planning to keep an eye on him in case he planned any "discussions" with anyone else in Paris. So, in the afternoon of 16 May, Fred checked out of the hotel and started thumbing his way out of town. Hacqueville was roughly 70 miles away in the general direction of Camp Lucky Strike.

Fred had planned on going there once he concluded his business, whatever it was, in Paris. Fred had little trouble getting close — the main road he'd taken from the Camp passed reasonably close to Hacqueville — but the last four miles or so were on an unpaved side road that left the main road to Rouen near Villers-en-Vexin. He hadn't walked far before his feet made it impossible to continue, so he stood in the shade by the side of the road hoping for a lift. Late in the day he managed to get a ride in the cab of a rickety farm truck. The farmer recognized him as a member of the Allied military forces, and he was only too happy to drive Fred wherever he wanted to go. His gratitude was almost embarrassing, as if Fred had singlehandedly driven the Nazis from Normandy.

Fred left the truck with a wave in the center of the town, near the school and within sight of the church. He was suddenly unsure as to what he should do next — if the Raulins and their friends had been executed, he wasn't sure he wanted to know. But he had come all this way, and there he stood, so he walked up and knocked on the door to the schoolhouse, where the Raulins had been living. There was no answer, which he thought was an ominous sign.

Fred went to the church grounds next, and tried the pastor's residence. To his relief, Simone answered the door and was struck speechless at the sight of him. She hugged him tightly, then brought him inside and sat him down at the kitchen table while she got them glasses of wine. When Fred asked about the Raulins, Simone told him that Max had been appointed the head of the aerodrome in Chartres, and the family had relocated. She assured him that they were all doing fine, and that she would send them his best wishes when they next corresponded.

Simone started to ask Fred about what happened after he left Hacqueville, but then decided that everyone should get the news. So she left Fred with the bottle of wine and scooted out of the house, returning 20 minutes later with Mr. Lesouer, the Brochonds, and Jacquelin Robert. Over the next few hours and several bottles of wine, bread, and cold meats, Fred gave an overview of what he'd experienced, glossing over his time in Buchenwald both to spare their feelings and to avoid making the nightmares worse.

The group listened with rapt attention, asking occasional

questions but otherwise simply absorbing the information. Fred finished with his departure from Camp Lucky Strike and his failed attempt to find the traitors who had betrayed him to the Gestapo. He said that he had come back to Hacqueville to see if everyone had survived, or if they too had been rounded up and imprisoned or worse. Fred then asked them if there was any chance that Desoubrie was hiding somewhere within reach. If he was hiding in France, Belgium, or Holland, Fred was prepared to track him down. But if Desoubrie was in Germany, he was out of reach — Fred would never return to Germany, under any circumstances.

The consensus among the group was that if Desoubrie was in France or Belgium, he would soon be captured, and if he was in Germany, his fate was still sealed, but it might take a bit longer. At the risk of causing offense, they pointed out that Fred was obviously in no condition to go traipsing around Europe hunting for traitors who were likely to be in good shape, heavily armed, and alert to any suspicious activities. The detective in Paris was right, such men should be left to the authorities or to the members of the FFI whose networks they had betrayed. All of the escape networks knew about Jacques Desoubrie and his various aliases, and if he were found by a member of the FFI rather than the authorities, it was unlikely that he would live to stand trial. Their advice was for Fred to leave Desoubrie to them, and to go home, live a good life, and always remember his friends in Hacqueville.

It was time for the visitors to leave and for Fred to get some sleep. Before going, Mr. Lesouer told Fred that he was the first sheltered airman to return to check if they were OK, and his arrival (and survival) should be celebrated. They would spread the word, and the next afternoon they would invite the town to attend a reception in the schoolhouse.

Fred bedded down for the night in the guest room. He awakened around 0300, bathed in sweat, with Simone standing at his bedside looking scared. He'd been screaming and calling out, and she had rushed in to see what was wrong. As he got his breathing under control, Fred assured her that it was just a nightmare and that she could go back to bed. Before she left, Simone suggested that perhaps he hadn't told them everything that had happened to him.

The reception the next day was a festive event, with a pot-luck style dinner enhanced by bottles of champagne used to toast Fred, Hacqueville, Charles de Gaulle, General Eisenhower, the Allies, and France. There were also pledges of eternal friendship and undying gratitude. All this took considerable time and even larger volumes of champagne. So much warmth and good humor was apparent that

Fred was overwhelmed, and he wound up spending two days in Hacqueville. They were busy days, as he went to visit each of his friends and their families to hear their stories about the months after his departure.

With the traitors out of reach and his French family doing fine, Fred felt free to return to Camp Lucky Strike. Simone passed the word, and soon Fred was waving goodbye from the passenger seat in another farm truck that took him all the way to Camp Lucky Strike, with his belongings on the floor in front of him. He was a bit nervous about his reception after being AWOL.

When they got to the entry, Fred climbed down from the cab and simply walked into the Camp past the guard-post by the main entry. Back by the tent, Fred saw the officer in charge, Lt. Sherwood, who told him to check the bulletin boards. To his delight, Fred found his name on a list for departure on 25 May on a ship bound for Boston via Southampton.[133]

Fred was also on a list ordering him to report for departure processing. On finding the office, the first thing he did was to complete a report on his experiences between the time he landed in France by parachute and his betrayal to the Gestapo. The form provided, titled Helpers and Betrayers, asked him to list everyone who had helped him evade the Germans, and to provide information on those people involved in his betrayal. After he completed that form, he was told to read and sign a secrecy agreement issued by the War Department. This three-page document prohibited any communication or publicity regarding his experiences. The last page required his signature and the signatures of authorized witnesses, certifying that he had read and understood the regulations. There followed a review of his paperwork, next of kin, his plans for the period of leave after arriving in the US, and whether or not he intended to stay in the Army (Fred was quite clear that his answer was NO).

Before leaving, Fred was handed a pamphlet "You're Staging for the States," which summarized the steps he must take and the forms he must complete before boarding a ship from Le Havre to the US. Afterward, Fred returned to the base HQ to send a telegram to Lucille. It was short and sweet: "Dear Lu, Well and on the way home see you soon love to all S/Sgt Frederic Martini"

Fred later recalled little about the troop ship voyage other than

---

[133] There is no record of the name of the ship. For unknown reasons, in 1952, the US government ordered the destruction of all passenger lists and troop transport records from WWII and the period immediately following the end of the war.

the fact that it was a rough Atlantic crossing, and since he was totally immune to seasickness (one of the lucky few on the voyage) the galley was his to command. For 11 days, he spent extended mealtimes in the mess area, with the cooks happy to give him as many eggs or steaks or scoops of ice cream as he desired. By the end of the voyage, his stomach had stretched to near normal proportions, although he was still much skinnier than normal. It would take another three months for Fred to regain his normal weight.

Troop ships arriving in New York City docked at midday, and arriving RAMPs were given a hero's welcome. But when the ship delivering Fred, Ed Ritter, and several other Buchenwald airmen to Boston reached port at 2200 on 11 June 1945, the docks were deserted. The RAMPs left the ship in darkness, and scattered as their orders directed. Fred's orders were to go to the train station and take the first available train to the Army Processing Center in Dover, Delaware, a distance of roughly 375 miles. Fred boarded the train in the wee hours and arrived in Dover on 12 June 1945, one year to the day after the downing of Crashwagon III. After he was logged in and provided with new uniforms — Fred was surprised to find he had been promoted to tech sergeant — he was handed a 60-day pass. At the end of that liberty period, he was to report to the Army Separation Center in Newark, New Jersey, for further instructions.

As soon as he got his pass, Fred went to the phone and called Lucille to say that he was OK, in the States, and heading for Brooklyn. It was a very animated conversation. In the early evening, Fred, his new duffel bag slung over his shoulder, headed back to the train station for the ride home to New York City.

Lucille already knew Fred was coming home. But the first official communication Lucille had received about Fred's fate caused his family more worry, rather than less. On 15 May 1945, Lucille received a letter from the Kansas City Quartermaster Depot, Army Effects Bureau. It said:

DEAR MRS. VIRGILIO:

THANK YOU FOR THE INFORMATION FURNISHED TO THE ARMY EFFECTS BUREAU, TO ENABLE DISPOSITION OF PERSONAL EFFECTS BELONGING TO YOUR BROTHER, STAFF SGT. FREDERIC MARTINI. I AM RETURNING THE LETTER WHICH YOU SUBMITTED.

I AM ENCLOSING A MONEY ORDER FOR $50 PAYABLE TO YOU, WHICH WAS RECEIVED WITH HIS EFFECTS, AND A CHECK FOR $40.50, REPRESENTING FUNDS BELONGING TO HIM. THE REMAINDER OF THE PROPERTY IS BEING FORWARDED IN ONE

CARTON AND SHOULD REACH YOU IN THE NEAR FUTURE.

MY ACTION IN TRANSMITTING THE PROPERTY DOES NOT OF ITSELF, VEST TITLE IN YOU. THE ITEMS ARE FORWARDED ONLY IN ORDER THAT YOU MAY ACT AS GRATUITOUS BAILEE IN CARING FOR THEM, PENDING THE RETURN OF THE OWNER. WHEN DELIVERY HAS BEEN MADE, I SHALL APPRECIATE YOUR ACKNOWLEDGING RECEIPT BY SIGNING ONE COPY OF THIS LETTER IN THE SPACE PROVIDED BELOW AND RETURNING IT TO THIS BUREAU.

FOR YOUR CONVENIENCE THERE IS ENCLOSED AN ADDRESSED ENVELOPE WHICH NEEDS NO POSTAGE.

Lucille had Fred's belongings, but where was Fred? If they had sent his belongings, did that mean he was dead or that he was coming too? She wished the letter had contained more specifics. Then on 24 May, she received Fred's terse telegram, and things suddenly looked a lot brighter. Lucille quickly spread the word to the family that Fred was coming home. Her first official confirmation that Fred was returning from the ETO was a terse telegram from J. A. Ulio, the Adjutant General. Sent on 30 May, it told her that Fred had been liberated on 29 April 1945.

She also received a letter from Sam Pennell's mother, dated 3 June, which said that Sam had called home from New York, and she wondered if Lucille had heard from Fred. Sam had been shipped out on a troop transport while Fred was hunting traitors in Normandy, and as a result, he had arrived more than a week before Fred. Then on 7 June, another telegram arrived saying that Fred would be returned to the US "in the near future," and that he would be in touch on arrival.

When Fred arrived in Brooklyn at long last, he moved into a spare bedroom in the house with Lucille, Eddie, and their sons, Edward Jr. and Frederic. He was, in their view, different from the Fred they had known before the war. Some of the differences were physical — he walked gingerly and didn't like to stand for very long. There was also the matter of the chunk missing from his ear and the bulk missing from his frame.

But the big changes were in his personality. He was certainly glad to be home and happy to talk with everyone, and he enjoyed playing with the kids. But he was jumpy and nervous, and at times they found him staring off into space with a bleak expression on his face. When asked about his time overseas, he told a few jokes about events in England, and mentioned the Raulins and his other friends in France, but those stories were relatively brief, and he didn't want to talk about his time as a POW, other than to say it was OK and that he had survived.

Ed and Lucille were sure that there was more to the story. At night, they were frequently awakened by the groans and cries from his room, and they suspected that the nightmares were related to his POW period. But they figured they would wait him out, hoping that he would eventually provide the details. For the time being, they were simply happy to have him back and in one piece.

For the first couple of weeks, Fred stayed in his room most of the day, emerging for meals or when visitors came calling. He was having some trouble adapting to life as an American civilian. He found he couldn't bear to tell them what had happened to him. If they believed him, they would be horrified, and they would want to do something for him, although there was nothing to be done. He wasn't sure he wanted to expose them to the realities of Nazi Germany. How could they deal with that information, from a vantage point so far removed both physically and culturally? And if they didn't believe him, he wasn't sure he could deal with being "Crazy Uncle Fred." Besides, he wasn't totally clear about what he could or couldn't talk about after signing that Security Agreement.

In mid-June, Loren Jackson called Lucille to let Fred know that he and Alice would be coming through New York the following week on their way back to Arizona. Fred's sister Betty was available, so the two of them met the Jacksons in town, did tourist things together, and had a great dinner in the city. It was just a little awkward, because Loren's perspective and experiences as a POW were so very different from Fred's, even though both had been in Stalag Luft III and Stalag VIIA. Loren told Fred that he would be staying in the Air Corps and making it a career, while Fred wanted nothing more than to forget the Army and the war as quickly as possible.

Lucille had stored Fred's belongings from Great Ashfield in a footlocker in the guest room closet. In late June, Fred worked up the energy to face the memories, and he opened it up and went through the contents. It contained Army issue clothing, including his monogrammed leather bomber jacket, plus toiletries, souvenirs from London, and personnel files and papers he had accumulated while at the 385th BG. There was also a large packet of mail that Lucille had tossed into the locker for him. All of the letters were bound together by a ribbon, and they all had stamps indicating NO LONGER AT THIS ADDRESS. His eyes were wet; here was all of the mail he had longed for. Untying the ribbon, he laid the letters on the bed, sorting them into chronological order before carefully reading them. This was a great way to catch up on the year he'd lost.

Among those letters from Lucille and Liz, he found one with a return address he didn't recognize. The name was vaguely familiar — Betty Hover — and typed rather than handwritten. It said:

DEAR FRED,

I'M STARTING THIS LETTER OFF WITH NO IDEA IN MIND BUT THE DESIRE TO WRITE TO YOU. I MUST HAVE STARTED IT A COUPLE OF DOZEN TIMES, BUT EACH TIME I GOT STUCK FOR SOMETHING TO SAY. I KNOW BETTY MUST'VE TOLD YOU ALL THE FAMILY NEWS THAT YOU'RE INTERESTED IN, AND I CERTAINLY CAN'T ADD TO HER EXTENSIVE KNOWLEDGE. ALL I KNOW IS, YOU'RE PRETTY FAR FROM HOME AND I WANT TO WRITE TO YOU, SO HERE I AM. JUST TO ENLIGHTEN YOUR MEMORY, WHICH CAN'T BE VERY CLEAR ON THE SUBJECT, I'M THE CHARACTER KNOWN AS "BOOP" TO YOUR LOVING SISTER AND ASSOCIATES — I KNOW ALL HER FRIENDS THINK THAT'S REALLY MY NAME AND AT THIS LATE DATE I'VE FINALLY GIVEN UP TRYING TO EXPLAIN THAT I WASN'T REALLY CHRISTENED "BOOP" AND/OR IT ISN'T MY LAST NAME EITHER. IT'S A LITTLE WEIRD, BUT AFTER A WHILE YOU GET USED TO IT. YOU MAY REMEMBER VAGUELY MEETING ME IN FLORIDA THAT YEAR WE ALL SPENT THE WINTER THERE. I REMEMBER THOSE PALM TREES WITH LOVE AND LONGING UP HERE WHERE THE SNOW'S BECOMING DEEPER WITH EACH PASSING WEEK. I KNOW YOUR REMEMBRANCE OF ME MUST BE SHADOWY — IF I REMEMBER CORRECTLY, YOU WERE PRETTY WELL OCCUPIED WITH MURPHY AT THE TIME. HOWEVER, AFTER LIVING WITH YOUR SISTER SO LONG, BEING STARED AT BY YOUR PICTURE ON THE DRESSER EVERY MORNING AND NIGHT, AND LISTENING TO THE TALES ABOUT YOUR EARLY LIFE WITH WHICH I AM REGALED EVERY SO OFTEN BY BETTY & LUCILLE, I FEEL AS IF I KNEW YOU ALMOST AS WELL AS THEY DO. DO YOU MIND VERY MUCH? WE'VE BEEN HAVING LOTS OF SNOW THIS WINTER, MUCH MORE THAN I REMEMBER IN A LONG TIME (I'M FROM NEW JERSEY, SO I SHOULD KNOW WHAT TO EXPECT). THE OTHER NIGHT WHEN IT SNOWED LIKE MAD, BETTY AND I WALKED FROM 50TH ST. TO 70TH ST., BACK TO 66TH ST. AND AROUND THE BLOCK AGAIN, WITH THE POWDERY SNOW SIFTING HAPPILY AROUND OUR ANKLES. IT'S A WONDER WE DIDN'T GET PNEUMONIA, ESPECIALLY BETTY, WHO DIDN'T EVEN HAVE RUBBERS ON. WE SEEM TO LIVE RATHER A CHARMED LIFE; NEITHER OF US GETS SICK FROM DOING THINGS THAT MAKE OTHER PEOPLE VIOLENTLY ILL; EVEN THE BAGS WHICH SHOULD CERTAINLY BE UNDER OUR

EYES ARE MYSTERIOUSLY MISSING. WE CAN'T UNDERSTAND IT, BUT WE DON'T QUESTION IT. NO DOUBT IT WILL CATCH UP WITH US SOON ENOUGH.

HOPE YOU ARE FEELING WELL AND THAT WE'LL BE HEARING FROM YOU SOON. I'LL WRITE AGAIN IF YOU CAN STAND IT.

BEST OF LUCK,

BETTY ("BOOP")

The letter had been sent overseas to Stalag Luft III on 28 January 1945. It was amazing that the letter had been returned. Lucille had probably been visiting their apartment when it came back, and she had kept it for him, hoping that he would someday be able to read it. When he went to bed that night, he found himself thinking about that letter a lot. There was something about it that appealed to him. He knew "Boop" was still rooming with his sister. Maybe once he felt a bit better he would look her up and thank her for writing. It was the least he could do. That night his dreams were free of nightmares.

CHAPTER 18

The Spoils of Victory

THE MITTELWERK

As the war wound to a close, Major Hamill was following LtC. Toftoy's orders, busily crating up the components for 100 V-2 rockets on flatcars for delivery to Antwerp and shipment to the US. It was a labor-intensive process, but the work was done by former slave laborers who were, for a change, treated well and paid decent wages.

Hamill had still been unable to find any documents, schematics, or instruction manuals, so he tried to take everything rather than take a chance at leaving behind some critical widget. On 22 May 1945, trains began leaving for Antwerp. More followed each day, with the last departing on 31 May, only hours before Mittelwerk and the surrounding area was turned over to the Soviets. The accumulated rocket bodies, engines, and other components were soon on their way to White Sands Proving Grounds, near the Army base at Ft. Bliss, Texas.

Major Staver had left Major Hamill to deal with the packing and shipping of V-2 components so that he could focus on tracking down members of the Nazi brain trust hiding in the Nordhausen area. On 12 May, he located Karl Otto Fleischer, who had not been taken to Oberammergau. Fleischer, who may have felt slighted by his exclusion from the party, agreed to help Staver find others in the area. He led the US team to Eberhard Rees, another engineer, and Rees in turn led them to Walter Reidel, who was high on LtC. Toftoy's shopping list. Reidel was actually glad to be located, as he was already in Army custody. Mistaken for a scientist working on biological weapons, interrogators had beaten him severely and knocked out several teeth.

Major Staver was frustrated by the inability of interrogators at Garmisch-Partenkirchen to get anyone to talk about where he could find technical documents concerning the V-2 program. Like those interrogators, Staver felt certain that the Germans were holding out on him. So he started pressuring the lower-level staff to see what they knew, telling them that Wernher wanted them to tell him where the paperwork had been taken. After several failed attempts and some false comraderie, Major Staver convinced Karl Fleischer that he was telling the truth about von Braun authorizing the release of information. On 19 May, Fleischer finally admitted that he had heard from Tessmann and Huzel about the documents being placed in an abandoned mine in the Harz Mountains, although he didn't know the precise location.

On hearing this, Major Staver took off like a rocket and began searching the entire area with a contingent of troops. He was eventually able to locate the mine, clear the passageway, and load the crates into waiting trucks. The trucks then raced for the American zone, arriving just as the British formally took over jurisdiction and control of the area on 26 May. (Although the British were Allies of the Americans, the British and the French were both trying to get their hands on advanced German military technology, and the US was afraid that the information they obtained would not be freely shared.) The intelligence coup was nearly as important as the rockets themselves, for the documents established the theoretical basis for the design, the design modifications done over time, and the plans for future enhancements. There was no particular reason to mention the recovery to the German rocket team, but it confirmed the fact that the "volunteers for America" were keeping secrets and withholding information, despite their protestations to the contrary.

GARMISCH - PARTENKIRCHEN, GERMANY

Well before the war ended, the intelligence arm of the Joint Chiefs of Staff, the Joint Intelligence Committee, had established a subcommittee called the Joint Intelligence Objectives Agency. The JIOA was similar to the CIOS, but it was restricted to military intelligence personnel — the OSS, FBI, and British intelligence services were excluded. The JIOA had developed plans to bring key Nazi scientists to the US where they could be supervised while they revealed their secrets. LtC. Toftoy advised the JIOA on missile and rocket technology, and made lists of candidates for importation. Army Intelligence (G-2, Exploitation Branch) was responsible for monitoring and maintaining security.

Less than two weeks after Germany surrendered, LtC. Toftoy smuggled the first of the German scientists on his wish list, Dr. Herbert Wagner, into the US. Wagner had developed radio-controlled guided missiles that the Army felt had great potential for use against Japan. There was no way to bring him in legally — he was a committed Nazi and a member of the SA (a bona fide "storm trooper") — so the Department of State wasn't notified, no visa was requested, and Wagner was flown in aboard a cargo plane with blacked windows.

Toftoy had similar plans for von Braun's rocket team, but the situation was complicated by the fact that it involved a team rather than a single individual. Von Braun and Dornberger were obviously key members of that team, but the rockets were so complicated that many specialist engineers were required for successful production. They needed a better idea of the workings of the team before they could decide who to take, but as the daily round of interviews continued, it was apparent that no one was willing to provide the necessary information. Days turned into weeks without a breakthrough. Each of the members of the rocket team was interrogated separately and at length by intelligence officers from multiple agencies. It was slow, boring, and repetitious. The questioning yielded glimmerings and bits of technical information, but no major breakthroughs. The Germans didn't want to reveal too much until they knew what kind of a deal they would get.

After an interrogation on 10 May, Wernher felt that things weren't moving along as quickly as he would like. So he shifted into salesman mode, and on 15 May he presented a detailed memo to CIOS interrogators that touted a glorious future in which rockets developed from the V-2 would revolutionize civilian life as well as warfare. He described supersonic rocket-powered airliners, rocket-based surveillance programs, and space stations. Wernher's propaganda treatise had its intended effect, and serious discussions got underway to bring him and his associates to the US. It did nothing to reduce the frequency of interrogations, though, and in fact it may have increased them. He was questioned repeatedly through the rest of May and early June. He probably didn't mind, now that he was again being treated as a prime catch and an honored guest rather than as a suspect SS-major. The setting was grand, the hotel facilities superb, and Wernher and Dornberger put up with their daily interrogation sessions and spent the rest of the day enjoying the hotel services.

On 12 June, Lt. Walter Jessel, an American intelligence officer, reported that Dornberger had expected that the group would quickly be transferred to the US, and when they weren't he had told everyone to hold back information and say as little as possible until a deal was made. The rest of the report gave a rather negative view of the group as a whole. Arthur Rudolph was considered a Nazi fanatic ("100% Nazi, dangerous type. . . . Suggest internment"), and the others were loyal Nazis dedicated to the Hitler regime and to winning the war.

Wernher's screening report said, "Attitude characterized by the following quote: 'I always was a German and still am.' Considers

Germany dead as a nation. Only German hope: To cooperate with western Allies to act as bulwark against eastern hordes, and as beachhead for US and British forces in the coming struggle." Jessel felt that although von Braun recognized Germany's defeat, he didn't see anything wrong with Germany's actions during the war. He seemed to have adopted the rhetoric of the Nazi party — that Germany was the victim, that the V-2 was a defensive weapon, and that Germany and the US should have joined forces to battle the Soviet Union. He seemed totally convinced that war with the Soviet Union was inevitable over the short term, and he was amazed that the Allies failed to see that Germany had been trying to save Western civilization.

Jessel went on to warn that von Braun was conspiring with Dornberger to withhold information, and that he felt that it would be absurd to give the rocket group security clearances. He called von Braun a security threat, and recommended that he be detained for War Crimes review by Military Intelligence. But the advanced programs that Wernher had effectively promoted left LtC. Toftoy and his superiors just as bedazzled as Speer and Hitler had been. As a result, they repeatedly ignored both Jessel's advice and the incriminating information subsequently provided by Wernher himself.

In the course of the interrogation process, each of the men was required to fill out a detailed questionnaire that included their education, professional and technical training, employment, and involvement with the Nazi party. When von Braun heard that the focus of the session was his personal history, he was glad he wasn't going to be pestered about missing documents yet again. But when he started answering the questions, he decided he would rather be dodging technical questions. It was like walking through a minefield.

One of the questions concerned his membership in the Nazi party. Wernher admitted he was a member, but said he had been forced to join the Nazi party in 1939. Nazi party records later revealed that he had voluntarily joined the Nazi party two years earlier, in November 1937.[134] He was asked about his membership in the SS, and he gave a similar answer — he had been forced to join the SS as a lieutenant in 1941. That too was incorrect, as SS records indicated that he had rejoined the SS on 1 May 1940 after enlisting as an SS reservist while in college. As it turned out, neither 1940 nor 1941 were ideal answers given that membership in the SS after 1 September 1939 was a criminal

---

[134] This was one month after his brother Sigismund joined. His younger brother Magnus had joined the Nazi Party at 13, as a member of the Hitler Youth.

offense under war crimes regulations.

Those were just the warmup questions. The hard ones came after Wernher had recounted his educational history. What was his position and where was he employed? He had multiple titles and responsibilities, and he really didn't want to highlight his connection to Mittelwerk, Bleicherode, or CCDC-Mittelbau. He decided to keep it simple, and gave his current position as Technical Director at the Army facility at Peenemünde (a position that he had not held since August 1944, when he became Technical Director and Vice President of Elektromechanischewerk, GmbH). In followup questions, he admitted to having meetings with the director of EW GmbH in Bleicherode but implied that he was otherwise uninvolved. In a footnote, Jessel's report noted that investigations already completed indicated that the EW GmbH group at Bleicherode was "well supplied with cars and women."

Lt. Jessel then asked that if Wernher's job was at Peenemünde, what was he doing 300 miles from there? Wernher had left Peenemünde in late January, but admitting that would lead Jessel to ask what he had been doing since then. So Wernher got creative, confident that any contradictory paperwork had been either burned or buried. He told Jessel that he had left Peenemünde on 10 March 1945 to avoid the Russians, and that he had been heading for Bleicherode with about 100 of his staff when his car crashed, breaking his arm. At the time, Jessel had no way of knowing that this was a total fabrication. When Jessel asked, "Why Bleicherode?" Wernher said it was because he had been there previously, the area was close to the American lines, and it was always his intention to surrender. When asked where he had stayed in Bleicherode, he led Jessel to believe it had been in the home of a friend, Ernst Franck. Admitting that he had commandeered a large home abandoned by its Jewish occupants would have raised questions about his long plans and his role in Bleicherode. Asked why he'd left Bleicherode for Oberjoch, Wernher said that he had left Bleicherode because SS-General Kammler had ordered him to relocate to Oberammergau, and that he had escaped from the SS as soon as he could.

Wernher's creative, self-serving interpretations and omissions were repeated at every opportunity. In other interviews, Wernher (and members of his team) gave consistent accounts of historical events that had little basis in fact, but that helped create a benign public image. According to Wernher, the members of his rocket team were apolitical and uninvolved in Nazi activities. He said that slave labor at the Mittelwerk was mandated by the SS and completely out of his control, as were issues of discipline, work hours, and other factors. He was adamant that there were no slave laborers at Peenemünde, which was devoted to pure research.

As to the V-2, the answer varied. Sometimes he said it was created solely for defense, and at other times that it was created solely for research. In either case, he said he had never intended his work to be used for military purposes. It seems likely that Jessel had not seen the press briefing Wernher gave on arrival, where he had taken all of the credit for the V-2 and boasted that if he had had two more years, Germany would have won the war. Through it all, Wernher never mentioned the Mittelwerk, and despite mounting evidence to the contrary, decades passed before he admitted ever setting foot in the place.

A few days after Jessel completed his interrogation, Dornberger and von Braun met with a reporter from the *London Daily Express*. On 18 June 1945, the resulting story, "Dr. V2 laughs — at London," was on newsstands in the UK. It was based on Guy Eden's extended interview conducted in the sitting room of Dornberger's lavish suite. The most interesting aspects of the article were the observations about von Braun and the attempts of the von Braun-Dornberger team to recast their wartime work as humanitarian:

> IT WAS IMMATERIAL TO HIM WHETHER THEY WERE FIRED AT THE MOON OR ON LITTLE HOMES IN LONDON, SO LONG AS HE COULD PROVE HIS INVENTION WORKED EFFICIENTLY. HE FEELS NO GUILT AT ALL. . . . "AND NOW," SAID DORNBERGER, "WHAT WE HOPE IS THAT THE WORLD WILL USE OUR EXPERIENCES OF THE LAST 15 YEARS FOR ROCKET DEVELOPMENT IN TRAVEL AND OTHER WAYS." "THAT'S RIGHT," SAID VON BRAUN EAGERLY, "OUR ROCKETS ARE REALLY A GREAT BOON FOR PEACE, IF YOU ONLY LOOK AT IT THE RIGHT WAY."

Readers who had survived the V-2 bombardment of London and Antwerp were well aware that von Braun had indeed worked for peace, but for one imposed by a victorious Germany. After the *Express* article was printed, there were calls to bring both of the men to the UK for trial as war criminals.

After much discussion with higher-ups, Major Staver received permission to take Wernher to Nordhausen to help him round up engineers and technicians still in hiding. Over 19-21 June, Staver, with Wernher's assistance, collected 1,000 specialists. These men were shipped to the American zone ahead of the Russian occupation. Staver's main concern was keeping the Soviets from getting their hands on potentially important information and skills. What would happen to these men once they were under American control remained to be determined. While they waited for a decision, Wernher was moved around. He was briefly held and interviewed by British agents in Kransberg Castle, where Albert Speer and other high-ranking Nazis were held. The code name for the program was Operation Dustbin. Werner was then moved to a schoolhouse in Witzenhausen, with other technocrats and their families. It was crowded and difficult, but as usual, Wernher made the best of it, arranging for privacy and getting a new girlfriend.

Wernher was still unaware that his treasure trove of documents had been discovered, and Staver didn't tell him. He did, however, continue to ask Wernher if he knew of any hidden documents, and the answer was always no. Staver was convinced that more documents existed, so he sent teams with metal detectors into the area around Dornberger's former headquarters in Bad Sachsa. Purely by luck, one of his teams stumbled across a trove of five crates that Dornberger had buried, containing 260 pounds of technical documents. Dornberger's and von Braun's main caches had now been found without their assistance, and despite their repeated assurances that no hidden documents existed. This would have raised serious questions about their reliability, had the promise of advanced Nazi weapons been less alluring.[135]

On 29 June, Dornberger was interrogated by British officers working on Project Backfire. This project was designed to teach the Allies how to launch V-2 rockets. The British were taking the lead, in part because they had found several completely assembled V-2s on railroad cars within the British Zone. The Americans had plenty of parts, enough for 100 V-2s, but those parts, along with a number of complete rockets, were already in the US. Dornberger thought that cooperating with this program would increase his leverage with the Americans. If he could get the British to make him an offer, the Americans would have to stop dawdling and make one themselves. So Dornberger assisted the British, giving them tips on proper procedures and the names of staff members who could provide specifics on various technical details. It soon became clear to the British that the infrastructure and launch facility requirements far exceeded what they had imagined.

---

[135] Georg Rickhey, the General Manager at the Mittelwerk, had also buried important documents. A British intelligence officer got Rickhey to reveal where he had hidden 42 boxes of documents dealing with the V-1 and V-2 programs.

While the rocket team was held in limbo, the Joint Chiefs of Staff (JCS) were considering their options. Before the German surrender, an inter-governmental panel (the State-War Navy Coordinating Committee, SWNCC), issued a directive that captured Nazi scientists should not be involved in military research. That position was suddenly problematic, given that the JIOA had collected over a thousand German scientists, most of them Nazis and many SS or SA members as well. Even if the Joint Chiefs were to decide that Nazis could work on military projects, the Department of State, a member of the SWNCC, would refuse to issue US Visas. So what could be done to get these men into the country?

The answer they formulated and approved was called Operation Overcast, to be run by the JIOA. Although Overcast needed approval by President Truman, it was set in motion almost immediately. The goal was to shorten the war with Japan by utilizing a select number of Nazi specialists who would be brought to the US temporarily. Because it would be only temporary, and the specialists would be under military control, they felt a visa wasn't required, and therefore there was no need to involve or inform the Department of State. Once their work was completed the Nazi technicians would be returned to Germany, and any found or even suspected of being war criminals would be returned immediately. At least that was the stated plan, i.e. the one most likely to win approval. In retrospect, it seems likely that the real plan was rather different.

The JIOA anticipated bringing 350 Nazi scientists to the US, and distributing them among military research centers and companies engaged in military production. Roughly one-third of them would be assigned to LtC. Toftoy's rocket program. The political problems Toftoy faced were that the V-2 rocket program was inextricably interwoven with the horrors and abuses at Dora and the Mittelwerk, and that the slave laborers for the program had come from Buchenwald and Nordhausen, names all too familiar to war crimes prosecutors and to the American public.

Military Intelligence (G-2) had already placed a security lid over the Mittelwerk, and the presence of Allied airmen at Buchenwald had already been concealed. The information blackout had started virtually as soon as the Dora and Buchenwald camps were liberated. The names of American airmen at Buchenwald and the death of Lt. Beck were included in military intelligence memos in May 1945. Yet when a congressional committee published the official US government report on German concentration camps after visiting both Nordhausen and Buchenwald, the introductory section stated:

> BEFORE PROCEEDING WITH DETAILED STATEMENTS CONCERNING THE SEVERAL CAMPS VISITED, WE BELIEVE A PRELIMINARY WORD AS TO JUST WHAT THESE CAMPS ARE USED FOR WOULD BE OF VALUE. IN THE FIRST PLACE, THE CONCENTRATION CAMPS FOR POLITICAL PRISONERS MUST NOT BE CONFUSED WITH THE PRISONER OF WAR CAMPS. NO PRISONERS OF WAR WERE CONFINED IN ANY OF THESE POLITICAL PRISONER CAMPS, AND THERE IS NO RELATIONSHIP WHATEVER BETWEEN A CONCENTRATION CAMP FOR POLITICAL PRISONERS AND A CAMP FOR PRISONERS OF WAR.[136]

This categorical statement would henceforth be the official position of the US government. The British, who had their own plans for German rocketeers, placed a nearly identical disclaimer in an April 1945 report to Parliament.[137]

When Buchenwald was liberated, the US Army seized the entry log and the office files, so they soon had a complete list of the names of the Buchenwald airmen. War crimes investigators circulated this list to stations throughout the ETO, to determine whether or not the men were still alive. It was a rather short list, however, as it included only the names of the commissioned officers.[138] The Army Judge Advocate General's office scheduled depositions from these officers for potential use in war crimes trials. All of the related paperwork, including the war crimes depositions, was collected along with the captured German documents and the MIS/OSS interviews and reports, and classified Top Secret. As far as the American public was concerned, the Mittelwerk never existed, and American POWs were never held in concentration camps.

---

[136] Atrocities and Other Conditions in Concentration Camps in Germany, submitted to Congress on 15 May 1945 for approval and publication.

[137] Buchenwald Camp, The Report of a Parliamentary Delegation, published in April 1945. Given Eisenhower's position regarding Nazi criminality, it is likely that the existence of the Buchenwald airmen was withheld from Eisenhower, as well as from the congressional and parliamentary representatives.

[138] In WWII, noncoms were not considered to be as important or as reliable as commissioned officers. After the war, war crimes investigators primarily contacted noncoms who were named as witnesses in the depositions of officers.

Plans for Operation Overcast were finalized by 20 June, submitted for approval by the JIOA on 6 July, and formally approved on 19 July 1945. President Truman officially authorized Operation Overcast later in July, after receiving assurances that the Germans brought into the country would be on short contracts, and that dedicated Nazis and known or suspected war criminals would be excluded. In discussing this with Truman, Justice Robert Jackson, who would later be the chief prosecutor at the Nuremberg war crimes trials, wrote, "I have assurances from the War Department that those likely to be accused as war criminals will be kept in close confinement and stern control.[139]

What transpired was something quite different. Through a complicated agreement among the Allies, the US agreed to loan a number of rocket specialists to the British for Project Backfire. The plan was to have the detained German specialists teach the Allies how to assemble, prep, and launch three intact V-2 rockets that the British had located in their sector. The British had a wish list: they wanted Dornberger and Axster for three weeks, von Braun, Riedel, and Steinhoff (among others) for two months, and a larger group for the duration of Project Backfire. No firm agreement was in place when on 22 July, General Dornberger, Dr. von Braun, and 77 other German engineers and technicians were taken by truck to the Krupps Proving Grounds at Cuxhaven, a coastal town on the North Sea that sat within the British Zone of partitioned Germany.

Two days later, Dornberger, Steinhoff, Schröder, and von Braun were moved to London for two weeks of interrogations that resembled corporate negotiations. Wernher was wined and dined and had cordial meetings with the Minister of Supply, who took great care to avoid offending him. A report filed at the time makes interesting reading:

> I SAW VON BRAUN AND HALF A DOZEN OF HIS EXPERTS FOR A SHORT TIME WHILE THEY WERE IN THE COUNTRY. . . . THEIR REPLIES TO QUESTIONS CERTAINLY CONFORMED TO THE DIRECTIVE QUOTED AT THE FOOT OF PAGE 1 OF THE SPECIAL INTERROGATION REPORT. STEINHOFF WAS THE MOST WILLING TO TALK, AND I GOT THE IMPRESSION THAT WE COULD HAVE GOT MORE OUT OF HIM IF WE HAD HIM ALONE.

---

[139] SWNCC 57/3, September 12, 1945.

VON BRAUN SEVERAL TIMES INTERVENED TO EXPLAIN WHY IT WAS IMPOSSIBLE TO GIVE ANSWERS TO QUESTIONS WHICH I HAD PUT TO STEINHOFF AND THE LATTER MIGHT PROBABLY HAVE ANSWERED. I ALSO SAW DORNBERGER. HIS TECHNICAL INFORMATION WAS SUPERFICIAL AND SALESMANLIKE. HE WAS OBVIOUSLY FISHING FOR A BRITISH BID FOR HIS SERVICES, AND THOSE OF HIS SUBORDINATES, WHICH HE COULD USE TO MAKE THE AMERICANS RAISE THEIRS, WHICH HE WAS ALSO EXAGGERATING. HE WAS OBVIOUSLY CONFIDENT OF HIS PROSPECTS OF KEEPING THE OLD FIRM TOGETHER AND UNDER HIS OWN DIRECTION. IT IS NOT IRRELEVANT THAT THE PEENEMÜNDE SET UP WAS CHANGED FROM A GERMAN ARMY EXPERIMENTAL STATION (HAP 11) TO A SEMI-COMMERCIAL ORGANIZATION (ELEKTROMECHANISCHE WERKE [SIC] GMBH). THIS FIRM IS STILL TRYING TO DO BUSINESS.[140]

The British also held lengthy discussions with Paul Schröder about his involvement with the rocket program. Many of his comments could have raised red flags about von Braun's reliability as a resource, as he cited specific examples of instances where von Braun made wildly exaggerated claims about performance capabilities, accuracy, and project timelines, and highlighted Wernher's tendency to select a team of subservient dependents and to reject outside advice and opinions, even from qualified specialists. The British felt that this was in keeping with the profile they had already built of von Braun, and with Jessel's evaluation in early June.

None of the Germans had been looking forward to the trip to the UK. They knew that the British considered them responsible for the V-2 bombardment of London and Antwerp, which left them open to charges as war criminals. But in practice, things worked out quite well, other than for General Dornberger. The British disliked and distrusted him. Their suspicions were confirmed when secret recordings revealed he planned to play the British off against the Americans and spark a bidding war for the services of the rocket team. There was concern that Dornberger might prevent the German technicians from freely exchanging information, and his security report stated: "Consider likely to exploit his considerable influence over EW personnel against Allied interests. Therefore desirable he has no further contact with EW Personnel." As a result,

---

[140] Miscellaneous papers of Prof. R. V. Jones, Kew Archives, London, DEFE 40/21

Dornberger was housed separately, with his interactions restricted and closely monitored.

Meanwhile, the British in Cuxhaven continued to work with their German tutors, and new questions surfaced requiring additional expertise. Eventually the Cuxhaven program involved roughly 150 rocket technicians plus an additional 600 German POWs tasked with the manual labor involved. These laborers fared much better than the POW laborers at Peenemünde or the Mittelwerk, for all of the Germans were well paid, adequately housed, and well fed, and they received generous bonuses when the program ended.

The Cuxhaven program was still gearing up when two atomic bombs were dropped on Japan, bringing the war in Asia to an abrupt end. The pressure to use the German expertise to defeat their former allies in Japan was now relieved. But this did little to dampen the enthusiasm of the Allies for utilizing the captured German brain trust, which was now seen by the JIOA as a hedge against future confrontations with the Soviet Union.

By late August, the US was demanding that the Germans in London be returned to US control. It soon became a political hairball. The British Ministry of Supply had expected to divide the German technocrats evenly with the Americans, but now it seemed that the Americans wanted all of the key personnel. Cables flew back and forth, the British sounding slighted and aggrieved and the Americans unwilling to yield. Finally, a deal was struck where the Americans would get the specialists they coveted, but the British would be kept apprised of the developments and advances.

After much ado, in early September, the British returned Wernher and several of the specialists who had accompanied him to Cuxhaven to the Americans. But to Wernher's dismay, Walter Dornberger wasn't released.[141] Despite the political wrangling and secrecy concerns, Wernher's leverage improved, as the Backfire program successfully launched three V-2s. The rockets performed as expected, traveling up to 155 miles before falling into the sea. The last launch was attended by representatives of each of the Allied forces (the Soviets included), plus a press crew.

LtC. Toftoy's group was now gathering the specialists from Bleicherode and the Mittelwerk at Landshut, a river town four miles

---

[141] For the next two years, Dornberger would primarily be held at Special Camp 11, in Bridgend, Glamorgan, a POW facility set up to hold officers and noncoms under investigation for war crimes. His conversations with other officers were secretly recorded and analyzed.

northeast of Munich.[142] A German army barracks in Landshut had been commandeered and converted to "Camp Overcast." Wernher was impressed by how many Peenemünders had been collected. He knew that his report on the potential of his rocket programs had impressed Toftoy, and that the plan was for the rocket team to relocate to the US, but there were way too many people at the Overcast base. Would they all be relocating?

When he asked, Wernher was told that there were three tiers of personnel at Landshut. The first tier consisted of essential people who would be shifted to the US to maximize their value. A second tier was for scientists and engineers who were of value to the US (and thus potentially to the Soviets) but who could do their work under supervision at Landshut. And third were the engineers and technicians that fell somewhere in between — they would be nice to have in the US, but they weren't at the top of the priority list for transfer.

LtC. Toftoy had received approval to move only 100 rocket specialists to the US. Since he was #1 on the list, Toftoy gave Wernher the job of triaging the rest. The chosen few that Wernher selected would be hired on six-month before they left Germany. Because they were only entering on a temporary basis for military consultation, the men would not require visas from the State Department. After much deliberation, Wernher, who had expected everyone in the top tier to accompany him, was able to trim his list to 118 specialists, the most loyal and trustworthy members of his team.

The six-month government contracts were between German Nationals and the US War Department. Wernher read through the paperwork very carefully before signing. The government would pay transportation from and to a stipulated address in Germany and provide a transit allocation of $6 per day. In turn, he would agree to work on research, design, development, and other scientific work as assigned. His travel would be restricted, but he would not be confined. Standard military housing would be provided, with medical care and food, plus vacation time and sick leave. He could bring his family and any dependents with him. He was delighted to find that his contract stipulated that an annual salary of $9,600 (the equivalent of a $126,500 salary today). It seemed almost too good to be true — not only would he be paid a great deal of money, but he would leave Germany before any awkward questions were raised about his wartime activities.

---

[142] Ironically, this was one of the places Fred had been sent to clear bomb damage while he was at Stalag VIIA.

On 18 September 1945, Wernher boarded a plane to the US, accompanied by six other members of the rocket team and nine German specialists in other fields. The rest of the rocket men and their families would follow over the next two months, traveling by ship from Le Havre.

The group was flown to Delaware and then continued on to Fort Strong, a stark facility situated on a small island in Boston Harbor. Wernher spent two weeks there filling out forms and being interviewed by technical teams from various military departments. It was cold and boring, and he was very glad when Major Hamill, the officer who had packed up the V-2 components, arrived in early October. Hamill had come to escort Wernher and several colleagues to the DC area, so that Wernher could have meetings with LtC. Toftoy at the Pentagon. While in the DC area, von Braun and several others stayed at a secure government facility known as PO Box 1142, located at what is now Fort Hunt Park. This complex was originally a site where captured Nazi officials could be interrogated by Army officers fluent in German. Lt. Arno Mayer was assigned to the von Braun group, and he wasn't comfortable with his orders. Rather than aggressively interrogating them for critical information, his role during the war, he was to wine and dine them, and to convince them that working for the Army would have plenty of fringe benefits. In their spare time, Arno took them on shopping trips to buy gifts for their families, who were still back in Germany at Camp Overcast. Wernher and the rest relaxed enough to slip back int some old habits, and when Arno heard Wernher refer to him as a "little Jew-boy" he stormed out, only to be told by his superiors to swallow his pride or be court-martialed.[143]

Sometime over this period, Wernher learned that he was headed to Fort Bliss, in El Paso, Texas. Wernher was intrigued. Like the other Germans, he had heard of Texas, but only as the home of cowboys and banditos. Hamill and his charges boarded the train to El Paso on 6 October, arriving at Fort Bliss two days later. The group was not expected, because for security purposes, the use of Fort Bliss as a home for German scientists had not been announced, even to the base commander. For his part, von Braun was unimpressed by the desert location and the primitive base housing. He had been expecting something resembling Peenemünde in its heyday. There had been better quarters at remote V-2 test sites, and those facilities were nowhere near as dry and dusty.

---

[143] Oral interview from NPR This American Life, Episode 595: Deep End of the Pool, Act Two, 26 August 2016

The Nuremberg War Crimes Trials began on 20 November 1945 and continued for the next 11 months. Had their true histories been known, many of the men delivered to Fort Bliss would have qualified as war criminals under the criteria used at Nuremberg. The list of defendants could have included Wernher von Braun, Arthur Rudolph, Herbert Axster, Georg Rickhey, and Magnus von Braun. But the JIOA had fully committed to their plans to use these men. In their view, the potential benefits to national security outweighed any other ethical or moral considerations. All necessary steps would be taken to ensure that the German contractees would not be held accountable for their actions during the war.

CHAPTER 19

Re-entry, 1945-1948

Despite being safely home, Fred's nightmares continued with few interruptions, and toward the end of July, he began experiencing bouts of dizziness and sudden flashes of intense anxiety. These flashes could be triggered by anything sudden or unexpected, but they were especially severe when he was out of the house and moving along the local streets. If he caught a passing glimpse of a uniformed policemen or mailman, he reacted as if an SS guard was coming for him. Loud noises were bombs falling, and jackhammers were machine guns. More than once, he found himself crouching in a doorway or diving under a parked car, actions that usually attracted a small crowd of curious onlookers. He never tried to explain. He simply got up, brushed any debris off his clothing, and continued on his way, trying not to look anyone in the eye. He spent more and more time in Lucille and Eddie's guest room, coming out only for meals.

Once he was moved in, his sister Betty started to press Fred to ask her roommate, Boop, for a date. In the process, Fred learned some things about Boop that he found intriguing. He already knew she could write a good letter, but she had a lot of other things going for her as well. Before the war, she had worked as an executive secretary at Fort Dix, an Army base in New Jersey. While there, she had interviewed and hired Sheila, and the two had become pals. Sheila and Boop decided to enlist together, joining the SPARS (the women's Coast Guard Reserve), shortly after its establishment in November 1942. They went to boot camp together, where they were assigned to a three-person room with Fred's sister. The three women were soon fast friends, staying together for the rest of the war. After leaving Palm Beach, Florida, where Fred had first met Sheila and Boop, they were stationed in New York City, where they lived in a city apartment and worked on Governor's Island. Boop was the senior noncom, a chief petty officer (equivalent in rank to a staff sergeant in the Army). She was an artist, she played the piano, she had graduated from college, taking business and accounting — Fred thought Betty made her sound like Wonder Woman.

As he recalled, she was also very pretty, although when he met Boop, he had thought his sister's roommates were off-limits. So he allowed himself to be prodded into asking Boop if she wanted to meet in the city for dinner. While at dinner, he asked why she had written to him. Boop said that his sister was always talking about him and how much fun he was (and it didn't hurt that she thought he looked like a movie star, although she didn't say that to Fred). She had heard many tales of Fred's childhood escapades. According to his sister, he was always in trouble with their dad, and she was often the reason.

Fred and Boop had a lot of fun together, which got Fred out of his room. They visited the bars, nightclubs, and restaurants together that he had frequented before the war. He was greeted like a prodigal son returning — everyone thought he had been killed in action. Drinks and meals were often on the house. Fred was overwhelmed by the response, and Betty Boop enjoyed everything about the commotion except the showgirls throwing themselves on Fred. Things got even more celebratory when Fred received his back pay. While that lasted, the motto of the day was "When Martini drinks, everybody drinks!"

Over the same period, a movie documentary was produced that presented graphic images filmed at major concentration camps across Germany. Considerable time was devoted to Belsen, Ohrdruf, Auschwitz, Mauthausen, and Buchenwald, and several smaller camps were shown as well. Fred heard about it, but he had no interest in seeing it. Betty, Sheila, and Boop saw it, but they were so sickened by the experience that they dared not mention it to Fred.[144]

Once Fred and Boop were an item, everyone decided that Boop wasn't a great handle, so from that point on, Fred's sister Betty was called Liz, and Boop went back to using Betty. Although Fred didn't give her details of his wartime experiences, he did explain to Betty that he had lingering health issues, like his feet, and she already knew about his recent hospitalization. Betty slowly adapted to Fred's other quirks, although it was sometimes challenging. The slow pace and the fact that their brief walks were followed by taking a seat were easily accommodated. But once, while strolling down Broadway in their evening clothes, a car backfired, and the next thing she knew, Fred was dragging her under a parked car. He had no idea how he had gotten there. Fred was embarrassed, but the only harm done was the ruination of her nylons.

---

[144] The film made no mention of Dora or the Mittelwerk, although the discussion of Buchenwald mentioned that 34,000 prisoners from there had been relocated to work at a remote "munitions factory" without providing any details.

It was a whirlwind courtship, and by mid-July, they were engaged. But a minor crisis followed when he started experiencing a familiar stabbing pain in his abdomen and finding blood in his urine. He knew he had to do something, and on 18 July 1945, he forced himself out of the apartment and traveled across town to the Fort Hamilton Army Hospital. Fred, running a low-grade fever and in severe pain, was admitted with a tentative diagnosis of appendicitis and nephritis. While tests were conducted, he was kept quiet and simply endured the pain. As in previous episodes, Fred's symptoms gradually subsided, and on 25 July, he was released with the notation "Appendicitis and nephritis not found on discharge." Betty had written to him each day, sending the letters to "Fort Hamilton Hospital" and trusting they would reach him.

Fred's 60-day leave ended on 12 September, and he reported to the Dover Air Force Base to spend a week filling out innumerable forms and having a full physical exam. He did the rounds, visiting all of the various Army offices and getting signatures on a form certifying that he was ready to be discharged from military service. The process was eventually completed, and on 2 October, he was ordered to report to the AAF Separation Base in Newark, New Jersey, where on 8 October 1945, Fred received his Separation Qualification Record, listing his training and his responsibilities overseas. He was now out of the Army and unsure what would come next. But the rest of his back pay had arrived, so he and Betty spent evenings together several times each week, going out and having fun in the city.

Fred's back pay was just running out when he received notification of the determination regarding disability payments after separation from the service. His rating form documented that he was missing thirteen teeth, that he had pyorrhea (gum disease), and noted an observation for chronic appendix and nephritis observation in July 1945. It also cited evidence of malnutrition, mentioned the forced march he'd described, and noted his foot problems. In Fred's application for disability, he had mentioned his dental problems and the acute appendicitis attacks at Buchenwald and in the Stalag camps, but those do not appear on his final rating sheet. In fact, there was no mention whatever of Buchenwald in the rating form, nor was it considered in his disability rating, because the Veterans Administration was unable to obtain any confirmation of Fred's claims.

It was not through lack of trying. Before making their disability determination, the VA contacted the Army, requesting information confirming what Fred had told them about his experiences and treatment overseas. The official response came in

November 1945, from the office of Major General Edward F. Witsell (the Adjutant General). It was terse and to the point, saying, "Records of alleged treatment in Prison camp in Germany not now available. In the event that additional records are received, a supplemental report will be furnished to your office." No further information was supplied (then or ever). As a result, all that the Veterans Administration had to go on was the congressional report on German concentration camps, which stated that no POWs had been held there.

The conclusions reached by the Board of Review demonstrated how skeptical they were about Fred's story. They felt his Buchenwald story was either a lie or a delusion, and they felt that his foot problems had no "organic basis," which meant they were all in his head. They could not decide whether he was actually in pain or goldbricking (making something up to inflate his compensation). They could see that he was suffering from extreme anxiety reactions — nobody could fake those symptoms — so they grudgingly decided to base compensation on the basis of psychoneuroses, which included extreme anxiety reactions, the "imaginary" pain in his feet, and his stubborn insistence that he'd been in Buchenwald.

The Board of Review discounted the incidents of abdominal pain Fred had described, stating "No evidence of chronic appendix." The only concession made was to note that his problems were "incurred in the line of duty" and were "likely to result in partial permanent disability." Fred was told that he would be granted a 50% disability pension subject to annual review. To put this in perspective, a 50% disability provided a stipend of $59 per month (in today's terms this would be $778 per month).

Fred was scheduled for followup physicals at intervals. Living at Lucille's, he was able to get by on his 50% disability, but he was unable to find work that didn't involve spending the day on his feet. Fred filed another VA rating appeal, and was examined on 9 April 1946. The examining physician noted on his record that Fred's blood pressure was 132/80 (a bit elevated), and recorded that Fred had pains in his feet and lower back, frequent colds, and chronic abdominal pain. He had been missing work, primarily due to his inability to stand.

The doctor noted that Fred was irritable and jumpy, prone to sudden rages or sudden fears, accompanied by a pounding heart and a rapid pulse. The report continued in terse phrases:

> *Finds it difficult to adjust to noise or excitement. Psychoneurosis, anxiety state. Fear of Nazi soldiers or overhead planes, bad dreams of German*

Nevertheless, the physician did not see residual signs of malnutrition, and he concluded that there was no organic basis for Fred's foot problems.[145] The conclusions of the VA physician as to Fred's status mirrored those of the original committee: psychoneurosis and anxiety neurosis, with somatic complaints, referable to his feet. In other words, the pain in his feet, like his claims to have been in Buchenwald, were all in his mind.

There had been hundreds of thousands of pensions paid in England and the US after extreme hardships and combat in WWI. The symptoms were classified as "shell shock," "effort syndrome," "war neuroses," or "neurasthenia." At the start of WWII, there were still servicemen institutionalized for these conditions. These diagnoses were not considered appropriate for Fred, because with his Buchenwald history classified, there was nothing to distinguish him from the hundreds of thousands of RAMPs who had been held in POW camps. His physical and mental problems seemed so different from what the VA had come to expect, that they interpreted his claims to be exaggerations or fabrications.

The long-term pattern was now set in stone. As with any large bureaucracy, once a VA determination was made, it developed an inertia of its own. Each denied appeal would be cited as grounds for future denials, regardless of what new medical understandings or historical documentation Fred might provide.

In that same 1946 evaluation, the VA dentist recommended that seven of Fred's remaining teeth be removed due to the level of gum disease present. However, in his opinion, the dental problems were not service-related, so Fred was told that he would have to pay for the treatment. Fred put off the procedure while he filed an appeal to the VA.

In the late spring, Fred and Betty set the wedding date for 28 December 1946. The marriage was a Big Deal for Betty's family for many reasons. She was of English/Scottish descent, and one of her antecedents had arrived on the Mayflower. Before they met Fred, Betty's mother and father, Mildred and Harry Hover, had grave reservations about their daughter marrying an "Eye-Talian," and they tried to talk her out of such a rash step. When they met Fred, however, that problem disappeared — they were totally charmed by him. The

---

[145] Although the condition of peripheral neuropathy wasn't recognized by the VA in 1946, its relationship to vitamin deficiencies and frostbite would later be well established.

only other potential problem was that the Hovers were Episcopalian, and Fred's family was Roman Catholic. This was really a non-issue, as Fred had turned his back on religion while at Buchenwald. As a result Fred had no objection to being baptized into the Episcopal Church at the cathedral in Trenton.

Fred had continued to correspond with the Raulins after the war, and over the summer he got a nice letter thanking him yet again for not betraying them to the Gestapo. They also thanked him profusely for the portable AM radio he had purchased and sent them. In closing, they told Fred that little Lionel kissed his picture each night before going to bed. They hoped he would visit them at some point, but Fred had no intention of ever returning to Europe.

It took less than two months for the VA to deal with Fred's appeal regarding the coverage for dental work. After reviewing his dental record prior to his departure for the ETO, the Chief of Dental Service at the VA reversed their decision and authorized the procedure. When Fred finally braced himself and went into the dental clinic they removed nine teeth, rather than seven, and he was given upper and lower dental plates. At 28, Fred had literally given his eye teeth for his country, and by the end of the year he would have only six remaining teeth.

Betty got her discharge on 26 June 1946, leaving the SPARS and moving in with her parents in Trenton. She had been conservative with her pay while in the service, so when discharged, she had savings in the bank. Although Fred initially objected, Betty started picking up the tab when they went out, which helped him stretch his disability income.

In the fall, Fred read an article in the *Brooklyn Daily Eagle* about the German scientists that had been brought to Texas to work for the US government. He found the article interesting, but it didn't seem personally relevant as Buchenwald wasn't mentioned and these were intellectuals rather than Nazis. He had a deep distrust of Germany, but he knew that almost everyone in Europe was struggling to find work just as he was. These scientists had survived the war and were making the best of it.

Fred found work on the factory floor of a mattress company in mid-November. He lasted only two weeks because he could not stand for hours to operate machinery or lug heavy mattresses around all day. Shortly after leaving that job, in December 1946, Fred filed another disability rating appeal, citing his inability to work and his continuing problems with nightmares, anxiety attacks, and pain in his feet.

A week later, he was rushed to the emergency room at Mercer Hospital with acute abdominal pains and a high fever. He was put directly into surgery for acute appendicitis, but that was not what they found upon opening the abdomen. Fred's appendix had obviously burst more than a year before. The only reason a lethal infection had not developed was because the ruptured appendix had become trapped in a pocket of mesentery, created by scar tissue and fused to the abdominal wall.[146] Because the bacteria from his gut were released into a small sealed compartment, they were not free to cause lethal havoc in the abdominal cavity, and his immune system had been battling to prevent the bacteria from spreading through the bloodstream or into surrounding tissues. The ongoing battle accounted for the periodic attacks that he had suffered since the major incident in Buchenwald in the fall of 1944. Over the years since the appendix ruptured, Fred's body had continued to try and seal the area completely, and the scar tissue had thickened to the point that the surgeons found it extremely difficult to access and repair the damage to his gut. An uncomplicated appendectomy takes around 30 minutes, but Fred was in surgery for four and a half hours.

After the surgery, while Fred was in recovery, the Hover's family doctor, who had sent Fred to Mercer Hospital, had a heart-to-heart with Betty. He told her that Fred would make it, but that given Fred's condition and his war experiences, especially the malnutrition and physical abuse, that it was unlikely that Fred would be able to father children. Betty kept that information to herself, and decided to hope for the best. Fred was discharged and recuperated in Brooklyn, with Betty a regular visitor. He was back on his feet in time to be married on schedule, and in January 1947, Fred moved from Lucille's place in Brooklyn to Betty's family home in Trenton.

On 28 January 1947, Fred's appeal to have his pension increased was denied. Paying the hospital bill for abdominal surgery had exhausted their savings, but Fred was confident that the VA would reimburse them. Three months later, he received a letter telling him that because his appendicitis was not service-related, the VA would not reimburse him for the surgery. He appealed, but the appeal was immediately denied. His description of his POW experiences and the surgical report he had submitted were both ignored. Fred and Betty were back to square one. This made them very anxious, because their savings were exhausted, Fred had no job, and Betty was pregnant.

For several months, Fred tried to find work without success. It was terribly frustrating. He spent hours each day walking, or

---

[146] The survival rate for untreated appendicitis, with adequate supportive care, is roughly 25%. The survival rate under Buchenwald conditions must have been near zero.

standing on the train to get to interviews. The pains in his feet, the crowds, the uniforms of the conductors or policemen — by the time he got to the interviews he was in a sorry state. Again and again, he endured the stress and the pain only to find that nobody had a job for a high-strung, partially disabled veteran who hadn't finished high school. He had one really good lead, and the interview was going well, when a forklift on the factory floor dropped a pallet-load with a bang. Fred could remember the interview and the conversation up to that moment. The next thing he knew he was cowering underneath the desk looking at the legs of his interviewer. The rest of the interview was very brief.

In March 1947, Fred finally found a desk job of sorts as a shipping clerk earning $50 per week. It wasn't much, but his boss gave him a flexible schedule and tolerated his missed workdays. Things gradually got more difficult as the year progressed. Betty was having a difficult pregnancy, and over the summer, her doctor told her that she must quit work and stay in bed or risk losing the baby. That cut off their primary source of income. The situation became critical in November 1947, when Betty was rushed to the hospital for a premature delivery. Their son weighed just 3 lb 2 oz at birth, and the odds of his survival in 1947 were extremely low. He was in intensive newborn care for over a week, but somehow took a cue from his dad, beat the odds and survived. Fred and Betty named their son after their respective fathers, making him Frederic Harry Martini.[147]

Fred's physical and mental problems showed no signs of abating. At the March 1948 disability review, the VA doctor noted:

> *Gets occasional nightmares. At times becomes tremulous. Irritable at times. Has a tendency to minimize his complaints. "I get tired but I think that is normal". States that . . . he develops pains in his feet while riding on the train. States his pains do not interfere with his work because his employers are considerate and don't care when he loses time or lays down to rest. Marked tremors of extended fingers. Tremors of eyelids. hyperhydrosis,[148] sensation to pin pricks, touch, and vibration reduced.*

Despite these observations, his disability pension was cut to 30% on 18 April 1948, lowering the benefit to $41.40 per month. Compounding the financial strain, he lost his job when business picked up and his employer needed someone full time who could

---

[147] Fortunately he survived to write this story.

[148] Excessive sweating; all of these symptoms indicate autonomic 'fight or flight' reactions. All would now be considered evidence of severe PTSD.

work on his feet.

It had become abundantly clear to Fred that he needed better skills to get a better job that relied more on brainpower than physical stamina. Betty had attended Rider College after graduating from high school, and Rider offered night school programs in various subjects. The college was not far from the Hover household, so in February 1948, Fred enrolled in a two-year program in Commercial Science. The curriculum was heavy on accounting and business management.

Although he had been home less than three years, Fred had already learned not to discuss specifics of his experiences overseas, and especially not to mention Buchenwald to anyone. He had learned that if he did, the response would usually be scornful disbelief — "Gee, Fred, I didn't know you were a Jew!" and "So where's your tattoo?" were typical comments he received. So except when attempting to sway the VA or when sharing a beer with Eddie Virgilio, Fred kept his experiences to himself.

CHAPTER 20

Project Paperclip, 1946-1948

-⦿⦿-

*One lie leads to another lie that always is the case Your first lie for deception and
your second to save face
And when you are faced with the truth the truth you will deny And to lie to you
comes easy so you tell another lie.*

FRANCIS DUGGAN

The Rocket team members awating transfer to the US were living in and around Landshut, primarily in Camp Overcast. By early 1946, Wernher had orchestrated the transfer of another 90 engineers and technicians from his Bleicherode team who had traveled from Landshut to Le Havre to Fort Strong before heading to Fort Bliss. It was an odd assortment of people, united simply by the fact that von Braun wanted them. Of the 90, only fourteen held doctorate degrees, and the others included engineers and technicians, an artist, a lawyer, a few workshop foremen, and some skilled laborers. Roughly half of the men had been members of the Nazi party, 21 had been in the SA (storm troopers), and two were former SS officers. The inclusion of SS members also raised red flags at the Office of the Military Government, US (OMGUS), as those who were in the SS after 1 May 1939 were supposed to undergo a comprehensive review for potential war crime involvement. Moreover, government regulations explicitly prohibited military employment of former SS members. These discrepancies were noted by OMGUS in their Operation Overcast communications. In response, the two SS members were taken off the list and replaced by specialists with less controversial histories. Significantly, von Braun was not involved in these personnel changes, and nothing was done about SS officers who, like von Braun, were already in the US.

The main attraction of the Fort Bliss facility was the presence of the White Sands Proving Ground nearby. It was at White Sands that Wernher's hand-picked team would try and teach General Electric (GE) employees to assemble and launch V-2s, much as they had taught the British at Cuxhaven. Their main problem was that the scrounged parts that Major Hamill had taken from the Mittelwerk were not in the best of condition, after sitting around for nine months in a windswept, dusty environment.

Progress was slow, and Wernher was dissatisfied with his treatment. This was not the life he had bargained for - it was stiflingly hot, the air-conditioning wasn't always operational, and living conditions were primitive. He was continually being pushed to get the job done, and the fact that he had promised Toftoy things he couldn't deliver anytime soon didn't help a bit (as in Nazi Germany, Wernher's promises invariably outpaced his ability to deliver results). His family members, stuck overseas in the Overcast compound, were also unhappy with their lot. Food was scarce in postwar Germany and everyone chafed at the short rations. His six-month contract would expire soon, and he still wasn't sure whether he would be staying in Fort Bliss, tolerating the unpleasant environment, or returning to an uncertain future in Germany.

The JIOA was equally uncertain about how to proceed. LtC. Toftoy, in charge of the rocket team imported under Operation Overcast, could easily imagine what would happen if the rocket men went back to Germany: they would probably be hired or kidnapped by the Soviets. As none of the other JIOA programs relying on imported German specialists felt any more comfortable with the prospect of their repatriation, the JIOA decided to review and reconfigure the structure of Overcast, making it more flexible and giving them more control. What emerged was called Project Paperclip. The German contractees would be put on renewable annual contracts, rather than the current six-months then leave terms under which they had entered the country. The wrinkle in this plan was that for the German contractees to stay longer, they would have to apply to the Department of State for entry visas. They decided to move ahead anyway, on the assumption that something could be worked out.

Project Paperclip was proposed in March 1946. The JIOA was now thinking big. The project would cover not only the Germans already in the US, but allow the importation of another 750 specialists. Their list included the rest of von Braun's team collected at Bleicherode and Nordhausen, who were still warehoused in limbo at the Operation Overcast facility in Landshut.[149]

Wernher was unaware of the Paperclip proposal, but he knew that his future employment, not to mention his salary, depended on a

---

[149] Before the program ended, it would bring over 1,700 German scientists and technicians into the US. In addition to the rocket team working for the Army, there would be teams working with the Air Force, the Navy, and various military contractors.

perception of the potential military value of his team. Once again, he donned his showman's hat and put his marketing savvy to good use. Wernher had an intuitive sense of what buttons to push to achieve the best results from a particular audience, as evidenced by his pitch to the Nazi military about the Peenemünde project and the promotional essay written in Garmisch-Partenkirchen.

Wernher used a more subtle and gradual approach in his seduction of the American military. He started with a tantalizing memo stating that an A-10 rocket could be used to deliver an atomic warhead, and then in July, he provided a detailed report that concluded that it was likely that the Soviets could produce A-9 or A-10 intercontinental missiles using the materials obtained at the Mittelwerk. Then as a closer, Wernher promised that if he had his old rocket team working with him, he could deliver a functional A-10 intercontinental ballistic missile and an A-11 that could launch a satellite, both within ten years. Wernher knew he was ringing all the right bells, because the US was becoming increasingly paranoid about the Soviet threat. So he agreed with the military assessments that predicted a full-scale war within five years.

In early September 1946, President Truman approved the hiring and importation of up to 1,000 German and Austrian scientists and technicians of vital interest to national security. The unfortunate part, from the perspective of the JIOA and LtC. Toftoy, was that the SWNCC policy statements were too restrictive. Policy 257/22 stipulated that the War Department must screen the backgrounds of those selected, and that reports would be submitted to the State and Justice Departments who would then decide if the specified individuals were qualified to receive US visas. Those not qualified would be ineligible, and if already in the US, they would immediately be deported to Germany. It included a very problematic clause stating that no person who had been "a member of the Nazi party and more than a nominal participant in its activities, or an active supporter of Nazism or militarism shall be brought to the US hereunder." Policy 257/24 was also a potential problem, as it stipulated that "active Nazis," a term difficult to define, were ineligible for hire under Project Paperclip,

The JIOA was now between a rock and a hard place. On the one hand, they had the authority to bring Germans to the US, but on the other hand, many of the people they wanted, including von Braun, would fall afoul of SWNCC Policies 257/22 and 257/24. There were also problematic security leaks, and rumors were circulating in the US press corps that the Army was collecting Nazis and corralling them at Fort Bliss, Wright-Patterson, Aberdeen, and elsewhere. Before the rumors turned the issue into a public relations nightmare, jeopardizing Project Paperclip, the War Department approved a press conference at Wright-Patterson air base to showcase advanced German technology and representatives of the German rocket team. It was to be stage-managed, carefully controlled to conceal the truth under the guise of full disclosure.

The press conference at Wright-Patterson, and similar briefings at Fort Bliss, followed what would become the official "party line." The Paperclip Germans were introduced as apolitical scientists who had spent the war in academic pursuits at an advanced research facility at Peenemünde. The American public was assured that these men had been exhaustively screened, and that they were "ivory tower" scientists who were not involved with any nefarious Nazi activities. Much was made of the congenial working relations between the Germans and their American counterparts, despite the fact that those relations were often difficult and contentious. Staged PR photos were provided, and the resulting articles were carefully vetted by military censors.

With the leaks addressed and publicity managed, it was time to try to sort out the security clearances. On 26 October, the JIOA requested security reports from OMGUS for people on the Paperclip "shopping list" who were living in and around Camp Overcast. On 3 March 1947, a memo was sent from the JIOA to OMGUS requesting that von Braun's security report be revised, as it would never get past a State Department review panel. The same was true for many of the security reports prepared for members of the rocket team who were already at Fort Bliss. In many cases, the recommendations and conclusions reached by the investigators had been completely ignored since at the time, there was no need for outside review. But negative comments in a security report submitted as part of a visa application would cause major problems. For example, the conclusions of the Rudolph report included "100% Nazi. . . . suggest internment," and von Braun's report called him an ardent Nazi who was likely to constitute a security threat.

The request for another security report for Wernher came at a bad time. Since his surrender in 1945, Wernher had been asked repeatedly about missing or hidden V-2 documents, and he'd consistently denied having any information about them. The JIOA already knew that this was a lie, as Major Staver had recovered the 14 tons of paperwork hidden by Huzel and Tessmann at von Braun's orders. Since they already had the paperwork, LtC. Toftoy had no reason to confront von Braun about the discrepancy. But Wernher's web of lies started to unravel in January 1947 when he sent a letter through the US mail to Walter Dornberger's wife in Germany (Dornberger was still out of reach in a POW facility in Bridgend, Wales). With his letter, Wernher included a map, showing the location of a cache of documents buried in a forest near Oberjoch. He asked Dornberger's wife to get the documents and give them to one of the Germans who would be heading to the US under the Paperclip program.

The letter was intercepted by Army censors at Landshut, and alarm bells began ringing. LtC. Edward Tilley, in the Special Investigations section of the Army's Field Intelligence Agency, Technical (FIAT), was put in charge of the investigation. The resulting furor involved both Army security and British Intelligence, culminating in an investigation code named Project Abstract.

Five days later, LtC. Tilley and Dr. John Marchant arrived at Fort Bliss to interrogate von Braun. They wanted it to be a thorough interrogation, but LtC. Toftoy and Major Hamill refused to allow it. They considered von Braun to be irreplaceable, and they explicitly ruled out aggressive tactics.

Instead, Wernher was invited to a lengthy, sometimes rambling, low-key interview. Wernher was uncertain as to the intent of the interview, but the atmosphere was relaxed and congenial. The conversation covered a lot of ground, and Tilley felt it significant that von Braun's descriptions of his responsibilities and activities in Bleicherode were subtly different from those of the other Germans interrogated. When asked about the period before leaving Peenemünde, he spoke freely, but when questioned about the period after his departure from Peenemünde, he was evasive.

At several points, and in many different ways, Tilley and Marchant sought information about documents buried in or around Oberammergau, Oberjoch, Bad Sachsa, or Upper Bavaria in general. Wernher calmly and consistently maintained that he knew nothing whatever about any caches of hidden documents. This drove Tilley wild. Toftoy's ground rules prevented Tilley from confronting Wernher with the evidence of his own letter, nor could he mention the 14 tons of documents Huzel and Tessmann had buried on Wernher's orders. Tilley did ask about labor status reports from the Mittelwerk. Those reports, including death rates, had been forwarded to Wernher's office and recovered from that cache. Wernher said he had never seen any such reports. The question may have unsettled him — Why would they ask about labor reports? — because he lost track of what he had or hadn't said in prior interviews. For example, in 1945 he had claimed that he was in Peenemünde until his car accident, whereas in his 1947 interview, he said that he had gone to Bleicherode to arrange housing for his staff. Tilley knew both statements were incorrect, given the files and correspondence already recovered. Asked to draw an organizational chart for the V-2 program, Wernher failed to include Albin Sawatski, the head of production at the Mittelwerk and his co-chair on the A-4 Production Committee. The omission contrasted with similar charts drawn by other members of the German rocket team, which gave both Sawatski and von Braun considerable prominence. Wernher was clearly avoiding any questions regarding his relationship with Sawatski and the Mittelwerk, neither mentioning that facility nor acknowledging his position and responsibilities in the CCDC-Mittelbau.

Tilley also discovered that von Braun had been withholding information about several advanced German research programs that he had previously "forgotten" to mention, including plans for an atomic rocket. In short, the interview was superficially cordial but intensely frustrating for the interrogators. In the aftermath, Tilley was so infuriated with the dissembling, inconsistencies, and runaround he had gotten from von Braun that he advocated shipping Wernher to a military prison in Germany for more aggressive interrogation. The suggestion fell on deaf ears. If Wernher were treated roughly, Toftoy and Hamill were sure that they would lose the cooperation of the entire German team. Whether or not that was the case, Wernher had done a superb job convincing them that he was irreplaceable, which gave him both protection and leverage.

Over this same period, British and American investigators assigned to the project interrogated Walter Dornberger, several of Dornberger's staff officers, Dornberger's wife, personnel who had worked with von Braun, von Braun's parents, and Wernher's older brother Sigismund. Their statements independently confirmed that von Braun was lying outrageously. When the British asked Dornberger about hidden documents, he admitted that he, von Braun, and Axster had been together when they stashed documents at various locations. Dornberger was then taken to Germany to assist in locating the missing documents.

But when Dornberger took the investigators to the spot where the three men had buried a small tin containing a map indicating the locations of the caches, they found nothing. Dornberger thought it likely that von Braun had moved the tin, for reasons of his own. The project wasn't a total bust, however. When interviewed, Dornberger and Axster admitted that they had each hidden other documents, without telling other team members. With their assistance, Project Abstract recovered those documents for the British and American guided missile programs. However, due to the constraints imposed by LtC. Toftoy, the investigators were never able to determine what Wernher intended to do with the documents he was trying to reclaim.

FIAT was not the only agency concerned about the security of the rocket program at Fort Bliss. FBI agents in the area flagged many strange and suspicious activities involving the imported Germans over this period. For example, Magnus von Braun, Wernher's younger brother, walked into an El Paso jewelry store and sold the proprietor a bar of pure platinum for a small fortune. Nobody could figure out where he got it. Other members of the rocket team received wire transfers of cash from unknown persons in South America, or were found traveling off base carrying highly classified material, which violated multiple security protocols. The FBI was worried that the Texas Germans might be selling classified materials to make easy money, but the Army told the FBI to stand down. There was too great a risk of adverse publicity that would harm the program. The standing orders now appear to be: (1) don't upset von Braun, (2) keep the program on track, (3) avoid adverse publicity, and (4) maintain tight security, as long as it doesn't interfere with orders 1 or 2.

Wernher was totally oblivious to the wrangling that was going on between the Army, FIAT, and the FBI, and shortly after the visit by Tilley and Marchant, he asked to be allowed to return to Germany under military escort to marry his first cousin, Maria von Quistorp. She had just turned 18, whereas Wernher was 35. He later said that he'd fallen in love and decided to marry her when he held her as a newborn in his arms. A trip to Germany would violate the terms of his employment, which specifically prohibited him from returning to Germany while the contract was in effect, but LtC. Toftoy approved the trip by liberal interpretation of an emergency clause. Perhaps in his view, it an emergency — under the circumstances, getting Wernher safely out of the way of investigators not under Toftoy's control seemed like an excellent idea. The wedding took place in Landshut, Germany, in early March.

In April, Toftoy received a report from a counterintelligence team not involved with security clearances for Wernher and his team. It included:

IN PEENEMÜNDE THERE WAS THE V-2 RESEARCH GROUP UNDER THE COMMAND OF THE GERMAN ARMY AND A RESEARCH DEPARTMENT OF THE GERMAN AIR FORCE WHICH WORKED ON THE DEVELOPMENT OF AN ANTI-AIRCRAFT ROCKET WITH REMOTE CONTROL FACILITIES. THE SCIENTIFIC WORK IN THIS DEPARTMENT WAS UNDER THE DIRECTION OF

DR. NETZER.

SINCE THE PRESENT INTEREST TO THE UNITED STATES AND OTHER NATIONS IN THIS WORK HAS DEVELOPED, THE LEADERS OF THE PEENEMÜNDE RESEARCH GROUP HAVE BEEN CONSISTENT IN THEIR OPPOSITION TO THE GROUP UNDER DR. NETZER. PARTICULARLY HAS THIS BEEN TRUE IN THE CASE OF DIR. STEINHOFF AND DR. VON BRAUN WHO HAVE DONE WHAT THEY COULD TO MISREPRESENT AND DISCREDIT THE WORK OF DR. NETZER'S RESEARCH GROUP. VON BRAUN AND STEINHOFF ARE IN THE UNITED STATES.

IN CONNECTION WITH THE PROMOTION OF HIS OWN PERSONAL INTERESTS AND THOSE OF HIS PARTICULAR RESEARCH GROUP, DR. VON BRAUN HAS TWO MEMBERS OF HIS GROUP WHO ARE NOT SCIENTISTS OR TECHNICIANS. THESE MEN ARE DR. AXSTER, A LAWYER IN CIVILIAN LIFE AND A MAJOR IN THE GERMAN ARMY DURING WORLD WAR II, AND DIRECTOR STEINHOFF, A MERCHANT IN CIVILIAN LIFE AND AN OFFICIAL FROM THE GERMAN HIGH COMMAND WHO SERVED AT PEENEMÜNDE UNDER ORDERS FROM BERLIN.

IT APPEARS THAT DR. VON BRAUN MAY ATTEMPT TO PORTRAY THE BACKGROUND OF HIS TWO ASSOCIATES, DR. AXSTER AND DIRECTOR STEINHOFF, AS EMINENTLY SCIENTIFIC.

The agents had written because they feared that Wernher's discrediting of Dr. Netzer could impede proper exploitation of Dr. Netzer's work. Although they flagged the misrepresentation of personnel in his group, they made no further recommendations, saying only that they provided the information to support "such action as is deemed appropriate."

LtC. Toftoy must have decided that there was little to be gained by challenging Wernher at this stage, and the report was filed away. Similarly, no action was taken in response to negative reports about other members of the rocket team. OMGUS reported that Axster's wife was said to be a committed Nazi who physically abused prisoners assigned to her as servants, but that too was ignored.

A revised security report on von Braun arrived from OMGUS investigators in May, but an objective reviewer would have characterized it as lukewarm at best. The same point was made multiple times in the document (italics added):

A SEARCH OF THE FILES OF 7708 WAR CRIMES GROUP FAILS TO DISCLOSE ANY RECORD OF WAR CRIMES AND SUBJECT. NO

CIVIL CRIMES RECORDS WERE CHECKED BECAUSE SUBJECT FORMERLY RESIDED IN THE RUSSIAN ZONE. SINCE SUBJECT FORMERLY RESIDED IN THE RUSSIAN ZONE HIS EMPLOYMENT STATUS COULD NOT BE DETERMINED.

BASED ON AVAILABLE RECORDS, subject is not a war criminal. He was an SS officer but no information is available to indicate that he was an ardent Nazi. Subject is regarded as a potential security threat by the Military Governor, OMGUS. *A COMPLETE BACKGROUND INVESTIGATION COULD NOT BE OBTAINED BECAUSE SUBJECT WAS EVACUATED FROM THE RUSSIAN ZONE OF GERMANY.*

BASED ON AVAILABLE RECORDS subject has not participated in any party affiliations, fraternal, political, military, or other public or private organizations during or since the Hitler regime.

BASED ON AVAILABLE RECORDS, subject has no criminal record or charges of suspicion of being a war criminal.

In other words, the investigators in occupied Germany had no real way to evaluate von Braun. They had no information in their files regarding his activities during the war, and thus no way to decide whether or not he would be a security risk nor whether or not he was a potential war criminal. The only way to answer those questions would be to access records lying within the Russian zone, which was impossible.

A June 1947 memo from the Judge Advocate General's office concerning von Braun was equally circumspect, saying, "There is no positive information linking subject with War Crimes cases which this Group has developed." Use of the term *positive information* rather than *information* suggests that there may have been unsubstantiated reports, but as no clarification was requested, there is no way to be certain.

The Army staff in Germany were not thrilled about being pressed to revise security reports. In reviewing the reports, one lieutenant colonel wrote. "Your attention is invited to paragraph 2(a)(5) of SWNCC 257/24 which indicates that active Nazis are not qualified for exploitation under the Paperclip Program." The wishy-washy response to their whitewashing requests raised hackles inside the JIOA. Captain Bosquet Wev, the Committee Chair, complained that the fuss about a Paperclip candidate's past history was tantamount to "beating a dead Nazi horse."

The ongoing denazification program in Germany added to Project Paperclip's headaches. General Lucius Clay was in charge of the program managed by OMGUS. Under the regulations in force, all Germans over age 18 had to undergo a review of their record and affiliations to determine their level of involvement with the Nazi regime and their support of Nazi principles. Clay simply had too few G-2 investigators to deal with the demands of the JIOA, plus handle thousands of pending denazification reviews. So he took the lazy way out, deciding that from that time onward, Germans already in the US would be exempt from German denazification procedures, and that their security clearances would be the responsibility of US agencies. If they wanted these Germans so badly, they could write their own security reviews. He would, however, provide them with plenty of blank denazification forms.

Meanwhile, on 1 July 1947, Wernher signed his third six-month contract at a salary of $831.25/mo ($10,975/mo today). Three consecutive six-month contracts were difficult to justify under a six-month then home policy, so on 14 July, Army Ordnance recommended that Wernher be approved for immigration. The other good news Wernher received that month was that Walter Dornberger was en route to the US under Project Paperclip. He was soon working on guided missile development at Wright-Patterson air base in Ohio. The decision to release Dornberger to the Americans, rather than returning him to Britain for trial as a war criminal, was an indirect result of his cooperation with the Project Abstract investigation.

From April to August 1947, the Buchenwald War Crimes Trial was held at Dachau. One of the offenses charged was the detention and death of Allied POWs. It would be reasonable to assume that camp records about the Buchenwald airmen, depositions documenting the treatment of the 168 Allied airmen, and the deaths of Philip Hemmens and Levitt Beck would have been featured by the prosecution. However, when challenged for specifics by the defense team, the prosecution was unable to provide the name of a single Allied POW who had been held at Buchenwald, nor could they identify any airmen who had died there. Neither was there any mention, at any point in the trial, of the transfer of thousands of prisoners to Dora and the Mittelwerk for the V-2 program.

Thus in the long run, it didn't matter that Fred and most of the other sergeants hadn't given formal war crimes depositions. Through the summer of 1945, war crimes documents relating to the Buchenwald airmen had been assembled and classified Secret by the Judge Advocate General, for use in subsequent prosecution. But all of that documentation was subsequently collected and buried. The collection process was remarkably thorough. Eugen Kogon, a prisoner who worked in Block 46 at Buchenwald, prepared a comprehensive *Buchenwald Report* in April 1945. The report, written in German, had a section specifically addressing the detention of Allied airmen at Buchenwald. The completed report subsequently disappeared, although a few individual sections were made available to prosecutors at the Buchenwald War Crimes trial.[150] The Buchenwald file cards and records of the airmen were withheld. Even the relevant pages of the train manifest listing the prisoners transported from Paris to Buchenwald were excised.[151] By the time the Buchenwald trial got underway, there was no evidence to indicate that what Fred and the other airmen might claim to have experienced was anything more than a flight of fancy.

Orders for the collection of files related to the Buchenwald airmen have not been found, but such comprehensive record suppression was no accident. Moreover, the British, who expected to receive the rocket team's research data, also collected and suppressed the files of their Buchenwald airmen, withholding the names and depositions from war crimes prosecutors. It is hardly credible that two allied governments would collect and classify the records so efficiently and then simultaneously lose track of them. Nor was this the only case where national security concerns were placed ahead of justice for American POWs. Over the same period that the airmen's records and depositions were sequestered (1946-1947), the war crimes depositions from American POWs subjected to chemical and biological warfare experimentation in Japan were collected and suppressed, the related war crimes trials were cancelled, and the war criminals were pardoned. In return, the Japanese war criminals agreed to cooperate with the US government and share their experimental data.[152] The suppression orders were issued on behalf of the JIOA by Army Intelligence (G-2), which was responsible for security of both the Japanese programs and Project Paperclip, and it is undeniable that

---

[150] A single carbon copy of the manuscript was found in private hands in 1987, and it was painstakingly translated and published by Mr. David Hackett. Publication details are in Appendix 7, but the text associated with the heading Allied Airmen in Buchenwald was omitted.

[151] The manifest can be obtained from the International Tracing Service; the original German document ends at page 49, with prisoner 1574. At some later date pages 50-53, which contain the names of the Buchenwald airmen, were retyped, annotated, and appended. The last listed airman is James Zeiser, prisoner 1750. The fate of the original German pages, which would have included the airmen and several hundred additional French prisoners, is unknown.

[152] The US government vehemently denied that the surviving POWs were telling the truth about their experiences in Japanese hands until the associated memos and records were declassified in 2007.

publicity about the Buchenwald airmen would have led to questions that would have threatened the security of the Paperclip program.[153]

Given the subject matter, the drastic security measures imposed for the Dachau-Nordhausen trial were not surprising. The defendants in this trial, which lasted from August to December 1947, included Georg Rickhey, General Manager at the Mittelwerk. Rickhey had been high on the list of suspected war criminals sought by OMGUS, but Project Paperclip had spirited him away to work at Wright-Patterson air base. As if that weren't enough of a potential problem for the JIOA, the prosecution summoned Arthur Rudolph and Wernher von Braun to testify before the court.

Rickhey had only arrived at Wright-Patterson air base in July 1947, but he was already in hot water with his American associates for expressing offensive Nazi political and racist sentiments. Major Eugene Smith, an Air Force investigator assigned to review the case against Rickhey, headed to Fort Bliss to interview the Germans who knew Rickhey. Despite advance notice, on arrival he found that both Wernher von Braun and Magnus von Braun were unavailable.

Major Smith was able to interview Arthur Rudolph. Those interviews revealed many conflicting and self-serving statements that contradicted the information provided in the interviews of lower level German staff members at the Mittelwerk. The discrepancies were noted, but because Smith was supposed to be investigating Rickhey, rather than Rudolph, he dug no deeper. This was the second "free pass" Rudolph received. In 1945, Canadian intelligence officers had interviewed staff at the Mittelwerk and received information implicating Rudolph in war crimes, including the execution of slave laborers. By the time they were ready to interrogate Rudolph, however, he was at Cuxhaven helping the British launch V-2s, and the situation was deemed too politically delicate to pursue at that time. Afterward, Rudolph was spirited away to the US and became virtually untouchable.[154]

The attitude of the Army on this matter is reflected in a detailed memo requesting that von Braun and two of his associates provide testimony that would exonerate Rickhey and document that he had

---

[153] Paperclip recruited several Nazi researchers who experimented on concentration camp prisoners. The most prominent was Dr. Hubertus Strughold, a Colonel in the Luftwaffe, who was responsible for lethal high-altitude, oxygen deprivation, and explosive decompression studies on prisoners, including children. After a long career in the US he became known as the "Father of Space Medicine."

[154] As a result, questions that should have been asked in 1945 about his involvement in war crimes at the Mittelwerk were not posed until the 1980s.

nothing to do with the working or living conditions, discipline, or punishment of slave laborers at the Mittelwerk. The testimony was to be given by deposition, because the JIOA felt that letting Wernher von Braun or Arthur Rudolph attend the Nordhausen trial was too much of a risk: first, they might reveal something incriminating during testimony, and second, they might be recognized by prosecution witnesses who had been slave laborers at the Mittelwerk. So the decision was made to cooperate without really cooperating. Georg Rickhey was packed up and shipped to Dachau for the trial, but the Army refused to allow either Rudolph or von Braun to leave the US, citing national security concerns. (The Court may not have been aware that Wernher had been allowed to go to Germany to get married a few months earlier.)

Wernher von Braun and Arthur Rudolph testified by answering a list of prosecutorial questions that were vetted by the Army. They also wrote letters attesting to the fine, upstanding character of Mr. Rickhey. Wernher went so far as to mention how much conditions for the slave labor force had improved in 1944 under Rickhey's management. In that testimonial, Wernher admitted visiting the Mittelwerk 10 or 15 times but stated that he had never seen any bodies, hangings, or signs of prisoner mistreatment. That was quite remarkable, if not miraculous, given that he had visited the tunnels during their hellish expansion phase of 1943-44, in the Spring of 1944 when prisoner abuse by civilians was so bad that even the SS complained, and in the winter of 1944-45, when prisoners hanged for sabotage dangled just outside the windows of Rudolph's office.

Rudolph's testimony was almost entirely fabricated. He stated that when he first arrived at the Mittelwerk on September 1943, the tunneling was virtually completed, the air was clean, the floors were paved, sanitary facilities were excellent, and the food provided to the prisoners was as good as what German civilians received. From his description one would assume that the laborers found mints on their pillows when they returned from a shift on the assembly line. He said he had seen no prisoner abuse or mistreatment. Rudolph was committing perjury — the tunneling was just starting in September 1943, conditions for the prisoners were catastrophic, there was neither paving nor sanitation, and the food provided was so poor in quality and quantity that the workers were starving. The Army censors who vetted the questions would certainly have reviewed the responses, but no corrections were made. Further, the JIOA did not provide, nor did they mention, the tons of classified administrative documents from the Mittelwerk and Peenemünde in their possession that would have convicted Rickhey and Rudolph, and implicated both von Brauns.

Security concerns thus placed the US government in the curious position of withholding key documentation and facilitating perjury at an international tribunal that was supported by the US, and which ostensibly administered fair and impartial justice.

At the end of the trial, Rickhey was acquitted largely on the basis of his testimony and the glowing recommendations of von Braun and Rudolph.[155] The abuse of prisoners was blamed on the SS and on Albin Sawatski, the head of production planning, who had died in May 1945 while in American custody. However, Rickhey's testimony did include some aspects that made the JIOA uneasy. For example, he testified that von Braun had received reports that included weekly updates on how many deaths were occurring among the labor force, information on the 350 prisoners hanged in the Mittelwerk outside Rudolph's door, and discussed the fact that practically all of the civilian supervisors carried out beatings, and that some supervisors had asked the SS to hang prisoners for shoddy workmanship. In addition, Wernher had admitted on the record that he had been a frequent visitor to the Mittelwerk.

This was not a pretty picture, and if the press got wind of it, the program might become politically indefensible. So the US government, through the JIOA and the Judge Advocate General's office, took the unprecedented step of classifying the entire trial record and all related documents as Top Secret. The files were buried and inaccessible in the interest of national security, denying historians and the general public access to detailed descriptions and accounts of the Dora Concentration Camp and the Mittelwerk. For decades the whole complex, and the abuses suffered by the slave laborers, remained out of sight and out of mind.

When reviewing Wernher's visa application, the State Department felt that it contained insufficient background information. So the FBI was asked to perform security checks on Wernher and the other Paperclip candidates independent of those conducted by the military. The JIOA, at meetings held without the State Department representative, decided that the problem was one of interpretation. After all, what constituted an "ardent Nazi" was just a matter of semantics. So memos were issued, ordering a more thorough investigation of the Paperwork contractees. However, one memo explicitly stated that Wernher should be approved regardless of his Nazi past, and another urged investigators to look for "all

---

[155] Although it seems hard to believe, the testimony of one von Braun team member was routinely accepted without question as sufficient grounds to exonerate another team member accused of war crimes.

extenuating circumstances" regarding his membership in the SS. The Army had Wernher right where Toftoy wanted him, and they weren't going to give him up.

It is quite clear that the JIOA felt that the real problem facing the country was communism in the future, not Nazism in the past. There were still concerns that some of the Paperclip contractees might be pulled back into war crimes investigations or tribunals in Germany, but that problem was soon solved. In November 1947, the US government announced that war crimes investigations were no longer a priority, and that related extradition requests from Germany would no longer be accepted. Shortly after this announcement, the first batch of rewritten security reports arrived, but the von Braun file was held back as incomplete. Availability of the file notwithstanding, Wernher was given yet another short employment contract on 22 November 1947.

In early 1948, a meeting of the minds between J. Edgar Hoover, Director of the FBI, and the JIOA resulted in a policy change regarding the FBI's security clearances for Paperclip contractees. In the future, membership in the Nazi party and Nazi organizations, including the SS, would no longer automatically make someone a security risk. Assured that his past would no longer be an impediment to his continued employment, the JIOA presented Wernher von Braun with his first annual contract on 16 February 1948. His starting salary was $9,975 per year, plus a variety of attractive benefits and allowances, and it took effect shortly before Fred's yearly pension was reduced to $546. The past histories of both men had been classified by the US Government, but only one of them was benefiting from the secrecy.

The Paperclip program was still actively engaged in bringing German specialists to the US for the military and for commercial companies that had military contracts. In some cases, the Paperclip team had to work fast, spiriting their targets out of Germany before a scheduled hearing before a denazification court. In April 1948, the German government, concerned about a major "brain drain," prohibited its citizens from signing military contracts with foreign powers. The JIOA fought against its implementation. A 2 April 1948 memo said, "Since such a regulation would involve all Germans including Paperclip, which are working for intelligence agencies, suggest that you take such necessary steps to inform the proper authorities of the possibility of enactment of such a law. Col. Liebel proposes Office of Military Government for Bavaria be allowed to advise German authorities such regulation will not receive approval of US authorities." Although the regulation passed, it was blatantly ignored.[156]

In May 1948, Wernher's revised-revised security file went for State Department review, but it got bounced back because the State Department felt that his Nazi party membership and SS rank would make approval by the Department of Justice impossible.[157] The file needed further revision.

Wernher, meanwhile, thought that he wasn't being given enough resources to achieve his goals. It reminded him of the early years with the VfR, the amateur rocket society he had joined in college. What he needed was public interest that would encourage, if not mandate, military involvement in the space program. So he decided to write a novel about the colonization of Mars, hoping it would galvanize public support for rocketry.

The story, set in 1984 and ultimately titled *The Mars Project*, described a colonizing trip to Mars involving ten ships, 100 men, and a few women to do the housework. It was filled with technical details such as calculations of thrust and payload that made for heavy reading. He included a cost analysis that indicated it was beyond the capabilities of individuals or companies. Only governments could afford to underwrite such a program. Notably, the voyage to Mars was undertaken only after a lengthy and disastrous war that ended after the Communist Eastern countries were nuked into oblivion by atomic bombs raining down from orbiting US space stations.

There was the real message: military supremacy in space would make the US safe from the Communist hordes, and only then would it be possible to explore other planets. The fact that this required the obliteration of millions of people by atomic weapons was glossed over — a regrettable but necessary prelude to further progress. The parallels to his missile work for the Third Reich were chilling, but they apparently never occurred to him.

---

[156] The US assured the Germans that the acquisition phase of the program had ended, eventually changing the name of the program, but the recruitment of German specialists continued until 1973.

[157] Wernher's visa application had to be approved in principle by the State Department, pass a detailed review by the Immigration Department, and then be cleared by the Department of Justice before returning to the State Department for issuance of a visa.

CHAPTER 21

Divergence

—◆Ǯ—

1949-1951

FRED MARTINI

In 1949, the War Claims Commission was accepting applications for POW compensation payments of $1.50 per day. Fred carefully filled out all of the related forms, outlining his capture and the beatings, abuse, and forced labor that followed in Buchenwald, Stalag Luft III, and Stalag VIIA. He sent the forms off, but a response was not immediate because processing was slow.

With his pension soon to be cut to $13 per month, Fred filed another rating appeal, recapping his medical history and adding that he had been unable to find steady work over the last four years. His application was denied. When Fred went to bed each night, he tossed and turned, thinking about his options. Should he just give up? In the years since he left the Army, he had gotten nowhere — he seemed to be beating his head against a brick wall. But Fred was far too stubborn to give up. If he got through Buchenwald, he could get through this as well. He needed money, and a pension increase would be a lifesaver. But he also wanted the VA to admit they were wrong about him. His illnesses were real, not imaginary, and he wasn't a delusional nutcase who "alleges he was in Buchenwald."

By June of that year, Fred had completed 18 months of the two-year business program at Rider College, with a grade of A or B in every course. But money was tight, and Betty was a stay-at-home mom. So Fred reluctantly left the Rider program when he was offered a job as a clerk at Wilcox and Gibbs, a company that manufactured sewing machines. It was his first chance for a desk job, one that would keep him off his feet. He and Betty moved into their own place, a rented home in Nanuet, New York, a few miles from the company's facility in Nyack.

Fred's next VA rating evaluation was conducted in May 1951 at the VA offices in New York City. The physician noted his present complaints as pains in the feet, nervousness, occasional pain in the abdomen, heart palpitations, jumpiness, and being easily upset. Notes indicated that he was losing days at work due to nervousness, and observations included that Fred was very tense, anxious, and restless, all consistent with a chronic severe anxiety reaction. However, the physician felt he had made a "good social adjustment," and after review, his pension was cut to 10%, or roughly $14 per month. It was not what Fred and Betty had hoped for and desperately needed.

In June 1951, Fred finally received a response from the War Claims Commission regarding his application for POW compensation. They agreed to pay him $1.50/day for the period of 21 October 1944 to 29 April 1945, while he was at Stalag Luft III and Stalag VIIA. They refused to issue compensation for the period he spent at Buchenwald because he could not prove that he had been there. The commission did not go so far as to say Fred was lying, but they did say, "The above dates were determined after comparing the statements in your application. . . . with official records on file in the War Claims Commission."

Fred was furious, and tired of being treated as a liar or a lunatic, so he filed a formal appeal with the War Claims Commission. The anxiety reaction, the pains in his feet, his jumpiness, and his nightmares were bad. Having to explain what had happened to him to a system that seemed either to ignore or dismiss his problems was even worse. The more he thought about his treatment by the US government, the angrier he got.[158]

Over the next week or so, Fred and Betty reviewed their finances. Without a better job, they would be broke in six months. So Fred, Betty, and Ricky had no choice but to move back into the Hover family home in Trenton, leaving Fred with a long commute by train to Nyack (2.5 hours each way). His feet pained him, and once home, Fred was distracted and depressed about his situation and his failure to support his family adequately. Sometime in November, something snapped, and shortly after midnight on a cold night, Fred gathered up everything that reminded him of the military, including his uniforms and his medals, and burned them in the back yard. Betty saw this, but didn't try to stop him — she may actually have been relieved.

Fred got along well with Betty's mother and brother, but he was still desperate to get back out on his own. He started looking for a job closer to Trenton, filling out job applications without providing full details. For example, in the space for high school, he gave the name of the high school he'd attended (Abraham Lincoln High). That was accurate even though he had only completed year 11. Similarly, under

---

[158] The survivors of experiments in Japanese POW camps felt the same way. "We fought the enemy, then came back to find we were fighting our own government." Holmes (2010), p128.

tertiary education he indicated that he had attended Rider College enrolled in a two-year business program, without adding that he hadn't graduated.

This approach, which provided truthful, if incomplete, answers to the questions posed, seemed to work wonders. A month later he had his first promising interview. He was nervous and jittery, but that wasn't unusual among job candidates. He was hired by Roebling Wire Products, and entered their foreman training program in August 1951. The plant was relatively close, and although the starting salary was low, it was a desk job with only supervisory visits to the shop floor. He was 33 years old, and Fred felt he was finally on the right track. When he completed the trainee program in October 1951, Fred was appointed foreman for extra-heavy industrial cloth at the Roebling plant. He could spend almost all of his time seated at his desk, which was exactly what he needed.

WERNHER VON BRAUN

Wernher's immigration status was still in limbo, but newly revised security files had finally arrived. In the new files, notations like "ardent Nazi" had been changed to "not an ardent Nazi," and his SS membership was either ignored or downplayed. Wernher (and any other Paperclip contractee who had been in the US for two years) was considered to have proven himself worthy of security clearance. Lingering questions about Wernher's lying and dissembling about his past, his colleagues, and hidden document troves were brushed aside.

To summarize the latest von Braun report, it stated that he was not wanted by the German police and that his involvement in war crimes could not be determined because the relevant records were in the Soviet zone of occupation. Given that he had been working in the US since 1945, "he may not constitute a security threat to the US.[159] The way now seemed clear for him to apply to the Immigration Department for an entry visa. The file was forwarded to the Department of Immigration in July 1949, but his application was kicked back yet again, pending further evaluation and clarification. Although the Army was gung-ho on von Braun, the Immigration Department remained unconvinced. In September, the resubmitted file cleared that hurdle. It was then forwarded to the Department of Justice, and in October, with the DoJ onboard, the file returned to

---

[159] It is interesting that even at this late date and after multiple rewrites, they could not bring themselves to state categorically that he wasn't a security threat.

the State Department for final approval. With all of the check-boxes ticked, Wernher could be granted a visa, albeit based on a misleading, carefully crafted, repeatedly massaged, and falsified history. On 2 November 1949, Wernher von Braun and a security guard traveled to Juaréz, Mexico, to file immigration papers and receive an entry visa for the US. When the pair recrossed the border, and US Immigration stamped his visa, Wernher was elated. He no longer had to worry about being exiled to Germany, and in five years, he would be eligible for full US citizenship.

Wernher, Maria, and their new daughter, Iris, were finding the quarters at Fort Bliss unsuitably small, but he was assured that would change relatively soon. Thanks to the Communist takeover of mainland China and the Soviet detonation of an A-bomb, missile technology was back in favor with the military, the press, and the public. Plans were underway to move the entire German rocket team from Fort Bliss to a military facility known as the Redstone Arsenal, in Huntsville, Alabama. Wernher was told that the move would allow him to find much nicer housing in the surrounding community.

Wernher completed *The Mars Project* by the summer of 1949, but the manuscript was in German. A colleague had been translating completed chapters into English, and once the translation process was complete, Wernher was eager to submit the novel to a publisher. Before that could happen, however, it had to be reviewed and cleared by Army Ordnance Security staff to make sure that it didn't contain classified information. With that process behind him, Wernher began submitting his manuscript to US publishers in 1950, but one submission after another generated rejection letters. The technical details were overwhelming, the plot was strange, the human aspect was altogether missing — it had no future in the US market. So Wernher decided to try his luck with German publishers, since the original manuscript was in German anyway. This led to a publishing contract with a German publisher who would have *The Mars Project* rewritten by someone who had crafted Nazi propaganda during the war. The publisher felt that the rewriting would make the story more palatable to the general public.

Wernher was excited to start serious planning for the move to Huntsville. His first appointment would be as Project Director of the Guided Missile Center. In the early years at Peenemünde he had been a civilian Director reporting to Major Dornberger, and now he was a civilian Director reporting to Major Hamill. He had 300 German staff working for him, most of them ex-Peenemünders. It felt familiar and comfortable.

When the Korean War began in June 1950, the rocket team

dusted off the V-2 design and assembled a Super-V2 using more advanced versions of the engines that had been developed by a company called Rocketdyne. What emerged, called the Redstone, could travel several hundred miles with a payload 50% greater than the V-2. Unfortunately, the guidance system of the Redstone, adapted from that of the V-2, was wildly inaccurate.[160] Some of the early V-2 launches at Fort Bliss had wandered off into Mexican airspace and almost landed in Juarez. On a flight of 185 miles, the impact site could be anywhere within a radius of 10-20 miles of the intended target, a margin of error equal to 8-10% of the range. With a nuclear warhead onboard, a margin of error that large would have horrific consequences. The Defense Department wanted a weapon that could reliably strike within 150 yards of a specific target at a range of 185 miles, a margin of error of 0.04% of the range. Developing a suitable guidance system suddenly became a high priority.

Overseeing the Redstone development, pushing for advances in guidance systems, maintaining correspondence with other scientists, societies, and journalists — nobody could fault Wernher's work ethic. This was recognized and rewarded, as Wernher received an 8.8% raise, to $11,550 per year ($113,500 today). He did have some unsettling moments in 1951, however, when journalists, including Drew Pearson, began asking questions about the employment of former Nazis by the US military.

It made Wernher very uncomfortable to think that newsmen were investigating his background. He had hoped that his Nazi activities had been buried and forgotten. Negative press coverage could jeopardize his funding, and a big enough fuss could jeopardize his US visa. He needn't have worried, however, as the JIOA looked after their own. Military intelligence teams responded to the potential publication of an exposé by investigating and intimidating the journalists involved. These actions were considered justified in defending national security.

Interviewers from the *New Yorker Magazine* were allowed access to the program but given misleading information. For example, when asked about von Braun's salary, Major Hamill assured them that Dr. von Braun's salary was very modest. The implication was that Wernher was all but volunteering his services to help his adopted country. In reality, the average annual income in the US at that time was $2,799, whereas Wernher was making over four times that much and receiving additional benefits.

---

[160] Schröder had predicted this when Wernher proposed adopting the system. The resulting argument led to Schröder's transfer to another team.

Some details in the 21 April 1951 article slipped past the censors, however. The security officer at Fort Bliss made an interesting comment, "They seem to have a group spirit, based on the idea that on each one's model behavior rested the glory of the Third Reich." It was left to the imagination to decide how popular that spirit was with the Army personnel on the base. For his part, Wernher attempted to use the interview to defuse any rumors about his past. He retold and embellished the story of his detention by the Gestapo, claiming that Himmler thought he was planning to defect to the Allies by flying to England with secret papers.[161] When asked if he had considered surrendering to the Russians rather than the Americans, he said no, but added:

> WORKING IN A DICTATORSHIP CAN HAVE ITS ADVANTAGES IF THE REGIME IS BEHIND YOU. I'M CONVINCED THAT THE MAN BEHIND STALIN'S ATOM BOMB PROJECT JUST HAS TO PUSH A BUTTON, AND HE'LL BE SUPPLIED WITH A WHOLE CONCENTRATION CAMP FULL OF LABOR. WE USED TO HAVE THOUSANDS OF RUSSIAN PRISONERS OF WAR WORKING FOR US IN PEENEMÜNDE.

His intention was to highlight the fact that the Soviets had the labor resources to make rapid advances, which could only be matched by giving his team more funding. But to some readers, it sounded like a wistful remembrance of the Good Old Days in the Third Reich. Fortunately for Wernher, there were no followup questions about his greatest slipup — acknowledging his use of POWs as forced labor.

1952-1955

FRED MARTINI

As 1952 began, Fred had a steady job and was earning average wages ($2,900 per year, the equivalent of $28,500 today). His VA pension may have been reduced to a 10% disability, but his feet still felt like he had hot coals inside them, and he was still jumpy, anxious, prone to depression, and quick to anger. Although he never struck or abused his family during such episodes, the anger rolled off him in waves. The sudden bursts of rage worried Betty and terrified his son, as did

---

[161] This hadn't been mentioned in his earlier interviews, nor was it recorded in his interrogations or depositions, and it wasn't in the reports of other engineers detained with him. But it was great for his image.

the cries heard through the walls when Fred was having nightmares.

The Martinis were still living with the Hovers, and Ricky spent a lot of quality time with Betty's brother, his Uncle Dick. Dick had his own internal scars accumulated as a young infantryman in the Battle of the Bulge, but those combat memories hadn't affected his underlying personality. Dick loved kids, music, science fiction, humor, and storytelling — all things that Ricky avidly absorbed. Their closeness bothered Fred at some level, but he kept that to himself.

Every summer, Fred, Betty and Ricky would go to the Jersey shore where Mildred, Betty's mom, rented a beach cottage in Island Heights, on Toms River. Fred commuted to work from there. Late in 1952, Fred was recruited by a headhunter and hired by Air Associates, a company building electronics on contract to the military. Fred was put in charge of entire projects, from planning and budgeting through procurement and manufacturing. He loved the work, his employers were impressed, and raises followed. In 1953, the family moved out of the Hover household for the last time, shifting to an apartment complex in Union, New Jersey, a bit closer to New York City and to Fred's sisters. It was also within reach of Dodger baseball games.

In the fall of 1953, Ricky started first grade at the Franklin school in Union, New Jersey. He did not finish the year there, however, because early in 1954, Fred was offered an attractive position with another small electronics company. The increased revenue enabled them to buy a starter home in a new suburban development in the town of Pompton Plains, New Jersey. The community was situated near Route 23, and a quick connection to Route 46 made the commute brief. It also made it possible to get to New York City in 30 minutes or less. Pompton Plains had a progressive school system that Fred and Betty felt would be ideal for their son. The only downside to the community was that a store on the main street still had a sign in the window that said, "No Jews or Italians." Fred shrugged that off — he'd seen signs like that in many places in New York and New Jersey — and in all other respects, Pompton Plains was a great suburban community.

Most of the people in their development had children for Ricky to play with. Betty was a stay-at-home mom taking care of the house, cooking the meals, and driving neighborhood kids to and from the local primary school when the weather was foul. In fine weather, the kids could safely walk to school carrying highly decorated lunch-boxes. When Fred wasn't at work, he was usually to be found working on the yard. It was a small yard, so he didn't have to walk a long way to spread grass seed or fertilizer around. He found that the activity calmed him down, almost like meditation.

Fred also worked on their cars, his two Rambler and Betty's little baby-blue Metropolitan, which the local kids thought was cool. He was an excellent mechanic and could fix almost anything, but he didn't really enjoy the process as he did before the war. His son used to hang around him when he was tuning the engine or otherwise tinkering, and one day Fred confessed that he wanted a life where his hands and fingernails were always clean. He didn't like feeling dirty, even for short periods, as it sometimes reminded him of times he was trying to forget.

He never did manage to forget, however, and the echoes reverberated through his family life. Betty had been lobbying hard for a family dog since Ricky's birth, and finally got Fred to agree, although he was still uncomfortable around dogs, even small ones. They adopted a springer spaniel named Speckles who became totally bonded to young Ricky. One evening when Fred got angry about something and was walking toward his son, fuming, the dog, lying with his head in Ricky's lap, sensed danger and growled. That was all it took — Fred lunged forward, grabbed the dog by the neck, and stormed out of the house. Despite pleas from Betty and Ricky, Speckles went straight to the pound. No dog was ever going to growl at Fred again.

In August, Fred received a letter from the War Claims Commission stating:

> IT IS REQUESTED THAT YOU FURNISH THE COMMISSION WITH AN AFFIDAVIT SETTING FORTH THE CIRCUMSTANCES CONCERNING YOUR CAPTURE ON AUGUST 5, 1944 BY THE GESTAPO WHILE YOU WERE IN CIVILIAN CLOTHING. YOUR AFFIDAVIT SHOULD CONTAIN A STATEMENT SHOWING THE DATE YOU FIRST NOTIFIED THE GERMAN AUTHORITIES THAT YOU ARE A MEMBER OF THE ARMED FORCES AND WHAT DATE THE GERMAN AUTHORITIES FIRST RECOGNIZED YOU AS SUCH. YOUR STATEMENTS SHOULD BE CORROBORATED BY AFFIDAVITS FROM TWO DISINTERESTED PERSONS WHO KNOW THE FACTS CONCERNING YOUR CAPTURE AS A CIVILIAN AND SUBSEQUENT TRANSFER FROM A CONCENTRATION CAMP TO A PRISONER OF WAR CAMP.
>
> FURTHER ACTION ON YOUR APPEAL WILL BE HELD IN ABEYANCE PENDING RECEIPT OF THE REQUESTED AFFIDAVITS.
>
> VERY TRULY YOURS,
> LUCY S. HOWORTH, DEPUTY GENERAL COUNSEL

Fred had already provided those details in the letter that registered his appeal, but he submitted the information. Unfortunately, he had no way of finding "disinterested persons" who could validate his account. In November, he received a letter informing him:

> IN YOUR APPLICATION AND ON APPEAL, YOU STATED THAT YOU WERE CAPTURED ON AUGUST 5, 1944, AND HELD AS A CIVILIAN PRISONER UNTIL OCTOBER 21, 1944, WHEN YOU ARE RECOGNIZED AS A PRISONER OF WAR. HOWEVER, YOU FAILED TO RELATE THE CIRCUMSTANCES IN DETAIL.
>
> IT IS, THEREFORE, REQUESTED THAT YOU SUBMIT, WITHIN 60 DAYS FROM THE DATE OF THIS LETTER, A STATEMENT IN AFFIDAVIT FORM SETTING FORTH YOUR ACTIVITIES DURING THE PERIOD IN QUESTION AND THE CIRCUMSTANCES WHICH LED TO YOUR RECOGNITION AS A PRISONER OF WAR. AFFIDAVITS FROM PERSONS HAVING PERSONAL KNOWLEDGE OF THE FACTS MAY LIKEWISE BE SUBMITTED FOR CONSIDERATION.
>
> YOUR FAILURE TO COMPLY WITH THIS REQUEST MAY RESULT IN A DISMISSAL OF YOUR APPEAL, IN ACCORDANCE WITH THE GOVERNING REGULATIONS OF THE WAR CLAIMS COMMISSION.
>
> VERY TRULY YOURS,
> JAMES L. THOMAS
> ACTING CHAIRMAN
> COUNCIL ON APPEALS

Once again, he submitted the affidavit requested, and again noted that he had no access to supporting witnesses. He had no idea how to reach Paul Wilson or Alex MacPherson, and in any case, they could hardly be called disinterested. Why didn't they believe him? The Army had liberated Buchenwald. Surely they had kept records, and besides, he had been interrogated repeatedly in the ETO about what transpired. He knew that Ed Ritter, Sam Pennell, and many others had been interviewed as well. So what was the problem? He couldn't make sense of it.

After a long pause, he received notification that a hearing had been scheduled and that he could testify in person at that time. That would be a logistical challenge, as he would have to leave work to go to the hearing. But the real problem was that Fred would need to stand before a panel of skeptics and relate his story in person. The thought made him both anxious and angry. He decided that the safest course would be to sit down and compose his statement in writing and then read it to the panel. It was a brief summary, almost an outline of events. The whole thing took just two typewritten pages that had been carefully trimmed of any graphic or emotional content. He didn't want to think about such details, and he certainly didn't want to write them down or say them aloud.

Fred attended the hearing without Betty but with a representative from the VFW (Veterans of Foreign Wars) who provided physical and moral support — very useful, as Fred was extremely agitated. At the session, he stood and read his brief statement, knowing (as the panel surely recognized) that he was repeating verbatim what he had written in his application and his appeal. When he completed his statement, he was dismissed without receiving any comments or followup questions from the panel. He left the room just as uncertain of the outcome as he had been before he arrived.

After a month, Fred received notification that the committee had decided to award him the $1.50/day for his time from 5 August 1944 to 21 October 1944, but they did so without acknowledging that anything in Fred's testimony concerning Buchenwald was true. Buchenwald was never mentioned. The panel merely said that there was (undisclosed) evidence that Fred had been captured in Paris on 5 August 1944, and that they had no information indicating that Fred had been outside of German control between the time of his arrest and his arrival at Stalag Luft III.

Fred took that judgement as a form of closure. Although it still frustrated him that his stories of Buchenwald were considered fabrications, he decided to declare victory and get on with his life. He gave up trying to convince the VA that he was telling the truth, which meant he stopped talking about the war altogether. He tried to put the whole business behind him and focus on his career and his family.

Their house was a modest one with two bedrooms, two bathrooms, a kitchen/dining room, and a small living room furnished with two overstuffed chairs and a couch. Fred liked to keep up with trends in stereo equipment and other electronics, so they now had an 11-inch black and white TV in the living room. Each evening, the family would sit together and watch shows like Lucille Ball, George Burns, Ed Sullivan, and of course the Mickey Mouse Club and Disney specials. When there were reruns of the *Life in the Desert* documentary, Fred would get queasy and upset, leaving the room because the musical score included passages that had been broadcast over the speakers in Buchenwald, over and over and over.

In March 1955, the whole family was around the TV the night the first of a new Disney series premiered. It was called *Man in Space*. When Wernher von Braun appeared, impeccably dressed in a suit and tie, and the camera zoomed in for a close-up, Fred, in his recliner, couldn't believe his eyes. "Son of a BITCH!" he said, turning to Betty, "That's the guy, that miserable Nazi bastard from Buchenwald." Both "bitch" and "bastard" were new to his son's ears, as his parents watched their language around him. As the show continued, Fred got increasingly agitated and finally left the living room. He refused to watch future episodes, nor did he discuss the reasons with his son.

But Betty knew the story, and she and Fred wondered what he should or could do about it. How could the government not know about von Braun's background? Fred finally decided that they had to know, and even if by some miracle they didn't, somebody already considered a psych case had zero chance of convincing anyone of anything. If the government refused to believe that he had even been in Buchenwald, they'd never believe what he had seen there — especially when the guy in question was a friend of Walt Disney.

Fred was not the only member of the TV audience who thought he recognized von Braun from his days with the Third Reich.[162] Over the years, Wernher was recognized by many former concentration camp prisoners, although most, like Fred, chose to remain silent for decades.[163] Of course, in the absence of photographic evidence or written documentation, such claims would not be sufficient for prosecution. But it seems odd that from the earliest days of Operation Overcast, government security investigations on Wernher von Braun failed to include interviews with survivors of Peenemünde or Dora/Mittelwerk. Instead, they relied primarily on the supporting depositions of other Paperclip

---

[162] There is no way to prove that Fred saw Wernher von Braun. There are no travel records, gate logs, or other paperwork documenting Wernher's travel after late June, when he stopped flying and started using cars or trains. Wernher never admitted going to Buchenwald, but his letter to Sawatski proves that he went at least once, in late July 1944, and batches of prisoners were shipped to the Mittelwerk from Little Camp while Fred and the other airmen were held there.

[163] Examples include Alex Baum, who claimed to have seen him routinely while doing slave labor at Peenemünde and at the Mittelwerk; Tibor Munk, Dick de Zeeuw, and Albert van Dijk, who reported seeing him many times at the Mittelwerk; and Georges Jouanin, who recounted being struck by von Braun for standing on a servomotor assembly in the tail section. Guy Morand testified that he had been beaten by the SS on von Braun's orders, and Robert Cazabonne testified that von Braun was present when several prisoners were executed for sabotage. A few of these reports may have been cases of mistaken identity; the rest were credible but officially ignored or discounted.

contractees, thereby ensuring a successful outcome. The government already knew that Wernher had worked at the Mittelwerk and been involved in slave labor, and the JIOA was determined to keep the information secret. So there is every reason to believe that anyone making or reporting stories about the claims of former prisoners would have been discredited, and related publications suppressed.

WERNHER VON BRAUN

Wernher was convinced that there were too many different companies doing related research in widely separate locations. It was making it too hard for him to maintain managerial control. He advocated shifting to the "all in one place" approach used at Peenemünde before the bombing raid in 1943. But the Army wanted the production farmed out to an outside contractor, with the Redstone Arsenal remaining focused on design and development. Due to military politics (the Air Force wanted the Army out of the missile business) the Redstone group was given the OK to complete the first set of missiles while a new contractor geared up for the job.

Wernher understood that in contrast to the situation in Peenemünde, funding determinations in America were heavily influenced by public opinion and media pressure. So in 1952, he orchestrated a publicity campaign to rally the US populace around the space program. He was already writing to organizations and societies around the globe, and now he started writing articles for magazines in the US. He started with *Collier's Magazine*, a high-profile weekly magazine with a broad readership. He worked with the editors to organize what they called a "symposium," which was a collection of articles on space exploration and technology by multiple authors. Wernher's piece, called "Crossing the Last Frontier," was the centerpiece. It was by far the longest article and it was lavishly illustrated.

Based largely on the ideas he'd developed in *The Mars Project*, it included winged spacecraft resembling the A-9, a three-stage rocket to launch it (the second stage comparable to the A-10), rotating space stations, and a moon landing. In the first paragraph, he predicted a space station within 10-15 years that would be "the greatest force for peace ever devised, or the greatest weapon of war — depending on who makes and controls it." He was clearly pulling out all of the stops.

That issue of *Collier's* was extremely popular, and it was followed by radio and television appearances with the authors of other articles in that issue. Wernher wrote several other articles over the next two years. All of these articles and related public pronouncements promoted space exploration as the primary goal, but reminded the reader that if the US didn't do it first, their enemies could use the same technology to defeat them in the war that would inevitably follow. It was an effective onepunch: heroic romanticism and proud nationalism, followed by fear of Communist aggression.

In late 1952, Dornberger's book, *V-2* was published in Germany, recounting the heroic story of the development of the missile. Somehow he managed to avoid mentioning slave labor, Buchenwald, or Dora, and Mittelwerk was relegated to a side comment about it serving as a production facility. He also failed to discuss the targets or the casualties inflicted by V-2 strikes. The narrative glorified the scientific and technical achievements of the German rocket team and attempted to replace the wartime image of General Dornberger, the Nazi fanatic dedicated to the destruction of London, with that of Dr. Dornberger, the innovative apolitical scientist.

At around the same time, Wernher was pushing the "explore space or be annihilated" button during a well attended lecture in Washington DC. There were quite a few skeptical articles written that claimed his math was wrong, that the estimated $4 billion cost was too high (or too low). A few humorists noted that since he had lost the war for Hitler, why should the US follow his lead? But although his ambitious programs would not be funded, his ongoing promotional efforts popularized space exploration and indirectly, science fiction to a generation of Americans.

The first Redstone missile was successfully tested early in 1953. The program had expanded rapidly, and soon it was reconfigured. The Huntsville facility became the Ordnance Missile Laboratories, and Toftoy, by then a brigadier general, assumed overall command. In August 1953, there was a major launch of a Redstone at Cape Canaveral, the launch complex in Florida. Dieter Huzel, who had hidden the 14 tons of documents for Wernher, was by his side. After coming to the US under Project Paperclip, Dieter had taken a position at Rocketdyne.

Another big *Collier's* issue was planned, this one focusing on the *The Mars Project* at the same time Wernher's novel with the same name was published in Germany. Between the articles and his speaking engagements, Wernher was more than doubling his already sizable salary. He was well on his way to becoming a scientific rock star.

The German publication of *The Mars Project* came as something of a surprise to the FBI, who were concerned that it might contain classified information. The publication triggered an FBI investigation and background check in April 1953. The security check revisited Wernher's original declarations, noting that he had failed to disclose what he knew about hidden documents. It also acknowledged the lack of information regarding when and why he joined the SS. Investigators in Germany reviewed the Project Abstract paperwork and noted (1) von Braun's lack of cooperation with authorities, and (2) information from the Berlin Document Center regarding his SS and Nazi party affiliations. However, this was all considered "old news."

Whereas a background check that included interviewing survivors of Dora or Peenemünde work details might have caused serious concern, the FBI instead interviewed his contacts in the US. Among those interviewed were two men who had worked with von Braun since his arrival at Fort Bliss, and a General Electric contractor whose company had ongoing contracts with the Redstone Arsenal. The latter, Dr. Richard Porter, spoke of von Braun's apparent interest in becoming an American, but added: "caution should be taken if Germany ever becomes unified, as it is possible that [his] loyalty would revert to Germany." This was very close to the observation made in von Braun's first security evaluation by Lt. Jessel in June 1945.

In other respects, the three Americans interviewed repeated to the FBI what von Braun had told them regarding his apolitical work in the war and his involvement with the SS. The FBI then interviewed Wernher's German contemporaries, who were themselves Paperclip recruits. These included Steinhoff, Dornberger, Debus, Dannenberg, and several others. All were former Nazis, and most had worked for Wernher at Peenemünde, Fort Bliss, and Huntsville. Several had skeletons in their own closets. All had praise for Wernher's hard work and dedication to the US.[164]

Finally, the FBI team interviewed Wernher, who was well prepared for their arrival. He gave the same details as before but further embellished the story of his arrest by the Gestapo. He had decided that this was a story with legs, and if presented properly, it would show that he wasn't a committed Nazi. When he listed his previous employment, von Braun brazenly stated that he had worked under General Dornberger at Peenemünde from 1937 through the end of the war. This historical revision went unchallenged, no doubt

---

[164] It is ironic (to say the very least) that Fred was required to provide disinterested witnesses to support an appeal to the War Claims Commission for a compensation claim of $115.50, whereas the FBI took the word of men whose careers depended on von Braun to determine his access to the military and atomic secrets of the entire nation.

because the FBI had no access to the documents that the JIOA had accumulated and classified.

In the end, the remarkable thing about the interviews and the responses was not that they included glowing accounts of Wernher's sterling character and apolitical activities during the war and later in the US, or that everyone sung the same song. It was that they gave the same chronology that Wernher, Dornberger, and the rest had presented at the time of their surrender. They all agreed that Wernher had worked only at Peenemünde, and that the move to Bleicherode was merely an attempt to escape the Russians. Because their accounts went unquestioned, Wernher managed to get through the entire process without being questioned about, and without ever mentioning, the Mittelwerk, Dora, or his position and activities in the CCDC-Mittelbau in Bleicherode.

The FBI, faced with a consistent story told by multiple sources, and with no access to the captured and classified German records, closed the file and granted Wernher his security clearance. Wernher, delighted and no doubt relieved, subsequently assured reporters who posed questions about his past that he had absolutely nothing to hide, which was hardly the case. He also said that the government knew everything about his wartime activities. That statement was also rather disingenuous, given that most government agencies, including the FBI, knew next to nothing about those activities.

Wernher continued to make occasional trips to California to meet with Walt Disney, who wanted to have a series of specials on space exploration. Disney wanted to promote the Tomorrowland section of Disneyland, which would open in July 1955. Wernher immediately saw that television provided a new and effective way to shape public opinion and pressure the government to increase funding for missile technology and space exploration. He readily agreed to work with Disney and to appear on the shows. The first program, *Man in Space,* aired in March 1955. The audience was estimated in the millions, reaching a far greater number of people than had ever heard of, let alone read, his *Collier's* articles.

In April 1955, Wernher von Braun was sworn in as an American citizen along with over 100 other Germans brought to the US under Project Paperclip. With the granting of citizenship and the release of *Man in Space* von Braun's transformation was complete. He now had a fine home, a wife and two daughters, a job he enjoyed, and a remunerative TV career. He was making ten times the average family income in the US, he was becoming an international figure, and his lectures and articles were in demand. He was well on his way to becoming as famous in the US as he had been in Nazi Germany.

WWII had ended ten years before. The key "rocket men" had been assimilated, adapting to their new cultural environment. The Buchenwald airmen, like Fred, were disparaged, discouraged, and resigned to their fates. Yet all the security protocols and paranoia remained in place. The original decision had been to keep von Braun's background and the events at Dora/Mittelwerk a secret. After ten years, the fact that the JIOA was keeping secrets from Congress, the FBI, the VA, the Department of State, and the Department of Justice, while misleading the press, intimidating authors, and suppressing publications also had to be kept secret. Exposure of these morally questionable actions would have serious personal and professional consequences. Heads could roll, and funding for all of their programs could be jeopardized. So in the interest of "national security" the JIOA remained vigilant, and everything remained classified. Until that policy was changed, the Buchenwald airmen would be treated either as delusional liars or as grifters trying to steal money from the VA.

CHAPTER 22

Convergence

-◦⊐⊑◦-

1956-1960

FRED MARTINI
In 1956, Fred started a new job with Mars International in Piscataway, New Jersey. It was a better job with more responsibility, and it was a company with lots of activities for employees. Fred was delighted to learn that they had a pistol team, as he had been rated Expert Marksman in the Army, and his vision was 20/15. He started shooting in regional and statewide competitions. At first, he shot at events the company participated in, but before long, he was shooting at other competitions with the local police, who had made him an honorary deputy. The living room and dining room gradually started to fill with trophies and plaques.

When the Dodgers announced that they were headed to the West Coast, it was like a death in the family. Nobody could believe that such a disaster could befall Brooklyn. How could they support the Mets? Or, horror of horrors, the Yankees? Baseball was finished for the Martinis. Little League, baseball cards, handwritten play-by play records — all were gone as if by magic. The mourning period lasted several years.

Of course, Fred was chagrined to see von Braun on the Disney specials and the newspapers, hailed as an American hero, but his son was gaga over the whole space race concept. So Fred worked on putting the past behind him and didn't take von Braun too seriously. It did irk him, however, that none of the many articles about von Braun mentioned his activities during the war, treating his focus as pure science. That description could hardly be stretched to include recruiting visits to Buchenwald.

Over this period, Fred found that if he kept busy and stayed focused, his nightmares became either less common or less memorable, and his flashbacks occurred less often. He spent long hours at work, became an assistant scoutmaster, organized neighborhood parties, and joined bowling and pistol shooting teams. To the outside world, Fred seemed energetic and extroverted, although at times eccentric. For example, when he accompanied the scouts on camping trips, he always slept in his car, never on the ground or in a tent. Sleeping "rough" would bring back too many terrible memories. At home, however, things changed very little. Fred continued to have problems with his feet, either from infected cuts that went unnoticed or from standing around or walking more than a short distance. His hands no longer shook, but he was still prone to mood swings and sudden anger. Playing golf had a calming effect, so he started playing every weekend if an electric golf cart was available. As a fringe benefit, he found the sport was of particular value when socializing with representatives of other companies, and he started to get a reputation as someone who could charm his way to new business. But he also had a proven track record of organizing staff and driving projects through to completion on tight schedules and within budget. As a result, he remained in the project management arena with his responsibilities and his income gradually increasing from one year to the next. Unfortunately, his blood pressure continued to climb as well, as it had since the end of the war. The stresses of chronic anxiety were compounding the physical problems resulting from malnutrition and abuse years earlier. By 1960, his blood pressure reached 180/90, and he was put on medication to try to bring it under control.

At the time, Fred was being recruited by the Daven Company, which had been purchased by General Mills and rechristened the Daven Electronics Division. Daven was heavily involved in the manufacturing of switches and electronic components for the aerospace industry. As luck would have it, one of their major clients was the Army, and they were gearing up to make switches and other components for the Mercury space program, which intended to get an astronaut into orbit ASAP. Fred assumed the role of a project manager in the Operations Department. At the same time, Ed Allman was hired away from Bendix Radio to be Chief Industrial Engineer for Daven. Fred and Ed hit it off immediately and were soon good friends and golfing buddies as well as colleagues.

WERNHER VON BRAUN

Wernher was lobbying hard for the go-ahead to launch a small satellite, even if it could do nothing other than be tracked from the ground. His justification was that the Soviets would probably put one up in the near future, and if they were first it would be bad for American prestige. Four launching dates were projected over AugustSeptember 1957 as part of Project Orbiter. But inter-service rivalry was making life difficult. The Air Force was busy with the Atlas ICBM and had little interest, if not outright hostility, for the rocket proposals of the Army or Navy. They also failed to see the point of helping either of them launch a satellite for scientific purposes. Wernher thought that the rivalry was like those in the Third Reich. Then he had had to deal with the SS obstructing the plans of the Army and Luftwaffe, and now he had to deal with the Air Force obstructing plans of the Army and Navy. It was all about political power and influence rather than the job to be done.

The tag team of Toftoy and von Braun kept the pressure on, and even without the support of the Air Force, a satellite launch became a priority for 1957, the International Geophysical Year. President Eisenhower made the announcement about a pending launch to the press in late July 1955. But the decision about who would oversee the production and the launching was given to a "select committee." The candidates to run the satellite program were the Air Force, which had a rough plan based on their Atlas ICBM, the Navy, which had an untested design they called Vanguard, and the Army, with a proposal based on the Redstone program. It became a political cat fight that ended with the committee members voting according to their military service affiliations. The final decision was that the Navy would launch the satellite.

Wernher was terribly disappointed, but all was not lost. There was also a decision pending on who would build an intermediate range ballistic missile (IRBM) that could strike targets 1,500 miles away. The committee reviewed the Air Force, Army, and Navy proposals and offered a compromise. The Air Force would get the funds to build an Air Force IRBM, while the Army and Navy would develop a shared design that would have land based and sea based versions. This would guarantee continued funding for the Redstone facility, and the IRBM would be very similar to the rocket von Braun had planned to use to launch a satellite.

With the IRBM program underway, the Redstone Arsenal was reorganized, becoming the Army Ballistic Missile Agency (ABMA). Wernher was promoted again, to head the Development Operations Division. This placed him at an administrative level that brought a salary of $16,530-$17,570 per year ($143,742-$152,786 today) plus a 16% bonus for the high cost of living in the Huntsville metropolitan area. This salary, added to his income from popular articles, lectures, and additional Disney specials (the second would air in 1956 and the third in 1957), made him wealthy by the standards of the day.

Von Braun now had over 3,000 people working for him. He went with time honored tradition, appointing former Peenemünde/Bleicherode employees to key positions. The goal of the program was to deliver a nuclear warhead weighing 1,500 pounds over a distance of 1,500 miles to a specified location. There were many obstacles to overcome — not just with regard to rocket thrust, and thus range, but also to guidance systems.

Meanwhile, another Paperclip recruit, Dr. Paul Schröder, who was working for the Air Force at the time, started writing a detailed article about the origins and development of the V-2. In it, he claimed that von Braun had not invented anything about the V-2 but that he had taken credit for everything. He said that von Braun was domineering and that any Peenemünders objecting were forced to leave. He related stories of von Braun's technical incompetence and the arguments over von Braun's decisions regarding the guidance system of the V-2. Schröder felt that his career in the US had been sabotaged as a result of Wernher's animosity. He submitted the completed article for review by Air Force Security. They determined that it did not contain any classified information and told him he could publish it. His attorney, however, subsequently called him to say that the Pentagon did not want the article published and that if it were published, it would jeopardize Schröder's citizenship application. Schröder took the hint and, for the moment at least, suspended attempts to publish the article.

The Soviets had their first successful ICBM launch on 21 August 1957, and in October, they succeeded in putting a satellite named Sputnik ("fellow traveler") into orbit. As it happily zoomed around the planet, periodically crossing over North America, the US population reacted with shock, anger, and dismay. How had the Soviets beaten America into space? What was all that rubbish about our German scientists being better than their German scientists? There were no answers to those questions that were not embarrassing for the US military and the Eisenhower administration. The ABMA hoped that this would open the door to their launch plans — they promised a satellite aloft in 90 days or less — but instead, President Eisenhower downplayed the Soviet achievement.

The position changed when on 3 November, the Soviets launched a much larger payload containing the poor dog Laika, the first (and so far the only) orbiting fatality, since there were no recovery plans. The US public went into paroxysms of paranoia. Predictions were made that Americans had better learn to speak Russian. President Eisenhower promised a satellite by March 1958, but that promise did little to calm anxieties. When the third Disney show aired, von Braun was put on the cover of *Life Magazine*. In the *Life* article he predicted that unless the country changed direction, in seven years, the US would be part of the USSR. The *New York Times* called him a prophet of the coming space age, but Eisenhower called him a publicity hound.[165]

The Navy announced that the first Vanguard ICBM launch would be televised live on 6 December 1957. For the day, it was "must-see TV." After great anticipation, the imposing rocket climbed to an altitude of around six inches before the engine quit, it fell back on the launch pad, and the whole thing disappeared in a tremendous fireball.

While Wernher's team scrambled to get a backup rocket ready, Wernher was lobbying Congress for $1.5 billion to develop a national space program. Every week or so, the Vanguard project tried again, and after four unsuccessful launch attempts and four spectacularly embarrassing explosions on live TV, the ABMA team got the green light. On January 31, 1958, a Jupiter-C[166] lifted into the air. Fearing another debacle that would further humiliate the Eisenhower administration, the launch wasn't televised live. The rocket stages performed as intended, and the satellite, Explorer 1, reached orbit to the delight and relief of all concerned.

Wernher was now a national hero. Two weeks later he was on the cover of *Time Magazine*, where he was called Missileman Von Braun. This article, like a similar one published in Germany at the time, presented a carefully sanitized version of his activities during the war. Wernher's Nazi party membership was not mentioned, and there was no mention of the SS, the Mittelwerk, slave labor, or other unpleasant details. Biographies were written based on his previous heavily censored accounts. *The Mars Project* was updated and serialized, and a second book, dealing with a moon mission, found a publisher. He found he could make $2,500 ($20,000 today) for a single lecture. A studio deal for a biographical movie with Columbia Pictures promised $25,000 plus 7% of the profits. He got a bigger house and a white Mercedes, all the while complaining about the pressures of celebrity.

But in March 1958, the Schröder affair resurfaced courtesy of Drew Pearson, whose earlier investigations into the Fort Bliss team had been quashed. Drew had Jack Anderson, an investigative reporter working with him, call the ABMA and ask to talk to Dr. von Braun. The security chief who took the message called Anderson back to tell him that Dr. von Braun was unavailable. Anderson replied that he and

---

[165] Eisenhower hated Nazis and despised war criminals. It seems unlikely that he was fully aware of the backgrounds of Project Paperclip employees, especially Wernher von Braun, but he was clearly not one of Wernher's fans.
[166] The Jupiter-C was a three-stage rocket. The first stage was a modified Redstone, which used liquid fuel, and the second and third stages were smaller and burned solid fuel.

Pearson were about to publish a book, tentatively called *The Missile Mess*, and that it had a chapter on von Braun. He went on to say that they had received a lengthy report from Dr. Schröder and wanted to get Dr. von Braun's response.

The news hit Wernher like a bolt from the blue, and he hardly knew what to say. Any response could backfire. In the end, Wernher said that he had never met the man, despite the fact that Schröder had played an important role in the A-4 project at Peenemünde and it had been friction with Wernher that led to his transfer. When questioned, Arthur Rudolph and Konrad Dannenberg had nothing very nice to say about Schröder. So when Pearson and Anderson published *USA: second class power?* later that year, it included little about Schröder, and von Braun's history remained obscure.

This didn't mean that the Schröder problem had been solved, however. In July 1958, George McLanahan, the Chief of Army Ordnance, sent a memo to General Toftoy advising him that the FBI was investigating a letter from Schröder that contained explicit allegations about Wernher von Braun. Schröder claimed that after one of his meetings with officials about his grievances, someone had tried to kill him by cutting the brake lines in his car. The damage had reportedly been verified by the local police. Schröder was terrified and Senator Stuart Symington was involved. Once again, the Army somehow buried the letter and muzzled Schröder without generating any negative publicity.

Times were changing, though, and it was getting harder to control the news media. Claims similar to Schröder's concerning von Braun's management style in the ABMA program appeared in the press. The implication that Wernher was more concerned with self-aggrandizement and the control of a closely knit subordinate group than with scientific advancement could seriously impact his lobbying efforts and the support for his programs. Wernher, who expected loyalty from his subordinates, was disturbed to find that members of his team were making negative comments to the press.

His subordinates weren't the only ones breaking ranks. The unified "German front" was starting to crack. Walter Dornberger, who knew von Braun as well as anyone, was unusually candid with Delmar Fahrney, a retired rear admiral formerly in charge of the Navy's guided missile program. Dornberger said that von Braun had published no papers, made no breakthroughs, and personally designed none of the V-2 details. He felt that von Braun's true genius was in team building and staff motivation, and presenting a vision for a project that would resonate with his audience and secure funding. Albert Speer, in his memoirs, had said much the same thing —

that Wernher had mesmerized him, the Führer, and many others with his grandiose visions of rocket weapons.[167] Regardless of the truth of the other assertions, Wernher had certainly demonstrated his talents for showmanship repeatedly since his surrender to the US in 1945. He was in many ways the Pied Piper of Rocketry for generations of Americans.

Later in the year, the amount of money Wernher was making was so incredible, and the time he was devoting to lectures and appearances so extensive, that he was asked to cut back to a level that would not impact his work so severely. But they could hardly threaten to fire him, especially when progress at ABMA continued. Wernher's group was now working on the Pershing rocket, a replacement for the Redstone. The Pershing used the solid-fuel rocket motors used in the second and third stages of the Jupiter-C. The von Braun team also continued to enhance the Redstone and a version of the Jupiter-C for the Air Force. Wernher put Arthur Rudolph in charge of the Pershing and Redstone projects and gave the Jupiter program to Konrad Dannenberg. Soon, another program was added: a jumbo super-rocket that could provide thrust comparable to what the Soviet rockets were generating. The design, called the Saturn, was based on interlocking eight modified versions of the Redstone rocket engine. President Eisenhower awarded Wernher the Distinguished Federal Civilian Service Award in April 1959. Despite his personal dislike of Wernher's charismatic showmanship, Eisenhower understood his value and that he thrived on attention and accolades.

Big things were happening in the rocket world, and the biggest was the creation of the National Aeronautics and Space Administration (NASA). The fledgeling agency soon became embroiled in political intrigues — now there was a fourth agency that was seen as competing for funding and prestige with the Army, Navy, and Air Force. Turf battles erupted over just what personnel and responsibilities NASA would have going forward. In a compromise solution, NASA took over the Army's Jet Propulsion Laboratory (JPL) in California, and the ABMA was contracted to complete work as needed for NASA. That solution didn't last long, though, and soon the entire von Braun team at ABMA, almost 4,000 people, were transferred from the Army to NASA. However, when the Army transferred the personnel, they did not transfer the

---

[167] In retrospect, Speer felt that the labor, money, and materials committed to the V-2 should have been used to build jet fighters and anti-aircraft rockets that could clear the skies of enemy aircraft.

still-classified information regarding their backgrounds in Germany. All the NASA administration knew was what they were told by the German specialists themselves.[168] Now that NASA had a full staff complement, construction got underway for new headquarters. Still at the former Redstone base, the new complex was called the Marshall Space Flight Center, with Dr. Wernher von Braun as Director.

In 1959, Wernher found the time to travel to Germany with an escort to receive the Commanders Cross (the *Grosse Bundesverdienstkreuz*) from the West German government. It was his third German cross, but his first peacetime one and the only one the American public would hear about. While in Europe, he also worked on the movie about his life, which was called *I Aim at the Stars* This "biography" took many liberties with the truth, although Wernher had personally reviewed the script during development and had approved the variations. In the film version of his life during the war *years*, he was an anti-Nazi activist, Maria was his girlfriend rather than an eight-year old child, Nazi SS villains stomped around looking evil, there was no mention of slave labor or the Mittelwerk, and next to nothing was said about his rockets bombarding Allied cities. When it was released in Europe, the movie was a commercial disappointment, and there was negative publicity due to protests by Dora and Peenemünde survivors' groups at many theaters. Wernher's response at the premiere in Munich included, "A war is a war, and when my country is at war, my duty is to help with that war." The statement was not taken as a sign of contrition.

The protests in Europe were largely ignored by the US press. Things were more settled when the movie was released in the US, where von Braun brazenly defended the accuracy of the portrayal. *Time Magazine*, however, felt that von Braun was depicted as a cheerful accomplice to mass murder, who cared only about rockets, not people. They thought he could sue for libel, an interesting concept given that he had a financial stake in the movie and had approved the script. Neither his stalwart defense of the film nor their critique made any real difference — the film was as great a flop in the US as it was in Europe. It was often referred to as "I Aim at the Stars but Sometimes I Hit London."

Wernher's busy schedule continued through late 1960, when the pace and pressure increased further. In November 1960, President Kennedy announced the goal of landing a man on the moon by the end of the decade. NASA would have to start gearing up in earnest.

---

[168] Whenever von Braun appeared on TV in a news report about NASA, Tibor Munk, a survivor of the Mittelwerk, would say to his daughter "Why do they say NASA, he is NAZI."

FRED MARTINI

Daven Electronics had two facilities, one in New Jersey, where Fred was based, and another in Manchester, New Hampshire. In 1963, Ed Allman moved to New Hampshire to become the plant manager for the facility, which produced resistors. He and Fred remained friends, as Fred bounced back and forth between New Jersey and New Hampshire. Fred was given the option to move to Manchester as well, but he decided to postpone a shift until their son graduated from high school in mid-1965

In 1965, Daven Electronics was purchased by McGraw-Edison, a corporate conglomerate based in Chicago. The company name was changed to "Edison Electronics, a division of McGraw-Edison." The New Jersey facility was closed, and the company consolidated at a new complex built at Grenier Field outside of Manchester, New Hampshire.[169] Ed Allman was named President of the reconfigured company.

In the fall of that year, Fred and Betty put their house on the market and bought a place in Bedford, NH. When they moved in, Fred was the new Director of Operations for Edison Electronics. In that role, he was responsible for all standard products — attenuators, switches, laboratory and test equipment — and for related product engineering, manufacturing, purchasing, production, and quality control.

He was considered to be a valuable asset for the company, so they covered him with "Key Man Insurance," which would pay the company in the event something dire happened to Fred. As a policy requirement, Fred had to have annual physicals, with the results forwarded to Ed Allman. The exams were conducted by Dr. Paul M. Harkinson. In 1966, at his first physical, it was noted that his blood pressure was 130/80, and that it had been higher a few years earlier but had responded to medication.

In July 1967, an uncontrollable fire inside the Apollo capsule during a testing session killed three astronauts, Gus Grissom, Ed White, and Roger Chaffee. The entire NASA program was suspended for a month while an internal investigation was conducted. It was clear that a spark had ignited the pure-oxygen atmosphere inside the capsule, and it was also clear that the safety

---

[169] Grenier Field was one of the stops made by Crashwagon on the way to the ETO in 1944.

features inside and outside the capsule were poorly designed and woefully inadequate, especially regarding a potential fire. But just what had caused the spark that turned the inside of the capsule into a crematorium remained a mystery.

Edison Electronics manufactured rotary switches for the Apollo capsules. These switches were completely sealed, and thus theoretically incapable of producing a spark when operated. But nevertheless, Edison representatives, as well as representatives of other contractors providing electrical components for the Apollo capsules, were ordered to NASA Headquarters in Huntsville and told to bring their spec sheets and test results for review.

Fred was one of those sent to Huntsville by Edison Electronics. Fred could hardly object to that, given his job description, but he really had no idea how he would react to seeing von Braun in person. On the one hand, Fred wanted to confront him, then alert the press and expose von Braun's Nazi history, but on the other he knew that whether anyone believed him or not, it would be disastrous for his career and perhaps his company as well. So could he just ignore it, as if nothing had ever happened, while standing on feet of fire?

Several sarcastic, biting comments were floating around in his mind at the arrival meet-and-greet. But when Fred saw Dr. von Braun making the rounds, shaking hands with the representatives and generally playing the role of the welcoming celebrity, his mind went completely blank. All Fred managed to do when von Braun reached Fred and shook his hand, was to look him in the eyes and say, "Nice to see you again." Von Braun continued on his way, but his face was momentarily blank, as if he was trying to place a face without success. Fred was disappointed at first, wishing he had been able to come up with something better. On further reflection, he decided it was probably for the best. From his expression, von Braun had no idea where he'd seen Fred before, but if he had a guilty conscience, the comment might give him something to worry about.

Later that year, Fred was given the role of Director of Marketing, largely because his ability to connect with potential clients was unsurpassed. People instinctively liked him, and conversations were easy and congenial. He was in great demand, which led to a chaotic travel schedule and multiple strategic planning sessions. It paid off, and Edison Electronics continued to thrive. The success of the Apollo program was a feather in the corporate cap, and in 1970, Fred was promoted to Vice President for Instrumentation Products, the pinnacle of his career. His salary was $21,000 per year, the equivalent of $68,000 today (this was obviously before the days of runaway executive compensation). At his annual physical, his blood pressure had risen to 140/90 despite powerful medication. He was still mercurial at home, he was still plagued with occasional nightmares, and he still struggled to get his aching feet into shoes each day, but such things were kept in the family.

WERNHER VON BRAUN

Wernher von Braun's records had now been classified Secret for 15 years. On 5 January 1961, a memo was sent to the commanding general of the US Army Intelligence Center by Colonel Claude Barton, the chief of the Security Division. The topic was the continued classification of Wernher's dossier, which included the Schröder depositions and reports. The heart of the memo said:

THE MATERIAL CONTAINS DEROGATORY INFORMATION RELATING TO ONE OF OUR MOST IMPORTANT GERMAN SCIENTISTS WHO HAVE IMMIGRATED TO THE UNITED STATES SINCE WORLD WAR II. THIS MATERIAL REQUIRES A HIGH DEGREE OF PROTECTION IN THE INTEREST OF NATIONAL DEFENSE PARTICULARLY SINCE A US ESTIMATE OF THE SECURITY THREAT INVOLVED IN THIS SCIENTIST'S IMMIGRATION IS INCLUDED. THE UNAUTHORIZED DISCLOSURE OF SUCH INFORMATION WOULD BE PARTICULARLY DAMAGING TO THE CURRENT DEFENSE SCIENTISTS IMMIGRATION PROGRAM (DEFSIP).

DEFSIP was the new name given to Project Paperclip in 1957. Nothing but the name changed, and German scientists were still being recruited and contracted for transfer to the US regardless of any restrictions imposed by the German government. The security restrictions and classification would continue to be maintained for the indefinite future.

The Marshall Space Center was now structured to mirror Peenemünde, although lacking the relevant files, the NASA administration may not have realized it. Wernher was Director of the Center, Arthur Rudolph was the Project Director for the Saturn program, and Kurt Debus was Director of the Kennedy Space Center at Cape Canaveral, Florida. The rocket team was definitely in the spotlight now, which would make it all the more catastrophic if Project Paperclip was exposed. Wernher gave President Kennedy a personal tour of the Space Center, and rode in the motorcade by Kennedy's side. Would Kennedy have enjoyed the tour as much if he had realized that this was just what Wernher had done for Hitler at Peenemünde?

Wernher was now promoting a grandiose vision that would give the US space superiority. He had once thought $1.5 billion would be sufficient, but he revised that figure just to be on the safe side. He was still overselling the project and understating the likely cost. The original proposal draft gave a figure of $7 billion, but James Webb, NASA's director at the time, realized that this was ridiculous. He increased the budget to $20 billion before submitting it for approval. The actual cost was even higher. Getting the first men to the moon eventually required $24 billion, 400,000 people, and more than 20,000 companies and institutions.

Wernher had to apply for a security clearance, required under the Atomic Energy Act. This time, the FBI was given access to Army Intelligence (G-2) files on von Braun, albeit for five days only. The FBI objected, but to no avail. The FBI summary noted that Wernher had been the subject of complete or partial government security checks in 1947, 1948, 1953, 1954, 1958, and 1959. They proceeded to re-interview the same people they had questioned in 1953 — Dornberger, Debus, Dannenberg, and the rest — and received predictably glowing recommendations, plus the same cautionary note from Dr. Porter. As before, Wernher received his security clearance.

The next step for NASA was Project Mercury, a manned orbital program. The Soviets again beat the US, putting Yuri Gagarin into orbit. After a test flight to near orbit with Alan Shepherd onboard, John Glenn became the first American to orbit the globe, on 20 February 1962. That same year, the JIOA was disbanded and the oversight of the Paperclip/DEFSIP program transferred from the Joint Chiefs to the Director of Defense Research and Engineering, a branch of the Department of Defense.[170] However, the Army remained in charge of ongoing DEFSIP programs, and security protocols were unaffected.

Wernher continued to add to his collection of shiny awards. In October 1962, the Franklin Institute awarded him the Elliott Cresson Medal for technological invention or improvement. Had Wernher's history not been classified, the Institute might have reconsidered, given that Elliott Cresson was a Quaker who campaigned against slavery. And even with his records under wraps, it was becoming more and more difficult to avoid questions about his wartime

---

[170] The best known branch of this agency today is DARPA (Defense Advanced Research Projects Agency), which funds research projects that have potential military, intelligence, or national security applications.

activities. The layers of secrecy were cracking. An East German magazine ran a series of articles using excerpts from a forthcoming book by Julius Mader, *Secret of Huntsville: The true career of rocket baron Wernher von Braun*. Fortunately for Wernher and for NASA, the articles were in German and the book was written in Czech. The problem was that the cover had a painting of Wernher in an SS uniform wearing his Knight's Cross, and the narrative included coverage of Dora and the Mittelwerk. Buchenwald, the Mittelwerk, and Peenemünde were in the Russian zone of occupied Germany, and the East Germans could hardly care less about the security concerns of the US Defense Department. But when the US media mentioned the German articles and the book, published in 1963, little credence was given to the content. The government had assured the press that anything coming from East Germany should be dismissed as a fabrication intended to cripple the US space program. After all, Dr. von Braun was a great hero, and his background had been thoroughly vetted multiple times by multiple agencies. Wernher was for the moment still protected, but the defenses were under siege.

In 1965, Wernher's past was again spotlighted when Tom Lehrer's comedy music record included a song about him with the line: "Once the rockets are up, who cares where they come down? That's not my department, says Wernher von Braun." Many people laughed — it was a clever reminder that Wernher had worked on the rockets used by the Nazis — but the fact that he'd been a Nazi party member and an SS officer was still a closely kept secret.

Later the same year, a French group representing the Dora/Mittelwerk survivors wrote letters to the magazine *Paris March,* to protest Wernher's celebrity status. Wernher responded immediately, saying that he was horrified by their accusations and that the US government had investigated his past and found him to be blameless and uninvolved in Nazi crimes.

In January 1967, a deadly fire in the Apollo capsule killed three famous astronauts. Operations were suspended for months while an incident analysis was done, and more detailed reviews continued for some time afterward. The cause of the fire was never determined, but a number of design flaws were found, and investigators were blunt in their analysis of the failings in terms of safety equipment and procedures. During the review, inspection teams came and went, and contractors showed up for interrogation armed with test results and specifications. Wernher attended as many of those sessions as he could, meeting dozens of executives and forgetting most of them immediately.

While this was going on, another foreign movie, *Frozen Lightning,* was released in Europe. The movie, filmed in East Germany with a substantial budget, was stimulated by the success of Mader's book about von Braun. Fearing lawsuits, Wernher's name wasn't used, and the main character was an unidentified Nazi rocket baron, but it included graphic scenes in the Mittelwerk.

Although few in the US heard about *Frozen Lightning,* Wernher felt compelled to put any rumors to rest. He issued a statement that said the accusations and portrayals in the film were completely false. He added that in his visits to the Mittelwerk, he never saw a dead prisoner, nor a beating, nor a hanging, and he never participated in any prisoner abuse. He assured everyone that claims to the contrary coming from survivors of the Dora camp were cases of mistaken identity. This was the first time in 21 years that he said the word "Mittelwerk" in public, and the first time he admitted to the press that he had been there. The official government opinion was unchanged — anything originating in East Germany was a fabrication with political motivations — and journalists covering the story neglected to ask *why* Wernher had visited the Mittelwerk.

Wernher had contacts all over the world, and to his delight, he continued to be showered with honors. From Germany, he collected an honorary degree from a prestigious German university, a medal from the German Society of Inventors, and an award for promoting the public understanding of science. In the US, he received the Langley Medal from the Smithsonian, the same medal given to the Wright Brothers. He went on hunting and fishing trips with corporate chiefs and congressmen, and he gave talks for hefty fees ($7,000 each) that promoted NASA and the space program. No doubt the more awards he received and the greater the public demand for his lectures, the less credence he felt would be given to rumors about his past.

By the end of the summer, the Apollo capsule and its safety systems had been redesigned, and after six test flights and an orbital mission, Apollo 8 headed skyward on 21 December 1968, and the crew returned safely after orbiting the moon. After two more test flights to practice protocols for landing and retrieving personnel, the Apollo 11 crew landed on the moon, returning home on 24 July 1969.

Two weeks later, Wernher wrote a letter to retired Major General Julius Klein, who was active in lobbying to promote reconciliation between Germany and the Jewish community. Wernher's letter discussed allegations that had been appearing in the press over the last decade, most recently in a 15 July column by Drew Pearson. In his letter, Wernher admitted being a member of the SS but asked that this information be kept confidential to avoid affecting his work at

NASA.

Wernher had reasons for concern. Another Dora war crimes trial was underway, and West German prosecutors wanted him to testify. Sending Wernher to a packed courtroom in Germany seemed to be a very bad idea for all sorts of reasons, press coverage among them. So the US government negotiated an agreement with West Germany. The West German court was told that Wernher could not leave the US for national security reasons, but he could be interviewed under oath in the West German embassy in New Orleans. That location happened to be as far from the paparazzi gang as possible, minimizing coverage by the US media. In his sworn testimony, Wernher admitted going to the Mittelwerk "approximately 15 times" and admitted that he had been in the tunnels in 1943 while the prisoners were living and working there. But he stuck by his claim that he had never seen a dead prisoner, or an execution, or any abuse or maltreatment of laborers.

Asked about sabotage reports routed to him by Sawatski and recovered at Peenemünde, Wernher replied that he didn't remember ever seeing them. He also stated under oath that there had been no slave laborers at Peenemünde. If the attorneys had challenged this assertion — there was irrefutable documentation and testimony confirming slave laborers at Peenemünde — he could have been charged with perjury.[171]

Six more Apollo missions followed, but none had the worldwide impact of the first. It was certainly a grand moment for all involved, but the future wasn't looking all that bright. By the time the first Apollo blasted off, there were problems with budget allocations, as the Russian space program seemed to have stalled. Now that Kennedy's goal was reached, enthusiasm for the space program and tolerance for the huge expenditures involved both began to fade. NASA began to cut back aggressively. Apollo missions continued until 1972, and there was talk of a space shuttle and a space station, but things would have to be done at lower cost and with fewer employees. Efficiency became the order of the day.

The team that Wernher had held together for 25 years started to fall apart. Some retired on pensions, but many took positions with private industry. Von Braun was put behind a desk in Washington, DC, as Deputy Associate Administrator for NASA and tasked to do future planning. He hated losing his team, and he was being forced

---

[171] From the outset, all of the Germans brought with Wernher in the Paperclip program had made the same assertion, although repetition and truth were in this case entirely different things.

into a role where he could propose projects without being directly involved and without any assurance that funding would follow. As public enthusiasm for space waned, more disturbing questions were being asked. Holocaust survivor groups were becoming active, and during a TV appearance, he had to field probing questions about the V-2 strikes on London and his relationship with the Third Reich. Albert Speer's memoirs were published, and they included some comments on von Braun's history as well as his charismatic promotional skills. In Speer's opinion, Wernher had charmed and deluded Hitler's inner circle into believing he could deliver on impossible promises.

Some combination of optimism and self-delusion was certainly involved. Given the modest payload of the V-2 (2,000 pounds vs the 8,000 pound bomb load of a B-17 or the 12,000 pound bomb load of a British Lancaster), and the fact that bombers can be reused while V-2s cannot, the only justification for the program would be using V-2s to deliver the chemical, biological, or atomic weapons that were under development in Germany at the same time. Fortunately, the war ended before a decision was made to launch missiles armed with chemical or biological weapons, and before Germany's atomic bomb program produced an operational device.

Funding was drying up, his team was falling apart, and his image was under siege. Wernher's rocket launches might be going fine, but down on terra firma, things were not looking so good.

CHAPTER 23

Unraveling

-=ᴑᴕᴐ=-

1971-1977

FRED MARTINI

Fred's new position as Vice President for Instrumentation at Edison Electronics became effective on 1 January 1971, and he moved into a larger office with a secretary outside his door, making appointments and filtering calls. Fred traveled extensively and was heavily involved in decision-making at the corporate level. He conferred often with Ed Allman, both officially and unofficially over meals or games of golf at the Manchester Country Club. By 1973, transition plans were being discussed in anticipation of Ed's eventual promotion to a position with the parent company, McGraw-Edison, headquartered in Chicago. It was generally assumed and accepted that Fred would be heir apparent and take over as president when Ed left.

Fred and Betty had long conversations about this. Betty had never been particularly fond of the weather in New Hampshire — she didn't play golf, she hated cold weather, and she really missed beaches near waters warmer than the Gulf of Maine. Their son, who was completing his doctorate at Cornell, had done much of his research work at the Mote Marine Laboratory in Sarasota. Like Betty, he hated cold weather, and they expected him to move there eventually. Sarasota was near where Fred's sister Liz, recently widowed, was living with her four children, and Lucille and Eddie spent winters in a condo near Liz's house. They weren't getting any younger. Fred's blood pressure was already way too high, and if he took Ed's job the stress levels would be even higher. After much discussion, Fred decided to quit while he was ahead. In early 1974, he and Betty threw their bags in the car, leaving most of their belongings in the house, and drove south. They stayed with Liz for a brief period before getting a mortgage on a house on a saltwater canal in the outskirts of Bradenton.

Fred dusted off his resume and started looking for part-time work, but the only jobs available were as a traveling sales rep, which was out of the question because, in addition to his chronic foot problems, his legs were now bothering him. Walking even a short distance was tiring and painful. While at loose ends, he started doing unpaid work for the local VFW, POW, Purple Heart, Disabled American Veterans, and American Legion groups.

Fred and Betty enjoyed Florida and being near Liz and her kids. Betty loved the warm weather, and Fred could take a small trailer boat out into the bay to fish. The only thing that really bothered Fred about their move was the bugs. Fred disliked bugs in general, but he absolutely could not abide the sensation of bugs crawling on his skin. Ants or, worse yet, fleas triggered immediate panic attacks. The sensation dropped him right back into the barracks in Buchenwald, and each time he would rush into the house, his heart pounding and his hands shaking as he tore off his clothing. Fred soon got rid of both the lawn and the garden, replacing them with stones and a no-maintenance xeroscape.

With Fred doing volunteer work, Betty decided to reenter the workforce, and soon had a good job. Her prior experience landed her a position at Arvida Corporation, a major property development firm. She became the executive assistant for the head of the Sarasota operation. That position kept funds coming in to keep them afloat. But it got harder and harder for Fred to leave the house. He was losing weight, and because he was having problems with his dentures, he contacted the VA dental clinic in St. Petersburg to get an appointment. The VA response, received on 11 November 77, said that, "Final determination of your entitlement to dental care must be delayed pending legal rating action to establish service connection." They told him to stand by and not have anything done unless he was prepared to pay for it himself. The form sent to the VA record center said: "Vet Alleges POW." Request complete dental rating on all teeth for all periods of service." Fred was told to expect that processing would take at least 90 days.

WERNHER VON BRAUN

Wernher did not particularly enjoy his new position. It was a difficult time for NASA. The 1960s had seen the civil rights movement and the assassination of three prominent figures — President Kennedy, his brother Robert, and Martin Luther King, Jr. — and the US had become involved in a war in Vietnam that was as expensive as it was unpopular. By 1971, space exploration was seen as interesting, but it no longer held the public's attention as it had during the go-go years of the Mercury, Gemini, and Apollo missions.

With public interest flagging, congressional interest followed suit. Wernher did his best, proposing several grand projects with equally imposing budgets, but none of them went anywhere. Worse yet, after being called to testify before Congress, word spread that he had seemed arrogant and dismissive of committee members' questions. This further eroded his effectiveness and his reputation, which was already under siege from the press releases and rumors concerning his testimony in the Dora trial. The situation wasn't helped by the publication of Clarence Lasby's book, *Project Paperclip: German Scientists and the Cold War*

Professor Lasby, a historian, had begun his research in 1959, and found it to be very difficult to get complete answers to questions about the importation of German specialists and an operation called Project Paperclip. In his research, Lasby met with the director of the then-current iteration of the Paperclip program, but remained unaware that it continued to operate, albeit under another name. All of the records of the JIOA and the dossiers on individuals recruited for Paperclip remained Top Secret, so Lasby had no way of knowing the Nazi histories of von Braun or the other rocket specialists in any detail. He only knew that lots of German specialists had been imported after the war in a highly secretive program of that name. He completed the manuscript in 1969 and submitted it for review and approval. Six months later, approval was granted.

When the book was published, even though detailed background information was absent, the mere fact that large numbers of former Nazis had been employed by the US government after the war caused a sensation. This wasn't great publicity for many programs, but it did raise additional questions about Wernher's past history. Wernher thought it was all too clear that the government no longer valued his services as they had in the past. He didn't know the reason, but he was getting pointed questions from the press that ten years ago would have been vetted and discouraged. He was stunned when he learned that President Nixon hadn't included him among the recipients of the National Medal of Science in 1971. How could he have been overlooked?

After a year and a half of frustration, Wernher decided to leave NASA and go into private industry. He was hired by Fairchild Industries as their Vice President for Engineering and Development, putting him once again in a position to develop, monitor, and coordinate multiple programs underway in the various company subsidiaries. Projects included satellites, drones, and military ground-support aircraft.

In 1974, he became involved in the formation of the National Space Agency, which was designed to promote public awareness and enthusiasm about space exploration. NASA supported it, with the understanding that the benefits of the space shuttle (sometimes mocked as a bus with wings) would be emphasized. Wernher kept up his frenetic travel schedule, giving lectures and TV appearances in the US and abroad. He continued to be in demand, but there were too many rumors circulating about his past for him to regain the idol status he had enjoyed in the period of 1959-1969. Things slowed down dramatically after mid-1975, when he was diagnosed with colon cancer. After the diagnosis, Wernher gave a reflective interview to the *Washington Star* in early 1976 where he seemed less concerned about editing his history. In that interview, he mentioned visiting the Mittelwerk and spoke of the hellish conditions there. That part of the interview was not released to the public, however, for fear it would raise questions about the Paperclip project in general. The government was still committed to keeping the program secret, for protecting its image meant protecting Wernher's.

With his life expectancy now a matter of months, his supporters at NASA, who either forgave, discounted, or ignored his wartime history, encouraged the Ford administration to award him the Medal of Freedom. That was ruled out in no uncertain terms, as it hardly seemed fitting to give such an appellation to a former Nazi who had worked hard to defeat the US in WWII. They got a warmer reception with their next proposal, which was to include his name among the recipients of the Medal of Science. The proposal posed political problems for the administration, however. After extensive deliberations, a panel of experts had already selected 15 scientists to receive the award. Von Braun's name wasn't on the list, and there was concern that adding him through executive decision would circumvent an established policy. The other problem was that those awards were going to be presented by President Carter in early 1978, and nobody expected Wernher to live that long.

A memo was distributed to cabinet members asking if Wernher should receive the award. There was one abstention and one objection (Bob Hartmann, President Ford's Chief of Staff, wrote "No medals for repentant Nazis!!"), but the others agreed, and the plan moved ahead. To reduce media coverage and possible controversy, the award was to be presented to him in the hospital by a government official other than President Ford or a cabinet member. The plan was then modified to have the award delivered by the chairman of Fairchild Industries, Dr. Edward G. Uhl, who had hired Wernher when he left NASA. The official announcement released to the press about the award included a one-page biography that omitted his Nazi history entirely. Shortly after receiving his last award, Wernher von Braun died in the hospital on 16 June 1977.[172]

---

[172] For a list of the awards given to von Braun during his career in Nazi

How to sum up his life? Wernher was a talented engineer with great organizational and marketing skills. He was also an opportunist who took every step necessary to accommodate his obsession with rocketry. Although he has been called "apolitical," the term is misleading. Wernher was always very political, but his political views were shaped by the combination of his society and self interest. He changed countries, allegiances, languages, politics, religions, and when expedient, his personal history. He was a German patriot and nationalist during WWII, accepting and endorsing the ethical standards of the Third Reich and working tirelessly to defeat its enemies, and then transformed himself into a defender of freedom for the United States. That transformation, which took him from a stellar career in Germany to an equally stellar career in the US, was facilitated and actively promoted by the JIOA and Project Paperclip through secrecy, dissembling, and "alternative facts."

Wernher's wartime activities would not have placed him in the top tier of Nazi war criminals, although other Germans sheltered by Project Paperclip would have qualified for that distinction. Yet his membership in the SS and his involvement in requesting and utilizing slave labor merited judicial review as thorough as that conducted for Speer and other prominent figures in the Third Reich. His actions should have carried consequences. They did not because the JIOA decided that he was essential to the compliance of the German rocket team. His false or misleading answers to questions about his past may actually have worked in his favor. He was already on Toftoy's wish list, and such blatant historical revisionism was evidence that Wernher would be as eager to follow the orders of the US Army as he had the orders of the German Army.

The JIOA could have treated him as a POW while allowing him to pursue his passion for rocketry. Instead, he was coddled and handsomely compensated, his personality quirks tolerated, and his secrets protected. All this was done on the grounds of national security. Whether or not those decisions were necessary, appropriate, and legal, and whether Wernher was a hero, a villain, or something in-between, is still debated by pro- and anti- von Braun groups.

In the final analysis, Wernher was brilliant but deeply flawed. One thing is certain: for both Wernher von Braun and the JIOA, the end justified the means. Wernher's lifelong goal may have been space exploration, as he often claimed in the US, but the means involved convincing the Third Reich — and later the US — that he could build them shortrange, medium-range, and intercontinental ballistic missiles

---

Germany and in the post-war period, see Appendix 5.

that would provide military superiority, if not outright world domination. Privately, Wernher may have felt that deaths during the production and use of those weapons were regrettable, but there is no indication that he would have felt any more remorse about raining nuclear fire on the Soviet Union than he felt about the bombardment of London and Antwerp.

1978-1995

FRED MARTINI

In January 1978, the VA reversed their 1947 decision regarding Fred's dental treatment, and limited coverage to the teeth he had lost overseas, not those lost to pyorrhea and complications after his return to the US. It was yet another blow from the VA and another strain on Fred's finances.

Since moving to Florida, Fred's blood pressure continued to climb despite medication. Increasingly powerful drugs were used, but their effectiveness declined quickly. He found it too painful to stand and walk, and by 1979, he was in a wheelchair. His primary physician, Dr. Mike Holsworth, had Fred check into Manatee Memorial Hospital in October for an arteriogram. Severe blockages were found in the major arteries supplying his legs, and he was scheduled for bilateral aortofemoral grafts to replace the clogged sections of those arteries. There were complications during the surgery, and when his kidneys failed, he was put on dialysis.

Meanwhile, the furor resulting from the gradual release of information about Nazi war crimes and Project Paperclip led the Justice Department to create the Office of Special Investigations (OSI) in 1979. Its stated goal was to track down and prosecute any Nazi war criminals living in the US. Fred wished them luck but was sorry that Eli Rosenbaum, the chief investigator, hadn't started investigating decades earlier.

In January 1980, still hospitalized, Fred had a stroke that left his speech impaired and his right side paralyzed. The report from the attending physician reviewed a longstanding history of hypertension and noted that despite treatment his blood pressure had been consistently above $200/100$. In the ICU after the stroke, he was very disoriented. Thinking he was back in Buchenwald, he tried to keep the staff away, telling them in German to leave him alone.

When he got out of the ICU and back into a regular ward, Fred regained his equilibrium. Over the next six months, he gradually regained his speech. With physical therapy, he became able to stand and walk for short distances, although every step was painful. He knew his health was failing, and he worried about what would happen to Betty if he died. Fred's blood pressure at the time was ranging between 160/70 and 190/90 despite multiple anti-hypertensive prescriptions. The VA denied his application for Housebound Aid and Assistance, with the rejection letter including the smug statement that, "In addition you are not entitled to any other benefit based on the application you filed." Betty was furious. "It's not fair!" she said, a phrase she had used often over their decades together. Fred's response was the same as always — "Betty, life doesn't have to be fair."

As Vietnam veterans returned and reintegrated with life at home, the issue of post-traumatic stress disorder (PTSD) became of general interest. By that time, much more was known about the longconsequences of combat, stress, severe physical abuse and malnutrition. The diagnostic criteria for PTSD included: (a) persistent remembering (reliving") the original experiences through intrusive flashbacks, vivid memories, recurring dreams, or extreme distress when exposed to circumstances even remotely similar to the original stresses, (b) difficulty in falling and staying asleep, (c) irritability and outbursts of anger, (d) difficulty in concentrating, and (e) extreme nervousness and exaggerated response to sudden stimuli.

Dr. Hallsworth (an internist) and Dr. Berkes (a nephrologist) explained to Fred and Betty that malnutrition and vitamin deficiency often resulted in peripheral neuropathy and kidney damage, and that combination causes chronic hypertension. The signs were there in his VA health record, but in 1945, the correlations were not understood. They assured him that he had grounds to have his VA disability rating elevated and his pension increased. In the final analysis, all of his problems were service-related.

With their assistance, Fred applied to the VA in March 1980 to get his 10% pension increased. In his application, Fred stated:

> *I am only allowed to leave my home to make visits to the Doctors Office for appointments. I have great difficulty walking due to the painful condition of my feet. I went when my country called. Now I am being ignored about the condition I am in due to my time as a prisoner of war.*

His application was accompanied by medical records documenting chronic hypertension, chronic renal insufficiency, interstitial nephritis, and arteriosclerosis, and medical opinions from an internist, a nephrologist, and a surgeon that his chronic hypertension and renal insufficiency were attributable to the abuse and malnutrition during the war, and to the severe PTSD that continued to affect him since his liberation. He was, in their opinion, totally and permanently disabled.

The VA remained obstinate:

> WE HAVE GIVEN CAREFUL AND SYMPATHETIC CONSIDERATION TO YOUR CLAIM FOR SERVICE CONNECTION FOR YOUR KIDNEY CONDITION AND HYPERTENSION WITH RENAL FAILURE. A REVIEW OF YOUR SERVICE MEDICAL RECORDS DOES NOT SHOW ANY FINDINGS OF NEPHRITIS OR HYPERTENSION WITH RENAL FAILURE DURING YOUR MILITARY SERVICE OR WITHIN ONE YEAR FROM THE DATE OF SEPARATION. THEREFORE, SERVICE CONNECTION MUST BE DENIED.

Fred might be disabled, but he was still mad and still stubborn as a mule. So he filed two appeals in 1981 — both were denied. The primary reason given for these denials was that a "service connection for a foot condition was previously denied as no organic foot condition was found in the evidence of record." That seemed a rather odd justification, given that the neurological basis for Fred's "organic foot condition" was not understood at the time of his separation physical.

In May 1982, a Memorial Day insert to his local paper ran an article about Fred and about his time in Buchenwald. The article was seen by John Chalot, another Buchenwald airman, who was living only 10 miles from Fred and Betty. John contacted Fred, and the two started corresponding and talking on the phone about their problems with the VA. Fred's network started to expand in late 1984, with the arrival of a letter that said:

> DEAR FELLOW KRIEGIE,
> THIS LETTER IS TO ADVISE YOU WHAT HAS BEEN ACCOMPLISHED MOSTLY BY OUR FELLOW CANADIANS, IN MAKING THE KLB CLUB MORE ACTIVE.
> IN AUGUST 1983, I AND THREE OTHER AMERICANS, ALONG WITH 10 CANADIANS ATTENDED THE CANADIAN POW CONVENTION IN HAMILTON. THE OTHER AMERICANS WERE ROY ALLEN, MYLES KING, AND T. C. RICHIE. A MEETING WAS HELD AND IT WAS DECIDED TO EXERT MORE EFFORT TO ORGANIZE THE KLB CLUB.

At that time, the core group had been able to locate 42 other

Buchenwald airmen. They started by contacting bomber group associations and local POW and VFW chapters to publicize the reactivation of the KLB Club. Like John and Fred, Buchenwald veterans had sometimes lived within a few miles of one another for decades, totally unaware that there were others nearby whose medical illnesses were also being dismissed by the VA as not being service-related.

Fred started corresponding with Art Kinnis, who was leading the push to create an active group. The KLB Club had very basic goals. First, they wanted to locate all of the surviving Buchenwald airmen, and second, they wanted the US government to acknowledge that they were neither hallucinating nor lying about their wartime experiences.

Fred began thinking about the medals and awards that he had burned so many years before. If they had been available, perhaps the VA doctors would have been less skeptical. So he wrote to the Army to get replacements, including copies of his discharge papers and the testimonial letters. Fred soon had the American Defense Service Medal, the Purple Heart with two oak leaf clusters, the Air Medal with oak leaf cluster, the WWII Victory Medal, the European African Middle Eastern Campaign Medal with 2 bronze service stars, the American Defense Service Medal, the Expert Marksman ribbon, and the Good Conduct Medal (Fred and his son had a good chuckle about that one).

Fred was convinced that, with the Buchenwald airmen supporting one another, the VA would be more reasonable. So he filed two appeals in 1983, focusing on seven problems his physicians felt were directly related to his service experiences. The first appeal was denied immediately, primarily because previous appeals had been denied. The second appeal was denied in 1984. The accompanying letter, signed by Earlie Walker, Jr, Adjudication Officer, made several interesting points: (1) the evidence of record did not warrant any change in his service-connected nervous condition, (2) service connection for hypertension, neuritis, appendicitis, renal failure, heart condition, and stroke had already been denied, and (3) perhaps most amazing of all: "Your head injury condition and shell fragment wound conditions were not incurred or aggravated during your service."

The reviewing doctor's notes revealed that he thought Fred's story was a complete fabrication. The notes included:

Alleges POW. . . . claims to have suffered from intimidation, beatings, physical torture, and inadequate diet while in prison. He also claims to have suffered a flack wound to the head. Wounds to leg and head could be

from other sources, no evidence to support SC [service connection].
Malnutrition was not found on last examination.

Fred had grown used to having his problems discounted, but now they were questioning his military service and the injuries for which he had been awarded the Purple Heart. He wrote to Loren Jackson, the pilot of his air crew, who wrote a letter testifying to the fact that Fred was a veteran who had been wounded when his plane was shot down. He also contacted LtC. Millikan, who had seen the condition Fred was in when he arrived at Stalag Luft III, and obtained a letter testifying to the fact that the arriving sergeants were in terrible shape, and that Fred had an appendicitis attack while at the camp.

Throughout this period, the OSI continued to investigate, and Nazi war crimes continued to be in the news. OSI investigators confronted Arthur Rudolph with the war crimes evidence they had accumulated, which included material from statements he had voluntarily given in previous interviews. Rudolph faced trial and probable imprisonment for his activities as production manager at the Mittelwerk, his sign-off on sabotage reports that resulted in hangings, his control over the hours worked by the slave laborers, and other related offenses. Rather than face trial, he renounced his US citizenship and returned to Germany. Because he had left voluntarily, without trial and conviction, he was able to keep his sizable federal pension. The lead investigator of the OSI, which had been created two years after Wernher's death, noted that if von Braun were still alive, he would be near the top of their list. Fred just shook his head in amazement when he heard about it.

What was going on with OSI seemed to have little to do with his physical problems or advancing his appeals with the VA. Fred and many other WWII veterans were interviewed in May 1984 as part of a Memorial Day article in his local paper. Although his friends at the POW society and the VFW encouraged him to try an appeal one more time, Fred wasn't sure he had it in him after so many defeats.

Rather than tackling the VA again, Fred became involved with the KLB Club's campaign to get congressional recognition of their service and correction of the official US position as published by Congress in 1945. This involved writing letters to congressmen and senators, announcement in POW and other veteran's magazines, and newspaper coverage. A flurry of news articles about the Buchenwald airmen resulted. The first appeared in the *Sarasota Herald Tribune*, after Fred, Ed Carter-Edwards, and John Chalot reconnected through the KLB Club. The headline read, "It took almost 42 years, but three who survived World War II POW camp are reunited." In late January 1987, the *News-*

Press in Tampa, Florida, ran, "Ex-Fliers Recall Concentration Camp at Reunion" after 12 of the Buchenwald airmen met at a reunion in Fort Myers, Florida. In mid-February, the *Lee Constitution* in Ft. Myers ran, "GI Ghosts of Buchenwald."

This was followed by two articles in the *Bradenton Herald*. "The Nazis Made Them Suffer" appeared at the end of February, 1987, and "Kept at Buchenwald, POWs Want Their Imprisonment Recognized" appeared in April 1988, with interviews and photos of Fred, Ed Carter-Edwards, and John Chalot. Fred and John were also featured in "Pilots Captured During WW II Feel for Allied POWs in Iraq." All of these articles made a point of saying that the airmen wanted the government to acknowledge that they had been in Buchenwald.

Ed Ritter, his old friend from Buchenwald, found Fred's address from the KLB Club, and they started corresponding. In 1987, Ed sent Fred two documents that he had obtained through a Freedom of Information Act request submitted to the US National Archives. The first was the list of arriving prisoners at Buchenwald on 20 August 1944, noting the amounts of money confiscated, and the second was the appendix on Buchenwald taken from an MIS-X[173] report on Stalag VIIA. That report described conditions at Buchenwald and listed the names of several airmen, including Fred. The documents were declassified in 1981, but nobody had asked for them, because nobody knew they even existed. Fred now had proof that he had been telling the truth.

Although Fred was now in and out of the hospital, each time emerging thinner and weaker, he continued corresponding with the KLB Club and writing letters to pressure Florida legislators to take steps to correct the official record. Finally in 1993, the efforts paid off with H Con. R 88, introduced on 27 April 1993 by Congressman Gillespie V. Montgomery from the state of Mississippi. It acknowledged and commended their service and authorized a proclamation by the President to honor their bravery. No financial compensation was proposed, simply public recognition of the Buchenwald airmen.

The resolution was approved by the 103rd Congress and was forwarded to the Senate for approval, where Senator John McCain had agreed to coordinate its passage. Letters of support were written by 21 of the surviving Buchenwald airmen. Once in the Senate, it was referred to the Senate Judiciary Committee. That committee either

---

[173] Military Intelligence Service branch X was responsible for intelligence concerning, and communication with, American military personnel held in German POW camps.

never got around to it or killed it for unknown reasons. It was a major blow to the airmen who had invested so much time and effort in the campaign. Fred was notified that the bill was dead in a letter that arrived on 30 November, which said that they would try again in 1995.[174]

Fred was deeply disappointed. How could this keep happening? How could an SS officer deserve presidential awards and buildings in his name, while the sufferings of American veterans were officially denied and bureaucratically ignored? He was already depressed and housebound, and the injustice of the situation made his physical limitations even harder to bear.

In 1994, Fred decided to give it one more try to appeal the VA decision. He knew he was near the end of the line. His liver had failed,[175] Betty's job had vaporized (the company had folded up after local development was completed), and Fred was afraid that what little money they still had in the bank after paying his medical bills would not be enough for her to live on.

He was well aware that it was a long shot, as the KLB Club had failed to gather sufficient congressional support for the recognition bill, and he had been even less successful getting support for his campaign against the VA. In March 1986, Betty wrote to Senator Paula Hawkins, who was known to be sympathetic to veterans issues:

THIS APPEAL IS BEING DIRECTED TO YOU, AS AN AVOWED ADVOCATE OF VETERAN'S RIGHTS, IN THE HOPE THAT YOU WILL BE ABLE TO CRACK THE FACADE OF INDIFFERENCE MY HUSBAND HAS BEEN ENCOUNTERING AT THE VETERANS ADMINISTRATION.

After summarizing his wartime and postwar difficulties, she continued:

ALL HIS DOCTORS HAVE CERTIFIED THAT HIS PROBLEMS ARE SERVICE-CONNECTED. . . . HE HAS HAD TO DIG OUT ALL HIS OLD PAPERS TO PROVE HE WAS EVEN IN THE ARMY, LET ALONE A POW. . . SENATOR HAWKINS, I BELIEVE THAT MEN LIKE FRED MARTINI HAVE VIRTUALLY GIVEN THEIR LIVES FOR THEIR COUNTRY AND THEIR COUNTRY SHOULD ACKNOWLEDGE ITS RESPONSIBILITY IN TIMES OF TROUBLE.

---

[174] See Appendix 6 for the text of the 1993, 1995, and 1997 resolutions.

[175] He had been diagnosed with hepatitis C in the 1980s. There was no way to tell if he had contracted an aggressive strain from a transfusion in surgery or if it was a smoldering case from the shared needles used to give the chest injections in Buchenwald.

WHAT MY HUSBAND AND THOSE OTHER PRISONERS WENT THROUGH IN BUCHENWALD WAS SO UNSPEAKABLE THAT EVEN NOW IT IS DIFFICULT FOR HIM TO TALK ABOUT IT; BUT HE HAS NEVER FALTERED IN HIS LOYALTY TO HIS CREW AND HIS COUNTRY.

She closed, begging for assistance. In May, Fred sent a letter to Senator Alan K. Simpson, detailing his military service and that of Betty and his sister, Liz. He gave an overview of his medical issues and the lack of support from the VA. Simpson was on record, saying:

SHOW ME A COMBAT VETERAN FROM A COMBAT THEATER WITH ANY TYPE OF AILMENT OR MALADY OR CONDITIONS AND I SAY GIVE HIM EVERYTHING IT TAKES — ANYTHING THEY NEED — AND I SHALL BE RIGHT THERE TO DO THAT.[176]

So Fred devoted four pages to summarizing his wartime experiences and the problems he had encountered convincing the VA to treat his conditions seriously. He closed with, "I honestly believe that the VA operates on the belief that if they wait long enough, problems will resolve themselves through attrition."

Several months later, having heard nothing from either senator, Betty sent a second letter to Senator Paula Hawkins, attaching a copy of the letter to Senator Simpson. In her cover letter, Betty wrote:

I FIND IT ALMOST INCOMPREHENSIBLE THAT THERE HAS NEVER BEEN A MENTION OF THE FACT, IN ANY SPEECH OR PUBLICATION I HAVE SEEN AT ANY TIME SINCE WORLD WAR II, THAT A FEW AMERICAN SOLDIERS WERE IMPRISONED AT THE INFAMOUS BUCHENWALD CONCENTRATION CAMP. . . . THOSE WHOM I HAVE MET HAVE, WITHOUT EXCEPTION, BEEN VICTIMS OF PHYSICAL ILLNESSES OVER THE YEARS WHICH, DOCTORS AGREE, ARE DIRECTLY RELATED TO THEIR INCARCERATION IN A CONCENTRATION CAMP. IN SPITE OF THIS, THE VA INSISTS ON TREATING THESE MEN AS NORMAL PRISONERS OF WAR DETAINED IN NORMAL CAMPS WITH THE NORMAL TREATMENT SUPPOSEDLY RECEIVED THERE. . . . SOME OF MY HUSBAND'S CONTACTS ARE CANADIAN VETERANS OF BUCHENWALD. THEIR GOVERNMENT GIVES

---

[176] Fred was probably unaware that although Simpson made those comments in a discussion of the Gramm-Rudman Amendment, they were made to deflect criticism from his assertion that most veterans' disability payments were awarded without sufficient justification.

THEM SUPER-SPECIAL TREATMENT, SPECIAL PENSIONS, AND
EVEN LAST YEAR FLEW THE ENTIRE GROUP TO EUROPE FOR A
REUNION WITH OTHER ALLIED BUCHENWALD SURVIVORS,
PAYING ALL THEIR EXPENSES. . . . I SEE HIM EACH DAY
FORCING HIMSELF TO WEAR SHOES WHEN HIS FEET ARE SO
PAINFUL THAT HE WINCES IF ANYONE TOUCHES THEM. . . .
EVEN AS I WRITE THIS, I FIND MYSELF CRYING. . . . WE
HAVEN'T HEARD FROM SENATOR SIMPSON.

Neither Senator Hawkins nor Senator Simpson responded to these letters.

Fred went before the appeals board in his wheelchair to give testimony in person, with Betty accompanying him. It was very difficult for them to talk about their situation in a public forum, and in the end, they shouldn't have bothered. The VA flatly refused to reconsider Fred's pension rating. As it had since 1947, the VA cited previous denials as sufficient evidence that no increase in rating was justified.

The only bright spot in his last year came in late January 1995, when Fred became a grandfather. To his great delight, his new grandson was named Frederic. Buoyed by this, Fred filed another appeal with the VA. He was determined to go down swinging.

On 25 May 1995, another Concurrent Resolution was introduced, as H Con. R 73, by Rep. Tim Hutchinson (R-Arkansas). In his introduction, Representative Hutchinson acknowledged the recent death of Michael Petrich, a Buchenwald airman who had been instrumental in reactivating the KLB Club. The resolution was referred to the Committee on Government Reform and Oversight and then to the Committee on Civil Service the next day. It went no further.

A few months later, on 21 September 1995, Fred died when multiple systems collapsed. His last VA appeal was still being processed. Fred died frustrated and angry about his treatment by the US government, and completely baffled by the government's refusal to correct the historical record. Yet that frustration and anger had never impacted his love of country, nor was he embittered by his experiences with the VA. He had often told Betty "Every day of my life after leaving Buchenwald was an unexpected gift." Fred always knew he was on borrowed time — he was simply trying to make the best of it.

EPILOGUE

In the aftermath of Fred's death, I flew from Hawaii to Florida and found boxes of correspondence and files and newspaper articles among his effects. My mother, still distraught, told me many things that she and Fred had kept to themselves. I decided to try to carry on the battle my father had started.

On 2 February 1996, I wrote to the Hawaii congressional representatives, Neil Abercrombie and Patsy Mink, and enclosed news articles about Fred and his experiences. I asked why the existence of the Buchenwald airmen had been kept secret for 40 years, even from other branches of the government, and why Congress had failed to pass a resolution that would set the record straight, despite the fact that it would cost nothing and require no payments to the survivors? I sent similar letters to the offices of Hawaii Senators Daniel Inouye and Daniel Akaka.

I received responses from all four. Rep. Abercrombie had contacted Ms. Sandra Stuart, Assistant Secretary of Defense, posing these questions. Rep. Mink reported that H Con. R 73 had stalled in committee, but that if it emerged, she would happily sign on as a cosponsor. She had also written to Ms. Stuart seeking answers. Senators Akaka and Inouye had written to the Department of Defense as well.

On 20 March 1996, James D. Wold, Deputy Assistant Secretary of Defense (POW/MIA Affairs) responded to Senator Akaka, with copies to Senator Inouye and Representatives Mink and Abercrombie. Mr. Wold said that he had checked with the Army and with the National Holocaust Memorial and verified the existence of the Buchenwald airmen. He also said, "None of those offices, however, could explain why the information has been withheld for so long." He said he had also checked with the VA, but was told that they could not research the case without a claim number.

On 22 March, Terrence J. Gough, Chief of the Staff Support Branch of the Department of the Army, responded to Representative Mink. The letter said, "A search at the Center for Military History files revealed no information on this subject." Mr. Gough then contacted a historian at the Holocaust Museum who advised him that approximately 500 American airmen and ground troops had been held in up to ten camps, including Buchenwald, Dachau, Flossenberg, Mauthausen, and Nordhausen. Mr. Gough was told that official documents were in NARA Record Groups 238 and 338, but he had no information as to when the records had been declassified.

On 9 May, Senator Akaka wrote to summarize the letters he had received, saying that the Buchenwald experience was confirmed, but that it was not known why it had been classified for so long. He said he had contacted the Army Center of Military History for further research.

On 20 June, Senator Akaka received a response from Mr. Joe We, Acting Chief of the Staff Support Branch. A search of their files contained no information pertaining to secrecy regarding liberated POWs. He went on to list the Record Groups at the National Archives where documents might be found, and quoted a senior archivist who said that the Buchenwald records had been officially declassified in 1974,[177] but that they were not consulted until the late 1980s. He felt that this might have contributed to Fred's frustrations, adding that after declassification, the records would have been accessible to the VA — if they knew who to ask and where to look for them. He did not attempt to address the question of why the existence of the Buchenwald airmen had remained classified for 30-40 years.

H Con. R 73 was not passed by the 104th Congress. In July 1997, it was reintroduced as H Con. R 95 early in the 105th Congress, with twenty-six cosponsors. Surviving members of the KLB Club were in attendance, as were representatives of the ex-POW and VFW organizations. The bill passed the House of Representatives on September 16, 1997.

In the Senate, the concurrent resolution (Sen Con. R 32) was again referred to the Senate Judiciary Committee. Once again, it died there for unknown reasons. The net result was that the Buchenwald airmen would receive no recognition, although the 103-105th Congresses did manage to find the time to commemorate the achievements of astronauts and contributions made to country music. No corresponding bill has since been introduced, and the official US historical record has yet to be corrected.

Ironically, soon after Fred's death, the German government initiated a program to provide compensation for victims of Nazi abuse and a second program for POWs assigned to forced labor kommandos. Buchenwald airmen alive at the time could receive generous compensation (up to $50,000) from each program. Betty wrote to ask if surviving spouses could be considered for such

---

[177] Despite this assertion, the earliest declassification date on documents obtained from the National Archives was 1981.

awards. She was initially told that it was likely, but by the time she received the application forms and started gathering the required documentation, the submission period had ended.

In 1999, Congress passed the Nazi War Crimes Disclosure Act, mandating the declassification of all related documents. An Interagency Working Group was established to oversee the review and declassification of these materials. The process was cumbersome, slow, and delayed by obfuscation, interagency squabbling, and outright stonewalling, particularly by the CIA. A final report, released in 2007, acknowledged that despite the best efforts of the IWG, not all records had been released.[178] What released was sometimes of limited value. For example, the FBI file on Wernher von Braun included a 48-page translation of an article published by Julius Mader, 43 pages where the entire contents of a memo or report had been redacted, and 31 blank pages inserted to signify that material was withheld due to security concerns — 62 years after WWII ended, 30 years after von Braun's death, and eight years after passage of the Nazi War Crimes Disclosure Act.

One by one the Paperclip Germans faded away. Walter Dornberger died in 1980, Kurt Debus in 1983, Ernst Steinhoff in 1987, Magnus von Braun in 2003, Ernst Stuhlinger in 2008, and Konrad Dannenberg in 2009. Arthur Rudolph fled the US in 1984 to avoid prosecution by the OSI, dying in Hamburg, Germany, in 1996, As the Nazi technocrats passed away, they took with them their claims of innocence and their stalwart defense of Wernher's reputation.

The image of Wernher von Braun as an American hero has continued to be eroded. In 2007, Michael J. Neufeld published what is often cited as the most authoritative account of Wernher's entire life, *Von Braun: Dreamer of Space/ Engineer of War*. He took pains to present the historical record of events dispassionately and to let the reader evaluate the evidence. In 2009, Michael B. Petersen published a lesser-known volume called *Missiles for the Fatherland* Petersen constrained his focus to von Braun's activities through the end of WWII. He included important details concerning the cultural environment and ethos in Peenemünde at the time. Together, these two books provide both the documented facts and the social motivation and context that shaped Wernher's attitudes and actions.

Many other books published in that same period took a much harsher view of von Braun.[179] In 2008, Aron Ranen released a video

---

[178] FOIA requests were filed over 2010-2013 to the CIA, FBI, Army, and Air Force. No new information was obtained, and the CIA responded that the agency "can neither confirm nor deny" the presence of classified information.
[179] See the reference listing in Appendix 7.

documentary called *The Lost Von Braun*. It included footage from wartime Germany and interviews with Konrad Dannenberg, Ernst Stuhlinger, and other German members of Wernher's team. These men repeated the false claims made since the end of the war: that there was no connection between Peenemünde and the Mittelwerk, that there were no slave laborers at Peenemünde, that they had been assured that conditions at the Mittelwerk were excellent, and that the SS must have been responsible for any abuses. The video then refuted those assertions by presenting documentary evidence provided by OSI investigators and the graphic testimony of men who had worked as slave laborers at both Peenemünde and the Mittelwerk.

In Germany, von Braun's complicity in Nazi war crimes is widely acknowledged, and streets and other public facilities given his name at the height of the Cold War have been renamed. Exhibits at the Peenemünde Museum have been revised to highlight the moral failings and the cost in lives, rather than simply to glorify the achievements of the rocketeers. In contrast, von Braun is still revered by the NASA community. The Marshall Space Center has the Von Braun Office Complex, where his birthday is proudly celebrated each year, conventions are booked at the Von Braun Civic Center in Huntsville, and the University of Alabama has a Von Braun Research Hall. Wernher's past has now been edited to the point where his professional life before coming to the United States is summed up on the Marshall Space Center website in three sentences:

AFTER GAINING HIS PH.D., VON BRAUN BECAME A CIVILIAN EMPLOYEE OF THE ARMY AND CONTINUED WITH THIS WORK. HE DESIGNED THE V-2 ROCKET THAT WAS USED SO EFFECTIVELY AGAINST BRITAIN DURING WORLD WAR II. AT THE END OF THE WAR, THE VON BRAUN TEAM AT PEENEMÜNDE ON THE BALTIC SEA HEADED SOUTH AND SURRENDERED TO U.S. FORCES RATHER THAN RISK CAPTURE BY THE SOVIET ARMY.[180]

The epitome of this kind of historical revisionism is NASA's official history, which includes:

BEFORE THE ALLIED CAPTURE OF THE V-2 ROCKET COMPLEX, VON BRAUN ENGINEERED THE SURRENDER OF 500 OF HIS TOP ROCKET SCIENTISTS, ALONG WITH PLANS AND

---

[180] http://earthobservatory.nasa.gov/Features/vonBraun/printall.php, and http://earthobservatory.nasa.gov/Features/vonBraun/vonbraun_3.php

It is difficult to reconcile this narrative with the fact that Wernher surrendered with six associates, he provided neither documents nor test vehicles, and he was fleeing Bleicherode and the Mittelwerk production facility rather than the Peenemünde rocket complex at the time.

The JIOA would have heartily endorsed these abbreviated and sanitized versions of Wernher's history. It is ironic that in general, Germany now has a more accurate view of Wernher's role in WWII than major government agencies in the US.

In many respects, these veterans were victims of "friendly fire," which can come in many different forms. Betty died in 2014, still hoping that Fred's story would someday be told and the service of the Buchenwald airmen officially commended. Few of the Buchenwald airmen are alive today, and with the KLB Club inactive, the US government is no longer under pressure to correct the official historical record and give the families a sense of closure. The treatment of these airmen, and the contrast with the treatment of those who had worked hard for Germany to win WWII, remains to be addressed.

Fred Martini and Wernher von Braun were enthusiastic patriots on opposing sides of the war. Their stories first intersected at Buchenwald Concentration Camp. Did Fred see Wernher there, as he believed? There is no way to be certain in the absence of documentation, but Wernher visited Buchenwald at least once, and Fred was held there. In the long run, it hardly matters whether Fred saw Wernher or if it was a case of mistaken identity. The fact remains that Fred, horribly abused by the Nazis during the war, was shabbily treated by his own government after he returned home, while Wernher, the most decorated and popular scientist in the Third Reich, was given a new career, a lavish salary, and further accolades in the US. The same government that accepted, forgave, and concealed Wernher's history told Fred that he was lying about his past.

Wernher was an opportunist who escaped justice; Fred was a survivor who was denied justice. Both were haunted by their past — Wernher by fear that his wartime activities would be revealed, and

---

[181] http://www.history.nasa.gov/SP-4223/ch3.htm
http://history.msfc.nasa.gov/vonbraun/bio.html

Fred by recurring visions of what he had experienced. Their respective fates were determined by decisions made in secret by US intelligence agencies. The JIOA and its predecessor, the CIOS, operated with little oversight and few constraints throughout the war. This fostered a siege mentality. Other agencies and branches of government were seen as potential impediments that could be circumvented without remorse. The decision to classify and withhold information not just from the public, but from Congress and from other government agencies, including the FBI and the VA, for 40 years cannot be forgiven and should not be forgotten.

In the end, who was betrayed? Everyone.

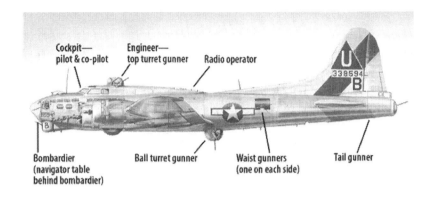

Figure 1: Crewmember position in a B-17G.

Figure 2: A B-17 crewman outfitted for a high-altitude mission.

Figure 3: Waist gunners in combat positions, viewed looking toward the tail of the plane.

Figure 4: The original Jackson crew during training at Drew Field, Tampa, Florida in February, 1944. Left to right: Lt. Loren E. Jackson, Lt. P. Hite,* Lt. J. Lindquist, Lt. Joseph Haught, Sgt. Armando Marsilii, Sgt. Frederic Martini, Sgt. Ervin Pickrel, Sgt. J. Rood,* Sgt Theodore Dubenic, Sgt. Felipe Musquiz. Asterisks indicate crew replaced before deployment to the ETO. (Lt. Hite was replaced by Lt. Ross Blake, Sgt. Rood was replaced by Sam Pennell.)

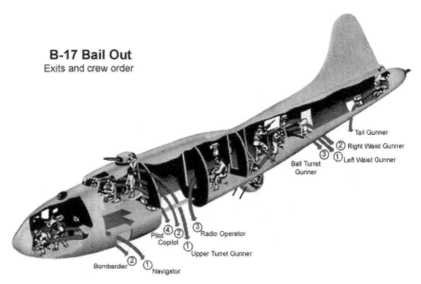

B-17 Bail Out
Exits and crew order

Tail Gunner

② Right Waist Gunner
③ ① Left Waist Gunner

Ball Turret
Gunner

Radio Operator

④ ② ③
Pilot
Copilot ①
Upper Turret Gunner

② ①
Bombardier ① Navigator

Figure 5: Diagram showing recommended bailout procedure from a crippled B-17.

Figure 6: General Walter Dornberger escorting Reichsführer Heinrich Himmler at Peenemünde. SS-Major Wernher von Braun, wearing his black SS uniform, is following closely behind Himmler. This is the only surviving photo of von Braun in uniform, although he wore it to SS meetings, on facility inspections, and at other times when the uniform helped him accomplish his goals.

Figure 7: A V-2 undergoing servomotor testing in one of the large halls in the Mittelwerk.

Figure 8: The Raulins and friends, 1945. Capt. Max Raulin is in the foreground on the left, standing next to his wife, Yvonne, while his son, Lionel, clowns around in the foreground. The names of the other people in the photo are not known.

Figure 9: A restored "40&8" boxcar from the train carrying prisoners from Paris to Germany, which departed on 15 August 1944.

Figure 10: Shaving and disinfecting arriving Polish prisoners at Buchenwald.

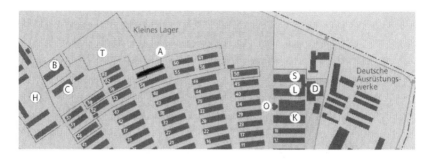

Figure 11 (below): A map of Little Camp (Kleines Lager) and the adjacent portions of the main concentration camp at Buchenwald in August 1944. D = Disinfection, S = Shower block, L = Laundry, K = Kitchen, O = Göthe oak, A = Abort, T = Tent area, B = Brothel, C = Cinema, H = SS Hospital.

Figure 12: A corpse wagon photographed at Buchenwald after its liberation in April 1945.

Figure 13: Barracks shelving in Little Camp.

Figure 14: Fred Martini, photographed on arrival at Stalag Luft III on 20 October 1944.

Figure 15 (left): Wernher von Braun and Army staff being congratulated after a successful V-2 launching at Peenemünde.

Figure 16 (below): A clandestine photo taken early on the march from Stalag Luft III to Spremberg.

Figure 17: POWs using a makeshift "kriegie stove" to heat water and cook meals.

Figure 18: The liberation of Stalag VIIA.

Figure 19: Emaciated bodies that were found in trenches by the entrance to the Mittelwerk and en masse within the Dora concentration camp. Some were killed by Allied bombing, others died of starvation or injuries.

Figure 20: V-2 engines within an assembly hall at the Mittelwerk.

Figure 21: V-2 components loaded for shipment to the US from the Mittelwerk, April/May 1945.

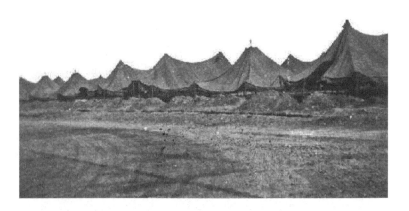

Figure 22: Densely packed tents at Camp Lucky Strike.

Figure 23: Wernher von Braun and Walter Dornberger at their surrender to the US. Wernher has his cast in place, Dornberger wears his tall hat, and to the left (uncovered) is Herbert Axster.

Figure 24: Betty and Fred at their marriage, 28 December 1946.

Figure 25: Wernher von Braun and Walt Disney.

Figure 26: The von Braun group of Paperclip contractees at Fort Bliss, Texas.

Figure 27: Wernher von Braun with President John F. Kennedy.

Figure 28: Fred Martini in 1965, at the time of his promotion to
Director of Operations at Edison Electronics.

Figure 29: KLB Club members (left to right) Bob Johnson, Ed Ritter, Fred Martini, Ed Carter- Edwards, and John Chalot, photographed at a reunion in Venice, Florida, in 1986.

Figure 30: Fred Martini with his son, daughter-in-law, and grandson, taken in Sarasota, Florida six weeks before his death.

Appendices

8th Air Force (Army Air Corps): The division of the Army Air Corps tasked with operations in the European Theater of Operations; based in the UK.

ABMA: The Army Ballistic Missile Agency

Abwehr: The German Army Intelligence section

A-4 rocket: The fourth iteration of rockets produced by Gen. Dornberger's Ordnance group under the direction of Wernher von Braun. *See V-2*

CIOS: Combined Intelligence Objectives Subcommittee; a subcommittee of the JIOA, consisting of representatives of the War Department, US Army, US Navy, State Department, Office of Research and Development, and Foreign Economic Administration plus the UK Foreign Office, Admiralty, Air Ministry, and various ministries concerned with the funding and production of war-related materials.

CJA: Command Judge Advocate, the chief legal officer of a military command, part of the JAG Corps

DEFSIP: The Defense Foreign Scientists Immigration Program, the name given to Project Paperclip in 1957; discontinued in 1970.

Dora: The concentration camp established to provide slave labor for construction of the Mittelwerk and other underground facilities in the Nordhausen area, and to provide skilled slave labor for the associated assembly lines.

ETO: European Theater of Operations

FFI: French Forces of the Interior, also called the French Resistance

FIAT: The Field Information Agency, Technical; an Army intelligence team working in the ETO searching for technological advances.

G-2 Army Intelligence (aka Military Intelligence)

Gestapo: The Nazi Secret Police, a plainclothes division of the SiPo, a branch of the Reich Security office (RSHA); primarily focused on combatting subversive elements in Germany and removing obstacles to Nazi policies by citizens of the Occupied Territories.

Heer: The German Army

JAG: Judge Advocate General, the legal corps providing advice and legal functions within a particular military service

JCS: Joint Chiefs of Staff, the heads of the various branches of the US military.

JIC: Joint Intelligence Committee, the Intelligence arm of the JCS.

JIOA: The Joint Intelligence Objectives Agency, a subcommittee of the JIC with members from branches of the military, the Department of State, and the OSS (Office of Strategic Services, which in 1945-46 became the CIA) tasked with the acquisition and use of German specialists. Disbanded in 1962 with responsibilities for DEFSIP/Paperclip remaining with the Army but oversight transferred to the Director, Defense Research and Engineering (Department of Defense).

Kapo: A trusted prisoner in a German concentration camp.

KLB: Konzentration Lager Buchenwald: the German name for Buchenwald Concentration Camp.

Kommando: A slave labor work group.

KriPo: The division of the SiPo responsible for dealing with domestic crimes.

Luftwaffe: The German Air Force

Milice: The Vichy French secret police who worked with the Gestapo and SD

MIS-X A section in the US War Department to keep track of and assist American POWs in the ETO.

Mittelwerk: The underground complex where A-4/V-2 production was done.

OMGUS: Office of the Military Government, US; the military administration responsible for governing the American zone of occupation in Germany after the war ended. General Lucius Clay was the head of OMGUS.

Operation Overcast: A plan to sequester German specialists collected by T-forces in a secure location within the American zone of Germany and pay them to work for the US government. The stated goal was to use their knowledge to help defeat Japan.

OSS: Office of Strategic Services, an espionage agency in WWII reporting to the Joint Chiefs. In late 1945, it was reorganized and placed under civilian oversight as the Central Intelligence Agency (CIA).

Peenemünde: German military research facility on the coast of the Baltic Sea in a joint venture between Army Ordnance and the Luftwaffe. Peenemünde East was under Army control and involved in rocket development; Peenemünde West was under Luftwaffe control and focused on cruise missile (V-1/Fi-103) and jet engine development.

Project Paperclip: An enhancement of Project Overcast that involved the recruitment of German scientists and technicians and their transport to the US to work in military and civilian corporate research facilities. Done without deNazification and in defiance of

US government policies regarding the employment and immigration of committed Nazis, SS officers, and suspected war criminals. The stated goal was to prepare for an eventual war with the Soviet Union; for this reason the intelligence services opted to circumvent both the letter and the spirit of the law.

RSHA: The *Reichssicherheitshauptampt* (Reich Security Central Office).

SD: The *Sicherheitsdienst,* or Security Service, a division of the SS responsible for counterterrorism and the destruction of resistance networks in the Occupied Territories

SHAEF: Supreme Headquarters, Allied Expeditionary Force

SiPo: The *Sicherheitspolizei,* or Security Police, a division of the RSHA that was in charge of the KriPo (domestic criminal police) and the Gestapo.

SOE: Special Operations Executive, an intelligence agency of the British military staffed by volunteers.

SS: The *Schutzstaffel,* the paramilitary arm of the Nazi Party, organized parallel to the Army but reporting to *Reichsführer* Heinrich Himmler instead of the German Military chain of command. There were three main divisions of the SS: (1) the *Waffen-SS* which had units in the Occupied Territories working alongside or replacing Army units, (1) the *Allgemeine-SS,* which included the administration staff of the RSHA, SD, SiPo, and (2) reserve units, and (3) the *Totenkopfverbände,* which operated the concentration camps and extermination facilities.

Tiger Teams T-forces: Groups of intelligence officers traveling with Allied military forces and tasked with finding German specialists and their equipment. There were groups looking for biological weapons, chemical weapons, atomic weapons, rockets, jet engines, aircraft design, and so forth.

V-1: The "buzz-bomb," a primitive cruise missile launched from rails and able to fly 200 miles before crashing and detonating its 500-pound explosive payload. Slow moving and subject to attack by fighter planes en route, but relatively cheap to produce in large numbers.

V-2: The A-4 rocket, capable of traveling around 200 miles carrying a one explosive payload. It was supersonic and impossible to anticipate or deflect, but its guidance system was poor, and it was impossible to aim with precision.

VA: The Veterans Administration, a branch of the US government intended to deal with veteran support and services.

Vichy Government: The puppet government of occupied France.

Wehrmacht: The German Military, literally "war machine," consisting of the Army (Heer), the Air Force (Luftwaffe), and the Navy (Kriegsmarine).

KEY PERSONNEL, WWII:
ALLIED FORCES
William "Wild Bill" Donovan: Director of the Office of Strategic Services in WWII
Dwight D. Eisenhower: Supreme Commander of Allied Forces, WW II, became President of the United States 1953-1961
Charles "Rojo" Goodrich: Army Colonel who was the Senior American Officer (SAO) in South Camp of Stalag Luft III. **Walter Jessel:** Army intelligence officer (G-2) who conducted the first security evaluation of Wernher von Braun in June 1945.
Philip J. Lamason: Squadron Leader, Royal NZ Air Force, who was the leader and ranking officer among the Buchenwald airmen.
Holger Toftoy: US Army officer (LtC. initially) placed in charge of the portion of Operation Overcast/Paperclip involving the V-2 rocket team; head of the ABMA.

> **Major James Hamill** and **Major Robert Staver:** deputies to LtC. Toftoy; Hamill took care of packing up materials at the Mittelwerk and shipping them to Fort Bliss while Staver sought German personnel and documents. Maj. Hamill became the program officer at Ft Bliss.

Bosquet Wev: Chairman of the JIOA; a US Navy captain

NAZY GERMANY
Walter Dornberger: Army Ordnance officer in charge of Peenemünde from 1937-1944; thereafter in charge of related special projects including mobile V-2 launch systems; spent two years in British POW camp, then moved to the US with Project Paperclip. After a career that took him from the US Air Force to a VP role at Bell Aircraft Corporation, he retired to Germany, where he died in 1980.
Joseph Göbbels: Propaganda minister for the Nazi government; on 1 May 1945, he committed suicide with his wife after killing his children in Hitler's underground bunker.
Herman Göring: Head of the Luftwaffe and Hitler's second-in-command; committed suicide in prison after sentencing at Nuremberg trials in 1946.
Henrich Himmler: Head of the Nazi Party, its paramilitary forces, and civilian and secret police forces; committed suicide after capture in May 1945.
Hans Kammler: SS-general, in charge of major construction projects including Auschwitz, the Mittelwerk, and various industrial facilities;

disappeared in April 1945.

Georg Rickhey: General Director of the Mittelwerk in 1944-1945. Brought to US under Project Paperclip but returned to Germany in 1947 as a defendant in the Dora war crimes trial. Acquitted but was not brought back to the US afterward. He died in 1966.

Arthur Rudolph: Responsible for A-4 production at Peenemunde, reporting to von Braun; became head of assembly and production at the Mittelwerk, reporting to Sawatski. Moved to US under Project Paperclip to work for von Braun; was placed in charge of the Saturn-V program. Renounced US citizenship and fled to Germany in 1984 to avoid prosecution for war crimes. He died there in 1996.

Albin Sawatski: Head of production planning for the Mittelwerk, co-chair with von Braun on CCDC Committee; presumed to have died in US custody in May/June 1945.

Albert Speer: Minister of Armaments and War Production, exercising financial and resource allocation for the Nazi government; served 20 year sentence for war crimes and died in 1981.

Magnus von Braun: Responsible for servomotor assemblies at the Mittelwerk 1944-1945. Brought to the US under Project Paperclip. Worked at Fort Bliss with his brother, then went to work in the UK for Chrysler; retired to Arizona and died in 2003.

Wernher von Braun: Technical Director at Peenemünde 1937-1944, Vice President and Technical Director of Elektromechanischewerk, GmbH 1944-1945, Technical Director of CCDC-Mittelbau 1945. Brought to the US under Project Paperclip to lead rocket team from 1945-1972. Retired to private industry and died in 1977.

Equivalent Ranks in the SS, German Army, and US Army

Waffen-SS rank	German Army rank	US Army rank	Rank Code
	Soldat	Private	The enlisted ranks are only approximately equivalent because the SS and German Army had numerous transitional ranks plus ranks assigned to specific tasks. For example, *Rottenführer* designates a Squad Leader, a position that some sources consider to be a Private First Class and others a Corporal. The officer ranks are direct equivalencies.
Sturmmann	Gefrieter	Private Second Class	
Rottenführer	Obergefrieter	Private First Class	
Unterscharführer	Unteroffizier	Corporal	
Scharführer	Unterfeldwebel	Sergeant	
Oberscharführer	Feldwebel	Staff Sergeant	
Hauptscharführer	Oberfeldwebel	Sergeant First Class	
Sturmscharführer	Stabsfeldwebel	Master Sergeant	
Stabsscharführer	Hauptfeldwebel	Sergeant Major	
Untersturmführer	Leutnant	2nd Lieutenant	O-1
Obersturmführer	Oberleutnant	1st Lieutenant	O-2
Hauptsturmführer	Hauptmann	Captain	O-3
Sturmbannführer	Major	Major	O-4
Obersturmbannführer	Oberstleutnant	Lieutenant Colonel	O-5
Oberführer	Oberst	Colonel	O-6
Brigadeführer	Generalmajor	Brigadier General	O-7
Gruppenführer	Generalleutnant	Major General	O-8
Obergruppenführer	General	Lieutenant General	O-9
Oberstgruppenführer	Generaloberst	General	O-10

APPENDIX 2: THE FRENCH RESISTANCE VERSUS THE NAZI SECRET POLICE NETWORK

⋅⊟⊟⋅

The SS was created in 1929 from volunteers who provided security for Nazi meetings and demonstrations. After Hitler's rise, the number of members grew exponentially. By 1940, it was a paramilitary organization with three major divisions (*Waffen-SS Allgemeine-SS*, and *Totenkopfverbände*), sharing a common fanatical mindset.

There were 38 Waffen-SS divisions, and in 1944, the Waffen-SS had roughly 1 million men under arms. Membership in the SS was not limited to German nationals; more than half of the Waffen-SS divisions were staffed by enthusiastic French, Polish, Hungarian, Dutch, and Russian volunteers. Waffen-SS units operated in the field alongside the much more numerous Army units. The Army, organized and staffed with traditional military personnel, was comparable to the British or American Armies. In 1944 the German Army consisted of roughly 12 million soldiers. Relations between the Waffen-SS and the Army were somewhat strained, as the senior officers of the regular army tended to consider SS men to be fanatical soldier-wannabes.

Heinrich Himmler, as head of the Nazi Party (*Reichsführer*), had control over the civilian police force and all divisions of the SS. The *Totenkopfverbände,* or Death's Head unit, was responsible for the administration of concentration camps. The Waffen-SS was originally the combat arm of the SS operating outside of Germany. The Allgemeine-SS originally formed as a "home guard" for the Führer but soon operated throughout Germany, and additional units staffed by local volunteers operated in the Occupied Territories. This division of the SS included the various security forces of the Nazi Party. The operatives of the Gestapo, or *Geheime Staatspolizei*, were primarily members of the civilian police, but they were awarded Allgemeine-SS ranks. The 150,000 Gestapo agents investigated treason, sabotage, espionage, and other domestic crimes that challenged Nazi authority. The SS had its own secret police known as the SD, or *Sicherheitsdienst*, which focused on counterintelligence operations such as arresting foreign spies and evading military personnel, as well as neutralizing the resistance networks involved. Although they held SS paramilitary ranks, they often operated in plainclothes like the Gestapo, rather than wearing uniforms. SD agents also accompanied the Army troops, acting as Nazi political officers responsible for ensuring compliance with party attitudes and directives. An especially fanatical division of the SD called the *Einsatzgruppen* was responsible for atrocities, killing any individual or groups seen as opposing the Nazi regime. This included implementing the Final Solution in the Occupied Territories.

The Gestapo and the SD both reported to Waffen-SS *Obergruppenführer* (Lieutenant General) Ernst Kaltenbrunner of the Reich Main Security Office, or *Reichssicherheitshauptamt* (RSHA). Both agencies relied on a network of paid and unpaid informers and sympathizers, as did other agencies of the civilian police that were given shorthand names that included KriPo (criminal police) and the OrPo (order police).

The SD was also assisted by the Vichy government's security police, the Milice, a paramilitary organization modeled after the SD and tasked with the suppression of the FFI. An embarrassing number of French civilians were willing to provide information to one of the above groups, in exchange for special privileges and cash payments. The Army also had a security police known as the Abwehr, which was primarily responsible for military intelligence, and the Luftwaffe, which ran the POW camps for allied airmen, had special interrogators who focused on gathering intelligence relevant to air operations.

The responsibilities of these various agencies often overlapped or competed. Early in the war, the Abwehr dealt with captured military personnel, the Luftwaffe with captured airmen, the Gestapo watched for treasonous activities, and the SD pursued resistance networks with the help of the Milice. But as the military situation deteriorated and Germany shifted from offense to defense, the Abwehr in France lost personnel and authority, and the Luftwaffe's influence waned as their air operations lost effectiveness. The power vacuum was filled by the Gestapo and the SD, and by early 1944, both agencies were heavily involved in the detection, capture, and interrogation of downed air crews.

Unfortunately, because most of the FFI members were amateurs and civilians with good intentions but zero background and training in covert activities and security, the German intelligence agencies found it very easy to corrupt and infiltrate the resistance networks in occupied France. By 1944, virtually all of the resistance networks in France involved in sheltering Allied airmen had been compromised. When it became clear that they would soon be leaving, the Germans made it a high priority to wipe out all remnants of the resistance networks before their departure.

The Germans had many methods of penetrating resistance groups. Many members of the SD had at one time lived in the US or the UK and were fluent in English. These agents would present themselves to the French as downed airmen or British special operations agents who had parachuted in to help Allied airmen escape. In addition, under threat of imminent death, a small number of resistance members decided to change sides. The Germans also had a small number of dedicated volunteers who believed strongly in the fascist cause and were all too happy to assist the Nazis.

Seventy years after the fact, it is difficult to obtain complete details about the betrayal and capture of all 169 of the airmen evacuated from Fresnes Prison on 15 August 1944. Many of the accounts written following their liberation have been lost, most of the airmen have died, and the Germans were very effective in destroying Gestapo records in Paris prior to their retreat. Yet the accounts that have survived share common features that indicate the existence of a carefully contrived, well orchestrated entrapment program in operation from June-August 1944.

Jacques Desoubrie, a young Belgian, played a pivotal role in dozens of betrayals. In 1944, Desoubrie was 22 years of age, a classic sociopath, and a savvy opportunist. He was quick witted, ruthless, and a superb actor. He volunteered his services to the Gestapo in early 1941. At the time, he was a member of an extreme right-wing group and sympathetic to the Nazi cause. With a command of French, German, and English, and his abilities as a chameleon, he was pre-adapted for the life of a spy – a life he seemed to relish.

In mid-1941, claiming to be an escapee from a German prison, he became involved with a French resistance group called "True Liberty" that was moving evaders (downed airmen) into southern France, which was administered by the puppet Vichy government rather than the Germans. In late November 1941, 75 members of this resistance group were arrested, and 12 of them subsequently executed. After this success, under the name of "Jean Masson," he started carrying false papers along the Paris-Brussels corridor for the Comet Line, a resistance network that was smuggling downed airmen to Allied forces by moving them across southern France and into Spain. In June 1943, the Paris chiefs of the Comet organization were seized and shot, more than 100 members of the network in France and Brussels were arrested, and a group of British and American airmen were captured and imprisoned as POWs.

Desoubrie then shifted to Paris as the main Gestapo agent in the area. In early 1944, he had rented an apartment as "Pierre Poulain," and was also called "Pierre du Nord," but after giving the Gestapo information about a resistance group in southern France, rumors began to circulate that Poulain was a traitor. So Pierre Poulain disappeared, and "Jean Jacques," a quiet fellow living with his wife and two children, magically appeared. (Although his "wife," Marie Verger, was married to someone else, the two children were his.) For an introduction to the remnants of the Comet Line (which he had largely demolished), he relied on Maurice Grapin.

Resistance members seldom used their real names, even when dealing with other resistance agents; Maurice called himself "Henri Grampon." Henri was a minor player in the local resistance network who had been arrested in early 1944 and decided it was time to change sides. His return with a story about a narrow escape was unquestioned, and he was welcomed back into the fold.

As an agent of SS-Colonel Hans Kieffer, deputy head of the Paris Gestapo, Grapin's role was to serve as the intermediary between Jacques Desoubrie (or whatever name he was currently using) and the German security police. To establish "Jean Jacques" as bona fide, Henri introduced him to Collette Marie Orsini, a young woman whose parents had sheltered airmen who later escaped through Spain. Mme. Orsini then introduced Jean Jacques to Louis Picourt, the head of the Eure FFI who was based in Chartres. Max Raulin reported to Picourt. With the Comet Line in disarray, Picourt had airmen hiding in multiple locations but had no secure way to get them out of the country. Jean Jacques claimed to have the solution to this, and offered to assist in getting the papers and connections organized to move the airmen to safety. He even had his own car and papers that would allow him free movement. Collette was, to use a then-popular phrase, "a looker," young, red-haired, and free-spirited. Although married, she and her new friend Jean Jacques were soon a couple.

Despite the obvious questions that might have arisen, Jean Jacques was so convincing and smooth that in short order, Picourt took him on a tour to meet the chiefs of resistance units in other parts of occupied France. Captain Max Raulin's base was one of their first stops because his far-flung network was hiding so many airmen; in mid-July 1944 he had at least 12 airmen, eight from the USAAF and four from the RAF. Jean Jacques was of course delighted to hear this. Each airman delivered to the Gestapo was worth a 10,000 franc "bonus," and with the Allies advancing rapidly, he needed to wrap things up and leave the country. He was on a roll — from late June to late July, he had spearheaded the collection and delivery of at least 38 airmen to the Gestapo in Paris. Yet no one in the FFI had as yet suspected that he was a double agent; for his efforts, he had been appointed the FFI chief for Aisne, a district near the Belgian border.

Jean Jacques was widely known as a trusted FFI transporter who, with Collette by his side, would pick up airmen in small groups from rural locations and deliver them to Paris (they first tried using the train, but the car was simpler and more direct). Jean Jacques usually delivered airmen directly to a hotel, but he occasionally used Collette's residence at 7 rue des Batignolles, Paris, as a way-station. The hotels were in a rather seedy, red-light district of Paris where few questions would be asked. One of the favorite destinations was the Piccadilly Hotel at 61 rue Pigalle, where rooms could be rented by the hour. Louis Gianoni, another SD agent, worked there and managed an adjacent bar/lounge, Le Prélude, at 59 rue Pigalle. If the airmen had already been questioned in some detail, they were left at the hotel until transport could be arranged — whereupon they were delivered to the Germans. If the airmen had neither been questioned nor given one of the bogus Red Cross cards used to collect information, they were sometimes kept there for days, awaiting the arrival of a British agent who, they were told, was the head of the local resistance network.

Desoubrie was primarily responsible for collecting airmen sheltered in Normandy, which included the Eure district where Fred was hidden. The "Comet Line" was the name of the resistance network that was attempting to repatriate the airmen, and Desoubrie had infiltrated the network very effectively. He was kept very busy because so many aircraft transited the area to hit targets in France and Germany. Other SD agents focused on other districts and escape lines, although all of their networks intersected in Paris.

A lot of confusion was caused by the names "Captain Jack," "Captain Jacques," and "Jacques" (as in Jean Jacques or Jacques Desoubrie). In practice, these names were used for convenience by several different traitors and SD agents operating in Paris and outlying areas. The man most often adopting the cover "Captain Jacques" was Guy Marcheret. Marcheret was tall – almost 6' – with brown hair and blue eyes. He was about 35 years old, and he spoke fluent English. He often claimed to be a British or Canadian Special Operations Executive (SOE) agent.

Marcheret often delivered betrayed airmen to 20 Boulevard de Sebastapol, a house where George Prevost lived with his sister Genevieve Rocher and her husband Jean. George was short, middle aged, heavyset (or fat), and balding, with thick glasses. He also had a prominent gold filling in his front teeth. His sister, older and matronly, did the cooking and cleaning. The Prevost clan was an established member of a resistance network; they had aided 28 airmen in the past, but at this point their cover was completely blown and they were being used, no doubt with great glee, by the SD. Here again, arriving airmen were told to await the arrival of a resistance chief.

The identity of the "head of the network" was largely a matter of convenience. For airmen delivered to staging areas by either Desoubrie or Marcheret, the resistance chief who showed up was one of the senior SD officers in Paris, Hauptmann (Captain) Christian Schnell. Schnell had relatives in Chicago and had spent considerable time there before the war. When operating undercover, Schnell was usually introduced as "Captain Jack," an American from Chicago (or occasionally Maine). However, if Schnell was unavailable, Marcheret might show up to interrogate airmen brought by Desoubrie, and Desoubrie could be introduced as "Captain Jacques" to airmen brought to the Prevost house.

As a result of this identity swapping, when the captured airmen were liberated and asked who had betrayed them, they all tended to say "Captain Jacques" or "Captain Jack" or "Jacques." It was initially thought that Desoubrie had been everywhere and done everything; had he survived (he was caught and executed — with Guy Marcheret —in late 1949), he probably would have been flattered by the padding of his resume. His record hardly needed padding — he was responsible for the capture of half of the Buchenwald airmen (84), almost twice the number of airmen attributed to Marcheret (43).

A third senior SD agent was known as Draga; his real name was Niodrz Yevremovitch. Draga was in his mid-30s about 5'10" tall, with short dark hair, grey eyes, and a pale complexion. Schnell had recruited him from the Marseilles jail early in the occupation. Draga usually introduced himself as "Dr. Maurice," a Spanish doctor working for the resistance; airmen were sometimes delivered to his Paris home at 2 Square des Aliscamps. At other times he, rather than Marcheret, visited airmen at the Hotel Piccadilly as the "resistance chief." In short, Desoubrie, Marcheret, Schnell, and Draga were busily disassembling escape networks, their paths in Paris intersected frequently in the hectic period of June-August 1944.

When Marcheret was playing the role of Captain Jacques, he was usually accompanied by Oberleutnant Wolfgang Brandstetter, a Lufwaffe reserve officer who had lived in the US. As a writer for an obscure German publishing house (owned by his family), Brandstetter appeared first in New York in 1936, but soon shifted to southern California until he was recalled to Germany in December 1938. He was about 6'2" tall, with fair hair, blue eyes, and a small scar on his forehead. Airmen often described him as very fit and good looking – a bit of a dandy who claimed to be "John," an American from Pasadena who had become a French air officer. John was often the person who did the subtlest interrogations, performing that role for "Dr. Maurice" as well as for "Captain Jack" and sometimes for "Captain Jacques."

In July 1944, Marcheret often traveled with Ivonne Lallier, a woman in her 30s whom he introduced as his personal assistant. Lallier was described as "unattractive;" she was short, had narrow shoulders and poor posture, and her red hair, obviously dyed, often assumed a peculiar shade of red-orange. Her eyes were distinctly yellowed, probably because in mid-1944, she was suffering from jaundice. Because she dyed her hair red, she was often confused with Collette Orsini, although detailed descriptions of the two were very different.

Whoever Captain Jack/Jacques might actually be, he attempted to get the men to fill out fake Red Cross cards, ostensibly so that the information could be radioed to England to establish that the airmen were who they said they were, rather than German spies. The airmen had been briefed on this tactic when they arrived in the ETO, so they often either refused to fill the cards out or filled in the minimal information required by the Geneva Conventions. Once that process was out of the way, the airmen were asked to hand over their dog tags and other identification – whatever they had kept – with the explanation that this would make their cover stories more believable should they be stopped at a checkpoint along the escape route. Few airmen complied with that request, but their refusal was accepted without a fuss.

The airmen were then delivered to the Gestapo. Small groups of 1-4 airmen were picked up by car, often a black 4-door Citroen. Most were driven directly to the Paris Gestapo either at 84 Avenue Foch or Gestapo headquarters at rue des Saussaies for interrogation before transfer to Fresnes Prison, although a few groups were taken into custody at a roadblock. On 15 July, 16 July, and 2 August, there must have been too many caught in the traps, because the Germans used covered lorries instead of cars. These vehicles gave them bulk transport capabilities, and more than 30 airmen could be collected in one sweep by driving from one pickup location to the next within Paris.

On 11 August, the last of the airmen within the escape lines were collected in a series of operations that included raiding the Prevost house and arresting the sheltered airmen along with George Prevost, Genevieve Rocher, and her husband Jean. After interrogation, the three were sent to Fresnes Prison and rode the same train out of Paris that carried the Allied airmen they had attempted to assist.

There were few happy endings to these stories. George Prevost died in Buchenwald Concentration Camp; although Genevieve Rocher survived Ravensbrük Concentration Camp, her husband died at the Dora camp. Louis Gianoni was killed on 16 August 1944 while assisting in the last-chance roundup of FFI members he had betrayed. Collette Orsini, although arrested and tried for her involvement with Desoubrie, was acquitted — a court decision that continues to stimulate strong disagreements among those studying this period. According to Collette, the Desoubrie-Orsini affair had come to a dramatic finale on 24 July 1944, when she finally realized he was working for the Germans. He had settled the matter by shooting her in the chest.[182] Although she was certainly injured and hospitalized, the circumstances remain obscure. It is difficult to reconcile her account with (1) the fact that she had shown her concealed pistol to a friend, a curious affectation for an innocent bystander, (2) that it was Desoubrie who took her to a hospital, and (3) that he later returned to try and convince her to flee Paris with him.

Guy Marcheret was captured and imprisoned in late 1945, but Jacques Desoubrie remained at large until his arrest in 1949, following a tip from his estranged wife. The two were tried separately but at roughly the same time perhaps the French wanted to get the Captain Jacques issue taken care of once and for all and both were sentenced to death by firing squad. The sentences were carried out at the Fort de Montrouge, near Paris, in December 1949. Desoubrie went to his fate completely unrepentant, and his final letter stated his undying dedication to the Nazi ideals and closed with "Heil Hitler."

Maurice Grapin was arrested, tried, sentenced to 5 years of hard labor, and then released. Draga was captured by the British in Italy in 1945 and "aggressively interrogated." His fate thereafter is uncertain. Brandstetter fared much better. He was no fool, and as things started looking bad for Germany he started hiding money in Paris. When France fell to the Allies, he deserted and waited for the right time to surrender. He was interrogated repeatedly, but after cooperating fully, he was released. He returned to Germany and to the publishing business that had provided him cover in the 1930s, spending the rest of his life in relative obscurity. Christian Schnell's story was the most remarkable of all. Schnell was arrested and held in a French military prison in Paris awaiting trial. In May 1949, on the day before the trial of the SD agents from Avenue Foch was to begin, Schnell was

---

[182] Some other reports say she was stabbed. There are also disagreements about the date of the incident and when she was hospitalized. Her story evolved over time; she later claimed that she knew Desoubrie was a German agent, but that she continued to assist him because he was blackmailing her.

released, for no apparent reason. It was either by design or the greatest stroke of luck imaginable. He was never seen again.

APPENDIX 3: BUCHENWALD AIRMEN

The Buchenwald Airmen			
Nationality/ Service Rank	**Name**	**KLB number**	**Unit Information**
New Zealanders/RNZAF (2)			
F/Lt	Cullen, Malcolm Ford*	78388	Typhoon, 257 Sq
S/L	Lamason, Phillip (Phil) John*	78407	Lancaster bomber, 15 Sq
Australians/RAAF (9)			
F/Sgt	Fairclough, Mervyn James*	78427	Halifax bomber, 51 Sq
F/Sgt	Gwilliam, James (Jim) Percival*	78423	Halifax bomber, 78 Sq
F/Sgt	Johnston, Eric Lyle*	78421	Halifax bomber, 78 Sq
F/O	Light, Kevin William*	78381	Lancaster bomber, 9 Sq
F/Sgt	Malcolm, Thomas (Tom) Alexander*	78379	Lancaster bomber, 463 Sq
F/Sgt	Mills, Keith Cyril*	78405	Halifax bomber, 78 Sq
P/O	Mills, Robert (Bob) Neil*	78426	Halifax bomber, 78 Sq
F/Sgt	Perry, Raymond (Ray) Walter*	78356	Halifax bomber 466 Sq
F/Sgt	Whellum, Lesley (Les) Keith*	78442	Halifax bomber, 102 Sq
Jamaican (RAF) (1)			
P/O	Guilfoyle, Michael (Mike) A.**	78393	Lancaster bomber, 12 Sq
Canadians/RCAF (26)			
F/O	Atkin, Harold*	78440	Halifax bomber, 427 Sq
F/O	Bastable, Harry*	78378	Halifax bomber, 640 Sq
WO	Clark, Don*	78364	Halifax bomber, 76 Sq
Sgt	Crawford, John	78406	Lancaster bomber, 106 Sq
F/Sgt	Compton, G.A. Edward*	78434	Halifax bomber, 424 Sq
P/O	Carter-Edwards, Ed*	78361	Halifax bomber, 427 Sq
Sgt	Fulsher, Frederick W.*	78418	Lancaster bomber, 100 Sq
Sgt	Gibson, William (Bill) R.*	78394	Lancaster bomber, 419 Sq

F/Sgt	Grenon, Leon (Leo) T.*	78438	Halifax bomber, 433 Sq
P/O	Harvie, John D.*	78412	Halifax bomber, 433 Sq
WO	Head, Les	78430	Lancaster bomber, 419 Sq
F/O	Hetherington, Stanley (Stan)	78436	Halifax bomber, 433 Sq
Sgt	High, Dave	78422	Lancaster bomber, 419 Sq
F/Sgt	Hodgson, Thomas (Tommy) R.*	78424	Lancaster bomber, 625 Sq
F/O	Hoffman, Charles Richard (Dick)*	78429	Halifax bomber, 432 Sq
F/O	Kinnis, Arthur (Art) G.*	78391	Lancaster bomber, 106 Sq
Sgt	**Leslie, Donald (Don) E.**	78404	Halifax bomber, 102 Sq
F/Sgt	McLenaghan, J. Ralph*	78373	Lancaster bomber, 514 Sq
F/O	Prudham, James E. (Pep)	78374	Lancaster bomber, 419 Sq
P/O	Scullion, Patrick*	78395	Halifax bomber, 433 Sq
F/O	Shepherd, Ernest G.*	78372	Halifax bomber, 640 Sq
F/O	Smith, James A.*	78428	Lancaster bomber, 419 Sq
WO	Sonshine, E.R. (Joseph)*	78343	Lancaster bomber, 12 Sq
Sgt	Walderam, Willie A.*	78402	Lancaster bomber, 106 Sq
F/O	Watson, Earl Carruthers*	78431	Halifax bomber, 432 Sq
F/O	Willis, Calvin E.	78342	Halifax bomber, 640 Sq

UK/RAF (48)

F/Sgt	Angus, Jack W.**	78390	Halifax bomber, 78 Sq
F/Sgt	Barham, Leonard P.**	78432	Lancaster bomber, 207 Sq
F/O	Baxter, Stuart**	78384	Lancaster bomber, 514 Sq
F/Sgt	Bennett, Geoffery	78344	Lancaster bomber, 57 Sq
F/Lt	Blackham, Thomas (Tom) Henry*	78380	Lancaster bomber, 50 Sq
F/O	Booker, Stanley Albert	78370	Halifax bomber, 10 Sq
Sgt	Bryden, Robert (Bob)	78365	Halifax bomber, 76 Sq
F/O	Chapman, E.W. (Ken)*	78409	Lancaster bomber, 15 Sq

F/Sgt	Chinn, Albert J.**	78433	Lancaster bomber, 207 Sq
Sgt	Clarke, John**	78385	Lancaster bomber, 514 Sq
F/Sgt	Davis, Eric*	78346	Lancaster bomber, 83 Sq
Sgt	Dowdeswell, Philip*	78410	Halifax bomber, 158 Sq
F/Sgt	Eagle, Douglas*	78403	Halifax bomber, 102 Sq,
F/Sgt	Fernandez, John Joseph*	78352	Halifax bomber, 158 Sq
F/Sgt	Gould, Terrance**	78386	Halifax bomber, 10 Sq
Sgt	Harper, Robert*	78414	Stirling bomber, 622 Sq
Sgt	Hegarty, Patrick W.	78420	Halifax bomber, 51 Sq
F/O	Hemmens, Philip D.*	78383	Lancaster bomber, 49 Sq
Sgt	Hughes, Ronald R.	78347	Halifax bomber, 76 Sq
F/Lt	Jackson, Edgar*	78392	Lancaster bomber, 100 Sq,
Sgt	Jordin, Douglas F.**	78341	Lancaster bomber, 12 Sq
Sgt	Joyce, Reg W.	78401	Halifax bomber, 102 Sq
P/O	Kay, William	78400	Lancaster bomber, 100 Sq
F/Sgt	Leverington Ronald (Ron) L.	78382	Halifax bomber, 102 Sq
Sgt	Lucas, Lewis J.	78389	Lancaster bomber, 106 Sq
Sgt	MacPherson, Alexander J.**	78435	Lancaster bomber, 207 Sq
Sgt	Marshall, Wilfred**	78417	Lancaster bomber, 12 Sq
F/Sgt	Measures, Dorak K.*	78413	Halifax bomber, 101 Sq
F/O	Mutter, Neville E.S.*	78375	P-51, 65 Sq
F/Lt	Nuttal, Cyril Worosley*	78366	Halifax bomber 158 Sq
Sgt	Osselton, John N.**	78371	Halifax bomber, 10 Sq
F/Sgt	Peirson, Frank	78362	Halifax bomber, 76 Sq
F/O	Percy, Douglas C.*	78411	Lancaster bomber, 630 Sq
Flight Sgt	Phelps, Edward K.	78419	Lancaster bomber, 207 Sq
Sgt	Reid, John D.**	78387	Lancaster bomber, 514 Sq
F/O	Robb, Ian A.*	78415	Stirling bomber, 218 Sq
Sgt	Rowe, Andrew**	78408	Halifax bomber, 640 Sq
F/Sgt	Salt, Frank**	78345	Lancaster bomber, 35 Sq
F/Sgt	Sharrat, William D.**	78397	Halifax bomber, 78 Sq

F/O	Spierenburg, Splinter Adolph (Dutch)*	78443	Lancaster bomber, 582 Sq
F/O	**Stewart, James (Jim) A.**	78416	Typhoon, 609 Sq
F/O	Taylor, Peter D.	78425	Halifax bomber, 10 Sq
F/O	Taylor, Ralph John (Bob)	78376	Halifax bomber, 10 Sq
Sgt	**Vincombe, V. (Frederick)**	78377	Lancaster bomber, 419 Sq
Sgt	Ward, John D.**	78396	Lancaster bomber, 576 Sq
Sgt	Watmough, George F.**	78439	Halifax bomber, 433 Sq
WO	Wesley, Laurice**	78399	Lancaster bomber, 207 Sq
F/O	Williams, Llewelyn**	78437	Halifax bomber, 102 Sq

Americans/USAAF (82)

S/Sgt.	Alexander, William*	78287	B-17, 489 BG, 845 Sq
1Lt.	Allen, Roy*	78357	B-17, 457 BG, 750 Sq
Lt.	Appleman, Stratton M.*	78314	Glider, 437 TCG, 85 Sq
Lt.	Bauder, Warren F.	78196	B-24, 44 BG, 506 Sq
1Lt.	Beck, Levitt C.*	78286	P-47, 406 FG, 514 Sq
2Lt.	**Bedford, Richard L.**	78283	P-47, 353 FG, 350 Sq
S/Sgt	**Bowen, Chasten (Chas) E.**	78336	B-17, 91 BG, 323 Sq
2Lt.	Brown, Robert W.	78295	B-17, 384 BG, 544 Sq
S/Sgt	Bozarth, James Walter*	78340	B-17, 401 BG, 615 Sq
2Lt.	Carr, Frederick W.*	78318	B-24, 489 BG, 845 Sq
Lt.	Chalot, John A.*	78278	P-51, 355 FG, 358 Sq
2Lt.	Chapman, Park*	78284	B-26, 322 BG, 450 Sq
S/Sgt.	Chessir, Douglas	78285	B-24, 489 BG, 845 Sq
S/Sgt.	Coats, Basil A.*	78308	B-17, 390 BG, 571 Sq
2Lt.	Coffman, J.D.	78319	B-24, 489 BG, 845 Sq
T/Sgt.	Cowan, Frank Kirby*	78271	B-17, 96 BG, 339 Sq
Lt.	Crouch, Marshall Jr. E.*	78277	B-24, 392 BG, 579 Sq
2Lt.	Dauteuil, Donat F.	78324	B-26, 391 BG, 547 Sq
2Lt.	Dearey, Ralph W.*	78316	P-51, 339 FG, 503 Sq

2Lt.	Denaro, Joe	78269	B-24, 801 BG, 850 Sq
2Lt.	Duncan, James H.*	78300	B-17, 390 BG, 568 Sq
Sgt.	Edge, William L.*	78267	B-26, 394 BG, 585 Sq
S/Sgt.	Fix, Earl Ellsworth*	78313	B-24, 489 BG, 845 Sq
Lt.	Fore, James W.*	78349	B-17, 91 BG, 323 Sq
2Lt.	Freeman, Elmer (James) C.*	78359	B-26, 397 BG, 596 Sq
Sgt.	Friel, Edward J.	78309	B-24, 491 BG, 852 Sq
2Lt.	Granbery, William L.*	78312	B-24, 801 BG, 850 Sq
S/Sgt.	Hanson, John P.**	78280	B-17, 385 BG, 548 Sq
1Lt.	Hastin, James (Jim) D.*	78354	P-51, 361 FG, 374 Sq
S/Sgt.	Heimerman, Lawrence A.*	78334	B-24, 487 BG, 838 Sq
2Lt.	Hilding, Russ D.	78326	B-17, 447 BG, 709 Sq
2Lt.	Hoffman, Robert B.*	78350	P-38, 55 FG, 38 Sq
2Lt.	Horwege, Glen L.*	78281	P-47, 362 FG, 377 Sq
T/Sgt.	Horrigan, Roy J.	78321	B-24, 493 BG, 862 Sq
1Lt.	Hunter, Harry F.	78337	P-47, 353 FG, 351 Sq
S/Sgt.	Johnson, Robert T.	78272	B-24, 448 BG, 714 Sq
1Lt.	King, Myles A.	78279	P-51, 355 FG, 357 Sq
Capt.	Larson, Merle E.*	78363	P-38, 474 FG, 429 Sq
S/Sgt.	Little, Bruce S.	78301	B-17, 379 BG, 526 Sq
S/Sgt.	Ludwig, Everett F.*	78339	B-17, 390 BG, 571 Sq
S/Sgt.	McClanahan, John H.*	78348	B-17, 384 BG, 544 Sq
S/Sgt.	Martini, Frederic C*	78299	B-17, 385 BG, 551 Sq
Sgt.	Mauk, William E.*	78298	B-24, 489 BG, 845 Sq
1Lt.	McLaughlin, Daniel (Whitey) G.	78338	B-17, 457 BG, 751 Sq
2Lt.	Mikel, George*	78266	B-17, 92 BG, 327 Sq
2Lt.	Mitchell, Gerald E.	78307	B-24, 801 BG, 850 Sq
1Lt.	Moser, Joseph (Joe)*	78369	P-38, 474 FG, 429 Sq
Sgt.	O'Masters, Lovell*	78290	B-17, 457 BG, 751 Sq
T/Sgt.	Pacha, Arthur M.	78288	B-17, 385 BG, 549 Sq
S/Sgt.	Paxton, S. Keith	78320	B-24, 493 BG, 862 Sq

Sgt.	Pecus, Steve*	78315	B-24, 489 BG, 845 Sq
2Lt.	Pedersen, J.W. (Charles)*	78351	B-17, 306 BG, 367 Sq
S/Sgt.	Pennell, Sam*	78289	B-17, 385 BG, 551 Sq
1Lt.	Petrich, Michael R.*	78325	B-26, 391 BG, 575 Sq
1Lt.	Phelps, Byron F.*	78331	P-38, 367 FG, 393 Sq
S/Sgt.	Pelletier, Arthur J.	78335	B-24, 487 BG, 838 Sq
Lt.	Powell, William (Bill)*	78296	B-17, 385 BG, 549 Sq
Sgt.	Reynolds, Leo J.	78292	B-17, 385 BG, 549 Sq
S/Sgt.	Richey, G. Thomas*	78317	B-17, 390 BG, 571 Sq
S/Sgt.	Ritter, Edwin W.*	78311	B-24, 93 BG, 328 Sq
S/Sgt.	Roberson, Charles William*	78327	B-17, 384 BG, 544 Sq
1Lt.	Rynerd, William H.*	78358	B-26, 397 BG, 598 Sq
T/Sgt.	Salo, Laurie H.*	78270	B-24, 801 BG, 850 Sq
S/Sgt.	Scharf, Bernard T.*	78353	B-17, 91 BG, 323 Sq
Sgt.	Scott, George W.**	78330	A-20, 416 BG, 668 Sq
T/Sgt.	**Shearer, Donald R.**	78332	B-26, 391 BG, 573 Sq
2Lt.	Smith, James W.*	78323	B-24, 493 BG, 862 Sq
S/Sgt.	Stralka, Paul A.*	78268	B-24, 801 BG, 850 Sq
T/Sgt.	Suddock, Dwight E.*	78273	B-17, 351 BG, 510 Sq
1Lt.	Sypher, Leroy Henry*	78276	P-51, 361 FG, 375 Sq
2Lt.	**Thompson, Warren A.**	78329	A-20, 410 BG, 647 Sq
1Lt.	Vance, Ira E.*	78360	B-26, 397 BG, 598 Sq
S/Sgt.	Vallee, Edward*	78293	B-17, 303 BG, 360 Sq
1Lt.	Vincent, Edwin H.*	78310	B-17, 381 BG, 534 Sq
1Lt.	Vratney, Frank	78328	B-24, 487 BG, 838 Sq
2Lt.	Ward, Robert	78355	B-17, 91 BG, 323 Sq
S/Sgt.	Watson, John Paul	78333	B-24, 487 BG, 838 Sq
S/Sgt.	Williams, W.J.	78294	B-17, 385 BG, 549 Sq
S/Sgt.	Wilson, Paul J.*	78297	B-26, 391 BG, 574 Sq
1Lt.	Wojnicz, Ray J.*	78367	B-17, 447 BG, 709 Sq
1Lt.	Zander, Arthur*	78368	B-24, 448 BG, 14 Sq
S/Sgt.	Zeiser, James F.*	78322	B-17, 91 BG, 323 Sq

* = Deceased ** = Not located after WW II Boldface = Known to be alive in Dec. 2016

APPENDIX 4: LAMASON, THE SOE, AND PLANS TO ESCAPE FROM BUCHENWALD

-ᘿᗷ·

Kenneth Burney, one of the SOE (Special Operations Executive) agents, had been in Buchenwald longer than the 37 in Dodkin's group, and he had some value to the Germans as a linguist. As a result, he was held apart from the rest, but he could wander freely within the camp. Using discreet bribes, Burney had been able to get the prisoner-guards responsible for security at Block 17 to allow Dodkin free passage into the main camp.

In short order, Burney convinced Lamason of his reliability by answering questions about minor details and personalities in the British organization that the Germans would be unlikely to know; Lamason had spent considerable time in the UK and had a capacious memory. But when Dodkin and Lamason spoke, Lamason was unusually reserved, if not outright hostile, and he seemed tense as he walked the two out of earshot to have a private conversation. A few minutes later, the atmosphere had changed, and the three were chatting like old friends.

Lamason's first impression had been that this man was a German spy, because he knew the real Kenneth Dodkin quite well from the time he had spent in the UK. Only after the two men had talked candidly and Burney had provided confirmation was he convinced that Dodkin was a dedicated British agent. The man posing as Dodkin was Squadron Leader Forrest Yeo-Thomas, age 42. He was probably the model for Ian Fleming's James Bond character — Fleming also worked for the SOE during the war — and Yeo-Thomas's exploits from age 18 onward resemble the script of one of the Bond movies.

Yeo Thomas and 36 other SOE agents had arrived from Fresnes Prison a week before the airmen, and like the airmen their fates remained uncertain. Yeo-Thomas, however, had used the last week to become familiar with the layout and organization of the concentration camp, and had worked out several escape scenarios. This was his third mission into Germany and the Occupied Territories, and the third time he'd been captured. Although this was his first time in a concentration camp, he was determined to escape and return to the UK just as he had on previous missions.

In the week following their shift into Block 58, Lamason had extended conversations with Yeo-Thomas ("Dodkin") and Burney. Yeo-Thomas had tried unsuccessfully to have his men shifted to Little Camp and combined with the airmen, but the SOE agents were classified as spies, whereas the airmen were logged as police prisoners, and the two were incompatible. Yeo-Thomas had received word from prisoner clerks in the main office that all of his men were to be executed, and he asked Lamason to try to intercede with the administration, bringing them under his wing (so to speak). After agonizing over the decision, Lamason decided not to attempt it. He was worried that linking the fate of the airmen to the fate of the SOE agents might jeopardize any chance they had of being transferred to a POW camp. This was a difficult decision for two reasons. First, Lamason had heard that execution orders had arrived in the file with the airmen, but that SS-Captain Schmidt would not sign the order until a date was specified by the RSHA (Himmler's office). (Lamason elected not to tell the other airmen as there was nothing to be done about this.) Second, the 37 SOE agents had now been released from isolation, and most of them had visited Little Camp to spend time with the airmen, swapping stories and making friends.

Just after lunch on 11 September 1944, an announcement was made, ordering 16 of the SOE agents to report to the front gate. On arrival, they were shackled together in pairs and then pushed into the punishment cells by SS-Hauptscharführer (Master Sergeant) Gustav Heigel, who was in charge of the prison and guard platoons. Heigel was rumored to be in charge of prisoners designated for "special treatment" (execution), and he had a penchant for beating and torturing prisoners before the sentence was carried out. The next day, the SOE agents were escorted to the crematorium by SS-Unterscharführer Wolfgang Otto and executed in the strangling room. Their bodies were presumably the ones Fred and Sam handled in the crematorium basement.

In the days that followed, Yeo-Thomas and Lamason met almost daily to compare notes and try to come up with a viable plan of action. The prospects were not good. Their numbers were already being whittled away; they had just lost 16 talented operatives and the surviving airmen and SOE agents had been weakened by malnutrition and disease. Most had dysentery, all had skin infections, many had rags binding festering foot wounds, others were coughing from respiratory infections, and those with minimal medical knowledge recognized the labored gurgling of pneumonia. The overcrowded camp was plagued by tuberculosis, strep infections, and pleurisy, as well as a persistent typhus epidemic that was barely kept under control by quarantining those infected in an isolation ward in Block 46. The two leaders agreed that their chances of a successful escape were now very poor. A surprise breakout by 200 trained, fit men backed by a Red/Green coalition might have a chance. But with their numbers reduced and their health failing, the ardor of their suitors had cooled, and their support was no longer guaranteed. Yeo-Thomas had tried to get the Reds to give him some of the weapons assembled by the airmen and now cached around the camp, but the Reds, who had hidden them, would not divulge their location.

In August, around the time the airmen arrived, Yeo-Thomas had met Professor Alfred Balachowski, a 55 year-old prisoner who had been a doctor at the Pasteur Institute in Paris. Balachowski, an Austrian by birth, was a portly and pleasant fellow with short gray hair and thick glasses. He was given special privileges in the camp because he worked in Blocks 46 and 50, manufacturing experimental typhus vaccines and monitoring experiments the SS doctors performed on prisoners. Balachowski was a member of a French resistance cell known as the Prosper Network, and he had volunteered to be deported to a concentration camp in Germany to save as many lives as possible.

In desperation, Yeo-Thomas prepared a coded message to the SOE, reporting on the bacteriological warfare work at Buchenwald and urgently requesting the assistance of paratroopers to break out of the camp with critical documentation. He entrusted the message to Hans Baumeister, a close friend of Balachowski's. Baumeister was a trusted German prisoner often sent out of the camp on assignments. With the message, Yeo-Thomas gave Baumeister a note verifying Baumeister's trustworthiness. The message and note were successfully smuggled out, but there was no response. (The message did not reach Britain until December 1944.)

While Yeo-Thomas was sending his message, Lamason was using a similarly circuitous method to send an uncoded message in German addressed to the Commanding Officer of the Luftwaffe base at Nohra, informing them of their plight and requesting that they be evacuated to one of the Luftwaffe POW camps. Time dragged on while Lamason waited in vain for a response to his message.

Yeo Thomas continued to look for a way to save the remaining 21 SOE agents. A plan began to take shape after Balachowski arranged a meeting in Block 46. Attending the meeting were Balachowski, Yeo-Thomas, Baumeister, and a prisoner-orderly, Dr. Eugen Kogon, who had survived in Buchenwald for many years. Kogon knew all of the angles, and together they decided that the best hope of survival lay in having SOE agents assume the identities of dying prisoners confined to the typhus isolation ward. There were several major problems facing them, however. The most obvious was that the plan would not work unless the SS doctor assigned to Block 46, Sturmbannführer (Major) Ding-Schuler would permit it. Dr. Ding-Schuler was Himmler's friend, but Kogon suspected that he had a strong sense of self-preservation. The proposed arrangement would be that Ding-Schuler would allow the operation to proceed, in exchange for a written commendation and possibly supporting testimony at his trial, if and when the Allies won the war. Thomas would also promise to try to protect Ding-Schuler from retribution by prisoners when the camp was liberated.

Kogon approached Ding-Schuler at his next opportunity, and the doctor agreed to the terms with the condition that the kapo of the experimental block, Arthur Dietsch, agreed as well. Fortunately, Baumeister and Dietsch were friends, and this obstacle was overcome. The only other problem facing them was the ticking of the clock — there were many typhus patients in isolation, but they were stubbornly clinging to life. But then Ding-Schuler had second thoughts; he would keep the bargain but he would only agree to save three of the SOE agents and one of them had to be Yeo-Thomas (otherwise he would have no to testify on his behalf). Yeo-Thomas reluctantly agreed, but continued to try to find a way to save the rest of his men while keeping the typhus plan secret from his men, Lamason and the other airmen, and the camp at large. And he knew all to well that secrets were very hard to keep in Buchenwald.

Yeo Thomas was now hiding in the Typhus ward, listed as a patient. Dietsche was giving him injections that gave him a fever, although Yeo-Thomas initially feared that it was a trick and that he was being executed. After much thought, YeoThomas decided to include Harry Peulevé and Stéphane Hessel in the plan. Once they were safe he would see if he could get Ding-Schuler to agree to increase the permitted number. Fortunately for the three SOE agents, a kommando returned to Buchenwald with a large number of typhus patients who were brought to the isolation ward. Several were close to death.

Unfortunately, time continued to work against them. On 4 October, 11 SOE agents were called to the main gate, but one of them, Peulevé, was in the isolation ward, supposedly deathly ill with typhus. A guard was sent to collect him, but Dietsch convinced him that it would be too dangerous to expose others to the disease. The others were never seen again. After the war, a German Private, Gerhardt Burkhardt, confessed to being part of a makeshift execution squad organized by an officer named Schmidt that killed roughly a dozen POWs that he thought were Americans in early October 1944. The men were brought out handcuffed together in pairs and shot in groups of four roughly 650 yards outside of the main gate of the camp. There are no records of any groups of American POWs in Buchenwald other than the airmen. However, the executed SOE agents included Canadians, and the distinction between American and Canadian accents could easily have escaped the ear of someone fluent only in German.

There were now 11 SOE agents remaining of the 37 who had arrived at Buchenwald in mid-August. On 6 October, Marcel Seigneur, Buchenwald 76635, died of typhus. The body was sent to the crematorium and a form sent to the camp administration reported that Harry Peulevé had passed away. Harry, now called "Marcel," miraculously recovered and rejoined the prison population.

On 7 and 9 October, SOE agents were told to report to the front gate, never to return. Only six now remained alive; Harry was safe, but the rest were still in jeopardy. Yeo-Thomas was relieved to learn that the three SOE agents not in the hospital (Guillet, Southgate, and Culioli) had been sent away on an extended work kommando outside of the camp, so for the moment, they were not in danger.

On Friday, 13 October, Maurice Chouquet, Buchenwald #81642, died in the isolation ward. This was unlucky for him but very lucky for Yeo-Thomas, who adopted his identity in the nick of time. "Dodkin" was called to the entry gate the next day, before the administration learned of his supposed demise. Finally, on 18 October, Michel Boitel died of typhus. When his body was cremated as Stéphane Hessell of the SOE, the last of the surviving agents was out of immediate danger. On the next day, 19 October 1944, Lamason and 154 other Buchenwald airmen were evacuated by the Luftwaffe. Levitt Beck died that night, but the others remaining behind in the medical tent were transferred to Stalag Luft III on 28 November.

The three SOE agents still had to "recover" and then find shelter where nobody could recognize the identity changes. Kogon and Baumeister quickly arranged for Seigneur, Chouquet, and Boitel to be transferred to a small kommando in Gleina, 34 miles from Buchenwald. From there, the men were transferred to other kommandos, and despite further hardships and abuse, they somehow managed to survive the war. Before leaving Buchenwald, Yeo-Thomas took a big risk and wrote a letter for Dietsch testifying that the man had given vital support to the SOE in general and Yeo Thomas in particular. He signed the letter with his real name, rank, and serial number. The letter was ultimately introduced at Dietsch's war crimes trial and largely ignored by the judges, who sentenced him to a lengthy prison term. Yeo Thomas was distressed but could do nothing about it. He never got to fulfill his promise to put in a good

word for Dr. Ding-Schuler, who committed suicide shortly after his
arrest.

APPENDIX 5: LIST OF AWARDS RECEIVED BY WERNHER VON BRAUN

NAZY GERMANY:
1943 War Merit Cross, First Class with Swords
1944 Knights Cross of the War Merit Cross with Swords

UNITED STATES:
1958 Honorary doctorates from the University of Alabama, University of Chattanooga, and St. Louis University
1959 Honorary doctorates from Canisius College, Pennsylvania Military College, Clark University, and Adelphi College
1962 Elliott Cresson Medal
1963 Honorary doctorates from Sunshine University and William Jewell College
1964 Lifetime Achievement Award, American Astronautical Society
Honorary doctorates from Iowa Wesleyan College and Brevard Engineering College
1965 Honorary doctorates from Iona College, Wagner College, Emory University, and Butler University
1966 Honorary doctorate, Bradley University
1967 Langley Gold Medal
1967 Honorary doctorate from D'Youville College
1969 NASA Distinguished Service Medal
1969 Honorary doctorates from the University of South Dakota and Rollins College
1970 Civilian International World Citizenship Award
1970 Gold Medal from the German Society of Pennsylvania
1971 Honorary doctorate from Pepperdine College
1972 Honorary doctorate from Belmont Abbey College
1974 Honorary doctorate from Notre Dame University
1977 National Medal of Science for Engineering

EUROPE:
1949 Honorary Fellowship, British Interplanetary Society
1959 Commander's Cross of the Order of Merit of the Federal Republic of Germany
1961 Gold Medal, British Interplanetary Society
1969 Hermann Oberth Medal
1975 Werner von Siemens Ring

OTHER:
1963 Honorary doctorate from Universidad Nacional de Cordoba

APPENDIX 6: CONGRESSIONAL FAILURES

H CON. R 88, INTRODUCED TO THE 103RD CONGRESS ON 27 APRIL 1993

Recognizing and commending American airmen held as prisoners of war at the Buchenwald concentration camp during World War II for their service, bravery, and fortitude.

Whereas, during World War II, 173 Allied airmen[183] were captured by the enemy and held as prisoners of war at the Buchenwald concentration camp in Weimar, Germany;

Whereas captured airmen included 81 Americans, 27 Canadians, and 65 Britons, Australians, and New Zealanders;

Whereas the facts and circumstances of their confinement are amply documented in the official records maintained by the National Archives and Records Administration;

Whereas a report from the international Red Cross concerning Stalag Luft III in Sagan, Germany, mentioned six American airmen held in Buchenwald, including one whose name does not appear on the list maintained by the National Archives;[184] Whereas, since the liberation of Buchenwald in 1945, numerous personal memoirs, scholarly books, and articles have been published describing the conditions of the concentration camp;

Whereas this extensive documentation records the extraordinarily inhuman treatment, deprivations, and personal suffering inflicted on prisoners of war and other inmates at Buchenwald; and

Whereas Allied governments and veterans organizations outside the United States have granted special recognition to their citizens and members who were held as prisoners of war in World War II concentration camps; now, therefore, be it

Resolved by the House of Representatives (the Senate concurring), that the Congress recognizes and commends the valiant American airmen held as prisoners of war at the Buchenwald concentration camp during World War II for their faithful service, personal bravery, and exceptional fortitude;

---

[183] The basis for this number is unknown.

[184] The missing airman was Sam Pennell. When prisoners left Buchenwald, their numbers were often re-used by new arrivals. Sam's name and details were crossed out and overwritten, but his entries can still be deciphered.

and request that the president issue a proclamation recognizing and commending the service, bravery, and fortitude of the American airmen.

Concurrent Resolution

Recognizing and commending American airmen held as prisoners of war at the Buchenwald concentration camp during World War II for their service, bravery, and fortitude.

Whereas during World War II 173 Allied airmen were captured by the enemy and held as prisoners of war at the Buchenwald concentration camp in Weimar, Germany; Whereas the captured airmen included 81 Americans, 27 Canadians, and 65 Britons, Australians, and New Zealanders;

Whereas the facts and circumstances of their confinement are amply documented in the official records maintained by the National Archives and Records Administration;

Whereas a report from the International Red Cross concerning Stalag Luft III in Sagan, Germany, mentioned six American airmen held at Buchenwald, including one whose name does not appear on the lists maintained by the National Archives;

Whereas since the liberation of Buchenwald in 1945 numerous personal memoirs, scholarly books, and articles have been published describing the conditions at the concentration camp;

Whereas this extensive documentation records the extraordinarily inhuman treatment, deprivations, and personal suffering inflicted on prisoners of war and other inmates at Buchenwald; and

Whereas Allied Governments and veterans organizations outside the United States have granted special recognition to their citizens and service members who were held as prisoners of war in World War II concentration camps:

Now, therefore, be it Resolved by the House of Representatives (the Senate concurring),

That the Congress —

(1) recognizes and commends the American airmen held as prisoners of war at the Buchenwald concentration camp during World War II for their faithful service, personal bravery, and exceptional fortitude; and

(2) requests that the President issue a proclamation recognizing and commending the service, bravery, and fortitude of those airmen.

Concurrent Resolution

Recognizing and commending American airmen held as political prisoners at the Buchenwald concentration camp during World War II for their service, bravery, and fortitude.

Whereas 168 Allied airmen captured by Axis forces during World War II were held as political prisoners at the Buchenwald concentration camp in Weimar, Germany;

Whereas of these captured airmen, 82 were Americans, 26 were Canadians, 48 were Britons, 9 were Australians, 2 were New Zealanders, and 1 was Jamaican;

Whereas the facts and circumstances of their confinement are amply documented in the official records maintained by the National Archives and Records Administration;

Whereas a report from the International Red Cross concerning Stalag Luft III in Sagan, Germany, mentioned six American airmen held at Buchenwald, including one whose name does not appear on the lists maintained by the National Archives;

Whereas since the liberation of Buchenwald in 1945 numerous personal memoirs, scholarly books, and articles have been published describing the conditions at the concentration camp;

Whereas this extensive documentation records the extraordinarily inhuman treatment, deprivations, and personal suffering inflicted on these 168 Allied airmen and other inmates at Buchenwald; and

Whereas Allied Governments and veterans organizations outside the United States have granted special recognition to their citizens and service members who were held as political prisoners in World War II concentration camps: Now, therefore, be it

Resolved by the House of Representatives (the Senate concurring), That the Congress--

(1) recognizes and commends the 82 American airmen held as political prisoners at the Buchenwald concentration camp during World War II for their faithful service, personal bravery, and exceptional fortitude; and

(2) requests that the President issue a proclamation recognizing and commending, by name, the service, bravery, and fortitude of those airmen.

APPENDIX 7: ACKNOWLEDGMENTS AND SOURCES

Those interested in digging further into this topic will find a list of reference books, relevant articles, videos, oral histories, and useful websites below. My mother, Betty Martini, and my uncles, Edward Virgilio and Richard Hover, provided information about my father's experiences and opinions. Adelaine Chéron Lavandier, Odile Lavandier, and Eva Brown assisted me in Eure; Lionel Raulin shared his memories and encouraged me to complete this project. My father's pilot, Loren E. Jackson, spent several days with me discussing the 385th BG and his aircrew's missions in the ETO. I have also had the chance to correspond with several of the Buchenwald airmen, including James Stewart, Ed Carter-Edwards (before his death in early 2017), and with the families of Ed Ritter, Sam Pennell, Richard Bedford, and Joe Moser.

I was fortunate to have the help of several professional archivists. Dieter Stenger, of Stenger Historica, spent months at NARA/College Park chasing down leads, photographing documents, and providing translations of captured German records and reels of microfilm. He did most of the heavy archival lifting for me. Steve Rogers, another archivist fluent in German, examined five microfilm reels from the NASM. Kevin Jones, Hywel Maslin, and Fred Greyer accessed files in the Kew Archives in the UK, and Franck Signorile provided files from the French archives in Paris.

Ian McLachlan, Bill Varnedoe, and Thomas Gagnon sent files and photographs from the 385th BG Association. Marilyn Walton, the keystone member of the Stalag Luft III Association, provided information and photographs, and cast a critical editorial eye over the final manuscript. Holm Kirsten of the Buchenwald Museum provided photographs and details of Little Camp as it was in 1944. Tracy Dungan, of v2rocket.com, provided editorial comments as well as photographs. Michael Leblanc provided information about the resistance network sheltering evading airmen, as did Edouard Renière, Bruce Bollinger, John Hill, John Howes, and Philippe Connart. I also appreciate the kind assistance of staff archivists at the National Archives at College Park, Maryland (William Cunliffe, Amy Schmidt, Christina Jones, James Kelling, and Paul A Brown) and at the National Air and Space Museum (Elizabeth C. Borja and David Schwartz).

In pursuing various leads and seeking additional information I had productive correspondence with staff of the Air Force

Historical Society/USAF Special Collections, SHAEF, JAG/UK, the Air University Library, the Air Force Academy, the National POW Museum, the Buchenwald Museum, the Mittelbau-Dora Concentration Camp Memorial, the US National Holocaust Museum/ITS, the Bundesarchive, Yad Vashem, and the Muzeum Zagan. I also corresponded with the US Army, the FBI, and the CIA.

I would also like to thank individuals (in alphabetical order) who were kind enough to respond to my questions and provide opinions, suggestions, and assistance: Gerald Baron, Richard Breitman, Mike Digby, Michael Dorsey, Thomas Hatfield, Colin Heaton, Clarence Lasby, Thomas Lauria, Dorothy Long, Tim Naftali, Tim Nenninger, Michael Neufeld, Mary Ruwell, Bernd Schmidt, Chris Simpson, Michele Troy, and Kenneth Waltzer.

Several people took the time to review the manuscript in development and offer suggestions for improvement. First and foremost is my wife, Kathleen Welch, who also put up with the time commitment and the expense of this project, followed by our son, Frederic P.K. Martini, who prepared the photographs for inclusion in the book and, more extensively, on the associated website. Mark Bennett reviewed an early version of the text and did copyediting on the final manuscript. His interest in the project and his attention to detail are both deeply appreciated. Doug Fudge, Dan Schiller, and Grey Wicker read early iterations and helped catch inconsistencies in the narrative. And last but not least, I would like to thank my agent, Webster Stone, for his astute editorial comments and advice.

References used are listed below, along with a listing of archival sources consulted. The tens of thousands of pages of archival materials took seven years to accumulate, and I see no reason that investigators whose interests overlap my own should be forced to go through the same costly exercise to access relevant materials. Anyone with overlapping research interests can arrange access to images of original documents through my website, https://www.fredericmartini.com

BOOKS, REPORTS, AND JOURNAL ARTICLES

Army G-2. (1944). Underground Factories Niedersachswerfen Area (July 1944) 9pp.

Army G-2. (1945). Final Interrogation Report No. 7: Prisoner O/Stubaf Arthur Scheidler. U. F. E. T. I. C. A. 635 27pp.

Army G-2. (1945). Final Interrogation Report Andreas Folmer. G.-. Twelfth Army Group SOI Detachment, CIB. APO 655 US Army 11pp.

Allen, Michael T (2002) The Business of Genocide: The SS, Slave Labor, and the Concentration Camps. University of No. Carolina Press; 309pp

Angier, J. F. (2003). Ready or Not Into the Wild Blue. The Aviation Career of a B-17 Pilot, 457th Bomb Group, 8th Air Force. South Burlington, VT, Success Networks International 292pp.

Anon. (1949) Das war Buchenwald! Ein Tatsachenbericht. Leipzig 130pp.

Arich-Gerz (2009) Mittelbau-Dora: American and German Representations of a Nazi Concentration Camp; 184pp; transcript www.transcript-verlag.de/ts1357/ts1357.php

Barkley, M. (1945). Atrocities and Other Conditions in Concentration Camps in Germany. U. S. Senate Committee on Foreign Relations, US Government Printing Office 18pp.

Beck, Levitt C. (2010) Fighter Pilot. Kessinger Publishing; 208pp

Biddle, W. (2009). The Dark Side of the Moon. New York, NY, W. W. Norton & Co; 220pp.

Birdsall, S. (1973). B-17 in Action. Warren, MI, Squadron/Signal Publications, Inc. 50pp.

Bode, V. and G. Kaiser (2008) Building Hitler's Missiles: Traces of History in Peenemünde. Ch. Links Verlag, Berlin; 143pp

Bodson, H. (2005). Downed Allied Airmen and Evasion of Capture: The Role of Local Resistance Networks in World War II, Macfarland; 224pp.

Bowman, M. W. (1992). Flying to Glory: The B-17 Flying Fortress in war and peace. UK, Patrick Stephens, Ltd; 224pp.

Bowman, M. W. (2000). Castles in the Air. Washington, DC, Brassey's Inc; 211pp.

Bowman, M. W. (2002). B-17 Flying Fortress Units of the 8th Air Force (Part 2). Oxford, UK, Osprey Publishing 96pp.

Breitman, R. and N. J. W. Goda (2009). "Hitler's Shadow: Nazi War Criminals, US Intelligence, and the Cold War." U. S. N. Archives 110pp.

Brown, P. B. (2008). Safehaven Reports of the War Crimes Branch 1944-1945. Washington DC, NARA 51pp.

Buchenwald Camp, The Report of a Parliamentary Delegation (1945). His Majesty's Stationery Office, Cmd. 6626: 8pp

Burgess, C. (1995). Destination: Buchenwald. Australia, Kangaroo Press; 184pp.

Caidin, M. Flying Forts. The B-17 in World War II. New York, Bantam Books 483pp.

Carr, E. C. (2002). On Final Approach. Recollections of a World War II B-17 Air Crew. Rochester, WA, Edward C. Carr 208pp.

Cawthorne, N. (2002). Fighting Them on the Beaches. The D-Day Landings June 6,1944. London, UK, Arcturus Publishing 239pp.

Childers, T. (2002). In the Shadows of War. New York, Owl Books; 443pp

CIA (1950+). Document file related to Project Paperclip released under FOIA 268pp.

Clark, A. P. (2004). 33 Months as a POW in Stalag Luft III. Golden, CO, Fulcrum Publishing; 207pp.

Comer, J. (1988). Combat Crew. The true story of one man's part in World War II's allied bomber offensive. London, UK, Penguin Group 268pp.

Cox, L. C. (1990). Always Fighting the Enemy. Baltimore, MD, Gateway Press, Inc; 363pp.

Crowley, I. F. and J. R. Trudeau (2011). Wernher von Braun: An Ethical Analysis; 52pp.

Cunliffe, William H. (2006). Select Documents on Japanese War Crimes and Japanese Biological Warfare, 19342006. National Archives and Records Administration; PDF available online, 170pp.

Dick, S.J., ed. (2008). Remembering the space age: Proceedings of the 50th anniversary conference H. Division. Washington, DC, Government Printing Office 467pp.

Durand, A. A. (1988). Stalag Luft III: The Secret Story. Baton Rouge, LA, Louisiana State University Press; 412pp.

Dyreborg, E. (2003). The Young Ones: American Airmen of WW II. New York, iUniverse, Inc; 618pp.

Feigin, J. Striving for Accountability in the Aftermath of the Holocaust. M. M. Richard, Department of Justice, Criminal Division, Office of Special Investigations 397pp.

Fore, J. P. (1996). Tragedy and Triumph. A Pilot's Life Through War and Peace. L. Jacks. Colorado Springs, CO, Skyward Press 294pp.

Gibson, G. (1946). Enemy Coast Ahead. London, Michael Joseph 302pp.

Gimbel, J. (1973). "Project Paperclip: German Scientists and the Cold War [Review]." Political Science Quarterly 88(3): 1.

Gimbel, J. (1986). "U.S. Policy and German Scientists: The Early Cold War." Political Science Quarterly 101(3): 18.

Gimbel, J. (1990). "German Scientists, United States Denazification Policy, and the 'Paperclip Conspiracy'." The International History Review 12(3): 24.

Goldhagen, D. J. (1997) Hitler's Willing Executioners: Ordinary Germans and the Holocaust. Random House; 634pp.

Harvie, J. D. (1995). Missing in Action: An RCAF Navigator's Story.

Canada, McGill-Queens University Press; 243pp.

Holmes, Linda Goetz (2010). Guests of the Emperor, The Secret History of Japan's Mukden POW Camp. Naval Institute Press, Annapolis, MD; 192pp.

Hunt, L. (1985). "U.S. Coverup of Nazi Scientists." Bulletin of the Atomic Scientists (April 1985): 8.

Hunt, L. (1991). Secret Agenda: The United States Government, Nazi Scientists, and Project Paperclip 1945-1990 New York, NY, St. Martins Press; 340pp.

Interagency Working Group (2007). Final Report to Congress: Nazi War Crimes & Japanese Imperial Government Records

Irving, David (1964) The Mare's Nest: The War against Hitler's Secret Vengeance Weapons. Panther Books; 378pp.

I.S. 9 (Awards Bureau), P. (31 January 1946). Recommendation for a pension in favor of Madame Veuve Genevieve Rocher, 20, Boulevard Sebastopol, Paris 4e

Jablonski, E. (1965). Flying Fortress. The Illustrated Biography of the B-17s and the Men Who Flew Them. Garden City, NY, Doubleday & Company 362pp.

Jacobsen, A. (2014). Operation Paperclip: The Secret Intelligence Program that brought Nazi Scientists to America New York, Little, Brown and Company; accessed as Kindle book.

JAG Report of the Deputy Judge Advocate for War Crimes, European Command; June 1944 to July 1948. Office of the Judge Advocate General 257pp.

JAG (1947). Review of Proceedings of General Military Court in the case of United States vs. . . . . [Dachau trial] 166pp.

JAG (1948). United States of America v. Kurt Andrae et al. (and related cases) April 27, 1945-June 11 1958, NARA 14pp.

Johnsen, F. A. (2001). Boeing B-17 Flying Fortress. North Branch, MN, Specialty Press Publishers and Wholesalers 104pp.

Kew Archives, London (online) British Response to V1 and V2 14pp.

Kinnis, A. G. and S. Booker (1999). 168 Jump Into Hell. Victoria, BC, Arthur G. Kinnis; 288pp.

Klaas, J. (2000). Maybe I'm Dead. New York, NY, Authors Guild backinprint.com; 408pp.

Kogon, E. (1945). The Buchenwald Report. Colorado, Westview Press; 397pp.

Kogon, E. (1950). The Theory and Practice of Hell. New York, Farrar, Straus, and Giroux; 343pp.

Laney, M. (2015) German Rocketeers in the Heart of Dixie: Making sense of the Nazi past during the civil rights era. Yale University Press, 302pp.

Lasby, C. G. (1971). Project Paperclip: German Scientists and the Cold War. New York, NY, Antheneum; 339pp.

Leverington, R. L. (1996, 1997) War Diary: A Year to Remember June 1944-June 1945; personal notes, 20pp.

Lichtblau, E. (2014). The Nazis Next Door: How America became a safe haven for Hitler's men. New York, Houghton Mifflin Harcourt; accessed as Kindle book.

Makos, A. (2013). A Higher Call. New York, NY, Berkley Caliber; 392pp.

Marshall, B. (1952). The White Rabbit: A British Agent's Adventures in France. London, Pan Books Ltd; 268pp.

McDole, M. (2005). Military Resistance in France 1940-1944 Corcoran Department of History. Charlottesville, VA, University of Virginia. Bachelor of Arts: 121pp.

McLachlan, I. (2004). Eight Air Force Bomber Stories: A New Selection. UK, Sutton Publishing; 212pp.

Michel, J. (1973). Dora. The Nazi Concentration Camp where Modern Space Technology was Born and 30,000 Prisoners Died. L. Nucera. New York, Holt, Rhinehart and Winston 308pp.

Miller, D. L. (2006). Masters of the Air. New York, Simon and Schuster; 671pp.

Moser, J. F. and G. R. Baron (2009). A Fighter Pilot in Buchenwald. Bellingham, WA, EdensVeil; 205pp.

Myhra, David (2012) Peenemunde: The German Experimental Rocket Center Introduction. RCW Technology Sales and Services; 99pp.

Myhra, David (2012) Peenemunde: The German Experimental Rocket Center & Its Rocket Assemblies A through A2, Part 2: Photos, Images, Drawings and Maps, Vol. 1; RCW Technology Sales and Services; 13pp.

Myhra, David (2013) Peenemunde: The German Experimental Rocket Center & Its Rocket Assemblies A through A2, Part 2: Photos, Images, Drawings and Maps, Vol. 2; Robert C Walters Technology Sales and Services; 15pp.

Neufeld, M. J. (2002). "Wernher von Braun, the SS, and Concentraiton Camp Labor: Questions of Moral, Political, and Criminal Responsibility." German Studies Review 25(1): 21.

Neufeld, M. J. (2008). Von Braun: Dreamer of Space/Engineer of War. New York, NY, Vintage Books; 588pp.

Neufeld, M. J. (2008). "von Braun and the lunar-orbit rendezvous decision: finding a way to go to the moon." Acta Astronautica 63: 10.

Neufeld, M. J. (2012). 'Smash the Myth of the Fascist Rocket Baron': East German Attacks on Wernher von Braun in the 1960s. In:

Imagining Outer Space: European Astroculture in the Twentieth Century. A. C. T. Geppert. Great Britain, Palgrave Macmillan pp. 106-126

Neufeld, Michael J. (2012) "Hitler, the V-2, and the Battle for Priority, 1939-1943." The Journal of Military History, Vol. 57 No. 3 (July 1993): 511-538

O'Leary, M. (1992). B-17 Flying Fortress, A Bombing Legend. Oxford, UK, Osprey Publishing 128pp.

Pearson, D. and J. F. Anderson (1958) U.S.A. second class power? Simon and Schuster, NY; 334pp

Pedersen, Hillary (2018) I Would Not Step Back. The Philip Lamason Heritage Centre Trust, Dannevirke, New Zealand

Perry, R. L. (1961). Origins of the USAF Space Program 1945-1956 Space Systems Division Supplement, AFSC Historical Publications Series 62-24-10. 5: 25.

Petersen, M. B. (2005)."Engineering Consent: Peenemünde, National Socialism, and the V-2 Missile, 1924-1945" Department of History, University of Maryland, College Park. Ph. D. Thesis: 451pp.

Petersen, M. B. (2009). Missiles for the Fatherland. New York, NY, Cambridge University Press; 278pp.

Piszkiewicz, D. (1995). The Nazi Rocketeers: Dreams of Space and Crimes of War. Pennsylvania, USA, Stackpole Books; 250pp.

Przybilski, Olaf H. (2002) "The Germans and the Development of Rocket Engines in the USSR." JBIS, Vol. 55: 404-427

Reuter, Claus (2000) "The A4 (V2) and the German, Soviet, and American Rocket Program;" PDF; Lulu.com, 209pp

Richey, Robert J. (2001). My Brother Glenn, a Prisoner of the Gestapo During World War II. AuthorHouse, Bloomington, IN; 150pp.

Roberson, C. (2005). Memoir. © C Robeson; 35pp.

Sanger, E. and J. Bredt (1944). A rocket drive for long range bombers [translated], Radio Research Laboratory 175pp.

Schmidt, A. and G. Loehrer (2008). The Mauthausen Concentration Camp Complex: World War II and Postwar Records. Reference Information Papers. Washington, DC, NARA 380pp.

Scofield, M. Project Paperclip 18pp.

Sellier, A. (2003). A History of the Dora Camp. Chicago, IL, Ivan R. Dee; 547pp. Simpson, C. (1988). Blowback. New York, NY, General Publishing, Ltd; 398pp.

Snow, N. (2009). The Rocket's Trail. Bury St. Edmunds, UK, Arena Books; 176pp.

Solasko, F., Ed. (1948). War Behind Barbed Wire: Reminiscences of Buchenwald; Moscow, Foreign Languages Publishing House;

156pp.

Stein, H. (2004). Buchenwald Concentration Camp 1937-1945 <u>A Guide to the Permanent Historical Exhibition</u> Frankfurt, Germany, Wallstein Verlag 320pp.

Stuhlinger, E. (2003). "Wernher von Braun and Concentration Camp Labor: An Exchange. German Studies Review 26(1): 6.

Taylor, B. (2010). <u>Hitler's Engineers: Fritz Todt and Albert Speer, Master Builders of the Third Reich</u>. Casemate Publishers; 272pp

Teare, T. D. G. (1954). <u>Evader</u>. London, UK, Hodder and Stoughton; 256pp.

Vance, J. F. (2008). <u>Unlikely Soldiers</u>. New York, Harper Collins Ltd; 309pp.

Varnedoe, W. W., Jr (2011). <u>The Story of Van's Valiants of the 8th Army Air Force: A History of the 385th</u> Bomb Group in World War II, Colonial Graphics Group; 156pp.

Walton, M. J. and M. C. Eberhardt (2014). <u>From Interrogation to Liberation</u>. USA, Authorhouse; 713pp.

Wright, Arnold A (1993) <u>Behind the Wire: Stalag Luft III South Compound</u> © Arnold A Wright (looseleaf, several hundred pages; transcript of Ewell R. McCright's handwritten journal)

ARCHIVAL RESOURCES

US National Archives, College Park, MD: Record Groups 18, 59, 60-65, 125, 153, 165, 210, 226, 229, 238, 242, 263, 319, 330, 331, 338, 342, 389, 407,466, 498, 549

Kew Archives (UK): Record Groups FO 1031, WO 33, 208, 219, 311, AIR 20, 40, 219, DEFE 40, HS 6

National Aeronautics and Space Administration, Chantilly, VA: Captured German documents: Microfilm Reels FE 28, 39, 40, 41, 54, 65, 66, 70, 71

ORAL HISTORIES:

Chasten   Bowen,
http://collections.ushmm.org/search/catalog/irn55166
Richard   Bedford,
http://collections.ushmm.org/search/catalog/irn57423
Ed   Carter-Edwards,
http://www.thememoryproject.com/stories/490:edward-edwards/
Arthur Kinnis,
http://contentdm.library.uvic.ca/cdm/ref/collection/collection13/id/2071

Alan Smith, http://www.thememoryproject.com/stories/557:allan-al smith/

Loren Jackson, extended taped personal interviews

DOCUMENTARIES

The Lucky Ones (1994), National Film Board of Canada, 50 mins.

Shot from the Sky (2004) History Channel, 96 mins.

The Lost von Braun (2008) Aron Ranen, 36 mins.

Lost Airmen of Buchenwald (2012) Michael Dorsey, 93 mins.

WEBSITE REFERENCES:

USAAF:

http://www.385bg.com/

http://www.39.org/Research/8th_AF_Formations_Description.html

http://www.303rdbg.com/crew-duties.html

http://www.303rdbg.com/crewmen-missions.html

https://www.youtube.com/watch?v=80SNbQmACZ0

https://www.youtube.com/watch?v=QL-zRFEt9lI

http://www.stelzriede.com/ms/html/mshwpmn1.htm#contents

http://www.398th.org/Research/8th_AF_Formations_Description.html

FRENCH AND FFI

http://www.conscript-heroes.com/escapelines/index.htm

http://www.aide-aviateurs-allies

https://en.wikipedia.org/wiki/Oradour-sur-Glane_massacre

http://www.cometeline.org/

http://theescapeline.blogspot.co.nz/2012/06/traitors-part2.html?m=1

https://catalog.archives.gov/id/5694055

https://www.evasioncomete.org

BUCHENWALD

http://www.scrapbookpages.com/Buchenwald/GettingThere.html

http://www.express.co.uk/expressyourself/282244/Sacrafice-of-Britain-s-bomber-boys

https://www.ushmm.org/search/results/?q=Buchenwald

https://www.ushmm.org/wlc/en/article.php?ModuleId=10005198

http://www.possumline.net/EscapersAndEvaders/robb/ownstory.htm

SL III AND S VIIA:

http://www.b24.net/pow/stalag3.htm
http://therealgreatescape.com/stalag-luft-iii/
http://www.usafa.edu/df/dflib/SL3/SL3.cfm?catname=Dean%20of
%20Faculty https://en.wikipedia.org/wiki/Stalag_VII-A
http://www.muzeum.zagan.pl/index.php?id=0&lng=eng
http://www.b24.net/pow/stalag7.htm
https://www.moosburg.org/info/stalag/indeng.html
http://b24boojum.com/prison.html

WERNHER VON BRAUN AND V-2 ROCKETS:

http://www.v2rocket.com/
http://www.newworldencyclopedia.org/entry/Wernher_von_Braun
https://en.wikipedia.org/wiki/Wernher_von_Braun
http://dora.uah.edu/engineers.html
https://www.ushmm.org/wlc/en/article.php?ModuleId=10007319
https://en.wikipedia.org/wiki/Mittelbau-Dora
https://www.ushmm.org/wlc/en/article.php?ModuleId=10005322
https://en.wikipedia.org/wiki/Dora_Trial

CAMP LUCKY STRIKE:

http://www.skylighters.org/special/cigcamps/cmplstrk.html
https://www.youtube.com/watch?v=4G_pReGM3uI

PROJECT OVERCAST/PAPERCLIP:

https://tinyurl.com/ycguoglo
http://www.greatdreams.com/blog-2012/dee-blog107-html
http://www.kbismarck.org/forum/viewtopic.php?f=26&t=2932
http://news.bbc.co.uk/2/hi/uk_news/magazine/4443934.stm
https://www.thisamericanlife.org/radio-archives/episode/595/deep-
end-of-the-pool

PHOTO CREDITS:

Figures 1, 2, 3: 385th Bomb Group Association; Figures 4, 8, 14, 24, 28, 29, 30: Frederic H. Martini; Figure 5: 381st BG Memorial Association, 381st.org; Figure 6: National Air and Space Museum, Fort Eustis microfilm collection; Figure 7: Photograph by Walter

Frentz. Courtesy of Hanns-Peter Frentz; Figure 9: Comite Du Memorial Du Dernier Convoi De Deportation En Seine-Et Marne; Figure 10: US Holocaust Memorial Museum, courtesy of Robert A. Schmuhl; Figure 11: From a map provided by the Buchenwald Museum; Figure 12: US Holocaust Memorial Museum, courtesy of Melvin Cohen; Figure 13: US Holocaust Memorial Museum, courtesy of Mary Dickinson; Figure 15: National Air and Space Museum, Fort Eustis microfilm collection; Figure 16: Stalag Luft III Association; Figures 17, 21: US Air Force Academy, from the scrapbook of General A. P. Clark; Figure 18: Moosburg Online; Figure 20: US Signal Corps/v2rocket.com; Figures 22, 23: v2rocket.com; Figures 25, 27: NASA; Figure 26: NACA

INDEX

Defense Foreign Scientists Immigration Program (DEFSIP), 298-299, 342-343

Degenkolb, Gerhard 58, 62

Desoubrie, Jacques, 221, 223, 350-353, 355

Dodkin, Kenneth 124, 364-365, 368 *See also Yeo-Thomas, Forrest*

Donovan, William, 205, 345

Dora Concentration Camp, 66-67, 88, 135, 200, 204, 269, 333, 376 *See also Nordhausen*

Dornberger, Walter, 48, 51, 54-57, 60, 64-67, 86, 90, 169-171, 194, 197-199, 201, 207-210, 232-233, 235-236, 239-241, 260-261, 265, 275, 284-286, 293, 299, 320, 326, 335, 342, 345

Elektromechanischewerk (EW), 89, 196-197, 234, 240, 346

Field Information Agency, Technical (FIAT), 260, 262, 342

Förschner, Otto, 67

French Forces of the Interior (FFI), 68, 71-75, 77-78, 84, 94-97, 100-101, 108, 116, 122, 124, 221, 223, 342, 349, 351, 355 *See also French Resistance*

French Resistance, 66, 75, 81, 83, 342, 348, 350, 366

Garmisch-Partenkirchen, 210, 230, 258

Gestapo, 66, 71, 75, 79, 81-82, 84, 92, 94, 124, 145, 157, 159, 164, 185, 194-195, 197, 218, 220-221, 223-224, 251, 277, 279, 285, 342-344, 348-351, 354

Gianoni, Louis, 78, 221, 352, 355

Gibson, William, 93, 101

Göbbels, Joseph, 58, 345

Goodrich, Charles, 159, 176, 180, 345

Göring, Hermann, 51, 65, 194, 201, 345

Grapin, Maurice 221, 351, 355

Grenon, Leo, 84, 93, 99, 102

Hamill, James A., 206, 230, 243, 256, 260-261, 275-276, 345

Hanson, John, 119

Harvie, John, 94, 122, 378

Head, Les, 98

Heimerman, Lawrence, 154

Hemmens, Philip 84, 97, 134, 145, 149, 265

Hilding, Russell, 119

Himmler, Heinrich, 51, 65-66, 71-72, 76, 87-89, 110, 138, 143, 168, 194, 201, 277, 326, 344-345, 348, 365, 367

Hitler, Adolph, 48, 55, 57-59, 65, 71, 75-76, 86-87, 89-90, 159, 165, 171-172, 189, 194, 196, 198, 201-202, 207-208, 214, 221, 232-233, 264, 284, 299, 303, 345, 348, 355

Hodgson, Thomas, 93, 122

Hoffman, Charles, 98

Hoffman, Hans, 121

Horrigan, Roy, 154, 156, 190

Hover, Betty, *See Martini, Betty*

Hover, Richard, 278

Hunter, Harry, 163

Jackson, Loren E., 21-22, 34, 166, 214-215, 227, 313, 325, 375

Jessel, Walter, 232-235, 240, 285, 345

Schutzstaffel (SS), 48, 50-51, 55, 57-63, 65-67, 71, 75-77, 79-81, 84-85, 87-90, 92-93, 95-102, 106-109, 111-114, 119-123, 125-131, 134, 137-145, 147-149, 151-154, 164, 168-172, 179, 184, 187, 192, 194, 196-202, 204-205, 214, 233-234, 237, 246, 256, 264, 268-271, 274, 282, 285, 290, 292, 295, 300-301, 308, 315, 321, 326, 329, 344-345, 347-349, 351, 365-367

Scott, George W., 154

Scullion, Patrick, 98

Shearer, Donald, 154, 161

Sicherheitsdienst (SD), 71, 75, 202, 221, 343-344, 348-349, 352-353, 355

Sicherheitspolizei (SiPo), 71, 342-344

Smith, Eugene, 267

Smith, James A., 98

Sonderinspektion II, 62, 65, 199

Sonshine, E. R. (Joseph), 93, 163

Special Operations Executive (SOE), 82, 124, 138, 143, 148, 344, 352, 364-368

Speer, Albert, 48, 51, 65-66, 89-90, 170-171, 194-195, 233, 236, 293-294, 303, 308, 346

Spierenburg, Adolf "Dutch", 93, 100-102, 104, 109, 112, 122, 126

Stalag Luft III (SL III), 152-153, 155, 158-160, 162-164, 166, 177, 184-186, 190, 215-216, 227, 229, 272-273, 281, 313, 330-331, 345, 368, 371

Stalag VIIA (S VIIA), 181, 184, 189-191, 214-216, 227, 242, 272-273, 314, 332

State-War-Navy-Coordinating Committee (SWNCC), 237, 239, 258, 264

Staver, Robert, 206, 230-231, 235-236, 259, 345

Steinhoff, Ernst, 67, 195, 239-240, 263, 285, 320

Stewart, James, 210

Suddock, Dwight, 154

T-Forces (Tiger teams), 205, 343-344

Taylor, Ralph, 93-94, 122

Tilley, Edward, 260-262

Toftoy, Holger, 205-206, 230-233, 237, 241-243, 257-263, 270, 284, 290, 293, 308, 345

Totenkopfverbände, 344, 348

Trautloft, Hannes, 145

Truman, Harry S., 237, 239, 258

V-1 (flying bomb), 49, 62, 88, 125, 168, 170, 196, 199, 206, 236, 343-344

V-2 (ballistic missile), 49-52, 58-62, 64, 67, 86-88, 90, 125, 168-173, 194-196, 198-201, 206, 209-210, 230, 232-233, 235-237, 239-241, 243, 256, 259, 261-262, 265, 267, 276, 284, 291, 293-294, 303, 321, 327, 331, 333-334, 342-345 *See also A-4, A-4b*

Vallee, Edward, 153

Veterans Administration (VA), 248-254, 272, 277, 281, 287, 305, 309-313, 315-319, 323, 344

Vichy government, 71, 344, 349-350

Virgilio, Edward, 32, 76, 254

Von Braun,

Magnus (father), 52-53, 55

Magnus (brother), 52, 169, 202-203, 208-209, 233, 244, 262, 267, 320, 346

Sigismund (brother), 52, 57, 233, 261

Wernher, 48-67, 86-90, 168-173, 194-203, 207-210, 230, 232-236, 239-244, 256-263, 265, 267-271, 274-277, 282-286, 289-295, 298-303, 305-309, 313, 320-322, 326, 331, 335-337, 342, 345-346, 370

Watmough, George, 98

Watson, Earl, 98, 122, 154

Weilheim, 203, 207

Wev, Bosquet, 264, 345

Whellum, Leslie, 93, 99

Williams, William, 119, 154

Wilson, Paul, 73, 80, 85, 93, 154, 161, 217, 280

Witzenhausen, 236

Wojnicz, Ray, 119

Yeo-Thomas, Forrest, 364-368

See also Dodkin, Kenneth

Zeiser, James, 93, 154, 190, 266

Made in the USA
Lexington, KY
31 July 2018